GAMBLING ON THE AMERICAN DREAM: ATLANTIC CITY AND THE CASINO ERA

T0330839

FINANCIAL HISTORY

Series Editor: Robert E. Wright

GAMBLING ON THE AMERICAN DREAM: ATLANTIC CITY AND THE CASINO ERA

BY

James R. Karmel

Routledge
Taylor & Francis Group

LONDON AND NEW YORK

First published 2007 by Pickering & Chatto (Publishers) Limited

Published 2016 by Routledge
2 Park Square, Milton Park, Abingdon, Oxfordshire OX14 4RN
711 Third Avenue, New York, NY 10017, USA

First issued in paperback 2015

Routledge is an imprint of the Taylor & Francis Group, an informa business

BRITISH LIBRARY CATALOGUING IN PUBLICATION DATA

Karmel, James R.
Gambling on the American dream : Atlantic City and the casino era. – (Financial history)
1. Casinos – Economic aspects – New Jersey – Atlantic City 2. Gambling – Economic
aspects – New Jersey – Atlantic City 3. Casinos – Economic aspects – New Jersey
– Atlantic County 4. Gambling – Economic aspects – New Jersey – Atlantic County
5. Gambling – Law and legislation – New Jersey 6. Atlantic City (N.J.) – Economic
conditions 7. Atlantic County (N.J.) – Economic conditions 8. New Jersey – Economic
policy
I. Title
338.4'7795'09749

ISBN-13: 978-1-138-66358-9 (pbk)
ISBN-13: 978-1-85196-926-5 (hbk)

Typeset by Pickering & Chatto (Publishers) Limited

CONTENTS

ACKNOWLEDGEMENTS

This book is dedicated to Naomi Ruth Karmel, my daughter and an amazing little girl who will turn eight in 2008. Her love and patience while I worked on this book meant everything to me and sustained me at crucial points over the past five years. Thank you Naomi for bringing me so much happiness.

There are many people who need to be acknowledged for bringing *Gambling on the American Dream* to completion. The research project that led to the book began in 2002 as the Atlantic City Project, involving archival research and oral history. I am very thankful for this support throughout the duration of the project.

Most importantly, I extend my sincere gratitude to Tom Eastep. As my dean, Tom decided to support the project and used his influence to secure a grant from Harford Community College (Bel Air, Maryland) through the College's 'New Initiatives' fund. Tom went out of his way to make sure that I had the financial support necessary and, later, the time (via sabbatical) to conduct research and begin writing the manuscript. Others at Harford who supported the project include Claudia Chiesi, Rusty Stephens, Luba Chliwniak, Jim LaCalle Andrea Craley, and many of my colleagues on the Dean's group and in the Behavioral and Social Science division. I am also very thankful to the New Jersey Historical Commission for an individual research grant for the project.

Many people in greater Atlantic City lent their considerable time and energy to this project, beginning with the reference librarians at the Atlantic City Free Public Library. Most importantly, I want to thank reference librarians Ali Smith Finkbeiner and Heather Halpin who were incredibly supportive and helpful to me using the Heston Room materials. Others at the Atlantic City Free Public Library who supported the project in various ways include Maureen Frank, Julie Senack and Pat Rothenberg. I reserve special thanks to Barbara Devlin, Aura Sprague Osorno and Jay Sodha of Local 54 for sharing their own oral history stories and connecting me to numerous other casino employees through the union to take part in the project. Also, I express a tremendous thanks to Cathanina Tran of the Atlantic City Jobs and Opportunity Program for her efforts to support the project by connecting me to various people in the casino community. Key oral history participants whose voices enliven the book also include: Steve Perskie, Russelle Patterson, Richard Lopez, Dan Heneghan, Chhitubai 'Chito' Patel, Paul Tjoumakaris, Edna Hall, Harry Hasson, Isias Gomes, J. David Alcantara, Pierre Hollingsworth and Hilda Mayra Momperousse.

My thanks also go out to key figures in my development as a historian. At the State University of New York at Brockport, I was fortunate to have great mentors in Steve Ireland and John Killigrew, who taught me to understand History as a rich human story, as well as a science. At the University at Buffalo, Richard E. Ellis, Michael Frisch and Helju Bennett shaped my professional identity and helped me develop analytical perspective on all matters. My thanks also go out to Robert E. Wright, the editor of this series, a friend and magnificent historian whom I have always looked to as an inspiration. Historians Bryant Simon and David Schwartz were also very helpful getting this from proposal to book, as were participants at a 2005 Oral History of the Mid-Atlantic Region workshop and many other professional colleagues who have contributed to my thinking at various conferences and workshops. Thanks also to Michael Middeke, Will Padgett and the staff at Pickering & Chatto for all their support. Finally, I want to thank my parents, numerous members of my family, and the many friends who have supported me and this project in numerous ways at various times since 2002.

LIST OF ABBREVIATIONS

ACCA	Atlantic City Casino Association
ACCHA	Atlantic City Casino Hotel Association
ACCVA	Atlantic City Convention and Visitor's Association
ACHRA	Atlantic City Housing and Redevelopment Agency
ACOPPED	Atlantic County Office of Policy, Planning and Economic Development
ACIA	Atlantic County Improvement Authority
ACPOHI	Atlantic City Project Oral History Interviews
AFL-CIO	American Federation of Labor and Congress of Industrial Organizations
AGA	American Gaming Association
CANJ	Casino Association of New Jersey
CCA	*Casino Control Act*
CRAC	Committee to Re-build Atlantic City
CRDA	Casino Reinvestment Development Authority
CRF	Casino Revenue Fund
CTRs	Cash Transaction Reports
DGE	Division of Gaming Enforcement
MBE	Minority Business Enterprise
M/WBE	Minority/Women-owned Business Enterprises
NAACP	National Association for the Advancement of Colored People
NGIS	National Gambling Impact Study
NJCCC	New Jersey Casino Control Commission
NJP	New Jersey Comprehensive Management Plan
REACT	Reach an Early Abatement of Crime and Taxes
SARC	Suspicious Activities Report by Casinos
SIGMA	Stockton Institute for Gaming Management at The Richard Stockton College of New Jersey
SJTA	South Jersey Transit Authority
WBE	Woman-owned Business Enterprise

LIST OF TABLES AND FIGURES

CHRONOLOGY

1970   The New Jersey Hotel-Motel Association forms a commission to study casino legalization.

1971   The New Jersey State Senate holds hearings on a resolution to 'to authorize by law the operation of gambling games in Atlantic City'. The New Jersey State Legislature forms the 'Gambling Study Commission'.

1973   The 'Gambling Study Commission' reports back favourably on holding a casino referendum.

1974   The first casino referendum fails in a state election by 400,000 votes; it would have legalized casinos, but not exclusively in Atlantic City.

1976   The Committee to Re-build Atlantic City (CRAC) leads a campaign for casino legalization in Atlantic City. The second casino referendum passes by 300,000 votes; casinos are allowed only in Atlantic City. The Bahamas-based Resorts International acquires Chalfonte-Haddon Hall Hotel.

1977   The *Casino Control Act* (CCA) passes the New Jersey State Legislature and is signed into law by Governor Brendan Byrne; it creates the New Jersey Casino Control Commission (NJCCC) and the Division of Gaming Enforcement (DGE), and defines extensive guidelines for licensure and operations of casinos.

1978   Resorts International opens at Boardwalk and North Carolina Avenue.

1979   Caesar's Boardwalk Regency opens at Boardwalk and Missouri Avenue, but is initially denied a permanent license. Bally's Park Place opens at Boardwalk and Park Place, but is initially a denied permanent license.

1980   The Golden Nugget opens at Boardwalk and Boston Avenue. Brighton Hotel and Casino opens on Pacific Avenue and Illinois Avenue; it becomes the Sands by the end of 1980. Harrah's opens in the marina district. The ABSCAM scandal breaks.

1981   The Tropicana opens on Boardwalk and Iowa Avenue. Del Webb's Claridge opens at Pacific Avenue and Indiana Avenue. Playboy opens on Boardwalk at Florida and Bellevue Avenues. Caesar's gains a permanent license for the Boardwalk Regency.

1984   Playboy loses its bid for a permanent casino license; it becomes Atlantis
       casino. Harrah's Boardwalk Hotel Casino at Trump Plaza opens at
       Boardwalk and Mississippi Avenue. The US Supreme Court rules
       that the NJCCC can require registration of union officials. Atlantic
       City Mayor Michael Matthews is convicted of corruption; James Usry
       becomes the new mayor. The Casino Reinvestment Development
       Authority (CRDA) begins.
1985   The NJCCC denies Hilton Hotels' bid for a casino license. The planned
       Hilton casino opens as Trump Castle in the marina district. Atlantis
       casino files for bankruptcy.
1986   The Local 54 union holds a one-day strike with impacts on casino com-
       munity and industry. Trump Plaza replaces Harrah's Boardwalk Hotel
       Casino at Trump Plaza.
1987   Bally's buys Golden Nugget; Bally's Grand opens in its place. Trump
       strikes a deal with Resorts International for management of Taj Mahal
       (under construction by Resorts International). The Showboat casino
       and bowling centre opens on Boardwalk. The US Supreme Court rules
       in favour of tribal gaming in California vs. Cabazon.
1988   The entertainer Merv Griffin acquires Resorts International and cre-
       ates Merv Griffin's Resorts Hotel and Casino. Donald Trump and
       Griffin strike a deal for Taj Mahal between Resorts International and
       the Trump Organization: Taj Mahal becomes the Trump Taj Mahal.
       Congress passes the Indian Gambling Act.
1989   The COMSERV scandal breaks; it involves corruption in Atlantic City
       government, including Mayor Usry. The NJCCC denies Atlantis casino
       license renewal, forcing it out of business. Trump buys the property
       and turns it into Trump Regency (non-casino hotel). Steve Wynn and
       Golden Nugget open the Mirage in Las Vegas. A helicopter crash kills
       three top Trump executives. Merv Griffin's Resorts enters bankruptcy.
1990   Trump Taj Mahal opens on the Boardwalk and enters into 'pre-pack-
       aged bankruptcy. James Whelan is elected mayor of Atlantic City.
       Streamlining of the NJCCC and the DGE begins. New NJCCC chair
       Steve Perskie begins the casino deregulation process. Mississippi legal-
       izes riverboat casinos.
1991   The New Jersey Assembly passes the casino deregulation bill; weekend
       twenty-four-hour gaming begins; the slot machine formula is revised
       allowing more machines. The Trump Taj Mahal emerges from bank-
       ruptcy. Resorts emerges from bankruptcy.
1992   Major deregulation passes: the *CCA* is modified to grant the NJCCC
       more direct power to regulate; hotel rooms construction is tied to CRDA
       funding, gaming floor space and construction of new Convention
       Center. Foxwoods casino opens in Connecticut. Mississippi riverboat

casinos begin operations. The Trump group enters into a second bankruptcy.

1993   Foxwoods expands to slot machines. Racing simulcasting and poker are allowed in casinos. The NJCCC revamps the Minority/Women-owned Business Enterprises programme.

1994   Construction begins on new Convention Center. Lorenzo Langford runs against Whelan for mayor, Whelan wins re-election.

1995   Major casino deregulation: it allows continued expansion for slot machines and ends the three-casino limit per operator. Trump goes public, creating Trump Hotel and Casino Resorts, Inc. ITT Corporation acquires Caesar's

1996   Atlantic City government approves a deal between the city and the Mirage for Mirage's acquisition of the H-Tract in the marina district and construction of connector road between Atlantic City Expressway and the marina casino district. The Casino Association of New Jersey terminates operations. Hilton Hotels acquires Bally's Park Place. Mohegan Sun opens in Connecticut. Trump's World's Fair opens in a former Playboy/Atlantis property (then Trump Regency non-casino hotel).

1997   Governor Christine Todd Whitman supports Mirage's bid for the H-Tract, connector road. The CRDA approves funding for connector. The New Jersey legislature approves Transportation Trust funds for the connector. The Atlantic City Convention Center opens. Bally's Wild, Wild West casino opens along Boardwalk. The Sands enters into bankruptcy.

1998   Construction begins on the Atlantic City–Brigantine Connector through the city's Westside neighborhood. Harrah's acquires Showboat casino and implements the 'Total Rewards' players' club across the nation. Hilton spins off Bally's into Park Place Entertainment (PPE). Whelan defeats Langford in a mayoral election. Sun International Hotels acquires Merv Griffin's Resorts. Trump Castle becomes Trump Marina. A reorganized Casino Association of New Jersey starts up. Starwood Hotels acquires Caesar's via ITT acquisition.

1999   PPE acquires Caesar's from Starwood Hotels. The National Gambling Impact Study commission report is released. Trump's World's Fair casino closes. The Claridge enters into bankruptcy.

2000   MGM Grand acquires Mirage, creates MGM-Mirage; construction on 'the Borgata' continues in the marina district. Financier Carl Icahn purchases the Sands.

2001   Langford defeats Whelan in a mayoral election. The terrorist strike of 11 September has minimal impact on casino revenues. Construction is ensured on the Borgata, the Walk outlet center and Tropicana's 'The

Quarter'. The Atlantic City–Brigantine Connector opens for traffic. Colony Capital acquires Resorts

2003 The Borgata opens as a joint venture between Boyd Gaming and MGM Mirage. Governor James McGreevey's revenue plan passes the New Jersey Assembly: new tax on casino comps, new parking fee, luxury tax imposed on casinos. PPE acquires the Claridge.

2004 Local 54 strikes seven casinos for one month; the settlement does not link the new contract to Las Vegas culinary union contract. Tropicana's 'The Quarter' opens. The Pennsylvania legislature approves a casino legalization bill. PPE becomes Caesar's Entertainment. Trump Hotels and Casino Resorts, Inc. files for bankruptcy

2005 Robert Levy defeats Lorenzo Langford in a mayoral election. Harrah's announces acquisition of PPE, which creates the largest casino company in the world. Colony Capital acquires Atlantic City Hilton (formerly Golden Nugget and Bally's Grand). Hurricane Katrina decimates the Biloxi-Gulfport casino community.

2006 Pinnacle Entertainment purchases the Sands and adjacent property along Boardwalk. It closes the Sands. Harrah's is sold to two private equity firms in a $17.1 billion leveraged buy-out. Casinos close for three days due to a budget stand-off in NJ state government. Pennsylvania casino operations begin. Columbia Sussex acquires Tropicana parent corporation Aztar. The Pier at Caesar's opens. Atlantic City closes Bader Field airport to make way for redevelopment.

2007 NJCCC approves Harrah's leveraged buy-out. Casino dealers at Caesar's, Bally's, Tropicana and Trump Plaza vote to unionize with United Auto Workers (UAW). Mayor Levy resigns amidst scandal over false representation of military service. Pinnacle implodes the Sands to make way for a casino property scheduled to open in 2011. Revel Entertainment Inc. and Morgan Stanley investment bank plan a casino on the upper end of the Boardwalk above Showboat. MGM Mirage announces a mega-casino and condominium complex for marina district.

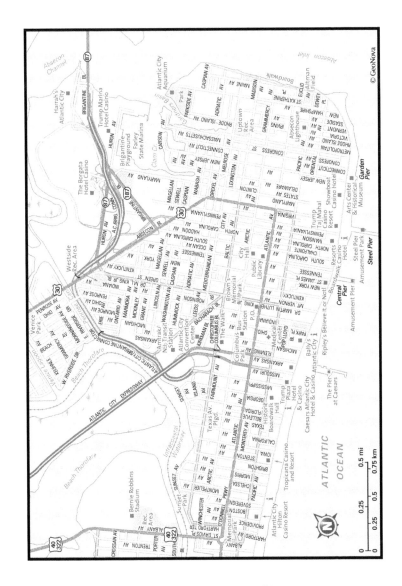

Map of Atlantic City, reproduced by permission of the GeoNova Group.

INTRODUCTION

Across the city a green and red sign lit up the night sky. 'Borgata' it proclaimed, brightly launching the casino era in Atlantic City into a new phase. The gleaming gold Borgata opened in 2003 and quickly became the symbol of a region's hope for its soul and sustenance. Would it finally be the solution to the city's long inability to restore itself as a 'destination resort'? Since the Resorts International casino opened in 1978, Atlantic City and its surrounding communities linked their fortunes, dreams and enduring vision of a bright future to casinos. As many have documented, that vision has been tested and, despite the money, often been viewed as bringing more problems to the people of the region than benefits. Yet, the story of Atlantic City in the casino era is a largely positive one, most clearly demonstrating an incredible faith in the power of energetic capitalism. The casino floor is a blur of market transactions, successes and failures. Money flies around in all directions, and always, the casino wins more than it loses due to the ironclad laws of probability. But money is just a means to an end. Money alone cannot bring happiness nor make a community whole. The story of Atlantic City in the casino era is therefore not just a story about making money. It is not a story about rich and poor, the community-haves and community-have-nots. Rather, the story of Atlantic City in the casino era is a story about people. It is a story about hopes and disappointment, opportunity and loss. It is a story about determination and desperation, strength and weakness. It is a story about brash, individualistic entrepreneurship and compassionate concern for others. It is an American story.

Before casino legalization in 1976, Atlantic City's economy was in shambles. Young people were leaving as soon as they left high school because there were simply no jobs to keep them around. The city had a three-month economy where residents tried to earn as much money as possible to get them through the long, cold winter, often relying on unemployment or public support to make it through each year. The surrounding region was largely farmland or remote Pine Barrens: there was no real substantial industry besides summer tourism, a few boat-making operations and agriculture. An oft-told account of the pre-casino 1970s is that someone posted a sign on the Albany Avenue bridge that connected the island town to the mainland that read 'Last one to leave Atlantic City, please turn out

1

the lights'.[1] After World War II, the region had sustained a series of hits and calamity of circumstances. The palatial hotels that once lined the Boardwalk eventually became deteriorating hulks along the shore as the summer crowds came in fewer and fewer numbers between 1950 and 1978. The gardens and pleasure piers were still busy, but, as the culture changed, attractive properties faded or were torn down and replaced. Forty years later, a former summer tourist recalled the transition that took place in the Chelsea section of the city in the 1960s:

> Another block or two at Morris or Brighton Avenue, on the north side of Pacific, stood the impeccably groomed gardens of the Gimbel Mansion and the Flamingo mansion, which later was demolished and became the Flamingo Motel. I believe that they were all gone by the early 60's.[2]

Moneyed tourists were scarcely to be found by the mid-1970s, and the old hotels were beginning to disappear.[3]

In the early 1960s, Atlantic City absorbed two major blows: one to its infrastructure and one to its public reputation. In 1962, a powerful nor'easter stormed up the east coast and broke the floodgate that protected much of the city's Inlet and uptown neighborhoods. The storm flooded a large part of the city, and also left it vulnerable to flooding from that point on, as the gate was not properly repaired for years. For the next two decades, the area would often flood as a consequence of normal tides, not just major storms. When the Inlet and uptown areas were massively redeveloped in the 1980s, crews first had to raise the entire streetscape by three feet and the houses even higher before residential construction could begin. Since many of the affected neighborhoods generally consisted of summer cottages to begin with, the urban infrastructure, already old and shaky, could not really withstand the storm's aftermath. The 1962 storm also washed away part of the famous Steel Pier. In 1964, another major blow hit the once-popular resort when the Democratic Party held its nominating convention in the city. That convention is probably best known for the uprising led by the civil rights-oriented Mississippi Freedom Democratic Party and for Fannie Lou Hamer's willingness to confront party elders, including President Lyndon B. Johnson. However, Democratic Party unity was not the only casualty of that convention. Reporters staying in the fading hotels wrote home about poor room conditions, service and the sorry state of their surroundings, thereby contributing to Atlantic City's already weakened reputation as a desirable place to vacation.[4]

By the early 1970s, the tourist industry could barely sustain itself, and could sustain the local workforce even less. Atlantic City was becoming a dreary nostalgia trip. Horses kept diving on the Steel Pier until 1978, but they represented a past era and were virtually isolated as a Boardwalk attraction by then. The show closed when Resorts bought the Steel Pier in 1978. The residents of greater Atlantic City wholeheartedly backed the casino legalization referendum. Jerseyites liked the unique requirement that casino 'win' (eight per cent) would be taxed specifically to benefit senior citizens through the creation of the Casino Revenue Fund. Bartenders gave out free drinks and people partied all night when it passed on the second try in 1976, this time limiting casinos to Atlantic City. Within eighteen months, the first casino opened and five years into the casino era, four times more visitors were coming to Atlantic City than the pre-casino era. But it did not happen as easily as the referendum backers had hoped. Overwhelming traffic, brutal real estate speculation, legal and bureaucratic obstacles made casino employment not easily attainable for many. In five years, the casino industry invested a few billion dollars to develop their properties and brought in five and a half billion dollars in revenue between 1978 and 1983.[5] Casino money flowed like oil through a gusher, but it did not automatically elevate the local population. Within two years, resentment and criticism of the casino industry emerged from Atlantic City sources. In the early 1980s, industry leaders also spoke up to complain about overly-strict regulations that limited casino operators on everything from the hours they could open, to the size of the casino floors, to the content of their advertisements. Meanwhile, the Golden Nugget casino also emerged as a model of new glamour and style, management, marketing and employee relations. It set an important tone for the industry and its president Steve Wynn set about training a whole generation of casino managers who later went on to success in other casinos.

By the mid 1980s, the casino era was advancing rapidly. Donald Trump had come to town and changed the local industry through his risk-taking, his brash personal style and his willingness to invest substantial capital. Acquiring three casinos by 1988, Trump also bailed out Resorts International by purchasing the Taj Mahal, a huge casino project at the far eastern end of the Boardwalk. Trump uniquely blended his personal charisma and celebrity with the marketing of the Trump casinos. Meanwhile, Harrah's bustling Marina casino slowly developed a brilliantly successful operation via smart, niche marketing and a comprehensive, independent approach to both employee relations and community involvement. Junk bond debt saddled many of the properties and the northeastern recession began to cut into gaming profits. After the Taj Mahal nearly collapsed in a heap of debt within a year of its 1990 debut, a new Casino Control Commission chairman, Steve Perskie, set about reigning in the agency and scaling back the original *Casino Control Act* legislation to empower casino operators to make business decisions that were good for the industry. Fifteen years after Resorts International's opening day, the casinos had twenty-four-hour gaming, a streamlined regulatory process, a more common-sense system of employee licensing and a new convention centre under construction. New immigrants by the thousands migrated to work in the casinos in the 1990s and created an international, cosmopolitan environment and a dynamic multi-ethnic immigrant community.

Deregulation set the tone for the booming mid-1990s when Wynn's Mirage corporation came to town and launched the casino industry on an expansion drive that continues to the present. Through incredible controversy, Wynn forged a deal with state and city officials for a mega-complex in the Marina that eventually opened as the Borgata in 2003. Along the way, the Atlantic City–Brigantine connector was built and a neighbourhood's streets torn up (the Westside). Through the 1990s, Atlantic County continued to prosper through casino wealth and the city's housing, crime and infrastructure problems began to improve through dedicated local and state initiatives and funding. The city's boom was slowed somewhat as the success of Connecticut's two tribal casinos re-directed a substantial portion of former Atlantic City gamblers to south-eastern New England. However, the opening of the Borgata, Tropicana's Havana-themed 'the Quarter' and a centrally-located retail outlet called the Walk spurred yet another Atlantic City renaissance in the mid-2000s before new slots parlours and racinos in Pennsylvania and New York threatened the industry again. Along the way, the casino companies merged and grew ever bigger. Harrah's emerged on top of the casino world in 2005 by purchasing Caesar's, instantly capturing 40 per cent of the Atlantic City gaming market.

What follows in *Gambling on the American Dream* is in equal parts an economic impact study, a community history, a financial analysis and a popular narrative. The business of the Atlantic City casinos has been a fascinating, exciting boom-and-bust tale, the cheers and moans of a casino floor writ large across coastal South Jersey. Economic data and financial results, coloured with contemporary and personal accounts of the casino industry, build the history of the casino era. *Gambling on the American Dream* highlights personal experiences wherever possible, and utilizes oral history to emphasize key aspects of the casino era.

Chapter 1 begins by discussing the decline of the region through the early 1970s, when discussion about legalized gambling as a cure for the city's problems picked up momentum. It focuses on the subject of illegal gambling as an important historical theme in the region's history and explains the ways in which gambling as a central component in Atlantic City economy and culture became embedded into the regional consciousness many decades before the casino era. In addition, the chapter examines early connections between famous regional political machines and gambling, the role of law enforcement and impact on average citizens. This helps develop an important theme of this book: that casino gambling, even though it was illegal, had been a significant and usually accepted part of the region's culture in the twentieth century. The chapter presents the pre-casino past as an important background for the campaign to bring legalized casinos to Atlantic City in the 1970s. The campaign actually began in the late 1950s with local business owners, but picked up a lot of support in the early 1970s when politicians began to champion the initiative at the state level. This led to a dramatic and interesting effort to convince New Jersey citizens to approve casino gambling generally across the state in 1974 (unsuccessfully) and specifically for Atlantic City in 1976 (successfully). The legislative hearings and oral history recollections from this period vividly reveal the opposition between pro- and anti-gambling forces, with a stark portrayal of the region's bleak circumstances set against apocalyptic predictions of a casino future. The chapter also addresses the passage of the *Casino Control Act* of 1977, defining the ways in which the state sought to regulate the casino industry at the beginning of the era.

Chapter 2 picks up the story in 1978 with the opening of the first casino, Resorts International. This was immensely successful, tapping into a huge market, and was the sole casino in Atlantic City for almost eighteen months. In the years 1978–9 the region experienced a wave of economic development and an influx of capital that created new jobs and new opportunities, in the midst of a slow national economy. By 1982, Atlantic County had become one of the fastest growing counties in the nation, and the number of casinos had increased to eleven, creating thousands of jobs through direct employment on the gaming floors, hotel and restaurant operations, and indirect employment in construction and other businesses throughout the region. Chapter 2 details this industry success, via the development of Harrah's, the Trump casinos and Showboat, and chronicles the attempt to establish Atlantic City as a 'destination resort' by re-opening the train link to Philadelphia, renovating the regional airport and establishing commercial airline service. It also describes the continued impact of a wave of real estate buying and selling: casino-related speculation that had winners and losers. Most famously, certain neighbourhoods were practically overrun with speculation, with tenants facing difficult consequences as a result.

By the mid-1980s, national media reports had become very critical of the city in the casino era, alleging continued urban blight. Chapter 3 addresses the substance of these perceptions, focusing on the impact of casinos on community life. The chapter also examines the change in city government that took place in the early 1980s from a commission to a mayoral system and includes information on the legal problems faced by Atlantic City politicians and other aspects of political corruption that were noteworthy of the time. While Atlantic City struggled with quality-of-life issues, the ring of suburban communities around it nevertheless kept growing and becoming wealthier. Casino wealth spread wide and positively impacted many people around the region, even if those people were disproportionately located outside the city. By the late 1980s, economic indicators for Atlantic County were quite good, and the county was advertising its status as a dynamic harbour for opportunity.

Chapter 4 reviews the turnabout that occurred in the late 1980s and 1990s, when the casino industry experienced a slowdown. One casino actually went out of business while others experienced problems. Meanwhile, the opening of the Trump Taj Mahal was a huge event in the casino era: at first promising, but soon disappointing. The industry was also impacted by a national economic slowdown and the drop in travel that accompanied the Persian Gulf War of 1990–1. The chapter addresses how average people handled these slow years by reflecting on growth patterns and individual stories about the city and region. It details the change in political direction that occurred with the election of James Whelan as mayor in 1990, and explores his executive actions and their repercussions. Whelan set a new path for Atlantic City's government by working more dramatically to bring the interests of the community and casinos together.

Chapter 4 also explains the cumbersome and unwieldy licensing process implemented for casino employment. Eventually, it led to long delays and political efforts to change the policy. The chapter develops themes from the previous chapter on the centrality of gambling to the regional psyche and on the role of casino gambling and the achievement of the American dream in the Atlantic City region. The late 1970s and early 1980s also included a crime spike caused by the influx of visitors and the relationship between casino management and labor unions. Chapters 3 and 4 also analyze new efforts at 'urban redevelopment' via the establishment of the casino-funded Casino Reinvestment Development Authority and its subsidized housing programs of the late 1980s.

Chapter 5 tells the fascinating and little-known story of the crucial role that immigrants have played in Atlantic City's casino era. Since the 1980s, immigrants from around the world have flooded into Atlantic City to fill 'back-of-the-house' jobs as cooks, cleaners and room service attendants at the casino hotels. Often, these jobs required little or no English language and paid relatively low salaries, yet they were stable and included valuable benefits. Many, by learning English, have worked their way up the job ladder, including a significant number of the higher-paid dealers in Atlantic City. Since the mid-1980s, specific communities have developed with immigrants from various countries in Latin America, South and East Asia. Prominent nations-of-origin for the casino era's immigrants include: Vietnam, the Philippines, India, Bangladesh, Pakistan, Columbia, China, Cuba, El Salvador and the Dominican Republic. Together and separately, they re-created Atlantic City as a diverse and international place. In recent years, many of the immigrants have moved beyond the casinos and opened businesses. Yet the casinos continue to anchor the diverse communities.

Chapters 6 and 7 tell the story of the casino community from the early 1990s to the present, as the existing casinos expanded and thrived in the prosperous tourist and business climate of the era. By 1999, the number of people in the region directly employed by casinos had increased to 47,366[6] and growth in the suburbs continued as new waves of casino employees became wealthier and bought homes outside the city . This was especially the case for those with young families, due to the perception that Atlantic City public schools were inadequate. Mayor Whelan's administration created a more harmonious relationship between the city and the casino community and sought to eradicate the city's over-supply of dilapidated structures. The Atlantic City casino industry faced a significant competitive threat when the Connecticut Pequots opened Foxwoods in 1992, yet gained new momentum a few years later when Steve Wynn's Mirage struck a deal to develop a few new casinos. The project also included the construction of a new roadway to the Marina district that divided the casino industry and city residents. The battle played out for four years in the late 1990s until one large casino was built along with the roadway that connects the Atlantic City Expressway to the Marina district casinos. This was a dramatic episode, with political and economic outcomes that impacted the region well into the 2000s.

Chapters 6 and 7 include an account of the drive to build the new Convention Center in Atlantic City and of the ways in which the Casino Reinvestment Development Authority (CRDA) has continued to impact growth and development in the region. They take the story up to the present, expanding on the newfound diversity of the city and region. Two large casino developments have opened in the recent past: the Borgata (2003) and Tropicana's 'The Quarter' (2004). Both are geared towards a more upscale casino clientele, *à la* Las Vegas, but are possibly at odds with the historic clientele of area casinos. In addition, the resort has shifted dramatically towards upscale retail shopping as a way to build a non-gambling clientele. Developments like the outlet centre called 'the Walk' and the Pier at Caesar's have become huge destinations unto themselves within the community.

Chapter 8 concludes the narrative by applying the story of the casino era in South Jersey to the burgeoning casino communities around the United States. It focuses on the Connecticut tribal casinos, the Mississippi casino industry and the nascent Pennsylvania gaming industry. Each of these casino locales has significant Atlantic City connections and each has impacted Atlantic City in different ways. Here, the book explains the role that the Atlantic City casino community has played in expanding the American casino age in the 1990s and 2000s.

Gambling on the American Dream makes extensive use of oral history to tell the story of the casino era. The oral history helps us understand that Atlantic City's casino era is a social construct – a collective marker of history for the residents of greater Atlantic City. This social construct leads to the establishment of certain themes and shared memories, something that historian Don Ritchie has defined as 'public memory'. In the case of Atlantic City, the 'public memory' consists of a historical understanding that the city was a faded, depleted, dying place in the years before the casino era began.[7] While 'public memory' may not always represent a completely accurate depiction of particular events and issues, it is reliably important for the creation of a meaningful narrative for historical participants. Some oral history narrators for this project who visited the region before the casinos came to town recalled a bleak setting for personal and professional prospects in the 1970s. They also remembered something of a golden age of glamour, wealth, beauty and easy-living along the Boardwalk in the mid-twentieth century.[8]

The pre-casino 'public memory' is very instructive and could be polished for tourist consumption, but the reality was a little different. People living in and around Atlantic City do not share the same idealized view – they recall a bleak and long decline for the region, from the 1950s through the 1970s.[9] In particular, Latino and African-American narrators from the period describe a bleak economic circumstance, shaded by segregation and exclusion. One narrator, Pierre Hollingworth discussed life in the segregated city:

> And actually, certain restaurants did not cater, nor did they want blacks. They didn't have no signs up there that said that, but they weren't very friendly about it. The beach was the same way. There was a certain section of the beach called Missouri Avenue, that was set aside specifically for black folk.

Hollingsworth's memories of economic poverty were tinged with racial exclusion:

> So in those days, it was – like I said, it was poor, but when you look right down to it, you didn't really know how poor you were until you start seeing the other side of town. And then, when you saw the other side of town, you began to really directly know what was [happening].[10]

Effective oral history demands that memories of the past are rightfully understood within the context of narrators' personal meanings and cultural perspectives.[11] In Atlantic City's casino era, one's perception varied tremendously based on cultural orientation, employment, location and family experience. Aside from the clear changes that took place when casinos appeared on the Atlantic City skyline, the casino era is often understood in highly subjective terms, depending on who is looking back.[12] Oral history excerpts throughout *Gambling on the American Dream* reflect this personalized view of history. The dramatic changes of fortune and upheaval experienced by longtime Atlantic City residents and newcomers in the casino era contributed to the creation of a powerful social narrative.[13]

The historical literature on Atlantic City's casino era is relatively scant, and until now, no book existed that effectively documented the entire time frame from the perspective of the casino industry, its employees and the public officials politically responsible for it. In the 1980s and 1990s, a number of writers published accounts of the early casino era that were invariably negative. They played up the unsuccessful attempts of the mafia to infiltrate the industry or the social problems that occurred as the casinos were built. These works did a fairly good job of detailing the harsher aspects of the early casino impact on the city itself, yet sometimes paid little attention to the more widespread economic changes being felt by people in Atlantic County and around the region.[14] Other treatments have presented the Atlantic City casino era, casino industry and socio-economic change more positively.[15] A few other works focus more specifically on the casino industry, its operators' and employees' perspectives and its marketing and financial strategies.[16]

More recently two good histories of Atlantic City came out that integrate the casino story into the unfolding story of Atlantic City politics and the decline of twentieth-century urban America: Hal Rothman's *Neon Metropolis: How Las Vegas Started the Twenty-First Century* (2003) and Bryant Simon's *Boardwalk of Dreams: Atlantic City and the Fate of Urban America* (2004). While making important contributions to our understanding of the casino era, Simon's emphasis is outside the industry, focusing more on urban development (or its opposite) and accentuating historical patterns of exclusivity and community indifference. The casino industry, however, really has defined the region since 1978 and, as such, Rothman's study of Las Vegas's casino expansion in the 1990s is closer in focus to *Gambling on the American Dream*. Finally, David Schwartz' comprehensive recent works on Las Vegas and the history of gambling provide effective brief analyses of Atlantic City's casino era.[17]

At a recent social gathering I participated in a conversation in which the topic of Atlantic City came up, as it often does in Maryland these days when people talk about casino or slot machine legalization. Invariably, opponents of legalized casino gambling bring up Atlantic City as a cautionary tale: we certainly do not want to bring that city's problems home, they say. It is understandable that Atlantic City has such a negative reputation in the mid-Atlantic region of the United States, its primary source of revenue. For thirty years, gamblers from New York City, eastern Pennsylvania, greater Washington DC and Baltimore have flocked to the South Jersey shore for fun and fortune, or, at least, the thrill of gambling and the chance for a windfall. As their cars or busses exit the Atlantic City Expressway and head towards a casino, they often see a bleak landscape of broken-down houses, a deteriorating commercial centre, ever-present 'We Buy Gold' jewellery/pawn shops, and other signs of urban squalor. Unfortunately, this impression is decidedly false. Much more has gone on in Atlantic City's casino era – most importantly, it has been a place to achieve one's American dream.

1 WE ARE FOR GAMBLING: THE PRE-CASINO YEARS AND CASINO LEGALIZATION

The casinos came to town in May 1978 after state residents passed a referendum allowing them into Atlantic City in 1976. They arrived into a landscape of decay and depression. Atlantic City was a very bleak place to live in the 1970s, having never broken away from its summer resort economy. There was little economic hope or opportunity outside the three summer months and the city never recovered its status as a premiere ocean resort in the early twentieth century. The situation in Atlantic City was such that the city's primary hospital barely covered expenses and a new medical centre it opened on the 'mainland' barely survived its first year of operation in 1976.[18] Atlantic City was also in the midst of a steep population decline that would lower its population by almost 50 per cent in twenty years, to about 41,000 in 1980 from over 60,000 in 1960.[19]

By 1976, the famous Boardwalk had become a platform for observing the city's decay. Garbage and debris littered the city and the once glorious hotels were barely surviving. Boarding houses and blocks bereft of human activity greeted visitors, including the early casino visionaries. Amidst the crumbling city of the era, the nation's racial and class tensions played out as urban blacks from around the mid-Atlantic flowed into the city on summer weekend bus trips. This alarmed city leaders who were trying hard to make the city once again attractive to middle-class white visitors. Steel Pier owner George Hamid Sr, for example, sought to discourage black day-tripping 'shoobies' (they packed their necessaries in shoeboxes), by re-creating his uptown Steel Pier as a quasi-Disneyland with an aquarium, petting zoo, even an ice skating rink operable in the summer. After all, how many 'shoobies' were ice skaters?[20]

Long-time resident Barbara Devlin recalled the slow-paced, summer-resort atmosphere of the pre-casino years after the resort's glory era in the early twentieth century:

> There were no casinos at that time, obviously, and they pretty much folded up the sidewalks after September, after the Miss America Pageant was over. That was pretty much it. So, it was real quiet.

Devlin was the type of aspiring entertainer that Atlantic City had drawn for years, in fact that it had become famous for developing. Her attempt to make it as a singing waitress followed in the tradition of her father, a singing bartender during the sunset of the 500 Club era, after its headliners Frank Sinatra and Dean Lewis had become big stars. She came for the summer with her family as a pre-teen and became so enamoured of the city that she returned on her own as a teenager. She was a singer and waitress who eventually found work in the casinos before becoming a union official with Local 54, the casino employees union. Her experience as a young woman in the pre-casino 1970s spoke to the city's lack of opportunity for year-round residents:

> The business slowed down significantly, especially in the dead of winter, December, January, February: that was real tough. Everybody lived on unemployment – so I was a professional unemployed waitress.[21]

By 1974, the city was known more for a dearth of human activity from September to June, when one 'could have rolled a bowling ball from one end of Atlantic Avenue to the other without hitting anything'. Indeed, it must have been difficult, as Devlin remembered, to eke out a living given the bleak setting: 'Across Atlantic Avenue and onto Baltic and Mediterranean, the buildings blurred into a huge pile of rubble making up a vast ghetto' dotted with 'abandoned churches, rundown boardinghouses, discount liquor stores and greasy-thumb eateries that closed down by dark'. By the early 1970s, Atlantic City had developed the lowest per capita income of any town in New Jersey, but the highest per capita quotient of contagious diseases. In addition, its infant mortality rate, crimes-per-capita and poverty rate also exceeded any other New Jersey city. In an age of national urban decay, Atlantic City was one of the most decayed cities in the nation.[22]

As a resort town, the city's economy barely existed without visitors and visitors were no longer coming in the numbers they once had. In the decade leading up to 1976, Atlantic City lost 6,000 hotel rooms – a decrease of 43 per cent from 1966. The lack of jobs outside a dying Boardwalk caused unemployment to skyrocket in the 1970s – up to almost twenty per cent. Meanwhile, approximately ten per cent of the city's houses had been abandoned by their owners by 1976.[23]

Barbara Devlin survived as a young adult in the midst of squalor and decay by maintaining a link to an earlier culture. For about eight years, she found work as a waitress and singer in the summer seasons. For Devlin, there was something unique and grand about Atlantic City, something that made it worth remaining:

> I liked the rhythm of the city. The city had a lot of soul, I thought, even pre-casino. You know, you still had the...the Boardwalk was still interesting. The hotels, the old hotels, were very stately. You know the town was unique ... So, I chose to stay, even though it was a bit of struggle to get through the winter.[24]

Another long-time resident, Russelle Patterson also became enamoured with the region as a young girl visiting from New York in the 1940s. Like Devlin, her childhood experiences, formed when the resort town was at its height of popularity amongst relatively affluent urbanites from the East Coast, created a sense of awe and majesty about Atlantic City. Patterson remembered that her father had been a judge for the Miss America pageant in the 1940s. She recalled coming from New York on the train to join her father. Her memory of Atlantic City at that time was that it was

> pure white, pristine, magnificent hotels, people well-dressed, a sparkling clean Boardwalk, people horseback riding on the beach, bands playing in the afternoon, tea in the afternoon out on the promenades. It was great.[25]

Later, Patterson's parents moved to Brigantine (outside Atlantic City) and she too decided to move to the area after a divorce, for opportunity and family. She came when she sensed the region was experiencing negative change and she wanted to be one of its reformers:

> And then, eventually, you take your stuff out of storage and you bring it down here and at this point in my life I thought I had dug a hole for myself, because Atlantic City was starting to change, and I figured I'm going to be one of the contributors to try and bring this city back. I stayed.

Patterson's decision to stay in Atlantic City was actually based on her desire to revive the city from its degraded state. It had to come back, she thought, to fulfil a historical promise:

> I could not believe what happened to the Boardwalk ... the deterioration, the blight in the city, the sad people. It was truly a queen that was dying.

To Patterson, there was an inevitability of sorts to casino era, as if the city really needed something to happen and that it would happen:

> you knew something had to happen or else the town would be no more. It was almost like the expression, 'last one over the bridge, make sure you turn out the light' ... that's what it was becoming. There were no jobs, a depressed population.[26]

As Boardwalk merchants like George Hamid tried hard to reinvigorate their turf, other parts of the city experienced some growth and dynamism in the pre-casino 1970s. Specifically, a growing Puerto Rican community sprang up in a part of the city called the South Inlet. The Latino community that emerged developed substantial neighbourhood institutions like Gil Maldonado's bodega and Spanish language churches, despite rejection and occasional hostility from non-Latinos. Historian Bryant Simon observes, 'a new neighborhood – albeit a poor and distressed one – was starting to take shape'. As well, the city's historical gay community experienced something of a revival in the pre-casino 1970s.[27]

The Hispanic community of the South Inlet was a vibrant and active one, if not especially wealthy. The culture existed in numerous small markets and restaurants, and neighbours knew each other – providing safety through familiarity. The barrio was separate from the city by way of a strongly understood racial divide, yet provided a welcoming and supportive environment for those residents willing to work hard to achieve, as was the case with future local attorney and Latino community leader J. David Alcantara:

> And people felt a need to associate with fellow Hispanics because you felt, at that time especially, even more limited, because there's just no Spanish to be spoken anywhere else but just that little group. We couldn't – and we had one or two stores that were Spanish-speaking stores ... it was amazing. At that time, I remember when we finally moved to Atlantic Avenue, there was an Acme, and that was where the Atlantic City Police Department stands. As a ten-year-old, walking with my mom hand-in-hand, and someone would go by and speaking Spanish, I say, Mom, Mom! Nudged her in the side and said they speak Spanish! And it was an amazing thing, because it's like going to China and you find somebody from New Jersey. It's like, wow. It was amazing. So people got to know each other, and it was a really warm thing to be able to talk to someone that understood at least the language, even if they were from a different sub-Hispanic culture.[28]

The new Puerto Rican South Inlet was an important forerunner to the immigrant communities that would become central to the city's identity in the 1990s. In the casino era, groups of Vietnamese and Central Americans similarly created supportive neighbourhoods, despite the constant economic struggle that comes with giving up everything in one part of the world for a new beginning somewhere else. The immigrant gamble is one of the core components of American history and provides a focal point of understanding the casino era. As the city itself turned to gambling to bring back its lost fortune, immigrants would soon play a central role. In helping the city start over, they too would be starting over: individually and collectively the people of Atlantic City saw in the casinos a brighter future.

When residents like Russelle Patterson made the decision to revive their town in the 1970s, gambling was a natural choice to channel their efforts. After all, Atlantic City built its reputation in the early twentieth century in large part on the widespread availability of gambling. Brothels replete with gambling, regular casinos, numbers games, illegal off-track horse betting and even full casinos were commonplace in the 1920s and 1930s, operating up and down Atlantic and Pacific avenues and easily accessible. In fact, the prevalence of gambling in the city was so intense in the early twentieth century that the political machine controlling the city catered directly to the gambling operators and brothels. Political leaders like the flamboyant Enoch 'Nucky' Johnson (the carnation-wearing 'Czar of the Ritz') shared openly in the profits in exchange for not challenging the legality of the gamblers. Historian Nelson Johnson notes that 'Gambling was Atlantic City's serious business' and that it had been central to the resort's economy for many decades by the 1930s. By then, gambling interests had become 'entrenched' power players within the neighbourhoods around the city.[29] In 1930, William Randolph Heart's *New York Evening Journal* ran an exposé on Atlantic City's gambling operations and the cover they enjoyed from local law enforcement. According to the paper, the city had 'Protected horse racing, slot machines, and municipal graft on a grand scale'. Reportedly, two mob outfits from Philadelphia had infiltrated the city to the extent that 'These groups now divide between them the gambling concessions in Atlantic City'.[30]

In 1936, the Federal Bureau of Investigation (FBI) launched an investigation that turned up eight prostitution houses and gambling houses. Around the time, an avenue stroller had his or her choice of 800 different businesses to play the illegal numbers game. Gambling houses varied in scope and sophistication, but most had roulette, blackjack, craps and racing results as a consequence of a wire service arrangement with Johnson. A few even paid round-trip train fares to their gambling customers – a stunningly close precursor to the mass-bussing in of gamblers in the legal casino era. Some of the bigger operations even developed a national clientele. They were illegal, but hardly secret and were an essential component to Atlantic City's economy beyond the resort's tourist bonanza.

According to long-time resident Gloria Vallee, the illegal casino era had a certain elegance to it. Vallee's 'Uncle Dan' ran Babette's on Pacific and Mississippi avenues. He was apparently adept at utilizing the corrupted legal and political network to further his casino's standing by protecting high rollers. In 1980 Vallee reminisced that the police constantly raided Babette's, but usually notified her uncle ahead of time so he could warn his gamblers. Nevertheless, escaping the authorities was an adventure:

> There was a trap door leading from the horse room ... You would go up a flight of stairs that led to the roof, cross the roof and go down the steps on the side of the building which led into Uncle Dan's and Babette's houses.[31]

'Uncle Dan' would have probably sprung quickly into action to protect his clients in a raid such as the following, documented in 1941:

> Excitement subsided last night after police raids on four alleged gaming establishments Monday, and of the 31 persons taken into custody, only four were still jailed as disorderly persons, undesirables or as gamblers.[32]

In the early 1940s, grandstanding mayor 'Two Gun Tommy' Taggart made a big show of personally leading raids on gambling houses around the city.[33]

Vallee also recalled the style of the earlier casinos and the influence of the era's mobsters. Like other recollections of Atlantic City's pre-casino decades, they are tinged with nostalgia for a more elegant, fashionable place populated by wealthy, rich vacationers:

> There was elegance to the people who gambled at Babette's. They were dressed, they wore furs; it was almost a formal look. You got people like the Wanamakers, Astors, Goulds and Vanderbilts, who came to the club every time.

The city's status as a safe, 'free city' for mobsters, as negotiated by 'Nucky' Johnson, played a role in its gambling culture, with a 1933 convention held at the Ritz Carlton hotel where he maintained a whole floor as his residence. Al Capone and other prominent mob figures of the 1930s were regular visitors and helped float the economy, though the public face of the town was something altogether different:

> the talk was that it was a resort and health spot, they [mobsters] all wanted Atlantic City to be one safe place where you could visit. And no one ever violated that truce.

In the resort town's twentieth-century glory days, gambling was both a central motif, drawing tourists, and an important economic engine:

> When we had gambling then, it was during the Depression. But somehow, [the Depression] was never felt down here. There were always jobs, people had food on the table.

As in the latter-day casino era, Vallee's recollections suggest that the city benefited significantly from positive public relations and the direct cash infusion that casinos brought. Vallee also spoke wistfully of a historic Atlantic City that self-regulated its excesses and thus ensured a quality standard of living for its citizenry. The casinos of that time successfully fulfilled their mission in her eyes, and the residents of the region realized both individual and collective benefits as a result. Her view of the illegal casino era reflected the 1970s debate over the merits (or lack thereof) of casinos in Atlantic City.[34]

While Babette's favourably impressed the teenaged Vallee, it had the opposite effect on the FBI, which ran a full-scale investigation of 'Nucky' Johnson and the illegal gambling business of Atlantic City from 1936 to 1941. Eventually, the investigation led to Johnson's conviction for tax evasion and a ten-year jail sentence, of which he ended up serving four. Meanwhile, the local political machine pushed 'Two Gun Tommy' out of his position and restored a certain order to Atlantic City under the legendary boss Francis 'Hap' Farley.[35]

The illegal casinos and assorted gambling operations never fully went away in the early 1940s. In 1949, a *New York Times* reporter noted that, in many of the 1,100 'tobacco, delicatessen stores, shoe shine parlors and newsstands', horse bets could be placed in addition to 'policy game' bets.[36] Public attention on the city's gambling operations picked up in the early 1950s. Beginning in 1950, a band of policemen took it upon themselves to enforce the letter of the law by raiding the gambling houses and making arrests. They became known as the 'Four Horsemen', and were possibly motivated by a desire for revenge following a failed city referendum that would have granted police and firefighters a guaranteed pay increase. The local Republican political machine now controlled by Hap Farley undermined the referendum, which was defeated in the 1950 election. The policemen may have honestly sought to enforce New Jersey's anti-gambling laws or may simply have desired to embarrass the political machine that remained supplicant and benign to gambling syndicates in the tradition of 'Nucky' Johnson.[37]

The police scrutiny on gambling continued despite the efforts of Farley, and his political associates to stop it. The Republican machine that ran Atlantic County included a protection operation that passed bribes to the politicians from the racketeers in exchange for salutary neglect by law enforcement authorities. The machine exercised its power over the police through 'Stumpy' Orman, a local real estate and hotel magnate, with offending cops assigned away from the gambling operations, eventually charged with misconduct and fired. It was, however, too late for the machine and their patrons – the police actions caused the state's attorney general to call for a crackdown on illegal gambling. Even more damaging to the gambling establishment, Atlantic City's gambling operations and compliant public officials became a focal point of the hearings on organized crime in the United States Senate that began in 1951, led by Tennessee Senator Estes Kefauver.[38]

The Kefauver hearings exposed the relationship between organized crime, gambling and the political machine running Atlantic City. They also marked the end of an era in gambling in Atlantic City by shutting down a number of major gambling halls. The episode wrought a clear shift in the mentality of many in the region, who had come to accept and even embrace the illegal gambling operations as a unique, dangerous but exciting feature of life in South Jersey. Recalling the hearings' impact, one resident likened them to a destructive force that forever changed the 'delicate balance of power' in Atlantic City. Local club owner Skinny D'Amato commented that the hearings changed the public perception of gambling:

> Before it was wide open. Then, all at once, gambling became dirty. Not just in Atlantic City, but all over the country. But it didn't matter to most cities, because gambling was only a small part of most cities. But it was bad here, because the casinos and the horse rooms were a big, big part of this town.[39]

Atlantic City's illegal gambling era provided a substantial legacy for the legal casino era that began in 1978. Most importantly, it created the identity of the region as one that included gambling as a natural feature. There was nothing wrong with it and perhaps it even contributed positively to the regional stability, well-being and sense of community. That the gambling operations were illegal and mob-controlled was irrelevant and essentially meaningless given the complicity of politicians and legal authorities. It was virtually legal. So where did concerned residents turn when they sought a remedy for the urban blight around them in the 1970s? Naturally, they looked towards history – they looked towards gambling. In doing so, they tied their own history to an optimistic future. They looked around and decided to gamble on restoring the American dream of opportunity and economic success to their faded resort city.

As gambling was virtually legal in Atlantic City through the early 1950s, the jump towards legalization seemed to be a natural leap for some. As early as 1949, the *New York Times* reported that there were 'extremists who would like to see a state law permitting Atlantic City to operate on the same plane as Reno or Las Vegas', although the writer was sceptical: 'It is doubtful if such a situation will ever develop.'[40] In 1958, the Atlantic City Women's Chamber of Commerce passed a resolution supporting legalized gambling in the city. Local hotel owner Mildred Fox pushed for the resolution and soon became a target of death threats and a candidate for police protection, possibly having been threatened by illegal gambling proprietors. Meanwhile, Hap Farley remained a powerful political boss and in the 1960s may have used his influence to prevent the spread of legalized gambling to Atlantic City out of fear of scrutiny of his local machine. Yet, as his career reached its twilight, Farley also unsuccessfully supported a gambling bill proposed in the state legislature in 1970. After he retired, the conversation opened again and picked up substantial momentum in the early 1970s, as the city plunged further into urban decay.[41]

In 1970, a new political push for casinos began, as North Jersey State Senator Frank McDermott sought to bring legalized gambling to Atlantic City under strict state control, and with dedicated taxes, in order to aid New Jersey's 'most pressing urban problems' and to 'provide housing for senior citizens, public safety and business and industrial promotion and development'.[42] The initiative quickly gained momentum in and around South Jersey and Trenton. In 1970 and 1971, the legislature held at least three separate hearings on resolutions in support of legalized gambling – a prospect that had already gained both grass-roots advocates and detractors around the state. A good representative statement in support of the idea is that of Gary Malamut, of the New Jersey Hotel-Motel Association, issued during a 1970 hearing. Malamut asked the legislators to 'Forget Nevada' and think about casino destinations around the world, notable for style and upscale relaxation like Monte Carlo, Curacao, Aruba and Portugal's Estoril. He argued that casino legalization was actually the best way to control organized crime from the business:

> The opponents, whatever their motivation, are unwittingly playing into the hands of organized crime by their objections. The objectors are perpetrating everything that they claim to be against: morality, corruption and narcotics ...

Malamut railed against the hypocrisy of those who both opposed legalization and denied the understood connections between the mafia and gambling. He appealed to the law-and-order sensibilities of the state senators:

> It's no wonder children say, 'Don't trust anyone over 30'. They look at hypocritical adults with our heads in the sand about organized crime, gambling and narcotics. Our public officials are doing a good job, but it would take thousands more. Many law enforcement officials endorse legalized gambling. They want to concentrate their time, money and effort on true crime enforcement. Raiding a bookie joint, or a numbers parlor versus a junkie assaulting and robbing a person seems a poor comparison.

Atlantic City Chamber of Commerce President Anthony Rey spoke directly to the economic impact of legal casinos:

> Not only would legalized gambling return employment on a year-round basis in the resort industry, which is either the number one or number two industry of our state, but would return the tourist who formerly filled our resort hotel and motel rooms twelve months a year and has now left our state to enjoy the gaming facilities in San Juan, the Bahamas and other such recreation centres here and abroad.[43]

At another 1970 hearing on casino legalization in Trenton, some 200 people came up from Atlantic City to demonstrate support for legalized gambling. 'WE ARE FOR GAMBLING * NOT MORE TAXES' read a large banner held up in the gallery by Democrats from Atlantic City. Sixteen witnesses testified, with fifteen in support and one in opposition to casinos on the Boardwalk. The hearing focused on the plight of state seniors, the inability of working people to pay higher taxes, and the possibility of permitting various shore towns (such as Asbury Park and Wildwood) to open casinos. Momentum for legal casinos was definitely on the rise in 1970 and 1971, despite the steady opposition of Republican Governor William Cahill.[44]

By early 1971, the State Senate was studying a specific resolution 'to authorize by law the operation of gambling games in Atlantic City'. Another hearing ensued to consider the efficacy of putting a resolution before voters to legalize casinos. Once again, supporting groups represented included firemen, business leaders, a teachers' union and the mayor of Wildwood, another shore town. Articulating opposition to the proposed referendum was a Minister with affiliated religious lobbying groups and members of the group Reach an Early Abatement of Crime and Taxes (REACT). The REACT witnesses opposed the resolution because it involved private enterprises to run the casinos, where they wanted the state to operate the casinos so that all employees would be public employees.[45]

The 1971 resolution did not pass, but it did lead to the creation of a 'Gambling Study Commission'. The commission reported back to the governor and legislature in early 1973. It backed legalized gambling based on its conclusion that substantial numbers of people gambled illegally but were mainly 'law-abiding citizens and do not nurture crime by choice'. The commission's report must have been joyfully received by the pro-gambling testifiers of earlier sessions as it came out against 'the hypocrisy and most of the corruption which the present anti-gambling laws foster'. The report also discussed the likelihood that compulsive gambling would become more problematic and laid the foundations for the eventual *Casino Control Act* and later revenue-generating programs. Finally, it left the question of state or private casino ownership open, though it was also very clear on the need for strict state supervision – probably because of the vocal argument of gambling opponents that gambling would naturally lead to more petty crime and organized crime.[46]

A legislative hearing subsequent to the commission's report in support of the referendum brought forth another motley crew of gambling opponents. These included the National Football League's Security Director, a fellow from the 'United Seniors of New Jersey', a number of clergy representatives, a lawyer from the horse-racing industry and a state police colonel. The policeman spoke out forcefully against the proposed referendum, previewing law enforcement's role in the statewide campaign. He presciently addressed a number of concerns, including high new costs for law enforcement, organized crime's inevitable influence, the attraction of unsavoury characters to the state and the general decrease in the community's living standards as measured by security and police interaction:

> we find that even in Nevada, as far away as it is out in the desert, their crime rate is real high in terms of the robberies and the muggings. Now relating that to New Jersey, wherever this casino may be, in terms of the millions of people that can be there in a half hour, there come the muggers, the robbers, the thieves, the shylocks, the hookers, all of those things that affect a community policewise.

Though clearly outnumbered, the referendum supporters developed a powerful and relatively simple argument for their side, easily expressed by Richard Lavin, Atlantic City bartender:

Let me again have a decent personal income. Let us again put the Atlantic County worker on the payrolls, instead of the relief rolls. Let us again increase our population. Let us again attract builders to give us the hotel rooms that we need. Let us again, have a year round economy. Let us have gambling.[47]

The line-up of the hearing probably foretold the immediate future of the first legalization referendum, which made it to the ballot in 1974. It also offered a glimpse of the underestimated power of a grass-roots idea that made tremendous sense. The increasing political and popular momentum in the early 1970s for legalized gambling was understandable given the powerful desire of the Atlantic City community to revive its town. The local pro-casino energy reflected a will and recognition of gambling as a natural fit for Atlantic City, probably based upon the city's history and gambling's demonstrated capability to draw visitors.

The movement to bring gambling to Atlantic City had a natural champion in Skinny D'Amato in the 1970s. By 1974, D'Amato's position as community leader was intact, despite his own personal difficulties following the decline and (after a fire in 1973) closure of his 500 Club. D'Amato had associated himself with the pro-gambling movement for a few years, and in the early 1970s gave quotes to the local press and even appeared on *60 Minutes* to support the cause. With his club gone and having personally experienced the region's decline, D'Amato now came out strongly for legalized gambling as a means to restore the resort in the image of Las Vegas. D'Amato distanced himself from those advocating state-owned casinos with an important point of logic: that they would have neither the capacity nor inclination to float large amounts of credit to gamblers ($50,000–100,000), and would therefore not bring in much revenue or operate very successfully.[48]

At the time, D'Amato had a bolder vision than others, like new governor Brendan Byrne. Governor Byrne, along with a broad coalition of groups such as REACT, had a more refined idea of legalized casinos. They pushed for legalized gambling in neat intimate clubs with limited hours and moderate-to-low public profiles. Some even sought vigorously to oppose slot machines, on the assumption that re-making Atlantic City into a town with 'Las Vegas-style, 24-hour-a-day string of casinos' would 'come not only as a nightmare to us, but to almost every other business undertaking in a community where casinos are a possibility'.[49]

But would the limited approach to legal casinos be enough to revive the city? D'Amato thought not and seemed to sense what was imminent, even if he was not in much of a position to capitalize on it at this stage in his life. D'Amato knew that the gambling business was as much about entertainment as it was the desire to bet. As a result, his notion of casinos drew upon the successful model of Las Vegas – a place where gambling, entertainment and culture had become intertwined to prosperous effect. Did Atlantic City ever become an eastern Vegas as D'Amato hoped? Partially it did, as the casinos that eventually dotted the Boardwalk and Marina district were mostly large, all-inclusive and certainly flamboyant. Yet, the casino community of Atlantic City eventually became something far different than anything imagined by D'Amato or anybody else in the early 1970s. It eventually became a dynamic setting for the American dream involving new players and new scenarios scarcely understood, yet fundamentally implied by the city's human links to its own history.

But getting to the desired outcome was no easy task, and the plan appeared to be stillborn when New Jersey voters rejected the first pro-gambling referendum in 1974 by 400,000 votes. Despite some receptiveness to the idea shown by the new governor, the movement for casinos never gained much traction around the state in 1974. It failed due to the inability of the local champions to convince state residents or to effectively oppose a fairly widespread anti-gambling movement, spearheaded by a coalition of New Jersey clergymen and law enforcement officials called 'No Dice'. The 1974 referendum also failed because it did not restrict legal casino gambling to Atlantic City, consequently spurring heavy statewide opposition. Nevertheless, local legislators Steve Perskie and Joe McGahn worked hard to organize the referendum and campaigned relentlessly around the state for its passage. They simply fell short to sharp opposition led in Trenton by rising political stars such as Thomas Kean, and media bulwarks from both New York and Philadelphia like the *New York Times* and *Wall Street Journal*. The Republican Kean led the fight in the state house:

> Gambling would become our primary business, we would become known as the gambling state, and all legislation would be discussed in terms of how the gambling interests feel about it.[50]

Meanwhile, state politics over a new state income tax also impacted the casino debate. How could the state raise more revenue without casinos? Looking back, Perskie recalled that

> there was a kind of a civil war going on in New Jersey politics in 1974 over the question of whether we should or should not have a state income tax. At the time New Jersey was one of only two states in the nation that didn't.

Perskie at first favoured the income tax, but he also understood that it was not really a question of one or the other (tax or legalization), even if others muddied the issue and hurt their own cause:

> we had a number of people coming out from Atlantic City who hadn't been trained and didn't know what they were talking about, who would go to a Lions Club in Ocean County, for example, and say if you pass casinos in Atlantic City, you won't need an income tax, which was sheer nonsense. It didn't make any sense, and people knew it.[51]

The 1974 referendum turned out to be more of a speed bump than a roadblock on the road towards casino legalization. Perskie, McGahn and their allies analyzed the loss and put together a much sounder campaign for a second referendum that eventually took place in 1976. The success of the second campaign also included a new, well organized pro-casino effort led by the Committee to Re-Build Atlantic City (CRAC). CRAC raised over $1.3 million by appealing to various pro-gambling interests, including Resorts International, a Bahamas-based firm looking to expand its casino operations inside the United States. CRAC consisted of a number of well-connected power players including Mildred Fox and Hap Farley. With Perskie's support, Farley spent thirty-four years of political capital to build support for the cause. In addition, CRAC hired an experienced, professional and exceptionally talented consultant from San Francisco, Sanford Weiner, to run the campaign: a good model for media-based politicking that effectively reversed the media advantage of the 1974 opponents. A CRAC brochure sought to assuage the fears of those who anticipated a wild and lawless Atlantic City:

> Fact: Tightest Controls in the WorldAtlantic City casinos would be governed by the tightest regulations in the world, including the creation of a Casino Control Commission to *license, regulate* and *audit* the operation of all casinos. Ownership will be private. Eligibility requirements for licenses will be strict and licenses will be subject to suspension or revocation at any time. Regulations will include full disclosure, unannounced inspection and subpoena power.[52]

Yet, all the organization and slick politicking in a century of American politics would not have made much difference without an effective message. Obviously, the 1974 message was not effective enough: that the state needed casino gaming to revive Atlantic City and perhaps preclude future tax hikes. Thus, Perskie and McGhan came up with a clever solution: to tie the casino tax revenues to a dedicated fund for senior citizens' utility bills and property taxes. In addition, the new proposal specifically designated Atlantic City as the site for legalized gambling, as opposed to 1974 when the amendment identified only 'specified municipalities' and left casino placement in the hands of local voters. The 1976 measure also resolved the public versus private issue definitively by allowing for privately-owned casinos. Perskie recollected that the referendum backers made this key decision 'in order to maximize the opportunity of attracting private investment capital into New Jersey in general and Atlantic City in particular'.[53]

Perskie recalled that between 1974 and 1976, casino backers developed a tight, effective strategy to win the next referendum. According to Perskie,

> Everybody who was anybody was represented in this committee and the committee assumed general responsibility for the conduct of the referendum campaign and raised the money and sent out the speakers.

CRAC leadership included people who realized that the key to a winning campaign was to address inevitable questions ahead of time:

> We knew from our '74 experience that there would be a gazillion questions
> from the electorate – how's this going to operate? Who's going to regulate
> it? What are the rules going to be? Where's it going to go? Who's going to
> get the license?

They addressed these concerns by drafting the first version of the law that would
eventually be known as the *Casino Control Act* (*CCA*). In the two months before
the 1976 referendum, CRAC members travelled the state with copies of the legislation, a move that Perskie believed was crucial for securing passage, because
they

> came across looking to the state by people who knew what we were doing and
> people who had answers to the various questions, and those answers were
> consistent and rational, and that gave people some measure of confidence to
> be able to vote yes.[54]

At a legislative hearing on the new referendum, many more business people
and others lined up to support legalized casinos than did so at similar hearings a few years earlier. Importantly, the new list included Atlantic City Police
Chief William Tenbrink, whose testimony must have helped to refute the law
enforcement opposition to the 1974 referendum articulated by Colonel Kelly –
opposition that had faced no rebuttal before. Tenbrink acknowledged that crime
would probably go up, but was optimistic that the police could handle a potential
crime increase:

> As far as the crime picture in Atlantic City – certainly we have crime in
> Atlantic City. The entire country has crime. Will casino gambling cause an
> increase in crime? I honestly, at this time, can't tell you it would not cause
> an increase in crime. However, I do not see it becoming a disastrous type of
> increase.

He also testified 'that the police department we have could handle the every-
day crime problems'. As he put it, 'the problems [of legalized casinos] are greatly
blown out of proportion'. Tenbrink then discussed his own view that unemployment and television inducements for commercial products were significantly
more responsible for causing crime than the potential problems spurred by the
casinos.[55]

At least one vocal opponent in the earlier debate made sure his voice was
heard by the politicians again, Dr Samuel A. Jeanes, of the New Jersey Christian
Conference on Legislation. Dr Jeanes remained far from 'neutralized' by the
additions to the amendment, arguing that the state should look to other opportunities for stimulating the South Jersey coastal economy and enhancing revenues.
As such, he advocated for the construction of 'the world's first floating nuclear

power plant' off the coast. He also had no patience for the proposed new benefits for seniors:

> Of course this gambling proposal has a carrot designed to capture the support of the Senior Citizens. It says that the State revenue from the gambling houses will provide reductions in property taxes, rentals, telephone, gas, electric and municipal utilities for eligible Senior Citizens and disabled residents. However, one of the sponsors of this resolution said on New Jersey television that the revenue from all the race tracks in New Jersey was but 'a drop in the bucket'. The rosy predictions of our politicians never materialized. And by the time the state funds another Bureau to handle whatever revenue it might collect, the Senior Citizens and disabled residents will find that this carrot has a great big hole in it.[56]

Also from the same hearing was an official letter submitted by Mildred Fox that called on the legislature 'to give the people of Atlantic City the right to decide their own destiny' arguing that 'It is time for North Jersey to help South Jersey survive by helping to rejuvenate and rebuild Atlantic City which is the largest resort in the state. And by so doing, every person in New Jersey will be a winner'. In profound opposition was the Reverend Jack Johnson of St Andrew's Methodist Church of Tom's River, who wrote in to say that 'We believe gambling is a menace to society, deadly to the best interest of moral, social, economic, and spiritual life' and that 'We believe the proposed "Casino gambling" will only increase the degree of corruption and decay in our state in terms of the presence of organized crime'.[57]

Around Atlantic City and South Jersey, the business community formed the core of the pro-casino movement. A 1976 Atlantic County Chamber of Commerce bulletin noted that efforts had been initiated 'to identify potential contributors to the Casino drive from throughout county'. The business argument was a dynamic force in and around Atlantic City to support casino legalization, whereas other reasons held sway around the state. Statewide, the proposed revenue fund made a huge difference for passage in 1976.[58]

Casino legalization heated up as Atlantic City's circumstances fell under scrutiny by a charter commission that studied the city and its form of government in the mid-1970s. In 1976, the commission produced a report entitled *Atlantic City on the Brink of Survival* and recommended a local referendum for the November election to institute a mayor with power, a change from the existing commission that ran the city beginning in 1912. The charter commission noted that

> each year our tourist oriented businesses are earning less and less money yet each year marks the closing of more hotels, restaurants, nightclubs, and other establishments which depend on tourists.

Since the late 1960s, the business climate had become considerably worse according to the report:

> Although our tourist industry has been experiencing a gradual decline ever since the days of the depression, this industry has displayed an unusually rapid decline beginning in 1968, clearly marking the turning point in our city's history.

The commission lamented the loss of the middle-class, 'young and middle-aged population of the city, both black and white', which it maintained was 'moving to the suburbs', and depicted a landscape of urban decay:

> Each year hundreds of buildings, hotels, businesses, and housing units are left vacant, vandalized, destroyed by fire, or demolished for some other reason [...] Virtually nothing has been built to replace them.[59]

Though the study did not mention casinos, the timing was certainly fortuitous for the pro-gambling forces, who were essentially making the same argument in the Trenton chamber rooms and to public audiences around the state. The study made clear that Atlantic City's economy was in a virtual shambles. Many restaurants and bars had already closed, and many of the ones left were barely hanging on. Many were neighbourhood hangouts, some had already filed bankruptcy petitions before casino legalization, while others stayed open just because it was cheaper to declare bankruptcy, and 'defer debt repayments and tax liabilities'. Without the major hotels operating, local businesses could barely sustain themselves. Between 1966 and 1976, fourteen of the city's biggest hotels had closed, including the Traymore, the Ritz-Carlton, Dennis, the Claridge, the Breakers and the President. Things were bleak, so the people rallied and casinos came to town.[60]

How was the referendum received in Atlantic City? In the words of Barbara Devlin, the scene was just amazing:

> That was an incredibly enormous party, all the bars and restaurants, hotels just opened their doors to people. It was open house in the town, when it passed ... We were thrilled! We thought our ship came in ... All the workers and all the folks who were local and had waited to see this town start heading up again, because it was going to be Vegas, I mean I didn't even think about Vegas, I thought about Monte Carlo! I really thought we were headed for great things here ... It was a great night; it was outstanding.[61]

But the casino era began slowly after the referendum passed. The first casino didn't open for eighteen months, and that surprised people. Russelle Patterson recalled that a lot of the population expected once they voted for gaming in Atlantic City that the next morning they would wake up casinos had magically risen out of the ocean. It seemed like the longest two years, waiting until May 1978 for Resorts to open.[62]

The day after the referendum, a national news service called the news desk of the *Atlantic City Press* to request a picture of people streaming into a newly-legalized casino.[63]

The optimism that hit the city with the referendum's passage soon translated into a wave of economic activity, as businesses geared up for the coming casinos. In 1977, the Chamber of Commerce alerted its membership that

> Chamber members will have access to the hundreds of inquiries from companies which have written the Chamber noting interest in locating here, offering their services and products to firms here located or planning to locate here, or from skills persons in the casino field seeking employment here.

The group also passed a resolution

> commending and supporting our legislators for their energetic commitment to the development of effective casino gambling enabling legislation and pledging our continued support for their efforts.[64]

While the Chamber was busy processing its business inquiries, some were starting to look at the city's dilapidated properties with a speculative eye. A real estate speculation frenzy was in its early stages as those with money began to look into purchasing lots and decayed buildings in hopes that one day some casino operation would set their sights on the currently undervalued land. Gaming operations were not necessarily getting involved in the speculation (though some did), but the decision to authorize casinos caused the speculation. The real estate speculators took advantage of a lax city government that did not quickly raise its property tax appreciation values. Consequently, some speculators bought property and paid low taxes for years, waiting for casino buyers to come along. This governmental property mismanagement contributed significantly to the real estate crisis that drove many out of their homes for inability to pay elevated rents or unwillingness to live in run-down, poorly-maintained structures. Some landlords preferred to push their tenants out and simply sit on the property until casino suitors came calling. Many of these landlords never did achieve what they had hoped upon legalization.[65]

The 1976 referendum cleared the way for casinos to open in Atlantic City but did not stipulate how they would operate or when they would begin operations. Although a legislative plan was already in place, the resolution of these issues eventually led to the creation and passage of the *CCA* in June 1977. The legislation set up the New Jersey Casino Control Commission (NJCCC) and its enforcement arm, the Division of Gaming Enforcement (DGE). The 1977 *CCA* also set forth a variety of regulations designed to both facilitate successful casinos and comprehensively establish control over casinos. The intent was to help the casinos and ensure that Atlantic City would not become inundated by visitors rushing in and out of the city for gambling purposes alone. Famously, the *CCA* called casino gaming 'a unique tool of urban redevelopment for Atlantic City'. It specified that casinos were meant to 'facilitate the redevelopment of existing blighted areas and the refurbishing and expansion of existing hotel, convention, tourist, and entertainment facilities'.[66]

Once again, nostalgia for a lost glamour influenced the perception of the future. The *CCA*'s designers sought to restore an ebullient panache to the city by re-building the city's tourist glory days, making it once again suitable for families on vacation. To accomplish these ends, they created a system in which the casinos would be strictly controlled via a ninety-six-page bonanza of regulations covering all aspects of the casino operations. The state came in with a strong hand to ensure clean and mob-free casinos, an especially important priority given the concerns over organized crime's perceived influence in earlier gambling operations. Additionally, the casino age in Atlantic City began in the wake of a major organized crime investigation of the Las Vegas casino industry. The regulations were massive, but they did reflect the mindset of the time, despite making life somewhat difficult – perhaps too difficult – for casino operators in coming years. Former casino reporter Daniel Heneghan commented on the many times he heard transplanted casino executives remark 'we don't do it like that in Vegas' in response to the state's regulatory climate.[67]

An introductory section of the *CCA* set a significant tone for the entire document:

> the regulatory provisions of this act are designed to extend strict State regulation to all persons, locations, practices and associations related to the operation of licensed casino enterprises and all service industries as herein provided.

The *CCA*'s heavy emphasis on regulation of all peoples and businesses related to casinos reflected the long debate over casinos in Atlantic City that had taken place throughout much of the 1970s. Casinos were coming to town under microscopic scrutiny. For example, the act's provisions regarding the physical casino space were exacting at a minimum and at times maddeningly precise. The *CCA* mandated that the casinos must 'Provide exterior public entrances to a casino only through an enclosed lobby or receiving foyer of not less than 400 square feet' and

> Establish a single room of at least 15,000 square feet as its casino, and provide the visibility between any two areas in the casino, whether or not contigu-

ous, may not be obstructed by partitions of any kind which cover more than 50% of the structural opening.[68]

The *CCA* also stipulated the exact amount of square footage a casino was allowed to allot for meeting spaces, 'Dining, entertainment and indoor sports' and casino space. Allotments for each category of space corresponded to the number of hotel rooms a facility would offer. The act also strictly limited slot machine space to 25 per cent of the first 50,000 square footage and 30 per cent of additional floor space and mandated the exact sizes of tables for baccarat, blackjack, craps, roulette and the 'Big Six Wheel'. It also defined the exact numbers of each game that casinos could have, based on the gaming room's square footage. It barred 'casino key employees' (employees directly involved with gaming) from gambling anywhere in the state.[69] The *CCA* also required that the casinos had to have 'high standards' as Perskie recalled,

> to maintain quality control enforced by the state: high standards in terms of how much money you had to invest, high standards in terms of what kind of facility you had to produce, high standards in terms of the investigative process that was unprecedented.

This was a very different approach from Nevada's looser regulatory scheme:

> What we did in 1977 in New Jersey in the Casino Control Act, in terms of setting up a new regulatory system was a radical departure from the only other American experience, which was Nevada at the time.[70]

By establishing full-scale resorts, the *CCA* also set up the casinos to become 'self-contained cities' where all of a visitor's needs (gambling, sleep, food, drink, shopping and entertainment) were taken care of. This approach tended to limit the success of surrounding businesses: after all, why go out into a depressed city when everything was available within easy reach of the casino floor?[71]

The *CCA*'s minutiae made sense in the context from which the Atlantic City casinos were born. Some involved in the legalization debate understood that casinos worked best in free-wheeling circumstances (like Skinny D'Amato) that allowed them to maximize entertainment and gambling proceeds. However, this was not the prevailing view in the state capital. In addition, the *CCA* set up the Casino Revenue Fund (CRF) to transfer eight per cent of casino gross revenues to senior citizens' programs and two per cent of revenues beyond initial capital costs for community redevelopment within five years. The latter tax would prove problematic and cumbersome and thus replaced with the establishment of the Casino Re-investment Development Authority (CRDA) in 1984.[72]

Much of the *CCA* was devoted to employee regulation and licensure, as state officials were extremely wary about allowing shady characters to become casino insiders. As such, the licensure process for all casino employees required certification akin to a security clearance from the Federal Bureau of Investigation (FBI). For example, the state law required each applicant to establish his or her own 'reputation for good character, honesty and integrity' by producing information about 'family, habits, character, criminal and arrest record, business activities, financial affairs, and business, professional and personal associates' for the ten years previous to application. In addition, the original *CCA* established a rather daunting process for prospective casino employees:

> Each applicant for casino key employee license shall produce such information, documentation and assurances as ... each applicant shall produce letters of reference from law enforcement agencies having jurisdiction in the applicant's place of residence and principal place of business, which letters of reference shall indicate that such law enforcement agencies do not have any pertinent information concerning the applicant, or if such law enforcement agency does have pertinent information, shall specify what that information is.[73]

The criminal background check and character references might have made sense at the time for the purposes of ensuring clean employees, but they quickly became a substantial burden for average people looking at work in the casinos. The new commission was serious about enforcement, as recalled by Russelle Patterson who remembered the bureaucracy and intense scrutiny:

> You had to pick up an unbelievable packet ... things to fill out in this packet, photographs, make four copies of this, which costs a lot of money; and return it to the Casino Control Commission. Then you had to wait and they would process and see if you were approved. They came to your home. They checked you out. They checked with neighbors[74]

Barbara Devlin had a similar experience:

> Now the thing there, was that the licensing process was a nightmare, a nightmare. Just for our end of things, which was not a key license but it was a casino license, you had to – it was a 26-page disclosure form ... I'm surprised they didn't take a blood sample. And then it took months and months for the process, because they were inundated, trying to open one casino.[75]

The licensing situation deteriorated to the point where a New Jersey Assembly committee actually stepped in to reform the bill within two years of its passage. At a 1979 hearing on *CCA* reform, city resident and casino employee Denise Dennis described her licensing nightmare:

> On April 3rd of this year I applied for a casino license and on April 17 it was received at the Casino Control Commission in Trenton. At the time, I didn't have promise of employment and then I was told that you did have a better chance if you did have promise of employment. Going back to Resorts, they

held interviews and I went and was given an official promise of employment. I
don't know if they submitted my name on a priority list … On August 3 I had
my personal interview at the Gaming enforcement trailer and Investigator
Robinson told me that as of that day my investigation was completed and
that she would be forwarding it to the legal department. August, September,
and October have gone by and I haven't received a letter … no letter.[76]

But all of these obstacles certainly did not stop the casino job-seekers. According
to Devlin, 'as far as the work force was concerned, they were coming back to town
in droves'.[77]

They came back for work, buoyed by the casino prospects and a long-term
outlook that looked promising indeed. Two years before Resorts International
opened, an economist noted that 'Casino hotels are very labor intensive businesses and on a per capita basis employ between four and five times the number of
employees of the traditional hotel or motor inn'. The economist's firm predicted
that the region would gain 22,000 to 29,000 jobs from 1977 to 1985. This would
reduce unemployment, provide 'a stable source of year-round employment', and
bring 'a strong stimulus to the overall economic revitalization of Atlantic City'. It
was really all about jobs in the beginning. The casino industry was labour intensive, and, apparently, South Jersey could provide the labourers.[78]

2 A MASTER PLAN: THE CASINO ERA BEGINS

The government economist writing about the Atlantic City area's economy in 1978 for New Jersey's Labor Department could scarcely contain the good tidings after the first casino opened (Resorts International). Casino development had brought a clear energy to the region, measured not just in terms of early, stratospheric casino revenue, but also in economic rippling through industries such as construction and transportation throughout Atlantic County. From the otherwise dreary semi-annual labour report came the exciting news:

> The rapidity with which Caesar's World and the Bally Corporation developments are proceeding has added an upbeat tempo to Atlantic City. The foundations for Caesar's are complete and the steel girder superstructure has been erected to three sections high.

Things were changing along the Boardwalk, and this was for the good of the region:

> Bally has demolished the Marlborough and parts of the Blenheim and Dennis hotels. Pile-driving equipment is in place and construction will start as soon as site clearance is completed. This is the first major commercial development in the city for at least two decades.[79]

On opening day, a line to get into Resorts stretched along the Boardwalk for blocks as the casino opened with Steve Lawrence and Eydie Gorme headlining the entertainment. Lawrence made the first bet, a $10 play on the craps table, but did not win. That did not stop the crowd, which waited patiently in line on the Boardwalk with signs advertising 'Waiting Time 2 Hour' and the like, as they slowly made it into the casino. The Boardwalk line was six blocks long. Crowding was a problem for a city that only had 50,000 parking spaces, but expected 150,000 cars per day. Within six days, the casinos made a record $2.9 million. On 27 May 1978, the banner headline of the *Press of Atlantic City* captured the mood well with a sly double-entendre: 'Queen of Resorts Reigns Again'. Now the action had really begun, and Atlantic City would no more be the place where, as one comedian joked in 1970, 'Every Friday night we shop till ten at the supermarket'.[80]

The upbeat state economic report was one of many in the first few years of the casino era, as the number of casinos increased quickly from zero at the start of 1978 to nine along the Boardwalk and in Atlantic City's Marina district of the city by the end of 1981. The increased economic activity translated into new jobs for a needy populace – a partial, but clear fulfillment of the pro-gambling promise of 1976. In August 1978 the Labor department noted that 'From June 1977 to June 1978 wage and salary employment increased by 5,700' due to the opening of Resorts and related activity. The coming casinos were already spurring new housing construction in Atlantic County such that the report also noted 'a perceivable increase in the construction of individual residential homes and townhouses'.[81] By mid-1979, the two-casino industry (Resorts International and Caesar's Boardwalk Regency) employed 7,000 people directly, and Resorts alone posted $224.6 million in gross revenues, likely a record for any casino over a one-year period at that time.[82]

Towards the end of 1979, the Labor department's report had an even more complete account of the casino era's dynamic beginnings in South Jersey:

> Atlantic County's economy over the past twelve months has been one of measurable growth. Residential permits issued are 10% higher than the previous year; 9,100 more people were employed in 1979 than in 1978 and though 400 more were unemployed than in the previous year, the unemployment rate has declined.

Yet, the state economists also noted considerable economic disruption as the region transformed from a seasonal and sleepy resort town to a bustling casino community with no climate-related limitations:

> There has been economic dislocation, particularly in Atlantic City, as the Boardwalk, for many years a 'summer shopping street' catering to beach and convention visitors, gives way to casino/hotel construction.[83]

The economic growth translated into numerous good jobs available to those with previously limited economic opportunities. For example, a city resident of the time described the impact on the region's Latin community:

> In terms of the Latinos, it was great, because now a whole number of jobs opened up in the casinos as hostesses, waiters, waitresses, kitchen stewards, kitchen workers, cooks, chefs, bar porters, busboys, waiters, cafeteria line-out persons, cocktail waitresses.

Moreover, these were decent jobs, many of them union positions:

> the Latinos had a boon with this, because these were, to a large degree, Local 54 business agent union, medically covered jobs, union-backed jobs. And they were also steady work. And in fact, there was an incentive to buy some

of the shares in the casino at that time, which a lot of people did, and some employees did rather well, actually.[84]

The casino impact on the region's economy was swift and conclusive. By 1980, the casinos had created almost 23,500 new jobs to provide the major portion of the area's economic expansion. But were these good jobs? According to state labour statistics, the casino jobs paid higher wages than similar jobs outside the casinos. In categories such as 'clerk-typist', 'computer operator', 'cashier' and 'restaurant manager' the casino jobs afforded people a higher standard of living. Overall, twenty-two out of twenty-six different occupations reported higher wages in the casinos than in comparable employers. For example, a casino electrician in 1980 averaged about $9.46 an hour compared to $7.71 an hour for an electrician outside the casinos. Similarly, a casino secretary earned $6.06 per hour while a non-casino secretary earned about $5.56 an hour. These statistics, along with other sources indicated that the casino jobs were well-paying jobs within the existing context of the South Jersey job market.[85]

The new casinos created new opportunities, regardless of existing skills or educational levels. For Atlantic City teenager Tom Gitto, the new climate was exciting and the casinos were easily accessible:

> But we were all excited about this vote that passed, and these that are going to happen. For us it was all pie in the sky, just talk. Then Resorts opened up, and one of our neighborhood guys, Joey ... We call him Joey Blackjack, because to learn – to help him learn [dealing], he would run blackjack games in his house. So all the neighborhood guys used to go to his house and play blackjack, so we call him Joey Blackjack. And Joey became a dealer, and then that's how I got interested, because he was telling me about it and things like that. So I went to school to be a dealer.[86]

At the Howard Johnson hotel, Barbara Devlin also pushed ahead for a new opportunity:

> And then we heard Caesar's bought Howard Johnson's and they were going to renovate and turn it into a casino, just like we'd heard; so we all thought we were going to have, you know, great jobs.

Yet, their initial optimism was not always borne out in reality:

> Those of us who were in Banquets immediately applied for other types of work. Nobody wants to shlep a tray deliberately, you know. So, we thought we'd all be cocktail waitresses or we'd all be bartenders, and we'll all get the benefit of the ... you know. But, that didn't exactly happen. Some of us kind of got left behind and had to stay where we were, which is what happened to me.[87]

With a monopoly on the casino business in Atlantic City that lasted over a year, Resorts International took in so much revenue that it could barely find enough employees to count it all. The casino grossed around $134 million in 1978 and $233 million in 1979.[88] The casino's savvy management quickly sought to take advantage of their company's success by diversifying into real estate. Resorts set about creating a virtual real estate empire in the city and ended up owning about 14 per cent of the land in Atlantic City by 1985, worth approximately $700 million according to the real estate valuations of that time. City government contributed to the acquisition by maintaining real estate valuations considerably low in proportion to the ever-increasing land values. According to one later investigation, the city government was at fault for failing to enforce a 1980 court order that had called for more current property tax appraisals.[89]

The problem was that the city indicated early that there were really no limits for casino zoning. Spurred by Resorts's success and the lack of clear zoning restrictions, casino developers and land speculators fuelled the rush, as one local observer recalled:

> The city sent out signals to speculators that we're going to let people open casinos anywhere. That dramatically fuelled land speculation.[90]

Another city resident at the time evoked an atmosphere so intense that it affected daily rituals like getting one's car serviced:

> I remember a very interesting situation when I was having the snow tires put on my car ... I was in the waiting room waiting for my car to be serviced and some gentleman in a suit came in with a clipboard, had a discussion with the owner for about ten minutes, and then everyone came back into the waiting area and said, Dennis, you just won't believe it, he says, what's going on in this town right now. And that was that the guy came in off the street and offered to buy his property.[91]

In the heavily Latino South Inlet neighbourhood, unscrupulous landlords cut off heat to tenants in the winter in hopes of driving tenants away. The idea was to get rid of tenants and level the buildings to have attractive empty lots available for sale to casino-struck speculators. Despite some resistance by the tenants, mainly the plan to move them out worked, even if most of the properties never did become casinos.[92] In fact, the situation devolved to the point that the state stepped in by passing a law in November 1978 requiring landlords to find housing for tenants within ten miles of their existing homes, let them stay for two years, stay for five free months or pay tenants the equivalent of five months' rent.[93]

By 1981, the real estate run-up and assorted problems had exacerbated the existing problems of the decayed community, to the laments of its residents who had expected a different experience. One magazine commented on the circumstances:

The Inlet, the once posh, now desperately poor black and Hispanic ghetto, much of which is zoned for casinos, is a wasteland of abandoned, burned, and bulldozed buildings. Elsewhere, rents have tripled.[94]

Looking back in 2005, a resident described the speculation and the long-term impact that impacted the neighbourhoods of Atlantic City, especially in the uptown and Inlet areas:

> So now all those – and they had a lot of slum landlords, and most of them lived out of town. So they wanted casinos over there. They didn't want to just sell their house. They wanted to make – get a $1 million for their home ... All they wanted was a casino. So that never happened. So they gave them more time. OK, another two years, and time went by. As you can see now nothing was ever done.[95]

Close to three decades after the casino land frenzy, many empty lots remained in the uptown Inlet neighbourhood –the casinos never having expanded into the Inlet section as speculated.

More positively, some made a great deal of money during this period, as early as 1977. Small hotel owner Tony Ranalli defined the fluid real estate situation well from a property-holder's perspective for a *New York* magazine article. A few years before casino legalization, he could barely sell his house for $5,000, but afterwards, he remarked,

> with all the big people coming in to invest their money, there's a feeling in the air that everyone wants to sell. There's a lot of cash floating around. I mean, it's a gold mine. I don't know who's making offers because it's all done through real estate agents, but I don't care. I'll sell to a Chinaman or an Arab.[96]

The agents Ranalli spoke about made a huge amount of money in the speculation craze. In 1979, real estate agent Paul Longo ('Don Paulo') posed for a magazine wearing a huge smile– likely due to his having sold $24 million of Atlantic City real estate in 1978. Other savvy individuals figured out how to play the speculation game quite well. Flamboyant art, china and glass dealer Reese Palley teamed with attorney Marty Blattto to come up (through various means) with $500,000 to buy the iconoclastic Marlborough-Blenheim hotel, ostensibly to develop a casino on the Marlborough site and preserve the Blenheim, with its white towers and unique style. Soon after, they managed to lease it to the Bally corporation and negotiated for Bally's to pay another sum on it, walking away with a great deal of profit to show for their investment. Others, like George Duberson, Pleasantville High School graduate, boat mechanic and part-owner of a boat rental operation and marina near the Atlantic City-Brigantine bridge, just stumbled into good fortune. When a 1978 master plan zoned the area for casino development, he and his partner quickly landed a deal with a hotel developer and sold out for

$8.8 million. Perhaps it helped that Duberson's partner was also Atlantic County Executive Chuck Worthington. Meanwhile, the money spread quickly within the region's professional circles. To handle increased real estate business, one law firm increased its staff from eight to nineteen lawyers within two years. A few people seemed to make a tremendous amount of money (like Longo), but many made just enough to substantially raise their standard of living.[97] In late 1978, a new casino industry newsletter noted that 'Even the banks are winners' and reported a surge in banking business by 63 per cent for Guarantee Bank, with others expecting similar results.[98]

Others played the speculative game, but lost. In 1979, a group of homeowners along Bellevue and Texas Avenues, just off the Boardwalk, held out too long for higher prices, rejecting a very lucrative offer floated by a casino development firm that eventually elapsed. Others resisted because they just did not want to leave their cosy, if ramshackle homes close to the beach. The Texas Avenue affair was telling, yet also complex. It demonstrated the impact that the real estate run-up was having in the community: sometimes pitting neighbours against each other and often causing difficult choices for people with little experience in such matters. These were not Atlantic City's poorest residents, these were blue-collar workers. Their experiences would strongly contribute to the perception of loss that began to emerge as golden expectations did not always come to fruition in the first decade of the casino era.[99]

The suburbs around the Atlantic City also experienced a wave of real estate activity with the early casinos, as all of Atlantic County's fortunes seemed to be improving with the coming of the casinos. In contrast to the situation in Atlantic City, the Atlantic County developments really did address the housing needs of the new casino employees. Unlike the city, the county did not have to contend with an entrenched and poverty-stricken population. Rather, its developers and planners could focus on open space available and build into the South Jersey pine-lands where it did not violate environmental restrictions. According to a housing official looking back, in Atlantic county

> You had no infrastructure problems ... There's nothing to demolish. There's nobody to move ... let alone environmental issues of buried tanks, things of that nature. It's much cheaper to do it on a raw land format.

Housing demand was high outside the city in places like Galloway township, and developers like Hovnian homes

> threw up tons of townhomes and tons of smaller homes that were very affordable ... The market forces really showed housing demand elsewhere than Atlantic City.[100]

Atlantic County was one of the fastest growing counties in the nation within a few years of Resorts' opening. The real estate boom coincided with the first wave of job creation around the region. Rural and slow-paced suburban municipalities soon became alive with the sounds of construction and related job opportunities. The casino construction spurred much more building: Atlantic City gave out 255 new residential permits in 1978, up from seven the year before. A similar boom occurred in Brigantine, with 242 housing permits in 1978, up from 167 in 1977. Pleasantville, Egg Harbor Township, Galloway and Hamilton all experienced similar increases in county-issued residential permits between 1976 and 1980, as demonstrated by the following table:

Table 2.1: County-Issued Residential Permits by Municipality, 1976–80[101]

Municipality/Year	1976	1977	1978	1979	1980
Absecon	24	37	31	58	28
Atlantic City	209	6	255	7	316
Brigantine	176	167	242	212	193
EHT	203	179	220	209	99
Galloway	99	98	135	237	205
Hamilton	105	85	111	293	219
Hammonton	49	44	52	28	12
Margate	17	55	41	58	27
Pleasantville	7	16	115	8	13
Ventnor	80	172	94	44	24
City Total	1210	1133	1710	1402	1290

In 1979, Atlantic County ranked first in the country in the rate of growth for personal income, with twenty per cent. The total hotel salaries and wages increased by well over 100 per cent, from $118,694,000 to $267,392,000 from 1979 to 1980.[102] By 1980, the casino industry had created some 5,800 building trades jobs, taking the region a long way from the pre-casino doldrums. A Boardwalk regular quipped that before the casino era 'when I saw a crane, I knew something was going to be torn down'. Now things were going ever upwards.[103]

Though the casino era began with a distinct lack of urban direction, Atlantic City officials did make an effort to plan for the growth by contracting with a specialist to develop an effective strategy for the future. The master plan that helped make boat makers and certain landowners quite rich was completed in 1978 by a Washington DC urban planner named Angelos Demetriou. The city turned to Demetriou after the 1976 referendum to study and devise a strategy for beginning the casino era. Demetriou's voluminous study expanded smaller planning studies on casino implications, such as an Atlantic City housing study in 1976. The 1976 report predicted the real estate boom, albeit with a mild tone that turned out to be quite an understatement:

> In addition, on the strength of the economic impact of the gaming program, it is anticipated that the value of real estate, both developed and undeveloped will increase.[104]

The 1978 *Atlantic City Master Plan* projected the specific ways in which the casinos would impact the city. It focused on showing city leaders how they could most effectively integrate the casinos into the community life of the city while ensuring that 'the environment and its offerings are so organized as to satisfy not only the outside tourist/visitor but also the local residents from the child to the adult and the senior'. The *Master Plan* laid out a comprehensive zoning plan for casino development along with 'a plan for an infrastructure (roads, parking, utilities and affiliated networks) that is capable of sustaining the magnitude of expected development'.[105]

The *Master Plan* also suggested a zoning map that took a decade to see realization, but basically laid out a successful geographic strategy for the casino era. It placed casino resorts along the Boardwalk and in the Marina district on the city's north side, surrounded by tidal marshes. The *Master Plan* recognized that casinos would clearly drive economic growth in coming years, yet that the city and region needed to adapt them to unique qualities of the community and integrate them into a larger framework of urban redevelopment. Demetriou's vision was for a casino community, not simply a casino resort. Thus, the plan sought to preserve the Boardwalk as a central feature of regional identity, economic activity and popular culture:

> The Boardwalk, representing a unique urban element of enormous value and service to Atlantic City is fully protected and enhanced by the new Plan, including the preservation of vital services and life-supporting establishments throughout its length. There is a risk of small shops being eventually extinguished (priced out) throughout the length of the Boardwalk and replaced by expensive hotels totally closed to this promenade and the beach – a possible development that would obliterate the attractiveness of one of Atlantic City's most vital parts and offerings associated with the experience of the Boardwalk.

Demetriou's planners also studied the city's housing stock, unfortunately finding 'massive deterioration in certain sectors of the city'. The *Master Plan* devised a substantive strategy for housing renewal that included a fourteen-point plan eventually leading to the construction of 15,000 thousand new homes by 1990, and the rehabilitation of thousands more. The plan was vague on financing this work, but its vision was clear and smart. For example, it proposed to 'land swap and/or to provide the replacement value of property to homeowners who must be moved' in the wake of redevelopment – a successful strategy employed eventually in the late 1980s and 1990s. It also called for disbursed public housing, construction of varied units to appeal to people of different incomes, senior citizen housing and the maximal use of public subsidies to achieve parity and to avoid the creation of new ghettoes. Its ideas even included 'bikeways, pedestrianways, skyways (bridges) and people-movers'.[106]

The *Master Plan* also included a proposal for developing the Marina region of the city by envisioning 'a casino entertainment center with the Marina at its core'. The planners had high hopes for the Marina district by recommending that it 'could become a very special pole of attraction' in the casino community. Yet, the obstacles for this were significant, because in the late 1970s the area was a mixed part of the city of semi-development, with land owned by various entities, a state-owned marina, an old landfill site and numerous individual land parcels. In contrast to the commercially-oriented Boardwalk, there had been minimal planning for the area. Now the *Master Plan* proposed a new land 'parcelization plan' to allow for three large casino hotels, three shopping and restaurant complexes and various recreational facilities such as swimming pools and tennis courts.[107] Significantly, the *Master Plan* also noted the importance of expanding the casino community up and down the Boardwalk and into the marina area and called for a new convention facility to replace the existing, dilapidated one – both concepts that would eventually become reality in the casino era. One important point of the *Master Plan* was a notion that the community should 'diversify, where feasible, in light of available market resources and financial considerations, the economic base of Atlantic City so as to avoid over-dependence on a few principal economic activities'.[108]

The extensive *Master Plan* ultimately proved too idealistic for the region in the early casino era. By the mid-1980s, the proposals to build infrastructure to match casino development were mainly forgotten as the rapid growth of the industry pushed aside many considerations beyond maximizing casino profits. While the casino industry in Atlantic City continued to grow, the failure of the city to adequately address key issues of housing and transportation in particular led to urban decay and decline. Five years into the casino era, most casino employees would not even consider actually living in the city where they worked, moving instead to the new homes of Egg Harbor Township and Galloway. Here, the quality of life was fairly good, infused with the dynamic spirit of young people with healthy disposable incomes. Others felt stranded and let down by the casinos, thanks in part to disappointments that plans such as the *Master Plan* were not actually implemented to the benefit of city life.

The casino industry's impact was felt everywhere, and seemingly by everyone in the region, regardless of age. The 1979 Atlantic City High School Yearbook ran a picture of the school's drafting club labelled 'Tomorrow's Casino builders' and showed a student reading a newspaper with the caption underneath: 'Before I line my canary's cage with this, let me see how my Resorts International stock is doing'. The 1980 yearbook included various pictures of casino construction sites along with an advertisement for the Harry Hasson and Son florist that announced its newest location at Caesar's in very large print.[109]

From the beginning, the casino industry faced extensive regulation from the NJCCC to enforce the *CCA*. With onsite NJCCC agents and DGE personnel, the early casinos faced severe limitations on their business operations, such as ones that ensured advertisements subjectively be 'in good taste' and that limited the actual gaming facilities to blackjack, craps, roulette, baccarat, the big six wheel and slot machines. The *CCA* required each casino to report monthly financial figures such as 'table win', gross revenue and money spent on promotions. The NJCCC's first annual report (1979) explained the original, quasi-public purpose of legalized gaming: to redevelop Atlantic City, and revitalize the region through job creation and tax revenue. The report also noted 'the law makes it clear that gaming is only to be a component of the new Atlantic City, and not its dominant theme'.[110] This was important because it reflected the original community focus of the casinos and underlined the ideal that the casinos had a much greater motive than profit. This approach proved to be limiting, and certainly inaccurate in the coming years. The casinos were entirely profit-oriented, and did become Atlantic City's only viable engine of economic growth, but this was to the benefit, not the detriment, of the region.

The huge casino revenue was the most significant feature of the first five years of Atlantic City's casino era. In late 1979, industry newsletter *Atlantic City Action* detailed the dizzying pace of construction pointing out that ten casinos were currently under construction and that Atlantic City was bucking the national economy with its growth:

> That's the story of the Atlantic City scene: Forms flying, steel swinging, the click of bricklayers' trowels, etc. The negative financial mood of the rest of the U.S.A. certainly has <u>not been felt in Casino City</u> with construction going full blast.

The newsletter predicted 50,000 new casino jobs within two years. In 1983, Atlantic City had 26 million visitors, compared to 7 million in 1978, an increase of 271 per cent in five years.[111]

Despite the construction, many casino visions never made it much past their blueprints. Within a year after Resorts opened, there were nineteen separate proposals for new casinos. These included plans by Benihana, Dunes, MGM, Penthouse, and the Ritz. One planned casino was called the 'Hi-Ho Hotel' and was set to replace the old Claridge with a brand new structure complete with a rotating bar on its roof. For MGM, the legal and financial fallout from a disastrous 1980 fire at its casino in Las Vegas effectively ended its Atlantic City expansion at that time, though not forever. In 1979, there were actually seven different casinos planned for the Marina district alone with a separate Boardwalk to link them together. By 1980, the successful casinos that would soon lead the industry to wealth and double-digit revenue growth were also in planning stages, open or already under construction. These included the Golden Nugget, Brighton (the Sands), Bally's Park Place and Caesar's.[112]

Two years after Resorts opened up; there were three casinos along the Boardwalk, with six more casinos in the works for completion by the end of 1981. The NJCCC's extensive reporting requirements ensured a wealth of data that showed that casino space increased from 100,000 square feet in mid-1979 to approximately 300,000 square feet at the end of 1980. Table games increased from 200 to 700 and there were close to 8,000 slot machines at the end of 1981, as opposed to just 2,500 a year earlier.[113] In the fiscal year 1980, Resorts alone increased its gross total revenue by 68 per cent in 1980 (to $273 million), and Caesar's revenue grew by 129.8 per cent in two years of operation. In two and a half years, the casinos had created 21,200 jobs that now represented 22.2 per cent of Atlantic County employment, up from 4.1 per cent after Resorts opened. The explosive growth's wealth effect also elevated per capita personal income dramatically in the region. At one point, a 20 per cent rise in the growth of this measure ranked Atlantic County first in the nation. Between 1979 and 1980, the total amount of salaries and wages of hotel and motel employees increased dramatically from $118.7 million to $267.4 million – that was all money floating around the regional economy.[114]

By the end of 1981, nine casinos had come online in Atlantic City with the opening of the Tropicana. Within three years of Resorts' opening, Atlantic City had become a major rival to Nevada for the country's gambling clientele and would soon surpass Las Vegas in casino revenue. The exuberance expressed in the *Atlantic City Action* was not irrational, but it was a little too optimistic. The region was growing fast and the casinos really did take off, though two years into the era, clear signs of problems began to emerge, and not just in the real estate sector. In late 1980, the *Action* mused that

> Hotel occupancy has been very low though the casinos have been packed. 'Day Trippers' do not fill the rooms; conventions must be booked, attractive travel packages must be offered and convention facilities expanded ... The very purpose of the gambling legislation in AC was to <u>promote tourism not bus travel</u>.[115]

The *Action*'s concern reflected an emerging sense of disappointment that the casinos had not yet renewed the city as a destination resort by spurring new visitors to the region's attractions beyond slot machines and gaming tables. It also signalled a renewed push in the casino industry towards building resorts that could rival Las Vegas casinos as places that visitors could come for two or three days, not just leave. For residents, this was much preferred, to stem the loss of external business outside the casinos. But this concern was based on an essentially false premise: that the casino industry would lead to success for the existing businesses along the Boardwalk and the faded shopping corridor of Atlantic Avenue, two long avenue blocks from the Boardwalk. Unfortunately for the business owners, this never happened.[116]

The perception that casinos were an endless source of wealth seemed to dominate the Atlantic City economic environment from 1978 to 1981, before reality caught up and the business dipped with the addition of the new casinos. Meanwhile, the NJCCC pursued its regulatory mission by seeking to determine at just what level the casino industry would reach a saturation point: i.e., how many casinos could the market successfully bear? Pushing the inquiry were the consistent requests for casino licences coming to the commission. Each request necessitated an exhaustive hearing into the personal background of the principals involved and financial analysis of potential impact. In 1980, the commission held hearings on Harrah's Marina Hotel Casino and the Golden Nugget applications for licences. In addition, it issued temporary licences for six more casinos and permanently licensed Caesar's and Bally's Park Place. Led by chairman Joseph Lordi, from 1977 to 1981, the NJCCC invented itself as the moral guardian of the casino industry. Always cognizant of the industry's historic reputation as tool for organized crime and for a wary New Jersey establishment, it pursued its mandate to ensure the 'maintenance of the integrity of casino gambling'.[117]

The first NJCCC Chairman was a prosecutor from Essex County in northern New Jersey. He served full-time, but presided over four other commissioners who only served part-time, despite the heavy workload as casino licence applications poured into the commission in 1978. Working with Lordi and the commission, the Assembly amended the *CCA* to speed up the licensing process and ease some of the background requirements for employee licence applicants. For example, it limited disqualifying convictions to a ten-year period and allowed for the granting of temporary licences.[118] The speed of this amendment to the *CCA* demonstrated the flexibility of the new regulatory system. Well-intended, the investigatory process was simply too strict and cumbersome in the beginning, hence it was changed rather quickly.

Soon after Resorts opened, the system faced a complex challenge with Caesar's World's application for a permanent casino licence for the 'Boardwalk Regency'. The Caesar's principals were Clifford and Stuart Perlman – two native Philadelphians who had profited well in Las Vegas with Caesar's World, which they acquired in 1969. They subsequently became involved with known mobsters through deals in Florida and Pennsylvania, thus providing a rationale for the commission to block their licensure, due to concerns that the deals 'may not have been isolated transactions'. After investing tens of millions in developing the former Howard Johnson hotel into its new 'Boardwalk Regency', Caesar's received an interim licence to open in May 1979. However, its opening was also delayed for a few weeks because many of its employees had yet to receive their licences. In addition, Clifford Perlman had to give up his business activities in New Jersey – as such he was effectively removed from Caesar's Atlantic City operations. Delays in granting licences to Caesar's employees led to the amendment which essentially gave the commission power to grant licences without the normal oversight process, if necessary. It also enabled the commission to override the licensure process for businesses involved with casinos. In 1981, the commission finally granted Caesar's its permanent licence pending a stock transaction in which the company bought back the Perlman brother's shares in the company for $99 million. As well, Clifford Perlman had to relinquish his role as chairman and CEO of Las Vegas' Caesar's Palace.[119]

After the decision to grant Caesar's World a temporary license, matters became very awkward for the casino industry and state regulators involved in a political scandal known as 'Abscam'. 'Abscam' was short for 'Abdul-scam', the FBI's term for a sting operation that involved the fictional Abdul Enterprises and a plot to bribe government officials, including Congressman, for various favours. Abdul's chairman was the bogus Emir Yassir Habib, a supposed sheik who wanted to buy into the Atlantic City casino industry. In March 1979, the pretend sheik and his associates arranged a meeting in Long Island with Camden, New Jersey's corrupt mayor and Kenneth MacDonald, a member of the NJCCC. There, the sheik's associate ('Jack McCloud') was waiting with a briefcase loaded with $100,000 in cash. In exchange for the cash, MacDonald supposedly offered to fix the subsequent NJCCC hearing so that Abdul would get its desired casino license. Abscam was a major sting that eventually led to corruption convictions for seven members of Congress, including a New Jersey senator (Harrison Williams). At one point, allegations surfaced that Joe Lordi gave preferential treatment for approval to the Benihana group that wanted to convert the old Ritz hotel into an Oz-like casino, a charge that Lordi vociferously denied. Though it only involved Atlantic City marginally, Abscam had understandable fall-out given the state's concern over organized crime and its new industry. MacDonald resigned from the commission, and the Assembly took action to redefine the commission, which formerly required only part-time work. As well, Lordi was put into a defensive position, having to distance himself from MacDonald, who he said was 'suckered' into the plot. With passage of the new legislation, all NJCCC members became full-time regulators and the *CCA* included a new prohibition on part-time state employees from representing or working for casinos. The amended act specifically barred commissioners from taking part in 'any other business, occupation or gainful employment'. It also barred public officials from accepting casino employment for two years following their public service.[120]

Like the Perlmans of Caesar's World, Bally's chairman Bill O'Donnell found himself under the investigatory spotlight due to a whole web of contacts that he and Bally's vendors had with organized crime figures. Most famously, he had met Genovese figures Gerardo Catena and Dino Cellini. In fact, Bally's had hired Cellini for its slot operations despite a past that included an alleged stint running a Havana casino for Meyer Lansky. Bally's eventually got its permanent casino license, but without O'Donnell as chairman. Like Perlman before him, the commission forced O'Donnell to divest himself of Bally's stock and step down before granting his company its permanent license.[121]

According to Steve Perskie, the exclusions were an example of the system working as it was designed to work:

> I felt very bad for them as individuals [the Perlmans and O'Donnell], I was kind of pleased that the message that was being sent out from New Jersey was we're not fooling around and you're going to have to meet the standards that we set and we don't care who you are, we don't care how much money you have.[122]

Though the accusations against the Perlmans and O'Donnell about mafia involvement were sketchy, it did not matter. The commission cared about upholding its standards, even at the expense of casino expansion, if necessary. The talent and success they demonstrated in the casino industry was secondary to the commission's concern for integrity, particularly in the wake of the Abscam affair. According to a close observer, looking back:

> Clifford Perlman, in particular, was at that point the genius behind Caesar's and he was in 1979 what Steve Wynn became in Las Vegas much later. He was the creative mind behind Caesar's and was one of the most influential citizens in the state of Nevada. We found him unsuitable for a license.[123]

The integrity mindset was understandable and worked by ensuring that organized crime made no significant inroads in the casino industry. However, from the perspective of the casino industry, there was a cost. Lordi's agency began the casino era identifying itself as the group to protect New Jerseyites from problems stemming from casinos, rather than as a body to promote the financial success of casinos. While this posture was a natural response to the mid-1970s debate surrounding legalization, it confounded casino managers who often came from Nevada and became frustrated with the regulatory climate. They had trouble understanding the reality of New Jersey's novel public-private casino scheme, a very different business model than had existed as Las Vegas' casino industry expanded after 1950. Daniel Heneghan remembered the mindset:

> That's not the way we do it Las Vegas. And I can't tell you how that rubbed people in New Jersey the wrong way ... But yeah, we wanted to set a different tone here than Nevada had.[124]

Las Vegas executives coming to Atlantic City took their business perspectives into a system consciously designed to prevent the influence of organized crime. Naturally, they chafed at having to negotiate the unique legal and economic framework established by both the first casinos and the commission. And all of this bothersome regulation added 40 per cent to the cost of running their businesses, according to an industry source in 1981.[125] A casino executive remembered the early years of the casino era and the contrast between the two different business cultures as it played out over regulating slots machines:

> You can imagine, an individual from Vegas coming in to run the slot operation. They were very accustomed for Vegas to do things unregulated, meaning they could bring in a new machine from this base to that base, and they could shift things around. The regulatory environment was totally different in Vegas. In the beginning, when the Resorts opened, they were just now, even though the regulations existed, as far as enforcing it and creating the details of the operational part of it, it was still not really mature. And I can remember, back in 1982, '83, I literally spent time with the DGE actually in developing a slot manual, slot operation manual. That manual specifically says how the procedures of things that were not covered under regulations. To this day [2005], we still use that guide, so to speak, that was originally created with the regulators and some of the operators, and I was part of that. And there was no frustration in my part, like it was for those people from Vegas.[126]

Success in this climate required the acceptance of NJCCC's regulatory regime as a unique system set up for New Jersey. It reflected the public concern over the industry at the outset, in contrast to the early years of Nevada's casino era.[127]

Between 1979 and 1981, the NJCCC's regulatory priorities drew increasing opposition from casino executives who questioned the benefits of such exacting control, especially after casino profitability dipped in 1980.[128] Petitions came in from various individuals and groups to alter the system. Why should the NJCCC have to examine the backgrounds of every employee, including valets, waitresses and janitors? The commission even admitted in 1981 that overly stringent requirements had probably reduced casino employment rolls by 10 per cent or more. Allied with the local Chamber of Commerce, casino executives also questioned the extent to which the Act regulated gambling operations and the ability to advertise, all heavily regulated under the 1977 *CCA*. In testimony before a state investigating committee, Chamber of Commerce officials expressed support for the 'removal of regulations no longer necessary to protect the public interest in area of advertising, hotel employee licensing and work permits, restrictions on airline promotion and 24-hour gaming, among others'. In response to these concerns, the commission held public hearings and eventually recommended that the state drop its pre-approval requirement for casino advertising. In addition, the NJCCC began to loosen up gaming regulation by dropping requirements for minimum bets and removing the 'early surrender' condition for blackjack.[129]

In this way, the Commission signalled a slightly modified approach to its purpose, even if its official pronouncements always underscored its integrity mission. It also continued to maintain its community focus, even launching a study of the region's housing problems as well in 1981. It was still fiercely interested in industry integrity, and this concern played out repeatedly in the 1980s in licensing hearings where principal industry executives faced serious personal scrutiny. In the face of industry pressure, the NJCCC bent slightly to accommodate the casino business and business people concerned with making money, who had come to resent the regulatory system as inhibitory. To some extent, this was the beginning of a decade-long and divisive tug-of-war between casino operators and regulators that would finally resolve in massive change in the early 1990s. The juxtaposition of public and private interests in the casino industry is vital for understanding the Atlantic City casino era. But what appeared to be separate interests were often the same: all had an interest in promoting and expanding the casino business, even if the community improvements did not come right away.

In 1982, the Atlantic City Casino Hotel Association's (ACCHA) annual report included a table showing the steadily increasing numbers of casino regulators and costs assorted with regulation, and sharply noted that 'These figures, which represent expenditures by the industry and not by New Jersey taxpayers, do not include internal costs incurred by the casinos in response to government regulations'. Between 1977 and 1982, casino-funded NJCCC and DGE expenditures increased from $12.3 million to $31.6 million, and the number of employees grew in accordance, as the number of casinos expanded from one in 1978 to nine by mid-1982. The association expanded the premise and offered a glimpse into a new counter-strategy of sorts – the casinos would monitor the monitors:

> The industry has also undertaken a study to monitor in-house costs of regulations unique to the casino industry. This will enable legislators and the public to evaluate the overall impact of regulatory costs on the industry.[130]

In 1983, ACCHA reported the amount of combined taxes and regulatory costs paid out by the casinos from 1978 to 1983, as follows:

Table 2.2: Combined Taxes and Regulatory Costs Paid by Casinos, 1978–83

Year	Combined Taxes and Regulatory Costs
1978	$10.7 million
1979	$33 million
1980	$68.7 million
1981	$86.5 million
1982	$117.3 million
1983	$139.5 million

In 1982, the trade group also addressed a difficult problem for the industry and its regulators over the industry's tax obligation to devote a portion of revenue towards Atlantic City redevelopment. The group was looking to Trenton to 'untangle a complex section' of the *CCA*, and briefly commented on the need for cooperation between politicians, regulators and the industry to resolve the problem.[131]

ACCHA's 1983 report also came out strongly for a new solution to the continued problem of casino re-investment in Atlantic City and included a pointed nod to Trenton to get something done to fix an 'unworkable and unresolved reinvestment program'. Industry executives argued that the state system was at fault, not them:

> The casino hotels, however, stand ready willing and able to carry out the mandate of the public, provided that workable and equitable legislation is drafted and implemented. State leadership is vital to successfully applying gaming industry resources to the needs of the local region, as well as to other deserving areas of the state.[132]

ACHHA and the state legislature hoped to resolve problems associated with the two per cent community reinvestment tax on revenues in excess of start-up costs. Since 1978, the tax on revenue was loaded with loopholes such as one that placed the money in escrow for five years, yet no casino had been operating for five years until 1983. At one point, Caesar's claimed it paid its tax by building a statue outside its casino. While Caesar's may have had a good rationale for viewing its new statue as an improvement over the bleak circumstances around the city, it drew ire and caused some to suggest that this was not the purpose of the tax as it was legislated in the 1977 *CCA*. Soon, the state began to focus on modifying the requirement to smooth the process and re-focus the revenue on its original intent – to redevelop Atlantic City – and the casinos came on-board.[133]

The need for a better system to funnel money towards housing development became evident a few years into the casino era. While casino revenue spurred new jobs and raised per capita income across the region, the new casinos often drew heavy criticism from those neighbourhood residents in closest proximity to them.[134] A 1981 NJCCC hearing brought out this criticism from citizens and commentators clearly upset by the casinos. One community organizer expressed a commonly held complaint, that the

> the industry has been in existence for three years and has apparently had the effect of displacing thousands of residents, many long time residents of Atlantic City and there has literally been no assistance from this body or any other governmental body.

The community leaders and activists complained that the casinos simply were not concerned enough with their housing situation; as one person commented:

> While I note that Resorts International and I believe Bally's and Caesar's World have voluntarily accepted a housing contribution condition attached to their casino license, as far as I understand it, none of these commitments

have been fully honored, nor has there been any Atlantic City lower or middle income housing produced by these commitments[135]

The disappointment over the housing problem was so deep as to call into question the entire experiment, as a neighbourhood activist explained:

> We had and have a hope of participating in this new birth of Atlantic City. The American dream is that we too as American citizens, whether we are black or white, whether we are rich or poor, can have a part in this dream and in the distribution of wealth and we are asking for our part, not let all the money pour to the coffers of the big casinos and the speculators.[136]

The housing complaints were symptoms of the broader malaise and mixed sentiments that many city residents held during the first five years of the casino era. Rising street crime due to the influx of visitors and noisy buses rumbling through residential neighbourhoods certainly added to community frustration. With the influx of so many new visitors on a daily basis, crime rose dramatically between 1976 and 1981, to the point where Atlantic City had the highest crime rate of any municipality in New Jersey, at 313 crimes per 1,000 residents in 1981, compared to 61 crimes per 1,000 residents statewide. The crime problem was exacerbated by the lure of the industry because the city lost veteran cops to the casinos, where they could earn approximately $5,000 more annually as security guards than they could as Atlantic City police officers.[137]

Frustration over housing and neighbourhood problems (such as noisy bus traffic) became a significant threat to the casino experiment by 1981. By then, the frustration was beginning to undercut the casinos' legitimacy as agents of positive change for city residents. Casino executives could not afford to maintain the status quo and hope that the new revenues alone would satisfy all comers without risking a severe curtailing of their business. Viewed from this perspective, the push towards a better governmental solution to the housing redevelopment issue was a natural outcome, even if it seemed to contradict the industry's other public prerogative: to lessen industry regulation and expensive oversight. This dichotomy demonstrated the mutually beneficial purpose of the unique mission and approach to casino regulation. To the industry leaders, it may have often seemed like overkill, but it did serve the purpose of directing energy and innovation always back towards the original motive behind legalization and capturing the broader public's support for the enterprise.

In 1984, the legislature finally altered the system, and responded to voices from all sides, by enacting a reform of the redevelopment revenue program and process. The end result was the Casino Reinvestment Development Authority (CRDA), established to direct 1.25 per cent of casino gross revenues towards Atlantic City redevelopment. Eventually it provided millions for new housing and community projects in the Atlantic City region. However, it got off to a slow start, due to a vague mission and the difficult, complicated and often conflicted relationship between the state and city governments.[138]

Governmental dysfunction at the state and local levels was major problem that hampered efforts to improve the casino community in the early 1980s. According to Steve Perskie,

> The state government's attitude through the '80s was we legalized casinos and now it's up to everybody else to go redeem the promises that were made about rebuilding Atlantic City. The city government's attitude through the '80s was we're in charge here. We don't want any help or interference from Trenton. Leave us alone and we'll do what we have to do.

Initially, the CRDA lacked

> a coherent strategy for marshalling the resources that were available and saying OK, our first priority is community redevelopment. Our first priority is housing. Our first priority is infrastructure. Nobody was answering any of those questions.

At one point in 1981, the city and state governments fought a political battle to retain control over the city's old convention centre at the middle of the Boardwalk. Though it cost the city millions annually in maintenance, the city government fought hard and won the right to retain control over the money-losing hulk of a building. In contrast, Philadelphia mayor Wilson Goode actually lobbied the state of Pennsylvania to take over his city's old convention centre, arguing that state residents who benefited from it should pay the cost.[139]

The expansion of the casino industry between 1978 and 1983 was remarkable. Casino players poured into town, and the casinos reaped the benefits financially. By 1983, gaming revenues in Atlantic City practically surpassed Las Vegas in casino revenue. In 1981, the Boardwalk Regency's $16.13 million profit was twice that of Caesar's two Nevada casinos (in Las Vegas and Lake Tahoe). Yet, revenues also began to slow somewhat after the first two years and when the market reached a saturation point of sorts nine casinos were operating. Resorts' International began the era by bringing in $162 million in gross revenue in 1978, with $134 million brought in from gambling. In 1983, the combined gross revenue of all the casino hotels had leapt to $2.23 billion, $1.76 billion from gambling. Net profitability went from $89.8 million in 1978 to $524.1 million in 1983. However, net revenues slowed down considerably as well in the same period as more casinos went on line from 1981 to 1983. With just one casino reporting in 1979 (Resorts) net revenue increased by 139.7 per cent between 1978 and 1979. With nine casinos operating in 1983, net revenues only increased 17.1 per cent from 1982 to 1983. However, profitability remained high throughout the period, averaging 63.7 per cent per casino in 1981, 35.1 per cent in 1982 and 41.1 per cent in 1983. In 1983, the casino industry had over $1.48 billion in costs and expenses, most of which flowed back into the local economy via wages, goods and services contracts.[140]

By 1983, Atlantic City's casino industry was very competitive, with the different casinos constantly trying to gain an edge over neighbours via marketing programs, entertainment and other enticements. In one memo from the early 1980s, a Harrah's analyst profiled the company's potential competition for its Marina casino and planned Boardwalk property. The analyst was particularly harsh on casinos identified with cut-rate promotions, lambasting Bally's, for example, because Sales Directors 'unnecessarily began, what we view a "Rate War" eventually effecting [sic] all properties – i.e. – $50 room rates for September business'. The memo also neatly defined some of the elements of success in the increasingly tight casino market, characterized by the Golden Nugget, for example: 'Marina's biggest competition with respect to corporate meeting and small groups business. Very attractive property to meeting buyer. Meeting/function space all in one area, same level. Good sales staff.' The analyst was less complimentary about the Tropicana ('very weak, inexperienced sales staff') and Playboy ('have weakest sales department – least of our competition'). The comments also demonstrated the significance of ties to Las Vegas for success in Atlantic City at the time – a benefit especially realized by Caesar's which brought in a lot of national groups via familiarity with its western property. The memo also discussed the potential for collaboration with proximate Boardwalk properties (such as Bally's, Playboy and Tropicana) for large meetings that required up to 1,200 rooms.[141]

So what did all the casino revenue mean for average residents of the area? For many it meant opportunities to restart their lives and careers. For others, it meant capitalizing on connections and seizing the moment, particularly for savvy businesspeople. One Margate retailer saw an opportunity to sell something, anything, in the new casino and was able to use a connection to plant a successful store at Caesar's. He used his skills and aggressive mission to forge a profitable niche at the casino selling women's clothing:

> Never sold a piece of women's clothing in his life, but he's a good businessman. He's a good marketer. He's a good salesman. He knows how to estimate a market and do what he has to do.[142]

Another local businessman also felt the pull of the casinos, but eventually landed in the slots side of the industry, taking advantage of electronics training he had received years earlier in the army. With a mixed record in the pre-casino restaurant business, he set out to work as a dealer when the casino era began, but that meant dealer school and at least a few unacceptable weeks before employment. So he successfully leveraged a background in electronics from the military into a position as a slot technician at Caesar's:

This impressed the casino's managers, imported from Las Vegas: Once they saw my resume, they really liked what they saw, because I had more electronics than any individual, including those that came from Vegas.

The pay was not very good – $5.35 an hour – but the excitement and potential of the casino experience proved compelling enough for him to take the job:

When he said, $5.35 an hour, I thought, gee, it's going to be a little tough for me, so I turned him down. I went home, a couple of days later, I realize that this is something maybe that I can get into because they talked about all the specific things that they had to offer in one major complex. The hotel, entertainment, food and beverage, gaming. It was just phenomenal to realize that one property can have all these things.[143]

Local florist Harry Hasson similarly saw his business go from a struggling small shop in the late 1970s to a bustling, busy outfit in the early 1980s thanks to a contract with Caesar's for flowers and landscaping.[144]

One individual with a clear vision to advance in the new environment was casino mogul and gaming prodigy Steve Wynn. Wynn had already made millions in Las Vegas as an executive with Caesar's and as a principal stockholder in the Golden Nugget before showing an interest in Atlantic City after witnessing Resorts International's initial success. Less than a month after Resorts opened in 1978, he came to Atlantic City and promptly made a deal to purchase the Strand Motel at prime site on the Boardwalk's western end for $8.5 million. Then, he convinced his investors to put up about $200 million to build the Atlantic City Golden Nugget, which opened in 1980. By 1983, it had edged out Resorts as the highest grossing casino, pulling in $260.5 million and stood out as a glitzy castle on the Boardwalk that incorporated imagery from Atlantic City's resort past into its casino present. In 1983, he signed Frank Sinatra to a $10 million deal. By then, the relatively small Golden Nugget's glamour-infused casino had taken root in Atlantic City, though only for a few years in the 1980s.[145]

Steve Wynn and the women's clothing retailer at Caesar's shared a vision that allowed them to play a dynamic role in the new casino economy. At the other end of the economic scale, others too were applying their skills and finding opportunity, as described by cocktail waitress Russelle Patterson:

Well, I knew I had to get a job as a cocktail waitress because I had come down here with knowledge and background in public relations from New York. I worked for the Visitors Bureau and the Convention Bureau for years. And, I was very good at working with the public and very good at working with entertainers because that's all I had been brought up with. But at that time, people who didn't have as much background, who were just from here, had all the jobs. And, they wouldn't even take your resume to put it away because if your resume got looked at in comparison with theirs, you would have gotten the job....So, a lot of these people stepped into places for maybe only one or two years, and then outside people started to filter in.[146]

An Atlantic City social worker noticed the difference in his low-income clients:

> I don't know whether the real estate change played out [with casinos], but I know that some of the people that I worked with did go and work in the casinos and were able to, because of that opportunity, were able to secure their own properties.[147]

Another narrator described the fluid employment situation, including the influx of casino veterans into the area for needed expertise:

> Well, in the first two or three years, there was a lot of movement, and the individuals that came with experience naturally got better positions in the new houses that opened. So it left vacancies and opportunities for the locals. Me and the people that started at Atlantic City, where they bring too many new, experienced people from Vegas, so therefore, they were looking for individuals that understand the business enough. The Resorts, for example, supplied a lot of the supervisor positions for Caesar's. Caesar's might have supplied some of the manager positions for the Tropicana and Golden Nugget, and so on. The people that actually came with experience, got even the higher position from managers to directors and so on.[148]

The influx of new jobs created plenty of opportunity and Atlantic County's unemployment rate dipped significantly in comparison to where it had been prior to the casino era. The following tables show unemployment rates for the state and Atlantic County in two five-year blocks before and after the casino era began, beginning in 1973. Atlantic County averaged close to 2 per cent higher annual unemployment than New Jersey for much of the 1970s. Beginning in 1979 (the first full year with operating casinos), the county still averaged a higher unemployment rate than the state. However, the difference had fallen considerably, and in two years (1980 and 1983), the difference between the state and county was negligible.[149]

Table 2.3: New Jersey and Atlantic County Unemployment
Rates in the Pre-Casino Era, 1973–7

Year	New Jersey Unemployment Rate (%)(July)	Atlantic County Unemployment Rate (%)	Difference (%)
1973	5.6	7.1	1.5
1974	6.0	8.2	2.2
1975	10.5	11.9	1.4
1976	10.9	12.2	1.3
1977	8.5	12.1	3.6
5-year average	8.3	10.3	2.0

Table 2.4: New Jersey and Atlantic County Unemployment
Rates in the Early Casino Era, 1979–83

Year	New Jersey Unemployment Rate (%) (July)	Atlantic County Unemployment Rate (%)	Difference (%)
1979	7.4	9.3	1.9
1980	7.8	8.2	0.4
1981	6.5	8.4	1.9
1982	8.4	10.1	1.7
1983	8.2	8.3	0.1
5-year average	7.7	8.9	1.2

As casino workers fanned out into Atlantic County, many long-term residents of the city remained disappointed. The bleak reality was that many inner-city residents were hopeful, but not successful in finding employment. Often, they could not meet the Commission's strict licensing procedures. Long-time uptown community and former chapter president of the National Association for the Advancement of Colored People (NAACP), Pierre Hollingsworth, explained the situation in a 2005 interview:

> Now, did it [casino industry] affect the unemployment rate of Atlantic City? Somewhat, because we still carried a double digit higher [unemployment rate] than the state of New Jersey unemployment rate. A lot of that's social problems, because some were unemployable. And then we had a aging population that was here. And so that, as far as employment was concerned, they employed more people than we had residents.[150]

Barbara Devlin also pointed out that a true employment picture was more than a matter of counting the new jobs created by casinos:

> There was always one faction in town that never seemed to get, never seemed to take advantage of or be part of the promise. And that percentage of people, mostly who lived right in Atlantic City, who didn't seem to benefit from casino gambling where jobs were concerned.[151]

Also disappointing to city residents was the closure of many local businesses, especially around the Atlantic Avenue commercial hub. In Atlantic City, the number of food and drink establishments dropped by half between 1979 and 1983, from 425 in 1979 to 222 in 1983. Hollingsworth reflected on the frustrating scenario and dashed expectations:

> It [the casino industry] wiped out the business district. Atlantic Avenue, where they had some businesses, department stores and everything, clothing stores, folk who businesses, department stores and everything, clothing stores, folk who had some – generations went out of business. They went out of business because they couldn't compete. Restaurants closed up because

they couldn't compete. They couldn't compete with free food ... We who are ignorant had no idea that it was going to be such a confined business.[152]

In 1984, a state Department of Labor analyst blamed the continued city problems on a decline in manufacturing jobs during the casino era and on incoming workers taking the new jobs. As well, some job loss was probably due to the 'loss of many restaurants and stores near and around the Boardwalk in AC that were demolished to make way for casino-hotels'. Other businesses failed because they could not compete with casinos.[153] Yet, less was also more in the exploding hospitality industry of the casino economy. In 1982, there were actually 26 per cent fewer total hotels and motels around Atlantic County than in 1975 (104 versus 140). Yet, they employed 27,849 people compared to 2,430 in 1975.[154]

Between 1977 and 1980, the total number of jobs in Atlantic County increased by 40 per cent, mainly due to the casino industry. Three of four casino workers commuted into the city and a 1982 state analysis listed the employment barriers still in place for many residents. Licensing fees, the licensing process, tuition costs, poor public transportation and low education level all contributed to the difficulties faced by many in finding casino employment, despite the booming casino industry.[155]

Many of the new hospitality employees were union workers, mainly due to one union's success working with the industry. Local 54 of the Hotel Employees and Restaurant Employees International included approximately one-third of all casino employees by the mid-1980s.[156] However, the unions did not organize gaming employees from dealers to slots technicians, probably because the wages and benefits for these positions were always fairly good. In addition, Local 54 became embroiled in controversy in 1982 when the NJCCC voted to cancel the group's registration (i.e. decertify it for the casinos) when the Division of Gaming Enforcement found that three of its top officials had close connections to Nicky Scarfo of the Philadelphia 'Bruno' crime family. The controversy went on for five years as the union appealed and the case worked its way through the courts. Ultimately the Supreme Court and relevant federal courts ruled in favour of the commission, that it did have the right to cast out the officials based on the original purpose of the NJCCC: to protect the integrity of the system. Once again, the public purpose of the casinos survived a significant test of its regulatory mechanisms and these worked quite well, despite a five-year legal effort by the union.[157]

While the casinos did not have the business multiplier effect predicted by some, they did positively reshape the local economy by 1983 and the industry as a whole was in a strong position. The NJCCC's 1983 Annual Report had a triumphant tone, reflecting back on the first five years of the great experiment:

> Casino gambling in 1983 in Atlantic City was a record year with win revenues climbing close to $1.8 billion, a growth of approximately 20 percent

over 1982. Equally important is the fact that the industry as a whole reported net operating income three times greater than in 1982 with eight of the nine casinos reporting a net profit during the year.

The Commission also reported on the industry's tax benefits to the people of New Jersey, such as the $460 million that the eight percent tax on casino wins had raised since 1978 for the CRF, benefiting senior citizens and disabled Jerseyites. Amongst the schemes aided by the fund were programmes helping seniors buy prescription drugs and offset high property taxes.[158]

3 A WINNING BET? SUCCESS AND STRUGGLE IN THE 1980S

Casino management was still restless in late 1983. Industry executives looked at the regulatory system established by the Commission with disdain. One major problem was the lack of twenty-four-hour gaming, a limitation originally put in place to allow some downtime for the industry, but now just viewed as an obstacle to success. While the industry had certainly done quite well in its first five years without twenty-four-hour gambling, now it was seen as one way in which the state continued to inhibit an even more successful casino business. A new industry journal editorialized that 'the city and the industry can probably develop more completely into the resort and convention centre which everyone wants, with twenty-four-hour gambling'.[159] The vision of an Atlantic City that existed as a tourist destination beyond gambling reflected the persistence of the original motivation behind casino legalization: to restore Atlantic City as a resort town. But the reality was different. By 1983, it had become a casino town, a lucrative business community, albeit with many challenges and problems, from political corruption to a tightening business climate. It had not become a destination resort.

Persuading people to remain in town for a few days was not so important, however, as long as the casinos were making money. Making money was the salient characteristic of the casino industry, despite a slowdown that occurred after the ninth casino opened in 1982. The gambling market was still in expansion mode between 1983 and 1987, with two more casinos (Trump Plaza and Trump Castle) coming online. The industry still increased its collective gaming 'win' proceeds from $1.8 billion in 1983 to $2.5 billion in 1987. Total revenue also increased in these years, from $2.2 billion in 1983 to $3.1 billion in 1987. In terms of growth, the casino industry's second five years in Atlantic City (1984–9) were more restrained, though also steady. As a whole, the casino industry's revenue growth rate averaged 11.4 per cent between 1983 and 1987, compared to 87 per cent percent between 1979 and 1982. The total costs and expenses of the industry rose considerably in the same span, from $1.49 billion in 1983 to $2.5

billion in 1989. These costs consisted primarily of money returned back into the greater Atlantic City community in the form of wages for regular employees, construction and maintenance, goods and services purchased and administration.[160]

Measured by profitability, the Atlantic City casino industry was successful from 1983 to 1989. Total gross operating profits rose from $524 million in 1983 to $667 million in 1989, after dipping slightly from $683 million in 1988. After start-up costs were factored in for opening years, every casino but one showed a profit every year in this span. Profits ranged from Atlantis's $2.9 million in 1985 to Harrah's $99.7 million in 1989. Profits were generally stable for the casinos in these years, but they did not increase much either, and the rate of profitability actually declined in some of the years by 1–2 per cent. The second half of the decade was especially stagnant in terms of profitability, with only one year (1986) showing an increase in the profitability rate (1.8 per cent).[161]

Profitability also varied considerably for individual casinos in these years, with some clearly taking off as more successful business models, while others lagged. For example, Harrah's showed an increase in its profit margin each year between 1987 and 1989, while the industry's margin rate declined for each year. Similarly, Caesar's beat the industry's profit margin increase every year from 1984 to 1988, actually increasing in three different years (1984, 1985 and 1987) when the whole industry's margin declined. On the other hand, Atlantis began its slide toward its ultimate bankruptcy in 1989 years earlier with growth falling almost 12 per cent in 1985 alone. Resorts International's fortunes also changed significantly in the late 1980s, underperforming the industry's growth rate every year from 1984 to 1989.[162]

Casino revenue translated into avenues of opportunity for local residents in many different occupations and at many different levels. Every new casino created thousands of new jobs for waitresses, accountants, dealers, secretaries, executives, chefs, valets, doormen and many other service workers. This shifted local commuters from looking west towards Philadelphia for work to looking east. Each casino was a plant of sorts, for managers and maintenance people alike:

> In Linwood, in Egg Harbor Township, in Hammonton, in Vineland. Instead of working in those towns or commuting west, they started coming east. Casinos offered a lot of opportunities at various levels.

As well, the casinos drew professionals in service areas that simply did not pay as much for educated workers capable of leadership. Thus one regional special educator took a position as an assistant supervisor of housekeeping and a Rutgers professor left a tenured position to become an executive with Bally's.[163] Many of these jobs were not very glamorous, but they were there, and that alone was enough to spur the local economy, as one local businessman recalled:

Casino gambling had a strong impact on all of South Jersey. We even had people coming from Philadelphia to work here. Once they came here, got their jobs, got their good paying jobs – some of them were good paying jobs. ... There was a lot of jobs in the casino industry that are not glorious or very financially rewarding. But they're still jobs that people are willing to sit on a bus, or carpool for half an hour, or an hour and half, just to get to work and back.[164]

With all the jobs came a dramatic rise in per capita income throughout the Atlantic County region. This increase easily outpaced both the state and nation between 1980 and 1986:[165]

Table 3.1: County, State and National Per Capita Income, 1980–6

Year	Atlantic County per capita income ($)	New Jersey per capita income ($)	USA per capita income ($)
1980	9836	10975	9503
1981	11251	12203	10544
1982	12163	13731	11470
1983	13189	14781	12093
1984	17010	16455	13116
1985	18092	17655	13190
1986	19229	18879	14639

While the casino industry was the reason for this great rise in cumulative wealth across the greater Atlantic City area, the financial realities of the individual casinos varied considerably. One strategy that worked involved marketing to create a solid identity that would lead to greater customer loyalty. In this way, Harrah's became the most successful casinos of the first-wave casinos (built between 1978 and 1983). Harrah's built a solid customer base by offering good odds on slots and focussing specifically on deals that helped build loyalty. As a result of its low slots 'win' (11.3 per cent) and its efficient business operation, Harrah's consistently beat the net profits' average for all the casinos. By the end of 1985, five years since it opened, it had earned about $211 million in net income, second only to Resorts International at $240 million (opened in 1978). By 1988, Harrah's was viewed by one analyst as having excellent future prospects.[166]

Harrah's approach to its casino was insular, specifically designed to lure customers away from the outside world and towards the gambling. With a convenient parking garage, it was built especially so that customers could drive up in their cars, a successful strategy in the age of drive-up convenience. Other casinos would soon emulate this strategy by focussing on parking garages, making casino access as convenient and easy as possible.[167] Another successful first-wave casino (in terms of net income) was Bally's Park Place. Bally's offered a different model of success – that of an efficient gambling operation that was sparing in its slots' payout. Bally's earned higher net income with low complimentary offers, tight slots, payroll and interest expenses, yet was not the best place for gamblers to win.[168]

The second-wave casinos developed in the late 1980s had mixed results within a few years of beginning operations. By 1988, Trump Plaza followed the parking garage formula to success and invested heavily in high-profile sports promotions like boxing matches held at the old convention hall. Yet, the other Trump property – Trump's Castle— did not fare well after opening in 1986 as a showcase for everything elegant. Steered by Ivana Trump, the Castle was meant to be the height of elegance, with imported materials and an upscale marina district with new shops and restaurants surrounding it. This investment, however, drove up its costs and so it began with a very high debt load. Also, according to one analyst, Trump Castle relied on bus traffic and the complimentary offers that came in with the bus riders to the extent that this hurt profitability. In its first full three years of operations (1987–9), its gross operating profit rate declined well beyond that of the industry as a whole.[169]

Change certainly had come to the Boardwalk and environs, mainly in the form of so many visitors coming in for day trips straight to and solely for gambling. In 1982, approximately 9.5 million people arrived in the city on buses alone, millions more than the total figure for 1977. In 1986, 16.4 million people visited the casinos on bus junkets, up from 2.8 million in 1980. In 1985, Atlantic City received over twice as many casino travellers as Las Vegas, Nevada: 29.3 million visitors total compared to Vegas's 14.2 million.[170] The total number of visitors coming to Atlantic City increased from approximately 7 million visitors in 1978 to 29.3 million visitors in 1985.[171]

Between 1982 and 1984, the casino industry and the NJCCC continued to clash over matters of regulation and business. Two major showdowns between the industry and the regulators highlighted the yet-unresolved relationship between the state and casino industry over the appropriate scope of regulation. In the first case, the commission rejected a permanent casino licence for the Playboy casino in 1982, based on its finding that Playboy chairman Hugh Hefner was unsuitable for licensure. The commission's case against Playboy relied on a 1960 charge that Hefner had bribed New York officials to gain a liquor licence for a Playboy club in Manhattan. As well, Playboy had recently lost gaming licences for two out of three of its London casinos for illegally allowing high rollers to write checks on bogus accounts as credit markers. Playboy's gambling operations in England were actually quite extensive with five casinos in total and eighty betting shops around the country. In 1980, the company made $30.7 million profit on its English gaming properties, more than double the profits from global sales of *Playboy* magazine. DGE director G. Michael 'Mickey' Brown and deputy James Flanagan interrogated Hefner about the allegation, but Hefner reportedly could not remember much about the case, or his management of the New York club. At one point, he explained that he could not recall many details 'because I was in love at that time'. The commission actually voted by majority in favour of Playboy's licensure (three to two), but Playboy still lost because the law mandated a four-vote majority for a permanent licence. Hefner appealed in various state and federal courts, but eventually lost the case and gave up after investing millions to build and briefly operate a sexy, shiny casino adjacent to the old convention centre. For the brief time it operated, the Playboy casino was an exciting place to be and its intimate, fun atmosphere was fondly remembered by employees a quarter of a century later. Hefner eventually sold out to the Elsinore Corporation, which re-named the casino Atlantis in 1984.[172]

The other case also reflected the commission's priority to ensure clean casino operations. It had to do with Local 54 – the main union for casino restaurant and domestic employees – and dated back to 1981 when the union took legal action to change the *CCA*'s mandate that all union officials be registered with the commission. The case involved the Local 54's president Frank Gerace, who was allegedly an associate of Nicky Scarfo, the Philadelphia mobster who had relocated to Atlantic City to run the family's operations in the new casino community. The NJCCC denied a few of the union leaders' registrations due to these allegations and Gerace and the union subsequently waged a three-year legal battle against the registration process for the purposes of retaining the union leadership. In 1984, the Supreme Court finally ruled in favour of the NJCCC to register union officials. Gerace and two other implicated union officials (Frank Materio and Karlos LaSane) subsequently resigned.[173]

The legal battle actually continued after the Supreme Court decision when the union sued in state court on other grounds. It lost again in 1985 because the question hinged upon whether Gerace's friendships could impact 'the policies intended to be served by casino gaming regulation'. Despite this, Local 54 continued to employ Gerace as a consultant, outside the reach of the *CCA*. What was ultimately important about the Gerace case? Firstly, it highlighted the benefits of the tight regulatory mechanisms designed by Steve Perskie and others in 1977 to keep organized crime out of the casino industry. Secondly, it displayed the lack of influence that organized crime held in the casino industry. Certainly, other unions also faced mob allegations (like the local Teamsters), but the casino business itself was the main enterprise driving the industry, employing 40,000 people by 1985.[174]

In the mid-1980s, casino industry supporters and insiders regularly lamented the NJCCC as a business liability. However, in this instance the agency clearly acted in the industry's interest, even as industry insiders assailed it on other matters like gaming floor regulations and licence oversight. To this effect, the Casino Association's Annual Report editorialized:

> The industry has supported all state efforts to insure the complete integrity of casino operations since its inception in 1976. However, the industry will

continue to discuss with the Casino Control Commission, changes to regulations affecting the industry's ability to make sound business decisions and the cost of regulation.[175]

To support its argument, the Casino Association also used its annual report to highlight the considerable regulatory costs of the New Jersey experience compared to Nevada. For example, in 1985 the NJCCC and the DGE spent $41.2 million on regulation, with 1,000 employees. In Nevada, the state's gaming board spent only $10.7 million for regulation, employing 350 people, despite the facts that there were many more casinos and gaming halls to regulate and that they were spread out across a much wider distance.[176] In 1984, casino executive Robert Maxey made the case in even starker terms, calling the system 'bureaucracy run amok' via an 'un-audited unlimited, self-determined budget which enables them to hire an enormous staff devoted to the nitpicking of an industry'. Maxey also joked that the commissioners 'have not been able to put us out of business yet' – an attitude that typified the unresolved conflict between the casinos and their regulators that persisted through the much of the decade.[177]

From the perspective of the individual employee, obtaining a licence to work in one of the casinos was not much easier in the mid-1980s than it had been in the late 1970s, despite some reforms. An average person seemed to face significant obstacles to work in the industry, as defined by the NJCCC. A 1986 brochure appeared to be designed to stave off potential casino employees as much as it sought to be instructive. It called all casino employee jobs 'positions of high visibility' to justify the need to have such thorough background checks and to 'eliminate persons with suspicious backgrounds'. Held up by the New Jersey Supreme Court, the commission reminded applicants that it had the right to investigate past employment records, military records, financial history, education transcripts, police and court cases, the backgrounds of family members, business and associates. In addition, the NJCCC also screened out applicants with immediate family members who worked in state government and barred anyone from casino employment who had worked in the DGE or NJCCC in the previous three years. The NJCCC also made clear that all casino employees essentially gave up their fourth amendment rights as subjects of warrant-less searches while working.[178]

In 1985, the commission made big news by denying Hilton Hotels a casino licence. The NJCCC made its decision based on the applicant's supposed associations with organized crime in its Las Vegas property and a Chicago lawyer (Stanley Korshak) with mafia connections. Although Hilton appealed, the hotel chain decided instead to sell the almost-finished property to Donald Trump, who turned it into the Trump Castle. The commission's decision faced instant rebuke by casino supporters, who viewed it as very characteristic of the self-defeating approach towards regulation they believed the Commission had towards the casinos. *Casino Chronicle* went a step further, issuing a blistering rebuke for the NJCCC's decisions on Hilton and Playboy. Among other reasons, the *Chronicle* objected to a minority of the commission blocking a casino's licence:

> The present system, under which two commissioners can block the licensing of a casino hotel is too reminiscent of a private club allowing a single member to blackball applicants with little or no explanation.[179]

Commission chair Walter Read responded to the critics of the Hilton decision by noting that it simply reflected the NJCCC's continuing mission to ensure integrity in the casino industry. In the 1985 annual report, he explained it in the context of other issues of that year, calling it a 'prime example of the Commission's emphasizing that it intends to continue to require strict compliance with the Casino Control Act'. Chairman Read briefly alluded to Hilton management not answering questions related to alleged improprieties on another matter – enough to raise a significant red flag in the eyes of the of the commission. Similarly, he noted that Resorts International's was only barely re-licensed following examination of company's dealings in the Bahamas. He also chose to highlight an extraordinary penalty levelled against Caesar's for giving special credit to embezzling Canadian banker Brian Molony: closure for one day. In 1985, some employees of Caesar's also drew the Commission's wrath for the casino's special treatment of Italian gambler Gaetano Caltagrione, who in 1983 asked for and received special conditions, such as his own room for gambling and all white dealers.[180]

The decision to deny a licence to Hilton resonated with many local residents as a symbol of the NJCCC's ineptitude for many years to come, as demonstrated by the views of one businessman from 2005:

> We could have had a Borgata here 20 years ago. Hilton came in and built Trump Marina. Came in, bought the land, built it, and then the state refused to give him a casino license. He's got a building that's 95 per cent completed, so he ends up selling it to Trump. At the time Hilton was – had the best databank of persons – of hotel guests that come to the city. And we say no to him.[181]

The commission's Hilton decision also led to a transaction between Hilton and Donald Trump that signalled Trump's ascendancy as the most powerful individual within the Atlantic City casino industry. Since 1982, Trump had partnered with Harrah's (then owned by Holiday Inn) and planned to split profits as the developer of Harrah's Boardwalk Hotel Casino at Trump Plaza, which opened in 1984. But the New York real estate magnate had developed a broader vision for his casino empire in Atlantic City by 1985 and had grown frustrated with Harrah's management of the Boardwalk casino. Harrah's operational style clashed sharply with Trump's over a myriad of issues. At one point, Trump objected to the size of his name on the building's logo, smaller than Harrah's and a bad marketing decision (he thought), given his rising celebrity from owning the United States Football League's New Jersey Generals. In turn, Holiday Inn CEO Mike Rose and Harrah's management were 'appalled' at the bright red, orange, yellow and purple wall treatments and chrome fixtures chosen by Ivana Trump for the casino. The divorce between the two companies appeared more imminent after Trump bought space adjacent to the casino for a parking garage and then declared that he would charge Harrah's for every car parked in the garage.[182]

Donald Trump wanted to be a casino magnate, not just a developer with his name attached to a casino. Barron Hilton's dilemma quickly became Trump's opportunity, as he outbid Steve Wynn and purchased the property for $325 million (loaned from Manufacturer's Hanover), then sold $350 million of junk bonds to assure the property, quickly named Trump's Castle Hotel Casino. It opened as an extension of his casino licence for the Trump Plaza property under management by the Hilton group, effective through 1985. Then, Trump went after both Harrah's and Bally's in takeover bids via stock acquisition. He acquired neither, but forced both to issue junk bonds and expand their debt loads to ward off the takeover attempts. Trump's bid also made Bally's look to expansion, which led to its 1987 deal to purchase the Golden Nugget. In the end, Trump took over neither Harrah's nor Bally's, but he did enrich himself by about $28 million through stock appreciation. This led to a Federal Trade Commission charge for stock manipulation that he settled for $750,000. Meanwhile, Trump the magnate was hardly finished building his casino empire in Atlantic City.[183]

Wary of the new competition in the marina district and possibly in disbelief over the aggressively competitive moves of its own partner, Harrah's sued Trump on the Castle's opening day for 'conduct detrimental to the partnership' to block the casino from using the name 'Trump'. The half-hearted effort ultimately failed and Trump labelled it a 'disgrace'. To finally dissolve the crumbling partnership, Trump then quickly raised more junk bonds and completed his corporate divorce from Harrah's by buying out its share of the Plaza. This slick financial manoeuvre made him the sole owner of two casinos within a few months.[184]

Trump's entry into the Atlantic City casino industry turned more dramatic in 1986 when he attempted to take over Holiday Corporation (Harrah's parent company) and Bally's via stock purchases, neither of which were successful. The moves caused real consternation within the Commission, and Read used his 1986 annual report to note that Trump's actions 'combined to force the Legislature to look more closely at the Casino Control Act'. Read also noted ambiguously that 'the regulatory system must be able to accommodate changes in owner-ship and transfers of interests in existing casino entities without sacrificing the paramount goals of integrity and public trust'.[185] But how did Trump's moves challenge the 'integrity' and 'public trust' of the casino industry? Actually, they did not – rather Trump's transforming entry into Atlantic City's gaming industry reflected the sophisticated nature of the casino business in a way that eluded the regulators. Though Trump was a private operator, his corporate approach toward business consolidation was inevitable in Atlantic City and ultimately led to a more focused industry that looked towards expanding the marketplace for all, rather than competing against each other for set gaming revenues. The *CCA* was designed especially to keep small-time mobsters from corrupting the new casinos, but the casino story of the 1980s was really about big time corporate operators like Donald Trump, Steve Wynn and the gaming gurus behind Harrah's.

In the late 1980s, the Trump Organization continued to expand its influence and ownership in the casino industry, most notably by purchasing Resorts International through a stock acquisition. Following the death of Resorts International's founder Jim Crosby in 1986, the first casino had faced major financial problems, stemming from costs related to the building of the Taj Mahal. The Taj began as a project in part to alleviate legal pressure on Resorts to build on its property known as the Uptown Renewal tract, to the east (up the Boardwalk).[186] The Trump group's move led to a dilemma regarding this construction project. Once the Taj was complete, technically, Trump would be the sole licensee for four casinos, a taboo according to the *CCA*. To get around this, Trump planned to close Resorts International while the Taj was still being built, a compromise approved by the Commission. Trump's attempted takeover of Bally's Park through stock acquisition actually led to the Resorts acquisition, as Bally's bought back Trump's stock, giving him a $30 million profit that he invested into the Resorts deal. Then, Bally's bought the Golden Nugget for $440 million, allowing Steve Wynn his exodus from Atlantic City.[187]

The 1987 Trump–Resorts arrangement gave Trump 1.75 per cent of gross revenue, 15 per cent of profits, and 3 per cent of the costs to build Taj Mahal in exchange for bringing management expertise. Trump's deal was, in fact, lucrative on paper, though a lot depended on the future success of the casino. In actuality, Trump was taking a huge risk by sinking $79 million into Resorts, a fading presence on the uptown Boardwalk by 1987. Resorts International's gross operating profit had declined every year but one since 1983 and at $69.5 million in 1987 was at its lowest point since 1982. But Resorts did own real estate – as much as 10 per cent of the city at one point – making it attractive from a development perspective.[188]

Trump's deal for Resorts also expanded the rift between the regulators and the casino industry. The DGE drew the ire of pro-casino forces for originally opposing the lucrative deal that Trump made with Resorts International as unnecessary and expensive. In fact, the DGE (not the NJCCC) had stepped in to oppose the manoeuvre originally, concerned about 'undue economic concentration within the Atlantic City market'. The NJCCC effectually overruled the DGE in approving the solution involving Resorts International's planned closure. But from the vantage point of some industry insiders, here was another good illustration of the counter-productive regulatory climate suffocating the casinos. Resorts needed Trump's managerial expertise and backing to get the Taj Mahal built; as one writer pointed out, the Penthouse and Dunes casinos were started but never finished. From this perspective, the Commission was again interfering in a management decision that was for the good of the casino industry.[189]

Early in 1988, a *Casino Journal* editorial articulated its sweeping and condemnatory position on New Jersey's casino regulators:

> It is equally dangerous and destructive to maintain regulatory agencies composed of people so philosophically opposed to the activity that they believe it is more important to prevent that activity from operating efficiently, than to insure that the public believes the maximum benefits from that efficient operation....the industry and its people are serious potential threats to his [CCC Chair Read] conception of the 'best interests' of New Jersey and its citizens.

It saw the myriad actions to regulate the industry as nothing less than an anti-casino conspiracy:

> To the DGE and NJCCC, the casino industry is an 'Evil Empire'. And they seek to no 'disarmament' treaties but, rather, act as if complete, **Unconditional Surrender** is all they believe, for the people of New Jersey to answer that call for surrender with the only response it truly deserves ... **Nuts!**[190]

The Trump–Resorts deal took new form in 1988 when entertainer Merv Griffin stepped in for the purchase. Griffin paid $300 million for Resorts stock, giving him control of Resorts International and an additional $63 million for Trump's management contract. As part of the deal, Resorts International went to Trump, and the Trump Organization became the exclusive proprietors of the unfinished Taj Mahal. This effectively alleviated the regulatory dilemma as Trump would only own three separate casinos, in clear compliance with the *CCA*. The deal took months of wrangling and near-collapses, but eventually transpired when both Trump and Griffin agreed to increase their personal contributions to satisfy the NJCCC. The Commission expressed concerns about the financial viability of both properties (Taj and Resorts), with both casinos highly leveraged. After months of declining stock value ($60 to $12), Trump's brief tenure as Resorts's majority owner and chairman appeared to be a disastrous financial move.[191]

Consequently, Trump tried to take the casino private by offering $22 a share in the face of opposition by Resorts International's stockholders and the independent directors who were the legacy of Jim Crosby, its deceased founder. When Griffin came in at $36 a share, compensation for the management contract and the split proposition involving the Taj Mahal, Trump had manoeuvred another savvy deal that extended his casino empire in Atlantic City while seemingly relieving him of a big burden, the revenue-losing Resorts property. The risk, of course, was the unfinished Taj: its outcome would ultimately determine the viability of the deal. Trump, however, was pleased in 1988, noting that 'it's going to be one of the most successful developments I've ever done'. Griffin walked away with a casino, but one with the second highest debt load of all the Atlantic City casinos (over $300 million) and stagnant revenue growth. He appeared less ebullient than Trump after signing off, commenting to a reporter that 'I'm just thrilled that it's over with. It's been a long hard pull and I'm relieved to get going'.[192]

An interesting sidebar to the Trump–Griffin deal concerned the Sands and its parent company, Pratt Hotel Corporation. According to Chairman Jack Pratt, Resorts (via the Crosby directors) originally came to Pratt with its offer to buy, but Resorts International's management rejected Pratt's offer at $600 million and Pratt was not willing to go beyond that figure. Pratt summarized his take on the deal, citing the Taj Mahal as a major factor in his company's rejection of the offer:

> The costs were just a runaway train. And when it got to $750–800 million, then the economics of the deal didn't make sense to us as a company, if you were going to operating them as casino hotels.

Later, Trump approached Pratt with an offer to buy Resorts that Pratt again refused (before the deal with Griffin was done). In August 1988, Pratt accurately predicted the impact of the vast project and its consequences for the Trump group and Resorts over the next few years:

> It's pretty hard to take a package that's gigantic in size and make it work. Even if you cut it in half, you still have two halves of a tough deal. So it will be up to Donald Trump to make his half work because he will have probably $750 or 800 million in it now, even buying at a discount. And when you look at what it costs to carry that amount of debt and what it will generate in gross operating profit, you have to step back and say there has to be negative cash flow for a considerable time. And when you step back and look at the other half that Merv Griffin has, you look at that and say he has to really depend on what the sale of those other assets are worth because he's got a lot of non-producing assets there that are not working now and won't be working for quite some time.[193]

The exchange between Pratt and Trump over the Resorts deal presaged a much more contentious conflict over the Penthouse property on Columbia Avenue and the Boardwalk. In the late 1970s, Penthouse purchased the parcel and began developing a casino. The development stalled due to inadequate funding, yet Penthouse held on to the land and the rusty, half-built casino until striking a deal with Pratt. Pratt and the Sands planned to develop a 'Hollywood' casino with a 'People Mover' monorail to connect it with a distant parking lot. Trump's group took advantage of a zoning board hearing and appeal process to delay the necessary approvals for the project. When they did not come through, Penthouse president David Myerson then swung the deal to the Trump Organization which bought the property in 1989 and planned a 1,000-room non-casino hotel. Complicating matters was Pratt's and Penthouse's joint ownership of a parcel on Columbus Place, tied to developing the Penthouse site. As always, Trump was blunt and clear about expressing his group's perspective:

> They had a contract and they had to close by a certain time and they were unable to do so ... it's [the Sands contract] a joke.

Meanwhile, the Sands issued a press release targeting Trump:

> This is but the most recent in a long-standing attempt by the Trump organization to oppose the development of the Sands Hollywood Casino Hotel Project, solely as a means of decreasing competition.

The Pratt company ended up suing both Trump and Penthouse for 'fraud, conspiracy and racketeering' consequent to the deal. Trump may have slowed the process, but in the end, he was right: the Sands had failed to come up with the money and approvals according to contract, thereby giving Penthouse an out.[194]

The contretemps between the Trump and Pratt companies signalled the intensifying competition of the time and also the stress of casino development in a time of slowing growth. Of the twelve casinos operating in 1988, only four made substantial profits, while four lost money and four barely made a profit. A close observer described the situation:

> casino patronage is not increasing in proportion to the increase in casino capacity. Nor is that patronage increasing in proportion to the increase in casino operating costs. These are most disquieting trends, in that they pose serious threats to the financial stability of every Atlantic City casino property. Unless new markets are opened beyond the day tripper draw of the Northeast, it is difficult to see how Atlantic City can expect to attract sufficient patronage to fill the Taj Mahal.[195]

The most powerful sign of trouble for the industry came in April 1989 when Elsinore's Atlantis lost its casino licence and shut down, a first in Atlantic City. Atlantis had been losing money since 1985, and had single-handedly shown that the mere existence of a casino did not ensure profits. The casino never really recovered after the Playboy debacle in 1984, with declining gross revenues at almost 30 per cent by 1987. In the meantime, it languished in bankruptcy from 1985 to 1988 and suffered a seven-month long employee strike by Local 54 from September 1987 to April 1988. The NJCCC denied its re-licensure on the heavy debt owed by Atlantis, steady losses (including $75 million in 1988), failure of a marketing program using tokens instead of coins for slot machines ('Hot Spots'), and connection to embattled investment firm Drexel Burnham Lambert. Facing legal action for its use of junk bonds, Drexel owned 4.7 per cent of Elsinore stock and 9.1 per cent of its bonds – enough for the Commission to call into question the casino's financial stability.[196]

In denying Atlantis re-licensure, the commission cited its 'failure to establish a financial stability' and 'state licensing standards' as a consequence of a DGE review.[197] The Commission appointed a conservator to oversee operations, effectively removing Atlantis's own management (led by CEO Jeanne Hood) from running the business. Atlantis had waged a long campaign to maintain its licence with 2,000 jobs at stake and employees operating in a state of disbelief that the Commission would accept the DGE's recommendation, especially given Atlantis's emergence from bankruptcy just five months earlier. In early 1989, the impending decision over Atlantis highlighted the influence of the biggest casino hotel union – Local 54— whose management encouraged the DGE to recommend a conservator early and supported NJCCC action to force Atlantic to go along with contract negotiations. Local 54 did not want the casino to use its financial weakness as justification for under-cutting negotiated salaries and benefits across the industry, though it was unsuccessful in precluding it from doing so by the NJCCC.[198]

In the NJCCC hearings over the licence decision, Hood faced long odds in turning persuading the Commission not to follow through on the DGE's recommendations. She argued that the casino just needed a few more months to find a purchaser to save the business. However, cash-flow projections showed that Atlantis would not make its bond interest payments by the beginning of May 1989, a foreboding piece of information that affirmed the state attorney general's conclusion that Elsinore had not 'demonstrated its financial stability, its financial integrity, its financial responsibility or its business ability'. Yet the doomed casino found a rescuer, of sorts, in Donald Trump, barely a week after losing its licence. Trump and Elsinore management quickly announced a deal in which the Trump Organization would purchase the hotel for $63 million, shut down the casino and operate it as a 'super luxury' hotel to serve as an overflow resource just down the Boardwalk from Trump Plaza. Along with the Penthouse deal, the sale also gave Trump complete control over four casino-zoned blocks on either side of the existing convention centre, a situation that prompted one gaming analyst to quip that Trump was 'playing Monopoly for real' but also risking the renewed ire of the regulators for attempting to corner the casino market by skirting the three-casino licence.[199]

Atlantis's collapse was an important milestone for the casino industry, the point at which the eleven-year-long streak of success came crashing down. It had a broad, negative impact on the industry as recalled by one observer:

> Well, in the second half of the '80s, we had the first bankruptcy of a casino, the Atlantis, which closed the year before the Taj Mahal opened. And that

certainly startled a lot of people. And there were vendors out there that weren't getting paid and stuff and … the failure of the Atlantis and – well there were vendors who were nervous. And some of them, I'm sure, didn't get the amount they were owed. And employees saw – and I don't know if – the rest of them cut back on their employees. And casinos aren't one of those just gushing cash.[200]

The DGE's successful recommendation to close Atlantis confirmed for regulation critics the view that the agency was anti-casino and seemingly corresponded with its previous actions targeting Resorts, Caesars, and even Steve Wynn, when Golden Nugget applied for its licence. The reaction against closing Atlantis also included rhetoric aimed at the state's politicians for distancing themselves from the industry:

> Yes, we have legalized casino gaming in Atlantic City. But we know we are going to burn in hell because of it. And we wish we didn't have casinos at all.[201]

At the time of Atlantis's closure, former governor Brendan Byrne weighed in on the decision, noting that 'I guess I would tend to let them sink or swim' and the state 'doesn't need to come in and supply the structure to make a casino go'. Byrne also commented on a number of issues often cited by regulation opponents, indicating that he was not especially happy with how the experiment had played out since legalization occurred under his watch. He supported twenty-four-hour gaming and suggested that regulatory costs were 'getting ridiculous and should be reduced'. Finally, he supported the establishment of a regional approach to problems faced in Atlantic City – noting that 'The failure to regionalize to solve some problems in Atlantic City was a major part if not the major mistake I made as governor'.[202]

The Atlantis's closure also brought attention to the significant problem of casino debt in the form of junk bonds. Though Atlantis's debt woes were especially egregious, other casinos also owed considerable amounts of money and, by the end of 1988, most were highly leveraged with junk bonds at interest rates as high as 17 per cent. The following table shows the outstanding debt obligations of the industry at the time:

Table 3.2: Outstanding Debt Obligations of the Atlantic City Casinos, 1988

Casino	Outstanding bonded debt	Bond interest rates (%)	Bond interest as % of net revenue
Atlantis	$144 million	13–15.5	N/A
Bally's Park Place	$156 million	11.5–13	N/A
Bally's Grand	$301 million	13.3	16
Caesar's	$67 million	N/A	3.5
Claridge	$128 million	12.5	31
Harrah's	$24 million (held by parent Holiday Corp.)	0	N/A

Resorts	$325 million	17	24
Sands	$187 million	11.75–16.5	10
Showboat	$180 million	10.4–11.25	9.5
Tropicana	$98 million	n/a	N/A
Trump Castle	$324 million	15	15
Trump Plaza	$275 million	10–13	10

Adding all obligations of the various casino parent corporations, Salomon Brothers pegged the entire debt at $5.3 billion in mid-1989. A gaming industry analyst cited the high debt figures as a portent of looming problems, especially as the economy appeared headed into a downturn. The situation clearly concerned DGE director Anthony Parillo, who commented that 'It is difficult to see how Atlantic City has benefited from all this financial engineering' and promised close scrutiny of future debt load increases. Yet, a Drexel Burnham Lambert analyst cautioned against overreaction by pointing out that the industry had always been highly leveraged and that it was better measured financially by cash flow income, before depreciation.[204]

In fact, the debt conditions did begin to have a major impact on the industry, leading to a round of restructuring via bankruptcy between 1989 and 1991. This phase began in late 1989, when Resorts filed for bankruptcy to restructure $912 million in debt. A year later, the Trump Taj Mahal followed suit. As the 1980s came to a close, the Atlantic City casino industry was in a difficult position. Although net revenue continued its long climb upwards (over $3 billion by 1988), revenue growth had dropped to 2.6 per cent by 1989, a number that signalled an industry slowdown that would last into the early 1990s.[205]

The problems experienced by the casino industry in the late 1980s mirrored the general discomfit affecting many in Atlantic City who had not reaped the benefits of the casino era. In one long-time uptown resident's eyes, the situation recalled a classic novel:

> Well, let me tell you, have you heard about the Tale of Two Cities? That was what happened when the casino started making money and everything was ritzy over there, and everything.[206]

At the time, the city's condition and prospects stood in stark contrast to the growing, prosperous suburban communities that ringed it. The impoverishment of the 1970s and real estate crisis of the first casino wave (1978–83) had not really been solved by the middle of the decade. In 1985, the poverty rate was close to 25 per cent in the city and 30 per cent of its housing units were government subsidized. Moreover, the city had no super market, nor movie theatre, in part due to the real estate run-up that had not fully abated by the mid-1980s. In 1986, television news reporter Bill Moyers filmed a special about Atlantic City and panned the casino era as an 'urban tragedy' when he found empty Boardwalk shopfronts, vacant uptown lots, distressed small businesses everywhere, a weakened church parish and disaffected residents who lamented lost city neighborhoods.[207]

What was news to Bill Moyers was glaringly obvious to people in and around the city and the casino industry in the mid- and late 1980s. Millions of people were coming to the casinos annually and for the most part, that was where they stayed. Many older businesses were shuttered, causing locals to lament over the mixed progress of their casino community. One resident discussed the bleak Inlet neighborhood, with sadness:

> At one time, our Inlet was one of the nicest sections of town with lovely homes, well-kept lawns and friendly neighborhoods. Over the years, it has fallen on bad times, and today is shunned by visitors and residents alike.

By 1985, the closure of two famous restaurants, including Pacific Avenue landmark Shumsky's, symbolized the downside to the casino experiment and the recognition that the casino industry had not benefited city businesses, despite early hopes.[208]

Mr and Mrs Al Cohen, owners of Polly's Dress shop on Atlantic Avenue, expressed their disappointment in the casino era:

> We thought it would be a panacea ... We thought the money would drop in our laps ... We thought it would rebuild the city.

But the Cohens instead found that that no one was leaving the casinos to walk a few blocks and shop at their dress shop. They survived by selling cheap merchandise but never hit the retail bonanza they had hoped for in the casino era.[209] Similarly, Bernard Josephson owned a print shop in the city and also supported casino legalization in 1976 only to find that business did not improve. But for Josephson, the story turned out positive:

> The owner of our building, just blocks from the Taj Mahal, wanted to make it condos to reap a fortune. I received an order from the county sheriff to vacate the premises in 30 days. There is an old adage 'When one door closes, another opens'. I took a job at Resorts as production expediter in the entertainment department. During my years there, I got to meet and greet such great personalities as Frank Sinatra, Don Rickles, Rodney Dangerfield, Wayne Newton, Liberace, and many more. I have great memories and stories that I'll never forget.[210]

An Atlantis employee reflected on the city's condition in 1986, commenting that

> In many ways, the city just isn't a convenient or pleasant place to live in. Who wants to spend two hours trying to go to the store on the weekends when traffic is congested?

According to another casino employee, the city's crime spike and general deterioration seriously impacted lifestyle choice:

> Who wants to live in a city that is dirty and sometimes dangerous? Any housing that's reasonable is down in the inlet, and the police won't even go there. I would like to live in the city and walk on the boardwalk, but right now, it is just nicer to live somewhere else.

Similarly, another casino worker commented on the negative qualities that the city had taken on:

> I don't feel that Atlantic City has a lot to offer people who want to live here. Not right now, anyway. The beach is eroding: it's very noisy; entertainment is limited to the casinos; there's nowhere to shop; and the city's very dirty. Also, I feel like I can't even walk or ride a bike here at night, as I can where I live. [211]

Another local observer juxtaposed the decaying infrastructure with the still-expanding casino industry:

> This time next year we will have yet another casino/hotel on the scene. Showboat will be open, followed shortly thereafter by Resort's overpowering Taj Mahal. Showboat will have a 60,000 sq. foot casino, while Resort's new facility will have, at its opening 90,000 sq. ft. [Taj project] ... These two new facilities plus some other minor additions will create a 26.7 per cent increase in market share of casino space in a town that has nothing else to offer but gaming. The Atlantic City boardwalk is dilapidated, the infrastructure is suffering from a 'a case of locked bowels', coupled with an airport that is not serviced by any scheduled airline. It would appear that the cart has been placed miles ahead of the horse, and the horse, trying to catch up, may have just tired in the stretch. [212]

To many in the casino industry, the city's problems could be attributed to highly dysfunctional city government. Casino champion Tom Carver summarized the long-standing industry attitude towards the city government:

> the number one requirement is, as it always has been for political stability in Atlantic City. That is the primary process that affects the casino industry and the entire development of Atlantic City. We must have political stability in AC so that the private business sector, other than casinos, will be willing to invest in the community. [213]

The industry's position on the local government was an important aspect of the early casino era. From the time that mayor Michael Matthews was led away in handcuffs from a celebrity roast by FBI agents in 1983, the city government was a constant object of blame for the resort's problems. The veneer of corruption and incompetence, cemented in Atlantic City's past, became a significant rationale for problems such as the low-income housing shortage, crime-ridden inner city and dirty Boardwalk. From the casino industry's perspective, the situation was bad enough to merit investment in an audit in 1985 by a private firm (Touche Ross). The firm concluded that 'local government is plagued with waste and inefficiency'.[214]

After taking over from the convicted Matthews in 1984, James Usry's first term as mayor did not bring the massive relief to the city hoped for by some in the casino industry. In backing Usry's opponent in the 1986 election, one commentator noted that:

> if Jim Usry is re-elected, we will have a Mayor who lacks both the will and the capacity to govern in the public interest because, as his first 2 years in office have so sadly shown, he lacks an understanding of where that public interest genuinely lies.

City government critics wanted the state to create a 'superagency' to deal with increased crime, congestion, pollution and higher property taxes vexing the local population. These critics had been somewhat underwhelmed by a perceived piecemeal approach to redevelopment by the state:

> an urban grant here, a beach erosion project there, a mortgage assistance project somewhere else. And every one of these State contributions has been trumpeted with an excitement we might expect to accompany the Second Coming, though, in fact, collectively they have amounted to very little.[215]

In late 1986, the atmosphere of urban crisis intensified significantly as Local 54 bar, restaurant and hotel employees staged a one-day walkout in response to stalled negotiations over a new contract. Fortunately for all concerned, union and management reached a settlement quickly and the workers returned to the casinos the next day. The sides agreed to a nine per cent contract increase over three years to end the strike. But the affair was shocking and violent with forty-nine people injured, thirty-nine arrested and rampant mob activity that included people being assaulted, widespread vandalism and damaged cars up and down Pacific Avenue.[216] The *Press of Atlantic City* reported on the travails of a Mary Romero, accosted in her car at a red light by a

> striking casino-hotel worker [who] slapped her in the face and tried to coax fellow pickets to help him overturn her van.

Sixty-two-year-old Mario Truscello of suburban Brigantine told a reporter that:

> the Local 54 guys were all around my car. They broke my window. They put dents in my car. One guy was jumping on the roof. That's when they dragged me out.

Another woman, defined as an 'outside vendor' with 'business in the casino' reported that a striker brandished a knife and scratched up her car's paint job with it.[217]

Though it was over quickly, the 1986 strike had a substantial legacy for the casino era and helped cement the universal perception that the city had gone awry and that the casinos had failed in their revitalization mission. Carver blamed the police and city government directly for allowing mobs to take over city streets. A North Jersey legislator opined in the *New York Times* that:

> The spontaneous violence supports my contention that there is rage beneath the city's recovery as a major resort and tourist mecca.

The assemblyman also framed the city's circumstance in precisely the way that casino backers suspected state politicians understood it:

> If there is a spirit of resignation among the permanent residents of Atlantic City, it may be shared by those of us from other parts of New Jersey who see a political change periodically bending itself to accommodate the casino industry's most visible needs while ignoring the needs of the people.[218]

Ultimately, the strike was probably more damaging to Local 54, as the most enduring legacy was the street violence associated with the strikers. From this point on, the casino sources often seemed hostile to the union and no union was successful in recruiting casino dealers until 2007. This had much to do with a perception that Atlantic City casino unions did not share a common vision of industry success. The strike also shone a harsh spotlight on the city's shortcomings, strife and even anarchy. A widespread notion spread through the community that things got out of hand because the police union was about to enter contract negotiations and thus sympathized more with the strikers, allowing things to spiral out of control. Casino customers experienced the disruption, and in one case, Lou DiLella (a Sands union representative) even wrote to two high rollers to explain the union's point of view. His version of the strike emphasized the chaotic city theme shared by casino management, and disowned the casino employees from the violence while putting the onus on street ruffians:

> As promised, here are some newspaper clippings of our recent 'ACTIVITIES'. I must tell you that most of the violence was not done by union members. I do not wish to make excuses for those actions since they should have never taken place however, it must be pointed out for the sake of fairness, that as things progressed on Monday nite/Tuesday morning, large bands of roving teenagers from the ghetto could be seen roving around the Hotels creating problems.[219]

By 1987, city hall's failures were widely acknowledged in many areas. The city government had not managed traffic flow well, planned for affordable housing or dealt with the crime wave that ensued following casino legalization.[220] Preventing the city's failure was now a high priority for the casino industry, according to a 1986 *Wall Street Journal* analysis:

> If the casinos themselves ever liked the resulting chaos, they don't anymore. The now-maturing casinos, which have a $3 Billion stake in facilities to protect, are beginning to see Atlantic City's fate as the key to their own.[221]

The initial crime spike in the city has often cited by casino critics as the major downside to legalizing casinos in Atlantic City, just as it was in the 1980s by outside commentators.[222] In 1977, Atlantic City police reported 4,391 index crimes and, in 1980, 11,899 index crimes. The collective crime index for Atlantic City shot up within a few years, mainly driven by a tripling of the number of larcenies that occurred between 1979 and 1982. These included muggings, purse snatchings and other types of petty thefts. In 1979, 3,869 larcenies occurred in the city, compared to 10,949 in 1982. While the coming of the casinos occurred concurrently with the crime spike however, studies conducted between 1985 and 1991 demonstrated that community crime rose due to other factors than the casinos. The crime increase of those years should also be noted within the context of a significant at-risk population (especially due to the crack cocaine epidemic of the 1980s), and the crimes themselves differentiated between those that were casino-based and those that were community-based. Visitor-inspired crime increased in Atlantic City's early casino era just as it increased in Orlando, Florida when Walt Disney World opened.[223] Moreover, the average crime rate per 1,000 residents actually *decreased* in Atlantic County from 1976 to 1981. Atlantic County municipalities had become safe bedroom communities in the casino era.[224]

After shooting up in the first few years of the casino era, the overall crime level actually levels off when it is visitor-adjusted and compared to New Jersey and national rates for the 1980s. Between 1979 and 1989, Atlantic City's visitor-adjusted crime rate increased just 0.01 per cent. This was poor compared to the state of New Jersey, which dropped 9.5 per cent in the same span, but actually better compared to the nation as a whole (which suffered a 3.1 per cent increase). When adjusted for the many millions of new visitors, the city's violent crime rate actually increased at a lower rate than the state and national increases in the first few years of the casino era. Between 1977 and 1981, Atlantic City's visitor-adjusted violent crime rate grew to 9.4 per 1,000 residents in 1981, considerably higher than the state index of 6.3 and the national index of 5.9 violent crimes per 1,000 residents in 1981. However, in the same period the rate of visitor-adjusted increase grew at a 29.6 per cent rate, compared to the state's huge 61.5 per cent increase. Atlantic City's increase in violent crime was actually on par with the national increase in these years (28.3 per cent) when adjusted for the approximate 42,000 extra people that populated the city on any given day

– more than doubling its residential population. In the 1980s, the number of violent crimes rapidly increased around the nation and in the state of New Jersey, rising 20 per cent and 10.9 per cent respectively between 1979 and 1989. Yet, in Atlantic City, visitor-adjusted violent crime in Atlantic City actually declined by 28.4 per cent in the same period, despite the fact that the actual number of violent crimes that occurred in the city was much higher per 100,000 residents than either the state or nation. Factoring in the actual daily population in the city, one was actually less likely to be victimized by a violent criminal than an average American in 1989.[225] However, despite the statistical reality, the perception of Atlantic City as a casino-driven, dangerous place, fuelled by Moyers's report and other accounts coming out of the region, could not have been more powerful by the late 1980s.

The city government had neglected to address the new circumstances of the casino era, with dramatic results. Its failure to effectively implement property tax revaluation had the negative impact of rewarding speculators who owned and sat on large tracts of property. To remedy the situation, a court finally ordered the city to do a massive revaluation in 1986, which led to property assessments going up from three to six times their previous valuations.[226] While this made up for years of stagnation and vastly increased revenues and the casinos' tax obligations, it also let to more housing problems for an already beleaguered local populace:

> Most thing they wanted to know about the taxes, because people's taxes were going up. And the casinos were making the money, and the people – the working people, the people – now the hard thing about the houses, is that they were building what they – they hadn't gotten to me yet for the houses.[227]

On the similar theme of local mismanagement, a 1989 *Casino Journal* editorial used a gubernatorial decision to override local officials on environmental preservation to make the point that the state had been way too lax by way of not intervening in the city's affairs earlier, thus obscuring 'the facts of Atlantic City's mismanagement of the industry'. From the mid-1980s, casino industry commentators had continually railed against the local politicians as a key source of the city's and the industry's problems. In short, the argument ran that the city government had failed to stimulate redevelopment effectively because of bribery, no-show jobs, poor fiscal decisions and 'politics of the lowest, most vicious order' conducted by self-interested, greedy politicians.[228]

Also in 1989, Ramada/Tropicana president Paul Rubeli articulated a 'Bill of Rights for the Casino Industry in New Jersey' that reflected, among other ideas, a local government and casino industry at cross-purposes. Rubeli's statement called for a 'five year management and capital plan for the city, county and state responsibilities in the South Jersey region'.[229] Similarly, Tom Carver sharply expressed the industry's dissatisfaction with the city in a *Time* magazine article, declaring

'This town is like an aging whore – Disrespect me, but give me something – just give me something' and arguing that the casino industry in Atlantic City was, like the British in Belfast, a universal target.[230]

As one former city official noted,

> one of the things that we learned, and we learned it first here, is that the help wanted sign does not cure long term unemployment.

The casinos never could be a panacea for the type of structural unemployment that impacted the city's population in these years, especially in the strict regulatory climate the persisted through the 1980s. Though well-intentioned, the laws that requiried legal purity for casino employment contributed to the difference between city and suburban casino impacts. Long-term unemployment in Atlantic City was a more deep-seated 'social problem' that defied a quick casino fix. Community leader Pierre Hollingsworth elaborated:

> A lot of them [city residents] did benefit. But a lot of them found out that they couldn't handle it, because in City Hall in particular, we had many people heard about being a dealer, you couldn't make this, and make this much money, and they flew out of City Hall, the casinos and work. And when they found out first they had to work – they had to really work, and also that the money wasn't all that great, and the benefits wasn't all they put up to be, they broke their neck trying to get back into City Hall. Now, did it affect the unemployment rate of Atlantic City? Somewhat, because we still carried a double digit higher than the state of New Jersey unemployment rate. A lot of that's social problems, because some were unemployable. And then we had a aging population that was here ... Crime was crime. Crime was bad prior to casino gambling, because naturally when you have poor folk living the way we were living and everything, it's always going to... that helps increase crime.[231]

The low status of city residents had racial implications. The decayed state of the city and continued high unemployment numbers in the city proper throughout the 1980s disproportionately affected African-Americans, approximately 50 per cent of the urban population at the time. The journalistic voice for that community was *Black Atlantic City* magazine, and later, *Black New Jersey*. For years, the magazine lambasted the casino industry for not doing enough to uplift the low-income black community, as in this 1982 commentary:

> On the other side of the coin lies the fact that Atlantic City residents who were unemployed in the pre-casino era, are the same ones now swelling the unemployment ranks.

A strong perception persisted through the decade that

the people who were supposed to benefit the most from casino gaming, have become the forgotten people.

Meanwhile, as it made clear, infrastructure problems that stemmed from the 1962 storm still had not been fully addressed:

> I see and talk to residents every day...when it rains our entire community floods. The streets are deplorable, and existing housing is in shambles.[232]

By 1987, the African-American community felt considerably more anger towards the casino industry for its perceived racism, initiated by Tom Carver's supposed attempt to have a black city manager removed from office:

> The real problem in this city as it relates to the casino industry is its failure and refusal to communicate with Black people, with any degree of dignity and respect, as it does with Jews, Asians and others ... This sad situation has only hit an impasse now because, for the first time in history, Black Americans are in positions of power and influence in Atlantic City, and the casino industry. While at the same time Blacks have eagerly sought out casinos for employment, gaming and entertainment ... When an industry fails to communicate with a significant part of the population, then animosity, distrust and dislike are bred.[233]

A magazine cartoon from the same time showed a young black man with his pockets out in front of a slot machine that came up 'H A A' in its three screens – not much of a jackpot. Looking back, NAACP leader Hollingsworth recalled the frustration of the black business community:

> We fought tooth and nail to create businesses, and we held all kinds of forums, opportunity, opportunity this, where we bought the persons and agents and the CEOs and everybody together, and said, hey, give some black folks some of that business. Give them some of those goods and services. It never really happened, to the success that it should have happened. We created all kind – everybody tried. Not only in town, but people came in from out of town, minorities all over, trying to penetrate this casino industry, and they never were successful, to any degree. Now you're going to find somebody who made a few thousand dollars, I'm not talking about that. But I'm talking about some real things.[234]

The evidence for racism in the casino industry is scant, but the perception was important for framing casino era of the late 1980s. It was also not surprising, given the substantial culture of racist posturing that lasted into the early 1970s, when some whites scapegoated young African-Americans for the resort's decline.[235] In reality, the Commission ensured that the industry strongly supported statutory goals of affirmative action and in fact devoted a large amount of effort and resources to maintaining that commitment. Affirmative action became a significant part of the agency's mission, especially as urban conditions deteriorated in the 1980s and there was a renewed spotlight on the struggling urban populace.

In 1987 the NJCCC reported that the casino industry employed 8,320 residents of Atlantic City, or approximately 39 per cent of the city's workforce, and that 38 per cent of the casino workforce was from a minority background. Moreover, 20 per cent of higher-income employees were minorities – a gain from 17 per cent over the previous year – along with 29 per cent of casino 'professionals'. In the lower rungs of employment, 72 per cent of 'laborers' were minorities as were 49 per cent of 'service workers', the largest employee category by far (numbering 13,837). A total of 30 per cent of casino dealers were minorities, up from 28 per cent previously. In commentary, the 1987 report noted that:

> While it is evident that the industry has become the largest employer of Atlantic City residents, unfortunately the bulk of those resident employees (57 percent) is concentrated in lower paying positions in the EEO job categories of Laborers and Service Workers.[236]

A Commission push that began in 1987 to improve minority representation in higher end jobs was slow to unfold through 1989, as the median annual income earned by casino-employed minorities actually fell in two years. At the same time, Read spoke to the NAACP to improve the commission's efforts in hiring minorities for higher-paying jobs. The drop occurred despite new regulations implemented in 1988 to create a higher and more independent role for affirmative action officers in the casino hierarchy. The NJCCC achieved more success in minority/women-owned contracting with 2.7 per cent and $27.3 million of the total amount contracted out by casinos going to minority/women-owned vendors, a rise from a negligible amount a few years earlier. The 2.7 per cent, however, fell far below new standards adopted in 1987, projected to raise the percentage of casino business for these firms eventually to 15 per cent of all contracting.[237] But the slow pace of progress in this area certainly irked those who were paying the most attention in the community, and cast a different perspective on alleged city government corruption. An investigation into city contracting inspired more negative sentiment with regard to the unequal situation:

> Already, local Black entrepreneurs are pitted against insurmountable obstacles in obtaining contracts from the city of Atlantic City and the Casino Industry. These two important entities could be the salvation for many Atlantic City based black firms that can provide the goods and professional services they purchase annually, by simply doing business with these companies.

Affirmative action made sense, but did it really make a difference in the 1980s? Some thought not:

Legislation regarding MBE [Minority Business Enterprise] utilization is rarely enforced, therefore the plight of Black businesses in Atlantic City continues to decline ... It is really an unsettling atmosphere for black business owners ion Atlantic City. Black Businesses are aware that Ernest English, a black business man, is fighting desperately to keep his battery-operated rolling chair company, on the Boardwalk, from financial failure.[238]

In 1988, presidential candidate Reverend Jesse Jackson came through Atlantic City on a campaign stop and, standing next to Mayor Usry and other community activists, rallied the crowd with a message bound to connect with the downtrodden of the urban community:

> We have a crisis and challenge when people are threatened by economic progress and they only have a job in exchange ... we had a job in slavery... today we need partnership not slaveship we need economic development, business opportunity and day-care for working mothers.

He also directed his rhetorical jab directly at the casino industry, to great cheers:

> I'm here to challenge the Donald Trumps and Merv Griffins, to be partners with the community.[239]

Jackson's voice was powerful and he easily captured the frustration that came with a decade of minimal progress in the black community since the casino era began. It was not racism that held back Atlantic City's black community in the decade since legalization, but a lack of opportunity for a variety of reasons. Overly restrictive regulations for casino licensure worked against many by keeping out anyone with a criminal record through the early 1990s when the NJCCC finally implemented a major regulatory overhaul that included more sensible employee requirements. An aging city population combined with higher rates of problems like drug addiction exacerbated the problem.[240] In addition, unrealistic expectations about casino work within the urban workforce also contributed to the frustration, as recalled a close observer looking back:

> We still got people, when there are jobs are available, it might not be what you want, but there are jobs if people want them. But they're still – you still get that group who just don't want to work. You can't make people, because even with the NAACP, we have job fairs. In fact, we have one coming up very soon. They're usually successful. Every – quite a few – the hotels have people who are less qualified, don't want to do menial work. They're not qualified to do anything, but they want to make the big bucks.[241]

Regardless, the reality that African-Americans in Atlantic City were not especially benefiting from the casinos spurred a serious effort to improve minority status within the industry through emphasis on better MBE efforts and upper-level hiring of minorities. To this end, NJCCC chairman Read spoke before an

NAACP meeting in 1989 and promised to move forward in the coming years. In the early 1990s, the industry did make strides to address the situation.[242]

Funded by 1.25 per cent of the total casino win, the CRDA began to form alliances with developers, casinos and the city housing agency to begin re-building Atlantic City in the mid-1980s to improve the housing situation. By the end of 1986, its primary reinvestment fund was capitalized at $95 million and the CRDA had about $11 million invested in various development projects. The CRDA's projects often came about through long-term bonds issued by the CRDA and purchased by the casinos to subsidize new housing construction. As well, individual casinos could satisfy their CRDA requirements by directly funding specific housing projects. Finally the casinos could provide cash in exchange for CRDA credits to offset future obligations. The CRDA's financial mechanisms gave the casinos a choice to be directly involved in redevelopment as developers or indirectly as capital sources for the CRDA, which then funded and organized construction projects.[243]

In 1986, Caesar's became the first casino to act as a housing developer via the CRDA by committing up to $34.2 million for the Caesar's Regency Tower and Caesar's Victorian Court for low- and middle-income rental units. Similarly, Bally's Park Place committed $7.5 million towards the Jacobs Family Terrace to build seventy-two town houses. In addition, the CRDA committed another $28 million towards two other projects: the Northwest Inlet Revitalization and Vermont Plaza housing projects, designed to create hundreds of affordable rental units and townhouses in the uptown section of the city. In addition, the CRDA announced comprehensive redevelopment plans for the Northeast Inlet neighborhood, its largest project in the coming years.[244]

Caesar's management was understandably proud when the projects were complete in 1989, with a press release noting that it was the first project of its kind. A year later, Caesar's also completed a companion project called Victorian II that created fifteen rental units for low-income families with rent not to exceed 30 per cent of their incomes. The company press release ballyhooed the accomplishment while also illustrating that demand far exceeded the scope of these projects:

> Fifteen low-income Atlantic City families now have a very special address. Victorian Court II, Caesar's Atlantic City's third investment enterprise under the guidelines of the CRDA is ready for occupancy.

Yet those fifteen families were chosen out of 400 that originally applied and thirty that interviewed.[245]

By 1988, the CRDA's efforts shifted to the massive, $500 million+ Northeast Inlet Redevelopment Plan, designed to eventually revitalize a 101–acre section of the Inlet area with 3,700 new rental and owned housing units and related commercial structures. The project began with $86 million in direct funding from Harrah's in combination with CRDA financing. The key to the plan's success came from the city government, which approved $17.2 million in October 1988 for bond-financed investment in the improvements in the infrastructure necessary to create viable housing. This piece was crucial for the first phase of the project to go forward and controversial, at one point pitting residents from downtown Chelsea against residents from uptown. A Chelsea group even threatened a petition drive to stop the project if the CRDA did not also meet demands to develop other parts of the city, a threat that Mayor Usry lambasted as overly divisive, pitting 'uptown against downtown, white against black, business against homeowners'. Squarely behind the bond issue and the Northeast Inlet project, Usry suggested that if it failed, 'you could say goodbye to redeveloping the rest of the city'. The conflict led the *Press of Atlantic City* to editorialize: 'Why does it always have to be 'We' vs. 'Them' in Atlantic City?' Never was a more appropriate statement heard for summarizing the contentious nature of the early casino era.[246]

The bond issue passed only after the CRDA agreed to also fund projects outside the Inlet over the following three years, but not before the debate exposed tensions in the relationship between the casino industry and city government and the overall discontent that industry leaders projected towards the Atlantic City of the 1980s. Harrah's executive Christopher Whitney expressed frustration with the process and difficulty getting the first phase started: 'I am stunned that it's difficult ... I am appalled that its this difficult to get a $17.2 million bond issue in return for an $83 million project'. Carver, a non-voting CRDA member, blamed small-minded locals and politicians for placing ward politics over the interests of the city and urged residents to 'let government do its work'. In fact, the government did do its work subsequently – the Council passed the bond-issuance two weeks later and the CRDA began implanting the plan soon after by contacting homeowners about buying their properties. Inlet homeowners seemed generally eager to sell out, to begin the process of demolition and to start the area's elevation, according to Carrie Frazier a local senior citizen who remarked 'We want the Inlet built up. It looks terrible up here.' Others, however, expressed regret and suggested that the CRDA's offers were too low. But reluctant property owners faced little choice as the CRDA soon started to use eminent domain to have the properties condemned to make way for the bulldozers, where necessary.[247]

The CRDA–Harrah's partnership on the Northeast Inlet redevelopment project was a good example of the kind of public–private cooperation that seemed so elusive in the casino era's first decade. It embodied the community revitalization promised by legalization and simultaneously acted on the industry's priority to improve the city for business purposes. A more attractive, less run-down environment was conducive for both the people who lived in it and for visitors. From Harrah's perspective, it fitted well into the company's image as a community-oriented business that cared as much about people, employees and local residents as it did about satisfying its customers and making profits.[248] But the CRDA was also controversial, viewed by the *Casino Journal* as 'one of the most tragic mistakes' of Trenton and somehow indicative of the governor's and North Jersey legislators' antipathy to the casino industry. From this view, the CRDA came into being as a political giveaway for the purposes of redeveloping places like Newark and Camden, given the development obligations spelled out for these purposes. More importantly, the CRDA was enacted to make up for the failures of the city and state governments in the first five years. The editorial brought the issue back to dysfunctional government, which should have redeveloped the city on its own terms, without charging the casino industry via the 'fiasco-fraud' CRDA obligation. According to this view, Atlantic City

> with its corrupt, ignorant, incompetent, and disinterested local government
> – looked worse in 1983 than it did in 1973. And the more glamorous the
> casinos became, the more painful and embarrassing the city's deterioration,
> decay and despair appeared to be.

It was also a distortion of the revitalization mission, something the casinos had fulfilled 'beyond the wildest imaginations and greatest hopes of the 'fathers' of the Casino Control Act'. *Casino Journal* placed its hopes for reform on the new governor elected in 1989, Democrat Jim Florio: 'Its up to you!'[249]

Another issue that brought forth questions over the relationship between the casino industry and the community was the proposed new Atlantic City high school. By the mid-1980s, the existing building at Albany and Atlantic avenues was decades old and suffering from major deterioration. Eventually, the decision came about to build an entirely new building at a new location that the city board of education decided should be Great Island in the southwestern part of the city. However, a problem existed because Resorts International bought the property during a land-buying spree in the early 1980s and had been holding it since, ostensibly for casino, marina and other commercial development.[250]

Nevertheless, in 1984 the city council passed a resolution declaring the island as a targeted spot for a new high school, and the school board was able to take the property through eminent domain in 1987 after years of failed negotiations between the casino and the city government. Much legal wrangling subsequently ensued between the school board and Resorts over its fair market value. Resorts declined a $5.72 million offer for the island, thus causing a judge to condemn the land until its fair market value can be determined to push the sale through. In late 1988, the casino's figure was $23 million, but the school board only offered $10 million. The matter was finally decided in 1990 when a jury set the price at $7.5 million for the land, a victory of sorts for the schoolboard. In the late 1980s, Merv Griffin's Resorts International faced considerable pressure to simply donate the land for the high school, a move the casino resisted.[251]

Casino Journal lampooned the city's efforts and supported Resorts over the school board. From the magazine's perspective, here was just another example of the city government butting heads with the casino industry – proof to support its ongoing narrative.[252] But was the narrative accurate? Perhaps, but Resorts's stubborn unwillingness to settle on the Great Island price cost the casino money and prestige. It also contributed to the alternative casino-era narrative that the casinos did not care much about the community's well-being. While the casino had a legitimate property claim and vested interest in the island, its public relations agenda could have been much better. In the end, the whole episode provided a solid example for the era's private-public dysfunction.

Not dysfunctional however, was the Sands's approach to outreach with the city school system. By 1988, the casino had established a successful partnership with Atlantic City High School. The Sands formed a career training program with the school and 'pledged to offer training and job placement opportunities' for new graduates. In addition, the casino assisted the school by holding a golf tournament to raise funds for a student trip to the Soviet Union. The Sands's community outreach to the High School was mutually beneficial, and also set a precedent for later casino efforts in the 1990s. The Sands was in its glory period in the late 1980s, making community connections and establishing a solid local clientele (and workforce).[253]

When Bally's bought the Golden Nugget in 1987 and transformed it into Bally's Grand, Atlantic City seemed to lose one of its more dynamic casino magnates in Steve Wynn. After missing out on the marina property that became Trump Castle, Wynn and the Golden Nugget's management team directed their energies back to Las Vegas to build the mega-casino hotel that would begin to transform that city when it opened in 1989 as the Mirage. The $440 million offer from Bally's was a great opportunity for the Golden Nugget, despite a successful strategy that had consistently placed the casino on top in terms of gross operating profit and growth between 1980 and 1987. As Bally's Grand, it never operated as profitably and was often in the lower half of the market in terms of profitability and profit growth.[254]

Meanwhile, Wynn's Golden Nugget maintained its property holdings in the marina, and was clearly transformed via the Atlantic City experience. Wynn's casino also stood out in Atlantic City's local industry for an outstanding customer loyalty program that Harrah's would later perfect. In a 1988 interview, Wynn recalled the Nugget's approach towards building and maintaining loyal customers based on an old American sales gimmick:

> I remember when we put in the 24 Karat Club, one fellow commented what an ingenious idea it was. I looked at him and said, 'Did you ever hear of S& H Green Stamps?' That gives you an idea of how far out of touch some of the casino people get when they're working all the time. Putting the S&H Green Stamp idea to work on the slot machines was just using an age old trick.[255]

Wynn also attributed Golden Nugget's success to dedicated reinvestment back into the casino:

> What did we do at GN? We reinvested every dime we ever made right in the neighborhood – we kept buying up the neighboring properties, building more garages, building more restaurants, redecorating. I redid the entire place every room, every corridor in the public area two months before we sold it to Bally. I always reinvested the money.[256]

Wynn jumped at another casino opportunity in Atlantic City when the Golden Nugget almost purchased Del Webb Corp.'s Claridge – a small casino operating between Bally's and the Sands in a restored old hotel In 1988, Golden Nugget reached a short-lived deal to purchase the property for $110 million. Wynn's attachment to the Atlantic City gaming scene sounded like both a business venture and personal game: as he put it: 'I'm a risk player and I'm dying to mix it up with the boys one more time'.[257] The deal fell through within a few weeks, however, because Wynn did not have enough security that his gaming strategy would work because of future uncertainty on the NJCCC. The Golden Nugget's marketing strategy involved offering '10 times odds' on craps, something new to the Atlantic City market, but not Las Vegas, where Golden Nugget-owned Binion's already had it in place. Wynn noted that the '10 times odds' led to 'big swings in wins and losses' and that casino operators 'need to be able to absorb $5 million loss on some days'. In this way, the game was better for casinos that could absorb the losses, something he could ensure with the Claridge. The problem was not with the game or the deal, however, but actually had to do with the temporal nature of the NJCCC:

> The offer was conditional upon certain operating procedures being approved by the regulatory authorities in New Jersey, under the internal controls submissions that are required of each prospective casino licensee. We didn't really need any regulations changed because nothing that we asked for was prohibited. But we also said in our offer to Webb that we would have to be certain that we would be allowed to implement our management program for five years.

Wynn's stated purpose in ending the deal involved the above critique of New Jersey's regulatory system, but he also took an opportunity to attack the entire industry's approach to promotions:

> Unfortunately, the history of casino gaming management in Atlantic City has been characterized, in terms of casino management, by a very obvious copycat kind of approach to everything. There has been very little original thinking. Every time someone has jumped on the bandwagon. The operators seem to have an unlimited appetite for giving coins away, and paying people to get on a bus. Yet they seem, for some strange reason, to want to avoid

completely the more obvious solution, to me, at least, which is to give folks better deals right at the slot machines. I don't know why that's true, but it is. They'll run helicopters, and comp suites, and do all kinds of things like that for people who really shouldn't get that kind of service. And yet, they won't give a guy a better deal on a craps table, which, in my view is a far more intelligent approach.[258]

Wynn's critique of the industry's approach to promotions reflected the rising use of coin/coupon giveaways for bus customers and overall increase in free perks for gamblers of all sorts. By 1989, the casinos spent an average of 24 per cent net revenue on these freebies. The failed Atlantis was at some level a testament to the over-use of comps, having given them away at one-third (33 per cent) of net revenue by the time it closed in May 1989. Between 1980 and 1989, average complimentary expenses for all casinos went from 10 per cent to 24 per cent of net revenue – a major expense.[259] But did this make for a better bottom line? That was not so apparent. In one contemporary report, a gaming analyst pointed out that comps were the second largest casino expense after salaries, and that the rationale for using them at all was questionable. There was no direct correlation between comp expenses and revenue, and some of the more successful casinos (like Bally's and Harrah's) had the lowest promotional expenses. On the other hand, mediocre-performing Trump Castle had a very high amount of promotional expenses. In 1987 alone, the casino free coin promotions for bus passengers totalled $218 million.[260]

Yet, effective promotions programs could be very successful for the purposes of maintaining a loyal customer base. Mary and Stan Sledak of Baltimore were customers of the Sands practically from the day it opened and enjoyed tremendous hospitality, special events and contact with Sands executives. Between 1980 and 1989, the Sledaks regularly visited, and in fact, were well aware of the mutually beneficial relationship they developed over the years. Their many years of frequenting the Sands also paid off in terms of personal friendships. Looking back in 2006, Mary Sledak explained:

> When we started playing, in the Atlantic City casino, we were not familiar with the comp system and had no idea we should ask for a drink, meal or room. We came, we played, and we left money behind or took some home. We enjoyed and got to meet nice people. As long as we enjoyed ourselves and did not lose to much, we were very happy with our trip. When we learned the comp. system, and started to get rooms and then meals or drinks, we said that if we lost as much as a good vacation, we were not big losers and/or gamblers ... As new casinos opened, we would visit them all one time, and usually not return. We would not play other locations because our comp value would then be too spread out over too many casinos. We would return to a few casinos when a Sands employee would relocate and invite us up for a drink. The Brighton employees are now spread all around in Atlantic City,

Vegas and other states that legalized gambling. We have visited an Illinois riverboat and Connecticut's famous Foxwoods. We would not have made these visits if there were not former Brighton/Sands employees/friends that we wanted to go and see.

The Sledaks' recollections also shed light on other ways in which the Sands pampered their best customers. In the 1980s, they attended parties with Bill Cosby, Wayne Gretsky and Jerry Vale, among others. They were also included in VIP functions such as the 1981 Larry Holmes-Gerry Cooney boxing match and a 1987 New York Giants football roast with quarterback Phil Simms.[261]

The Sledaks also received an invitation to come to the Sands as part of a junket aboard a DC-7 from Baltimore-Washington International (BWI) airport, with airfare, cocktails, a free room and meals, all compliments of the Sands.[262] The Sands's BWI junket represented an important part of the casino business of the 1980s. One insider estimated that 10–15 per cent of casino business was junket-related. Caesar's had a sophisticated junket program in place in which the casino determined each player's 'Earning Potential' (EP) by taking into account playing time, average bet, games played and betting strategies to assess the long-term casino gain for each junket customer.[263]

In the last half of 1989, three events occurred that significantly impacted the region, defined the early casino era in Atlantic City and contributed to its next phase. Firstly, in July, federal agents arrested Atlantic City mayor James Usry and thirteen other city government officials on corruption charges in a political scandal known as COMSERV. Secondly, in October, a helicopter crash on the Garden State Parkway took the lives of three top Trump Organization executives. Thirdly, Steve Wynn and the Golden Nugget opened the Mirage in Las Vegas.

The COMSERV arrests were a nadir for a city government bogged down by corruption and incompetence allegations for most of the 1980s. City governance was supposed to improve with a switch from commission governance to a mayoral-council system in 1982. Usry himself won a special recall election in 1984 after the first mayor, Michael Matthews, was indicted on federal charges and exposed to be much more interested in consorting with casino celebrities and mafia moneymen than actually running the city. Usry focused on the city's residents and was highly regarded in the black community, although he never did win over the casino people.[264] By 1987, he found staunch defenders in local residents who were disappointed in the casino experience and who lamented the sad state of their city and dichotomy between casino glitz and urban problems:

> There has been much frustration and anger directed towards the Usry administration from the people of Atlantic City because there has been no parallel growth between the two existing economies of Atlantic City. On one hand, you see as a setting the glamour of the casinos and on the other, you see the run down homes, the underdeveloped inlet and the overall

poverty that engulfs most of Atlantic City which sits beyond the eyesight of the Boardwalk. It seems that one side has all the money while the other has none of it and the only growth in Atlantic City is taking place on the Boardwalk.[265]

Mayor Usry eventually pled guilty to a campaign finance violation but remained in office until he lost the 1990 election. A corrupt contract process involving a mechanized electric cart operator led to the indictments. Many of the original charges did not stick and were eventually considered by many, including by some of Usry's loudest critics, to be the result of an overly zealous attitude on the part of the FBI. However, the affair appeared to confirm the judgment of casino industry insiders that the city government was a cesspool ruined by dishonest and self-interested politicians who perpetuated unstable politics to the detriment of the casino industry.[266]

The turbulent ending to the 1980s was also defined by the shocking helicopter crash that killed three of the Trump Organization's top executives. In October 1989, a helicopter shuttling the executives from New York crashed on the Garden State Parkway, killing all aboard. Steven Hyde (Trump CEO), Mark Etess (Taj Mahal President) and Jon Benanav (Trump Plaza VP) were highly regarded executives with considerable gaming experience. Hyde and Etess were both former Golden Nugget executives who switched to Trump soon after Trump outmanoeuvred Wynn for Hilton's marina property and began his drive to dominate the Atlantic City casino market. Both were known for their style and Hyde, especially, for his effective management of the Nugget, where he successfully managed the property using Wynn's marketing strategies through 1986. Etess had become prominent around town as the frontman for big sports and entertainment productions. He had grown up in the Grossinger's Catskills hotel family and had been around celebrity and the hotel business his entire life. Hyde, Etess and his Nugget colleague Jack O'Donnell successfully emulated the Golden Nugget's success at the Trump Plaza in the late 1980s. They created an opulent atmosphere catering to high rollers while simultaneously projecting a glamorous ambience that acted as an 'aphrodisiac' for mid-level gamblers. They also focused tremendous efforts at maintaining customer loyalty.[267]

The lives of the three Trump executives whose helicopter crashed that day in 1989 demonstrated the success of the casino era's first phase, even as the crash itself was a metaphor for the industry circumstances at the time. As executives at the Sands earlier in their careers, both Hyde and Benanav displayed a noteworthy personal touch that worked effectively to solidify good customers. This was on display when Benanav at one point responded to a specific comment from Mary and Stan with humour and offer for breakfast:

> So you think we need a cooler casino? Well, winter is just around the corner and with all the guests we have walking through our front doors into our

casino, that should bring a nice cold draft into that area ... Stan and Mary, in all honesty it is a pleasure having you as one of our regular guests and I promise next time I will join you for breakfast.

Hyde's drive towards promoting Wynn's innovative and personalized marketing approach was also shown when he responded to an elderly customer's odd letter asking the casino not to be angry over her $40 slot winnings. Hyde reportedly responded with a personal invitation to a gourmet restaurant, not something commonly issued to her class of gambler.[268]

Through their actions, the Trump three helped create casinos in the 1980s that were successful at making money by appealing personally to customers at every level. The better casinos, like Golden Nugget, Harrah's and Trump Plaza were very effective at tailored marketing programs and a personalized approach to the business. These executives personified that approach to the casino business and reaped its benefits personally and for the casinos they worked for. Through their careers, one can see the simple, day-to-day operations that built the industry and with it, the Atlantic City economy in the 1980s, as controversy swirled on a macro level. The Sledaks profoundly changed their casino habits after the crash, their personal feelings for Hyde and Benanav so strong that they could not easily enjoy the experience for some time afterwards. When they did resume their frequent visits to the Sands, they made more money and always felt more relaxed, believing that Jon Benanav was watching over them from above – their guardian angel in the casino.[269]

One of the biggest events to impact Atlantic City in the late 1980s actually took place thousands of miles away in the western desert. After two years of anticipation, a volcano began erupting every half-hour amidst a tropical setting and near animals such as dolphins, sharks and white tigers. Steve Wynn and Golden Nugget, Inc. opened the $630 million Mirage in Las Vegas in November 1989 and began a new phase of the American casino era. The Mirage changed the focus of Las Vegas by creating a new challenge for casino operators, now needing to entice customers to come out for reasons beyond gambling. The Mirage was a spectacle when it opened and represented a new approach to gaming that sought to generate revenue through attractions, entertainment and luxury – a new direction from the gambling-focused resorts of the past. Wynn's Golden Nugget used profits earned in Atlantic City to invent a new style in gaming in Nevada by actually creating a destination resort.[270] His Las Vegas competitors were already contributing to the new Vegas before the Mirage even opened. In May 1989, the city was alive with Rio and Excalibur going up, along with major expansions at the Riviera and Circus Circus. Within five years, Luxor, New York New York, and the MGM-Grand all opened up and by 1994, Las Vegas was a vastly different resort town than it had been in 1988: a real vacation spot, not a just a place where people went to gamble.[271]

The Mirage stunningly won $40 million in its first month of operations. The Mirage's opening success and Las Vegas's new vibrancy contrasted starkly with a seemingly bleak casino environment in Atlantic City. As such, Wynn's success also increased scrutiny of the ongoing Taj Mahal project, hundreds of millions of dollars over-budget by 1989, its sixth year of construction. Wynn's coup also created higher anticipation and higher stakes for the Taj opening, now scheduled for December 1989. Would the Taj's architectural opulence create enough of a sensation to match the Mirage's draws, such as an indoor rainforest? Would $14 million worth of German crystal chandeliers, 250 suites, and a vast 120,000-square-foot casino create enough buzz to justify a billion dollar venture? Would it generate enough revenue to make a profit over the estimated $1.2 million daily cost of operations? The transformative power of one blockbuster casino also highlighted the weakness of the overall industry with Merv Griffin's Resorts and the Claridge viewed as most likely to fold when the Taj came online. Yet, hope also abounded that the Taj would increase overall quality in the Atlantic City market, expand the market by bringing in new players and weed out the industry by improving the stronger casinos and expediting the collapse of weaker ones. Given the stakes, its no wonder that Trump commented that his Taj Mahal would be 'the most spectacular, the most phenomenal building ever opened in the United States'.[272]

Mirage's success also showed where Atlantic City could go, if the right things occurred. However, Atlantic City's casinos would have to deal with a revamped Las Vegas while still struggling with the junk bond debt problem exposed by Atlantis's failure. As the Mirage sought to successfully create an image – a glamorous experience beyond gambling – so too did the Atlantic City casinos need to sell themselves with creative marketing:

> Can these casinos survive while carrying this heavy debt load and the concomitant carrying charges? The answer is 'yes' under two conditions: first that the economic climate remains positive, and second that every casino continues to come up with creative marketing programs to attract more and more of the approximately 55 million people within three hours driving time of Atlantic City.[273]

Wynn himself was very clear on how the Atlantic City casino culture could take advantage of the Mirage's success for its own purposes. Mainly this meant that the regulators needed to drop their perception of the Atlantic City as the anti-Las Vegas casino town. This attitude prevailed at the outset, when the state essentially defined the industry as a partnership of sorts between the public (represented by the regulators) and private casino operators. According to Wynn, however, it was essential now to shift philosophy and emulate the westerners, especially as the Mirage and Las Vegas reaped the benefits of unleashed and creative entrepreneurial energy. Economic revitalization remained the mission, but the view was that it should happen with less government oversight:

> To the extent that you want to have any success in achieving the goals of the *CCA*, you better think about Las Vegas and understand Las Vegas. And learn from Las Vegas. Because the extent that this place is like Las Vegas, that's how close you'll get to fulfilling your goals of the *CCA*, which is redeveloping AC ... It took creative genius to retard the growth and the potential of that Atlantic City had and does have. I mean the DGE had to be standing up and galvanized every step of the way. Because the developers, if they were left alone, would have developed.[274]

Wynn's success as a casino operator gave him substantial credibility as an evaluator of the Atlantic City casino industry. Although he was constantly engaged in Atlantic City with initiatives to come back, his comments were much more than complaints from an industry source – they really did reflect the climate of the times in the casino era during the 1980's.

4 RECESSION AND RECOVERY: TURNING A CASINO CORNER

In November 1989, Trump Taj Mahal Vice-President Donald Buzney had a problem. The Taj was set to open within six months and it still had 3,100 unfilled positions. Buzney's solution was outreach. In an unprecedented strategy for Atlantic City casinos, he prepared the Trump Organization to recruit employees from outside the region. To fill the jobs, Trump would end up recruiting workers from Gary, Indiana, Washington DC, Puerto Rico and Ireland. Trump's outreach to Gary also highlighted the reality of looming competition for the Atlantic City casinos, as Gary residents had just voted in favour of casino gaming in their fading rust-belt city on Lake Michigan. Perversely, the possibility of Gary casinos actually served as a selling point for creative Trump recruiters, led by Donald's brother Robert. He suggested that Gary residents could take jobs at the Taj to learn the casino business in preparation for a future move back home to work in a Gary casino.[275]

The Taj's employment issues highlighted a broader crisis of uncertainty in the casino industry, at its lowest point since the era began in 1978. No one really know what impact the Taj Mahal's opening would have on the resort community and the broader casino industry, but it was hard to miss the potential danger and industry-wide anxiety as the 1990s began. Total casino revenue had essentially stagnated and actually declined when adjusted for inflation. The overall rate of revenue growth had slowed to 2.6 per cent, down from 9.5 per cent in both 1987 and 1988. Costs and expenses were rising at a faster rate then revenue growth in the same period. An Atlantic County report summed up the uncertainty and anxiety, especially with regard to the employment impact:

> The absorption of the Taj Mahal into the mature casino gaming market will
> have positive, though unknown, economic impact ... The economic impact
> of the Taj Mahal opening will depend on the degree that Taj Mahal employ-
> ment exceeds the contraction of employment in other casinos.[276]

As 1990 began, one casino had already closed (Atlantis) and a few others were struggling to survive; the Taj's opening crept closer amidst a northeast recession that tempered the enthusiasm for gambling. The city's ongoing political corruption and lack of progress on improvement projects like the new Convention Center and airport also contributed to the depressing atmosphere. Finally waking up to the reality of unprofitable bus charters, the casinos had cut back on these in 1989 to reduce costs. Comps remained very expensive and the casinos were not reaping returns for their investments in them. Finally, the corporate debt problem was viewed as 'an explosion waiting to be touched off' and was exacerbated by the late 1989 collapse of the junk bond market, consequent to Drexel Burnham Lambert's implosion and Michael Milken's legal problems. A few casinos, like Trump Castle, were paying millions more in interest alone than they could bring in via gaming and general revenues. As the nineties began, the Trump Organization alone had raised over $1 billion in junk bonds for casino development.[277]

At one point, the industry's prospects appeared so bleak that a north Jersey legislator proposed a three-year moratorium on new casinos – a proposition opposed by casino insiders and the NJCCC, but reflective of the mood. The suggestion also highlighted the extent to which the state viewed itself as an active player in the casino industry, with many officials not willing to let the marketplace alone shape its expansion. But the move was unnecessary and rightfully opposed by casino sources. The marketplace regulated the business properly on this front and there would be no new Atlantic City casino opening after the Taj Mahal's 1990 debut until 2003.[278]

Adding to the misery was Resorts International's decision to file for bankruptcy in late 1989 to escape its crushing $912 million debt. Resorts sought to erase $600 million debt outright by exchanging it for Merv Griffin's own stock in the company – 76 per cent of his shares in Resorts International. Resorts's troubles were the result both of the hard times of the industry as a whole and the deal Griffin had made with Trump in 1988 in particular. At the end of the 1980s, that deal appeared to be a real loser for Resorts, and a big unknown for Trump, dependent on the Taj's opening. Resorts's bondholders were angry enough to require the bankruptcy filing to include a $5 million fund for the sole purposes of taking legal action against Trump, on the dubious grounds that a fraudulent conveyance had occurred. The bondholders believed that Trump had unfairly bought the Taj Mahal for much less than its value and by doing so effected Resorts's insolvency in the process.[279] Resorts's investors were justifiably put off at the state of their casino, but blaming Trump for being a wilier dealmaker than Griffin hardly constituted an effective strategy for recovery. The legal action never went anywhere as Griffin and Resorts's new management threw a tremendous amount of energy into remaking their casino, successfully pulling it out of bankruptcy in two years. When Resorts's licence came up for renewal in 1990, the NJCCC rightfully questioned the legal fund built into the bankruptcy filing. Predictably,

Trump criticized Griffin for misplaced blame, suggesting that the entertainer needed to 'turn his attention to the revitalization of Resorts instead of pursuing wholly baseless and wasteful claims against me'.[280]

The hype surrounding Taj Mahal's opening actually began in late 1988, when construction resumed after a long pause during the Resorts–Trump negotiations. Trump and a host of local officials cut a huge ribbon suspended between two fez-wearing employees, offering a preview of the gold-braided uniforms future casino workers would wear. Trump acknowledged the high stakes involved with the project, and implicitly, his own exposure:

> We've been working for a year to straighten out what someday will be a very successful building. It better be.

Over the next year, stories drifted out about the $14 million Austrian chandeliers being installed and the Italian marble laid everywhere. Trump himself proclaimed it a splendid building ready to transform the gaming marketplace, yet also acknowledged the risk involved and exorbitant expense of the casino. At points, he lamented the cost and always mocked Resorts for wasteful spending:

> I always say if there ever was a nuclear war, I'm going to find a place somewhere within the Taj Mahal to be sitting because this frame is the heaviest, the most powerful, the most expensive structural frame I've ever seen.

By autumn 1989, the project was $300 million over-budget, in part due to the repairs necessary to infrastructure that was exposed to the cold and salt air for a year while the project floundered under Resorts's control.[281]

The picture for the Taj Mahal grew even murkier following the helicopter crash in late1989 that killed three Trump executives, as the Trump Organization had to scramble to replace the executive talent. Trump executives also found themselves looking for good mid-level managers in a tight labour market, sometimes offering 25 per cent more money to bring over talented people, despite official denials that they were only paying the prevailing wages. The casino labour shortage was a problem glaringly exposed by the Taj Mahal's coming debut. DGE director Parillo commented on the situation in a General Assembly hearing in early 1990:

> The <u>Good</u> news is there are jobs aplenty. The <u>Bad</u> news is that there does not seem to be enough people to fill them. Fueled by the casino boom, the expansion of positions has far outpaced the waning supply of workers – the so-called 'Baby Bust' phenomenon – resulting in what some experts say is a real labor shortage.

Parillo also noted that the DGE was sending fingerprinting agents outside the region with casino recruiters.[282]

The tight labour market naturally led casino employees to maximize their opportunities by taking the best offers that came their way. Two weeks before the Taj's April 1990 opening, the existing casinos had lost approximately 10 per cent of their employees to the new casino, with the weakest casinos (Resorts and Claridge) losing 15 per cent. The 1990 casino labour hearings exposed the difficulty the industry had in recruiting workers from outside the region, thus stressing the existing regional workforce. They also led to renewed scrutiny on the 'key' licensing process: the legal requirement that all gaming floor employees had licences gained from passing a DGE background check. Atlantic County Assemblyman Alfred Scerni called the licensing situation a mess, rife with 'horror stories of licensings that went well beyond 45 days', including one case where it took thirteen months for a casino employee to be relicensed after taking a two-year hiatus from the casino business. During the hearings, Scerni began an eventually successful process to improve the system, by proposing to allow temporary licences for all 'key' licence applicants while the DGE reviewed their applications.[283]

The Taj's labour demands led some of the other casinos to take defensive, and in some cases aggressive, measures to prevent their existing employees from leaving. Bally's posted a regulation in the dealer's lounge that specifically barred their dealers from working, or even training with another casinos. Claridge similarly warned its employees about moonlighting at the Taj. Resorts took a different approach by offering a slight carrot for employees staying on – a choice to receive higher wages in exchange for giving up some spousal benefits under the casino's health care plan – though they also used the stick, delaying first-quarter raises until after the April opening of the Taj, making them retroactive, but not paying out any employee who left to work there. Resorts's executive Al Luciani summed up the significance of the problem and emphasized the need to remove obstacles towards hiring workers:

> [its] no secret that there is a shortage of employees ... employee will greatly influence any future development and, in fact, determine the level of service offered.

Echoing Assemblyman Scerni, Luciani also cited 'entry level barriers', like the upfront costs of licensing, as making the situation worse.[284]

Other casinos responded to the tight labour market by ramping up incentives to maintain employee satisfaction, emphasizing their employee-friendly workplaces. Showboat, for example, went public with a new program called Career Path Planning to facilitate upward mobility for its employees. The Sands added a new employee concierge position and a childcare centre. Interviewed during the labour crunch, Bally's CEO Richard Gillman stressed his casino's team concept in making the case that it was a desirable workplace:

A lot of people who started with us are still with us, so our turnover has been 18 percent better than the next best casino relative to turnover lately. So I think people like us; they know we're here; we have an open door policy.

He made sure that *Casino Journal* readers understood that there were 'no superstars' at Bally's and that all employees knew what to expect in terms of job security, benefits and salary. Of course, all the extras could not hold back casino workers from seeking better opportunities with the new casino, as one dealer named Susan bluntly reported:

> The name of the game is advancement ... I'd like to get a promotion, but I might make a lateral move and hope for good tokes [dealer tips].[285]

Dealer Tom Gitto found the Taj's lure powerful enough to get him to leave a very comfortable position at Resorts, where he had built up a substantial network of friendly colleagues. Looking back in 2005, he described the intense competition taking place for skilled and experienced personnel wrought by the new casino's opening:

> I dealt for eight or night years [at Resorts], and then the Taj Mahal was opening up, and then Resorts offered me a supervisor position. So I was a supervisor at Resorts for about a year, and then once the Taj finally opened, the Taj made me an offer to come over there. So I took that. I remember it being the toughest thing, because I'd been at Resorts for ten years and all my friends were there, and I said, how am I going to do this, and all my friends are here and I really didn't want to go, but there was a better offer at the Taj.[286]

The Trump Organization's ambitious recruitment program led to the hiring of 350 people from Puerto Rico and Europe. Their experience did not start very well, however, as many could not afford the region's rents and had little means of transportation once they arrived. This led to a mini-scandal of sorts, about a month before the Taj's opening. The local press seized on the issue and soon interviews appeared with migrant workers who complained that they were, in effect, stranded by the Trump group, which covered them for thirty days in a hotel then cast them into the high-priced rental market with salaries too small to afford an apartment. Interviewed in 2005, a Puerto Rican native recalled the circumstances surrounding the Trump outreach and for those who responded:

> Because people they come here looking to better themselves looking for that opportunity, for a better job, better-paying job. And when you have, for instance, a teacher that is earning $600, $700 a month, gross, to come here and make $1100, so people come here. And unfortunately, the situation in Puerto Rico at the time wasn't so good either – there weren't that many jobs available. Criminality was beginning to go up, and people just wanted to come here. Some came and they were well-prepared. They couldn't teach because they didn't have the license here, but they were able to secure a job

as a dealer, casino dealer, and making $700 in Puerto Rico a month while making $700, $800, $900 a week here as a casino dealer, and people working in housekeeping department, making $100, $120 a day of tips. You don't see that any more, but at the time we did. And the lure of the casino industry, Trump, he hired people to come to Atlantic City to help build the Taj Mahal, and a lot of people got stranded. They were promised jobs, apartments, places to stay, and a lot of people end up at the mission, homeless here.

Close to a third of the workers actually went home before the year was over, experiencing a dislocation described by one to a local reporter:

> Everybody in Puerto Rico talks about Donald Trump, and when you think of Atlantic City, you think of the best hotels in the world. So I decided to come here, to take a chance. But so far, it's been really disappointing. A lot of people feel that way. Many are looking for jobs in other hotels.

Yet, the Trump group did make a substantial effort for the group, ultimately paying out close to $3 million in extended housing aid for the 1,066 relocated workers at the Taj months after the casino opened.[287] The foreign workers' story was a public relations problem for the Trump Organization, but it was also a harbinger of things to come in the casino industry. By the early 1990s, the labour shortage caused both casino managers to look for new sources of labour and potential casino employees to view Atlantic City as a place for work. As the 1990s, progressed, the casino community would become a magnet for immigrants from abroad and from other American locales seeking their versions of the American dream. The Taj Mahal's widespread call for employees and qualified success at attracting people beyond South Jersey was a powerful motivator for those who needed the workers (casinos) and those who needed decent jobs, replete with health benefits. In the 1990s, the two entities (casinos and their employees) became mutually reinforcing, as immigrants flooded into the community to meet the demand for workers. In the process, they transformed the community into a diverse and international dynamo (see Chapter 5).

The Taj Mahal's April 1990 opening was the biggest event to happen in Atlantic City since the opening of Resorts in 1978. It marked the beginning of the second phase of the casino era by bringing a new glamour to the Boardwalk. Yet it also took place at a time of financial insecurity for the casino industry and emphasized the extent to which the industry was corporate and therefore reliant on financial markets and the ability to capitalize debt. Of course, as it neared completion, the Taj had become a symbol of inefficiency to some business observers like *Forbes* magazine, which predicted bad things for the casino empire, given the Trump Organization's debt load, the soft New York real estate market and high cost of the casino's construction. In February 1990, Trump Taj junk bonds were worth 78 cents on the dollar, prompting one analyst to quip that 'The market is saying this is a very risky piece of paper, certainly not for widows and orphans'. Worse, respected casino expert Marvin Roffman predicted that the Taj would be in trouble once the free publicity of the opening wore off and the weather cooled. However, some were more optimistic, such as a Raymond James analyst who predicted that the industry was set to increase its revenue by 9 or10 per cent, and that the Taj will 'create the excitement that the city has been lacking for several years'. The new energy would uplift the upper and central Boardwalk casino zones as well.[288]

The *Atlantic City Action* summarized the diverse outlooks, with a unique prediction based on the recent perception that the comps marketing system had not worked well from a business perspective:

> Each opening of a new casino hotel facility in recent years has been countered by over-reactions and marketing strategies that were spearheaded by excessive bonusing in the form of comps and giveaways. There is no doubt in my mind that the Taj Mahal's entrance into the Atlantic City casino hotel market will be met in the same manner.[289]

The Trump Taj Mahal began operations on 2 April 1990 with a splendid flourish, though without some of the star power originally hoped for. By this time, the casino's fortunes were intertwined with the celebrity of its namesake and Trump made the most of it, beginning with an employee pep rally in a huge ballroom on 29 March, with a video genie named 'Fabu', laser lights, and rock music, in which 6,000 employees cheered him along. Opening day for Taj customers was not as celebratory. Amidst the excitement, the Taj's new automatic change makers were depleted quickly and could not be replenished fast enough by staff. This led to long lines at the only two change booths – a blot on the day that otherwise had Trump triumphantly leading reporters through the ornate casino and hotel, with its gleaming white elephants up front, glass towers the color of the blue sea, seventy-five-yard marble front desk and gilded touches everywhere. The casino reportedly spent $4 million alone on the sparkling, Indian-themed uniforms worn by the staff. Opening day was a triumph for Trump, the casino magnate: he had finished the mammoth Taj Mahal when Resorts could not and in doing so had elevated himself to pop-star status.[290]

The Trump Taj Mahal also debuted the concept of the 'theme casino' in Atlantic City, promoting an experience well beyond gambling. This was a novelty for the entire casino industry, pioneered in Las Vegas by Circus, Circus, and recently spun to a new level by the Mirage and the coming Excalibur. The Taj styled its entrance off Pacific Avenue from Disney as a grand promenade with trees, flowers, a fountain and two large white gates to go along with the bejewelled white elephants.[291] The new casino imported a more universal fantasy into a gambler's world. Taj staff studied at the Disney Business Seminars program to learn how to transform the gaming experience into more of a vacation escape for visitors. Taj patrons would find themselves surrounded by 'performers', not employees. They would gamble amidst an ongoing 'mingling theatre' with door-men wearing giant feathers on their heads and with Sinbad, Scheherazade and Ali Baba floating around the tables and slot machines. Taj managers worked with specialists to create the Disney-styled image by focusing on the employees' well-being. Speaking just before the casino opened, Antoinette Whiting, the casino's 'Image Programs Manager' sounded like a New Age version of a Harrah's executive in her focus on the Taj's rank and file:

> Everything in the environment, all of the vibes and feelings, affect the behav-ior of the individual. A lot of managers miss that. If they have programs, they often try to implement new training programs, and these work to a degree. But they work much better when the whole culture promotes it. Most peo-ple think image deals with makeup, but my concern is to help individuals from the inside out. A lot of people in this industry want to develop, but don't know how. So I help them develop trust, and look for ways to develop a better self-image.

Whiting even brought in 'makeup specialists' from New York to help shore up the casino employees' confidence and to protect them from surly gamblers and the trauma of having money thrown at them all the time.[292]

The new casino style of the Trump Taj Mahal emphasized the extent to which the Atlantic City casino industry was at a turning point in 1990. In the face of stagnating revenues and the threat of competition from out of state, it needed to do business a different way. The Taj Mahal was over-the-top, magnificent and expensive. But it was also different, new and exciting – and at that point in Atlantic City's casino era, there was an almost unanimous call for change. The opening of the Taj seemed to offer a new chance to make Atlantic City, via the casino industry, into a legitimate vacation destination, following the Las Vegas model – something New Jersey Casino Association president Tom Carver was publicly promoting, despite the critics who continued to say that a new Las Vegas was something the state definitely did not need.[293] Twelve years into the casino era, here was a chance for renewal, yet again – another shot at achieving an American dream of shared and individual prosperity.

Trump hosted the official opening of the Taj with a grand party in which Merv Griffin introduced his rival casino owner. With his company's bondholders still pressing for a $5 million legal fund to sue Trump, Griffin may have been in an awkward position that April night, but he hardly showed it, hopping on stage while his hit song 'I've Got a Lovely Bunch of Coconuts' played in the back-ground. Griffin quipped 'I used to have a lot of coconuts', thus reminding the crowd that Resorts was in bankruptcy court in part due to the fall-out from the Trump-Resorts deal of 1988. As always, however, business concerns took over and Griffin expressed the hopeful outlook that the Taj would uplift his casino and others by bringing hundreds of thousands of new players to Atlantic City – a message also expressed by other notables like Senator William Gormley and Mayor Usry. Later, pink and purple fireworks exploded and green lasers lit up the new hotel tower while 'Stars and Stripes Forever' and the Star Wars theme ushered in a new phase of the casino era.[294]

To some gamblers flocking to the Taj Mahal in its first week, the experience was almost overwhelming. Alma Guicheteau of Vineland wandered around the vast gaming floor looking for her friend to no avail, at one point complaining exasperatedly that the Taj was 'too big' and that 'Trump can keep this damn place'. Even she, however, was appeased by a Donald-sighting and autograph session, and she was of course taken by the slots action, as were the thousands who put their money in. The Taj was too successful for its own good in its first week of operations. By 7 April, the slots machines were down for hours at a time as employees tried to keep up with the demand for coins. On the second day of real gaming, the casino did not even open up until 4.30 p.m. as workers tried to reconcile the previous day's paperwork with all the money that had poured in. By the end of the week, the Taj was shuttling slots workers from the other Trump casinos and gamblers to the other casinos while its own slots operation was stuck. The money was flowing to a degree not seen since Resorts's opening in 1978. On its fourth day, the Taj Mahal's win topped $1.1 million – the projected amount to break even on its enormous construction costs. In one eight-hour test, the slots won $713,000, compared to $102,558 for the Showboat's premiere in 1987.

But what good was the opening bonanza if chaos reigned? Trump's management team knew that their customers would quickly turn away in the face of the problems and the early revenues would dry up fast. Meanwhile, NJCCC regulators were carefully observing and putting pressure on the Trump team to keep the slots going while accurately reporting the daily win. The hardships of the Taj's first week tested the strength of the organization, and executives like Trump Castle's Ed Tracy and Trump Plaza's Jack O'Donnell pooled resources and management tools to get the casino through the hardest part, even if that meant shutting down the slots for its entire first weekend of operations. The efforts to keep the Taj Mahal standing tall were a masterpiece of executive management by Trump executives and model of leadership acumen by Trump. By the end of the first week, Trump had replaced the Taj's top executives and shuffled Tracy to the CEO position in the Trump Hotel Corporation. Yet the casino won $4.9 million in six days, with sporadic slots operations that probably would have accounted for $2–3 million more in the win total. The good tidings lasted through April and the Taj Mahal's first month of operations was the best month ever for a casino in Atlantic City.[295]

For months before the Taj opened, the other industry operators had been preparing in different way. Resorts and Showboat, adjacent to the Taj Mahal, were ready for their own kinds of reopening, hoping to benefit from wandering Taj gamblers. Bally's responded by adding substance to its entertainment line-up for the remainder of the year. Harrah's did not make any noticeable changes, taking the long-term view that had built it into a successful operator, continuing in earnest with its 'People Place' campaign. Harrah's lost less than 100 employees to the new casino – the lowest loss in town – and had begun to shift away from busses in favour of emphasizing car passengers coming to town. According to Ron Lenczycki, Vice-President and General Manager, Harrah's would stick to its simple and successful formula that involved targeted customer marketing and employee satisfaction. Employee statements appeared to back up Lenczykci's confidence in Harrah's programme for absorbing the Taj's debut. According to Jane Gilmour, slots attendant:

> I love the people ... the customers, my fellow employees. It's so totally different than the other houses. The make you feel like you're a part of things. You don't feel like an 'employee'. There's not a door here they're not willing to open.

Gayle Columbo, food and beverage supervisor, echoed the sentiment:

> The people here are really nice to work with. I believe in Harrah's. It's a good company. Its always been good to me and the people around me.[296]

Unfortunately for Harrah's, the Trump group and the entire industry, the big winnings of the first week and the upsurge in casino revenue did not last long. By late summer, several of the direr predications that surrounded the Taj's opening appeared to be coming true: that the Taj would dilute the gaming market and that the demand increase it spurred would not enough to make up for the losses around the industry. Adding 20 per cent new gaming capacity to the Atlantic City casino only increased the total casino win by about 6 per cent. For the second quarter of 1990, the industry lost $1.2 million – the first time the industry had ever made a loss in that usually lucrative time of the year. The Trump casinos appeared to be in the worse shape, with Trump Castle and Trump Plaza dropping substantially in revenue from Summer 1989 levels and the Taj missing its approximate break-even mark of $1.3 million casino 'win' per day. The bad financial news completely reversed the labour problem of early 1990 posed by the Taj's debut, turning the shortage into surplus. By the mid-summer, talk of layoffs was in the air, and by September, Trump's new CEO (Ed Tracy) discussed reducing the Taj's workforce from 6,000 to 5,500 and cutting hundreds more jobs at the other Trump properties. In an interview published in the *Press*, he frankly explained the Trump's group's unfortunate circumstances:

> When the Taj opened, it appeared that we were growing in market. I think, in fact, the Taj masked the downturn in the economy that we saw really come to fruition at the end of June, and clearly in July and August. It's clear

that some of the business from the Plaza and some of the business from the Castle has gone to the Taj, as it has from every other establishment in town. The Plaza, for example, was down 27% in gross gaming revenues, which is a substantial reduction. That clearly has repercussions throughout the organization. In the month of August, it came back ... We clearly have a struggle on our hands, and we have to find new ways to attract business to our town, and clearly it appears that one way to grow market shares is to encroach on existing market share.

The casinos typically hired and laid off workers according to a modest seasonal effect, but now the cuts were more drastic and consequent to the 'recessionary trends and the dilution effect from the opening of the Taj Mahal', in the words of a Claridge executive. CANJ president Tom Carver partially blamed the industry's problems on casino overcapacity and a stagnant gaming market, noting that the resort had not sustained the big crowds of April enough to offset its expenses. Carver's analysis also touched on the downside of using star power as a primary marketing tool, commenting that people came when Trump himself was all over the new casino and that the drop-off occurred as his presence faded. In contrast, the Las Vegas casinos continued to ride a double-digit wave of increased win amounts in the same period over the year before, with the additions of the Mirage and the new Excalibur – the casino that made the Taj Mahal's claim to be the largest in the world short-lived.[297]

The industry's 1990 troubles came down on the Trump Organization hardest. Next to Merv Griffin, Trump had personally gambled the most in Atlantic City, hoping for the big casino pay-off, and now he was losing his gambit. As the Taj's fortunes went sour, the NJCCC called him in to justify his empire – apparently ready to collapse in a mountain of debt. The Trump group had barely kept the Trump Castle from going into default when Trump bailed it out with a $65 million loan in mid-summer and averted a major cash flow crisis. By September, a $47.3 million interest payment on Taj bonds was looming for 15 November, and the NJCCC was openly reviewing the financial solvency of the Trump empire. The bondholders were due $675 million, and increasingly concerned about their investment. Trump convinced the commissioners to accept his bank bailout, including a determination that a new Chief Financial Officer be appointed to manage the finances of his casinos, but the bailout did not cover the looming Taj bond payment that was causing a large amount of anxiety up and down the Boardwalk. Would Trump make the payment? If not, would the Taj be forced to shut down like the Atlantis before? How could the Atlantic City casino industry absorb this potential blow? How long could the Trump Plaza and Castle survive, given their own debt and decreased revenues? Meanwhile, the Trump groups had left numerous contractors unpaid, including the Ohio company that had made the white elephants outside the casinos. What would happen to them?

By mid-November 1990, prospects were very bleak for the Trump group with another $47.3 million payment to bondholders nearly due. Two days before the payment's due date, the Trump group cut off talks with the bondholders' negotiator and instead prepared a 'pre-packaged' bankruptcy filing. The filing would need to pass muster with the NJCCC, but was a better option for the Trump group than to be forced into regular chapter 11 proceedings by unpaid bondholders. Around the same time, the Trump groups scored some positive publicity for itself by closing a deal on the Evander Hoyfield–George Foreman boxing match scheduled for April, 1991. In addition, CEO Tracy personally delivered a $3.9 million tax payment to City Hall. The move helped dispel some questions over Trump's ability to survive the tough times, despite the fact that it was a few days late.[298]

By the end of December, the casino community had some answers to the questions raised by Trump's uncertain status. The Taj did not recover well enough to make the bond payment, but Trump managed to arrange the 'pre-packaged bankruptcy' that paid off the bondholders part of the money owed, lowered the interest rates and gave them half the equity in the Taj Mahal, while allowing Trump to remain in charge. The Trump group also reached a deal with the unpaid contractors to pay 30 per cent of what was owed, with the rest being paid over a five-year period. Collectively, the manoeuvres convinced the NJCCC that the Trump casino empire was financially solvent and therefore worthy of its licence. Finally, the Trump group managed to pay approximately $34.5 million to bondholders of the Trump Castle and Trump Plaza, with some help from an interest-free loan via a purchase of $3.45 million chips at the Trump Castle by a lawyer for the Trump patriarch, Fred Trump. It was very close, but the Trump group managed to stave off default, casino closure and get through the year.[299] However, the bankruptcy filing rippled through the region's business community, with many Taj suppliers left feeling unfairly treated by the Trump manoeuvres. A local car parts dealer recalled that

> a lot of people were upset with Donald Trump. They were happy ultimately, it was a great thing, and the world all knew about the Taj Mahal. But there was a lot of local businessmen that weren't getting paid.

The Taj's bankruptcy meant that some contractors

> couldn't pay me for their parts – their 55-gallon drums, the hydraulic wheels, or equipment I was selling, all that kind of stuff. It put some people out of business.[300]

The Taj Mahal's grand opening and its ensuing inability to generate increased business across the casino industry affirmed the long-standing view that the state's regulatory process needed a major overhaul. The Taj's struggle to survive its debut year and its failure to lift the industry out of its doldrums were significant factors in the calls for less micromanagement of the industry. Resorts's bankruptcy and the junk bond debt problem also contributed to the new energy for change. The shaky fortunes of the industry also generated new momentum for regional transformation via increased attention on the two big projects long viewed by many as the answer to Atlantic City's problems: a new convention centre and an expanded, modernized international airport. Despite the bleak circumstances, hope was strong as always for those in the casinos industry who envisioned a better future this time because of new political realities. The 1989 election of Governor Jim Florio and the 1990 election of Mayor James Whelan (both Democrats) were cause for no small amount of optimism from industry types for non-partisan reasons. Though it was not entirely clear what they would do in their new offices, both Florio and Whelan represented something very important from an industry perspective: they were a clear break from the past. City Councilman Whelan defeated the indicted Usry and Florio defeated his opponent (Jim Courter), who appeared to represent the anti-casino establishment personified by Republican governor Thomas Kean.

Amidst the opening week hoopla at the Trump Taj Mahal, Trump escorted Governor Florio around the new facility. Afterwards, Florio briefly explained his administration's intent on Atlantic City:

> We will be looking at all the things that have to be done to make sure that the benefits that come from these facilities really go out to all the people.

He also noted that Atlantic City 'should become a full-fledged convention center rather than just be totally dominated by the casinos' and that the Florio administration would push hard to create a 'world-class airport' along with a new convention centre.[301] Whelan also became mayor based on big vision of change. For him, this involved a shift in the orientation of the mayor's office towards integrity and a new attitude towards the casinos. Looking back in 2005, he recalled the novelty of this approach to the industry:

> I think one of the things that I brought to the table as mayor. And I guess to the extent, you always build on some of the things that go before, but I was unabashedly pro-casino ... .I think I was the first mayor that was unabashedly pro-casino. I think other mayors were – they would tell you that, yeah, casinos were good and so on. But they'd always temper it with they got to do more, or they're not doing enough, or we still have these other problems and so on and so forth. My take was, hey, the casinos came here. They said they were going to provide jobs and pay taxes and do construction. They've done all that, now we got to figure this out. We got to stop blaming them for the problems. We got to figure this out together.[302]

In the heated and decisive primary battle between the incumbent Usry and the other candidates, Whelan talked about solutions for the community that had little directly to do with the casino business. In a predominately Democratic city, winning the Democratic primary was the real election and Whelan attacked the current mayor over the basic conditions of the city. He focused on providing strong leadership and quality-of-life issues such as crime and street pollution. He talked about adding more police, cleaning up dirty public buildings and advertised in *Black New Jersey Magazine* that it was 'Time to Put Atlantic City Back Together'.[303] Significantly, the magazine failed to endorse the incumbent Usry in the primary and triumphantly reported the primary result in tandem with the opening of the Trump Taj Mahal and the unprecedented election of an African-American woman (Barbara Hudgins) to City Council:

> So much has happened in Atlantic City over the past year: A new mayor and the first African-American woman have been elected to office in Atlantic City government. And if that is not enough, casino magnate Donald Trump has opened what has been called the **8th Wonder of the World** in the Taj Mahal Hotel Casino.[304]

Despite Whelan's direct focus on the city and its residents, his winning message resonated with casino backers who had been blaming their industry's problems on the city's condition, and especially the city and state governments for years. Improving the relationship between the city and the industry, perceived as dysfunctional in the 1980s, was vital for the industry to gain a positive image. A 1988 *Casino Journal* article emphasized the connection and the sheer frustration heard repeatedly in the 1980s from industry sources:

> No Atlantic City politician runs for office today on his record of positive success in translating the economic BOON or casino gaming into social and ECONOMIC BENEFITS for Atlantic City, or for the state and its citizens. Even more significantly, all those politicians already in office are able to sustain themselves despite the physical face of Atlantic City, and despite the social conditions that sadly afflict so many Atlantic City citizens, because they place all blame at the doors of the casino industry and at the feet of its executives. And the people accept these charges as 'gospel' because the media regularly repeats those charges ... Because of 'moral opprobrium' the economic revitalization produced by casino gaming, instead of being cited as its greatest accomplishment is used as a club with which to beat the casino industry, because all that economic vitality exists in such glaring contrast to the backdrop of deterioration, decay and despair that are so obvious today in many non-casino sections of Atlantic City.[305]

As the 1990 mayoral race began, the *Casino Journal* editors at first withheld support from any of the candidates in the hope that the state would step in to create a 'superagency', to essentially take over regional governance on issues such as transportation, housing and political corruption. However, *Casino Journal* changed its position to a full endorsement of Whelan in its pre-election issue, naming him the candidate who 'had shown more positive thinking and genuine commitment to the public interest' than the rest, and especially more than the incumbent. As the primary approached, the editors re-thought their previous stance on the 'superagency' and developed more faith in a new city administration to take positive steps for the city, including a more cooperative approach to the Pomona airport. Still, after he won, *Casino Journal* editors made clear that Whelan would soon need to get things done, or risk the permanent disabling of city government:

> [the Whelan administration] had better be able to claim success in major areas where the city has been negligent or deficient in the past. For if it cannot claim such success, the new city administration will lose the right, perhaps forever, even to deal with those issues, much less determine their resolution.[306]

Whelan did not set out to become the candidate to champion the casinos, but he eventually won their support by forcefully changing the look and style of Atlantic City. The city began to move in a different direction politically and socially with Whelan's election, one that was in the interests of the industry and its residents, by now intricately tied into the casino's success. A 1991 city brochure captured the mood of his administration well and the collaborative, creative state efforts to improve the industry and city. It pointed out that

> A strong partnership has evolved among public agencies to support and guide the City's renaissance. This collaborative effort includes the Atlantic City Department of Planning and Development, the Casino Re-investment and Development Authority (CRDA), the Atlantic County Improvement Authority (ACIA), the Atlantic City Housing Authority and Urban Redevelopment Agency, the Atlantic City-New Jersey Coordinating Council and Atlantic County and its Agencies.

The list was a little overwhelming, but demonstrated the powerful and effective efforts by a host of public agencies and officials to stabilize and improve the casino community. By the time Whelan won re-election in 1994, the casino community had recovered dramatically from its crisis point. Whelan himself deserved a lot of the credit he received from casino insiders for changing the city in a positive way for the industry.[307]

In 1990, the other big story of the casino community was the beginning of a new approach to casino regulation, long called for by the industry. As the industry's revenue stagnation continued into the mid-summer, Tom Carver used the miserable revenue numbers to justify a call for dramatic policy revision at the state level. CANJ used the likely external competition from Iowa and Illinois riverboats, and from casinos in New Orleans and Gary, Indiana, to call for systemic change at the state level. The proposal included changes in the focus and make-up of CRDA and NJCCC operations and a streamlining of the *Casino Control Act* to ease business restrictions. On the subject of redevelopment, CANJ's 1990 proposal suggested that 'reinvestment and redevelopment must include more than housing if Atlantic City is to become the year-round destination resort as envisioned by the Casino Control Act'. In addition, the CANJ called for a 'greater state role' to coordinate public facilities and transportation infrastructure – code words for the Pomona airport and proposed convention centre. Finally, central to CANJ's concerns was its call for regulatory relief to alleviate the 'inability of the industry and the regulators to establish a "make it work" approach to casino industry regulation'. The state should adopt, it proposed, 'a positive, innovative approach to industry problems' while maintaining its integrity standards.[308]

The proposal reflected an emerging consensus for regulatory change from casino executives, the industry's journalistic advocates and even the NJCCC itself. In early 1990, commissioner and businessman Pat Dodd laid out a new vision for redevelopment in the wake of Chairman Stephen Read's departure:

> I am a firm believer in letting market forces go. You can't compete with a house that you would build tomorrow on the second block down that you can build for a fraction of that on the mainland, and have schools and safety and all that. Forced competition doesn't work. And there isn't enough money in all of Atlantic City to redevelop the housing neighborhoods in that fashion ... I've always looked at the CRDA as more of a tool to be use to lure private businesses as partnerships and develop that.

Dodd also criticized CRDA's signature accomplishment to that point – Harrah's Northeastern Inlet housing project:

> All the eggs! [in one basket] And committed for quite a while. We mortgaged the future on that. This is supposed to be a fluid thing, a living breathing document, not one thing that we start out with and we go for the next twenty years doing the same thing.

He noted a distinct lack of communication between the industry and its regulators and argued that the NJCCC and the DGE needed to eliminate redundancies while maintaining checks and balances over each other. Dodd reiterated the by-now commonplace 'competition is coming' mantra, noting that casino expansion had come to a halt in Atlantic City and that the city lacked sufficient hotel rooms for the future.[309] A major part of the dilemma had simply to do with relationships between the various entities involved, as Whelan recalled fifteen years later:

> We spent a good portion of time blaming each other. The casinos blame city government. The city government would blame the state. The state would blame the casinos. And everybody was right. And we also – there was no – the relationships and the trust weren't there to really harness the energy of the casinos.[310]

One controversial aspect of casino regulation had to do with the amount of space that casinos could devote to slot machines as opposed to table games on their gaming floors. The 1977 *Casino Control Act* limited the amount of space that casinos could devote to slot machines, a measure that did not garner much opposition in 1978 when the primary business of the casinos was in the table games. In 1990, however, things had shifted, as slots became more attractive and electronic technology allowed for easier tabulation of slots play for comps. Yet Atlantic City was always more slots-focused than Nevada: Resorts's 1978 slots' win was 43.7 per cent of total play – considerably higher than Nevada's slots take. The introduction in the 1980s of video poker along with Atlantic City's market-focus on low rollers also spurred the slots' expansion, which took off at the beginning of the 1990s. In 1989, Resorts's slots' win was at 55.3 per cent, just below the industry average of 56.2 per cent. The slots wins of a few casinos were upwards of 60 per cent, including Harrah's and TropWorld.[311]

The new popularity of slot machines may also have had something to do with a new generation of gamblers who grew up in the electronic age with video games a source of regular entertainment. In addition, the old training grounds for table games like back-alley craps seemed to have declined in the culture. Yet, the NJCCC permitted the Atlantic City casinos to allocate only 30 per cent of the first 50,000 square feet of the gaming floor to slot machines, and only 25 per cent of floor space for slots above the original space. Not surprisingly, casino executives sought regulatory relief to take advantage of the increasing demand for slots in the early 1990s. Trump Castle president Tony Calandra made the case for change, pointing out that

> with the rapid growth in popularity of slot machines, many casinos would like to see that rule [limiting slots machines space] relaxed or even abolished, reasoning that if customers want slots, the casinos should be able to provide them. In other words, let the markets determine the percentage.

The rising popularity of slot machines also amplified calls for the NJCCC to allow the casinos to offer new games like 'Pai Gow' poker to appeal to wider markets, especially Asian customers from the northeast. Many believed that good casino marketing programmes could bring the glamour of the casino experience even to slots players, and the casinos appeared willing to make this investment.[312]

By the end of the miserable summer of 1990, the industry was actively pressing for government changes to move it out of its 'crisis'. As the official spokesman for the casinos, Tom Carver publicly complained about 'no game plan' and rampant building with no city investment. He reiterated his call to make Atlantic City more like Las Vegas, echoing Steve Wynn, and once again sounded out for twenty-four-hour gaming and an 'intelligent regulatory attitude' and also lauded Mayor-elect Whelan for placing a Caesar's vice-president on his transition team. Carver noted that the market was not expanding, despite the Taj Mahal, and that the city was not yet a destination resort like Las Vegas, where people stayed longer. In Carver's view, Atlantic City also needed the

> beginning of intelligent governmental process towards the development of AC ... You can't advertise Atlantic City as a first class resort/tourist destination when you can't back up that claim.

Casino industry executives repeatedly backed up Carver on his points, noting the need for twenty-four-hour gaming and the need to clean up the city. The 'crisis' also renewed executives' calls for less regulation, an improved airport and, for some, real action towards the Convention Center. Harrah's Ron Lenczycki applauded Florio's establishment of a new New Jersey-Atlantic City Coordinating Council to help smooth over conflict. The council was headed up by Mayor Whelan and New Jersey Commerce Commissioner George Zoffinger. Local 54's president (Roy Silbert) also called for twenty-four-hour gaming, and also for sports betting, Keno and racetrack simulcasting. He lamented the casino's industry's supposed lack of common purpose with labour:

> It's tough dealing with the casino mentality, which regards the jobs of our members as just an ancillary service. It's different from dealing with hotel people in Chicago or New York, because with casinos, you're dealing primarily with economists and financial people. I don't have a community of interest with them.[313]

Within this advocacy group, there were certainly differences of opinion on how to proceed, such as on the wisdom of constructing the new Convention Center. But the relatively unified front and broad-based agreement on a number of issues (like twenty-four-hour gaming and looser regulation) propelled the casino industry forward from its desperation at a crucial point. The disappointment of the Taj's first summer quickly faded into a self-generated optimism and energy, now supported by public officials. There were plenty of detractors and certainly major battles loomed in the near future, but for now, the Atlantic City casino community came together and brought itself another chance. Though not similarly organized, it was reminiscent of the community efforts that led to casino legalization in 1976.

On the regulatory front, the NJCCC began to move almost simultaneously to a February talk in which Carver told an audience that a major difference between Las Vegas and Atlantic City was 'that the casinos are allowed to be what they are'. Chairman Stephen Read stepped down from the Commission in early 1990. His last annual statement, the NJCCC's 1989 annual report, echoed a number of recent *Casino Journal* articles in noting the importance of responding to the threat of new competitions. It also sounded defensive (not surprisingly), noting that

Casino regulation has worked in Atlantic City. It has given the industry credibility in the financial investment community and it has kept the industry
clean.

Read's acting successor, Valerie Armstrong, quickly began to reduce the size of the
commission by cutting over thirty jobs, including twenty-nine inspector positions,
to reduce its administrative costs by $1.35 million annually. Well-received by the
industry, the cuts appeared responsive to CANJ's 1988 audit that recommended
agency streamlining and reduction to save $3 million a year. Circumstances had
changed considerably in two years, and the regulatory changes appeared more
necessary given the state of the industry. A few months after the Commission's
streamlining, an industry analyst and former executive declared that casino gaming in New Jersey was now considered a 'legitimate business' in Trenton and that
legislation on the table would really boost the industry.[314]

The casino industry entered a new relationship with its regulators upon the
nomination of Steve Perskie to chair the Casino Control Commission in mid-
1990. Perskie left a judgeship in late 1989 to become Governor Florio's Chief
of Staff with some hopes that he could reverse the 'mistakes' of the 1980s with
regard to casino policy. Perskie's renewed interest in casino policy had a lot to do
with Florio's ascension to governor, bringing renewed hope at the state level. In
Perskie's eyes:

> you had a new governor who's a friend of Atlantic City, if you will, or at least
> a supporter of the idea that state government had a significant role to play in
> the redeeming of the promises.[315]

Perskie's nomination was accepted with broad support across the community,
from local officials like Whelan and Senator William Gormley and casino people
like Carver and new Trump Taj Mahal president Jack Davis. In something of a
consensus statement, Davis championed Perskie as someone with the 'understanding of the businessman's viewpoint and an appreciation of the state government
and public viewpoint'.[316]

Once installed as commissioner, Perskie could not afford any honeymoon, nor
would casino people give him one. Not long after taking the post, he outlined his
priorities as follows: resolution over airport expansion political stalemate, a new
Convention Center, a new Atlantic City High School on Great Island, NJCCC
consolidation in Atlantic City, a comprehensive review of *CCA* regulations and
procedures to sort out those that affected business aspects of gaming. Of these
priorities, the Convention Center was probably the most controversial in 1990, as
many in the casino industry opposed its construction in the absence of dedicated
funding and without the estimated 10,000 more hotel rooms it would require.[317]
The other items had almost universal support. Even Pierre Hollingsworth, often

a sharp critic of the casinos, was in concert with the industry on most of these points. He recalled the situation in 2005:

> the regulations were killing them. They told folk what color to paint their rooms. You could not walk into a casino – I mean, walk into a hotel and walk into the casino at the same – you had to walk past the lobby and everything before you can go to the casino. The restrictions were terrible, so – and they talked about keeping down organized crime, which was somewhat successful. But the restrictions were so unbearable that they were losing money. And then they didn't have 24-hour gambling ... were closing up at, I don't know, 3:00 in the morning or something like that.[318]

By the beginning of 1991, Perskie's NJCCC had begun its ambitious deregulation program, in concert with a supportive legislature in Trenton. To this end, it was investigating change on three fronts: a review of all integrity regulations, lessening regulatory interference in the casino business and staff reorganization and streamlining. Within two years of Perskie's nomination, the entire regulatory emphasis of the casino industry changed dramatically. Working closely with casino executives and the New Jersey legislature, Perskie was able to put through major changes to the *Casino Control Act* which led to the casinos themselves gaining much wider latitude in running their gaming operations. Twenty-four-hour gaming became a reality, as did a much quicker and more streamlined process to introduce new table games. Basically the legislature gave the NJCCC complete authority to approve new games, as opposed to requiring legislative approval as had been the case previously. Similarly, the NJCCC gained new authority to loosen up limitations on the amount of casino floor space that slots machines could occupy – bringing it up to 75 per cent of the gaming floor, almost double the amount of space allowed before. Perskie explained the re-engineered purpose of the NJCCC in the commission's 1990 annual report:

> The decision to streamline the staff and to move away from any involvement in purely business decisions by the commission is designed to provide a stronger basis for the redevelopment of Atlantic City as a viable and attractive resort.

Even the cover of the NJCCC's annual report signalled the new regulatory environment with the statement:

> The past year, twelve years after the start of casino gaming in this state, was a time of vast change – in Atlantic City, in the casino industry, and in the Casino Control Commission.

The report also demonstrated the quick progress made in a major and long-complained-about problem: employee licence processing. Between March and December 1990, the NJCCC and DGE cut the processing time for licences

almost in half. By the end of the year 41 per cent of all applications were proc-
essed in less than twenty-six days, up from less than one per cent when the year
began.[319]

In the 1991 annual report, Chairman Perskie was able to champion the
progress of deregulation and its impact, as he saw it, in producing a revenue
increase for the second half of the year. The key change, as Perskie understood
the commission's policy, was mid-year legislation that allowed weekend twenty-
four-hour gaming, new table games 'Red Dog' and 'Sic Bo', and a revised policy
to allow slot machines on the casino floor. The new slot regulations linked the
number of permissible slot machines to the number of hotel rooms a property
had – thus providing an incentive to add hotel rooms, increasingly important as
political momentum for the new convention centre grew. Additionally, the casinos benefited from a relaxation of the 'tape measure', rule which now allowed
casino operators much more flexibility for placing restaurants, showrooms, health
facilities and parking spaces on their properties.[320]

As always, the outspoken Wynn monitored the situation and expressed his
view, which finally seemed to resonate with the people that mattered. In 1991,
he sounded more hopeful than before, yet not ready to call Atlantic City a transformed community just yet:

> see the legislature in sort of a knee-jerk reaction, by dong things under the
> Perskie regime that will head off some more bankruptcies, if they can ... They
> should make sure that key employees are reputable, upstanding people; they
> should stop spending money and creating a bureaucracy to license dealers
> and waitresses and other non-management people; they should stop telling
> people how to build their buildings and what to put in them; they should
> keep their noses out of the business and let these people 'rock and roll' and
> market to their heart's content, taking advantage of advertising and market-
> ing strategies just like they do when they're running a state lottery.

Wynn had been saying for years that Atlantic City needed to emulate the Las
Vegas model, not reject it, and finally the state was responding.[321]

By the end of 1993, fifteen years into the casino era, the state had transformed
its entire regulatory process on casino gaming. After the initial round of legislative changes after Florio and Perskie took office, the state continued to modify the
CCA, shifting more authority to the Commission in a manner conducive to the
casino business. In 1993, casinos added racing simulcasting and poker to the gaming menus and also benefited from an important *CCA* amendment that allowed
expansion of the casino floor space in accordance with construction of new hotel
rooms. Significantly, the casino expansions could now take place before completion of the new rooms, thus providing an added incentive for the casinos to build
new rooms. In addition, the NJCCC allowed for the implementation of full
twenty-four-hour gaming and dropped licensing requirements for non-gaming

employees. Basically, almost all major regulatory decisions now passed from the New Jersey legislature to the NJCCC, as the politicians appeared to have gained 'great confidence in the abilities of the commission and Division of Gaming Enforcement to do quality work and to act in the public interest'.[322]

In a 1992 interview, the governor explained that the regulatory shift was designed to 'free the industry to be able to grow in a more marketplace-oriented way, which will help the industry grow and prosper'. He commented that casino executives he met with were happily surprised because before they had only met with the state's attorney general, which implied that they were a law enforcement problem 'there seemed to be an awful lot of appreciation that we were talking to them as business people, which they certainly are'.[323] The regulatory changes clearly improved the industry's attitude towards state officials and the regulatory mechanisms in place. Even Senator Gormley – so often criticized in the past by *Casino Journal* – was now heralded for his efforts and political leadership in convincing New Jersey legislators to shift business prerogatives to the casinos themselves. *Casino Journal* compared the new era to the old, giving a lot of credit to Steve Perskie:

> Perskie's solicitation of the industry's views, therefore, broke the evil precedent established under the hellish regulatory regime dominated by Walter 'One Note' Read and Anthony 'Piranha' Parillo. And when Perskie was appointed Casino Control Chairman, in 1990, he established what we considered to be the excellent precedent of listening to the industry's spokesman and responding to their requests for rational, reasonable, responsible and fair casino regulation. Not only did he streamline the commission's staff and procedures, but he pruned the overgrown regulatory tree of its least productive, and least essential branches. And when legislators like Essex County Senator Richard J. Codey, proposed wide-ranging revision of the *CCA* – increasing the prerogatives of casino executives with respect to the purely 'business' aspects of casino administration and operation – Steve Perskie was wholly supportive, both in securing the enactment of such proposals into law, and in implementing them through new legislation.[324]

Casino executives took notice as the regulations changed, and the industry's fortunes appeared to improve by mid-1992, after the casino deregulation bill became law. Amongst the senior casino staff, there was an entirely new posture towards the public sector. The situation was far removed from 1989, when the casinos called for their own bill of rights. Along these lines, Bally's president Richard Gillman noted that

> If we really continue on the path we've recently seen – the concept of 24-hour gaming, additional games, sports wagering and profitable simulcasting – then I think Atlantic City can re-group and ultimately be a huge success.

He also expressed faith in public officials like Perskie and Gormley to clear the way for a robust response to new competition and affirmed support for key recent decisions like the hotel room expansion ruling. Trump joined in the optimistic chorus of 1992:

> Steve Perskie and the commission have made really made great strides. And by the way, these are the strides to keep an industry strong so that when things get tough, the industry can pay taxes, take care of the elderly and do all the other things that it has done in the past. So, I take my hat off to Steve Perskie and the entire commission.[325]

Years later, a casino executive noted that deregulation had a positive impact on the Caesar's slot operations by empowering managers to make quicker decisions to maximize profitable use of slot machines on the floor:

> There were a couple of areas in the slot area where they would allow us to offer, for example, a large progressive jackpot and we were able to remove it upon notice. That could never happen before, and they were ... because we had issues with, hey, here's a big jackpot, and we want to remove the machine that that jackpot is associated with it, because no one is going to hit it, because it's not getting played as much as it used to. People are bored with that game, and I couldn't take it out, unless that jackpot hit, so I was a double sword here. Nobody would play it, and yet you couldn't hit it, so I couldn't remove the money.[326]

The revised regulations also empowered casino executives and managers by easing the hiring process to meet the needs of their businesses. Managers and supervisors could now hire whomever they wanted, a distinct change from before, when there were strict restrictions on hiring only slots technicians, for example, from specifically-approved schools:

> And that opened the gates, in my opinion, where you can have people with that kind of background, you can send them to CCI school [Casino Career Institute], get familiarized with the regulations before they even come onboard for you, and you can get them familiarized with the slot machines before they even come in the casino. And then you want to train them further, that's fine, you can train them.[327]

At the end of 1993, Perskie's outgoing report as NJCCC Chair sounded a triumphant note. He celebrated the beginning of poker and keno, approved in 1993 with the Commission's new authority. He also reported on new simulcasting programmes and commented on 'a growing confidence in the Commission by granting us authority to make decisions that had been previously been the province of lawmakers'. Perskie also alluded to the collaborative efforts between the state and the city, demonstrated by the Atlantic City/New Jersey Coordinating

Council. One important regulatory change allowed NJCCC 'principal investigators' on site in the casinos to approve changes in casino floor games or table games procedures quickly. In two years, investigators had approved 169 of these changes, demonstrating the efficient and casino-friendly posture of the new regulatory environment.[328]

A major difference between the late 1980s and the early 1990s was competition. For years, Atlantic City's east coast monopoly on casinos benefited the Atlantic City industry. The new competition posed by tribal casinos in Connecticut and the possibility of casinos in New York and Pennsylvania shook up the local casino industry. In the early 1990s, the success of the Foxwoods tribal casino drove deregulation in Atlantic City. Former New Jersey DGE official Mickey Brown led a major expansion of Foxwoods to better orient it to the New England market, directly competing for Atlantic City's slots' players. Foxwoods struck a deal with the state of Connecticut to add hundreds of hotel rooms and thousands of slots machines in 1993 – boosting its total employment to 7,000 – higher than any Atlantic City casino. Foxwoods also moved aggressively to sign a $113 million deal with the state of Connecticut for a virtual casino monopoly, a move designed to shut out the Mirage group, then looking to begin a casino in the Hartford area. By the end of the year, it had significantly peeled away Atlantic City's southern New England slots players.[329]

In the early 1990s, the industry also faced competition from the expanding casino community of coastal Mississippi, where a few 'floating' casinos had recently opened and soon begun to thrive. The debut of Biloxi's Casino Magic in late 1992 was part of a major casino expansion on the state's Gulf coast that would eventually lead to ten large casinos. Casino Magic included a 40,000 square foot casino floor with another 60,000 square feet of space for entertainment and restaurants – comparable to the smaller Atlantic City casinos. Along with Foxwoods, the Biloxi casino movement helped to justify increased pressure on officials and politicians to enact casino-friendly legislation. A casino employee who moved from Atlantic City to Mississippi compared the two casino communities and found a parallel on transportation:

> We have a similar situation in Atlantic City as regards to the airport ... Because of the high visibility of the military in southern Mississippi, the airport has runways that can handle any kind of plane, but there's not much in the way of terminals. But the local government is working closely with us to improve the airport, and hopefully, it won't take as long as Atlantic City.[330]

In 1992, before the Foxwoods expansion, the casino industry was clearly back on track, after a slow three years. Casino 'win' grew by 7.5 per cent after an anemic 1.4 per cent in 1991 and a low 5.2 per cent growth in 1990 that should have been much higher with the added gaming capacity of the Trump Taj Mahal. In 1992, every single casino increased its casino win from the year before, whereas in

1990, the casino 'win' actually declined from the year before in all but two of the casinos. Total revenue for all the casinos also increased at a healthy rate – 7.2 per cent from 1991, after a three year-decline in the total revenue growth rate from 1988 to 1991 that bottomed out at an actual decline of 0.1 per cent in 1991. The industry's total revenue for 1992 was just over $4 billion, more than double what it was a decade earlier. Profitability was also up substantially in 1992, with the Trump casinos leading the way: Trump Plaza was up 36 per cent and Trump Marina increased its profits an astounding 45 per cent in 1992. The industry average gross operating profit increased by 10.3 per cent, with all but one casino (the Sands) growing its profit, and six casinos increasing at a rate of 10 per cent or higher from 1991. On the gaming floor, the trend towards increased reliance on slot machines for profits continued unabated in the early 1990s. In 1993, slot machine win accounted for 67.1 per cent of the total casino win in Atlantic City, with a few casinos, such as Harrah's and the Tropicana earning about 75 per cent of their casino win via slot machines. In 1989, the industry-wide average for slot machines was at 56 per cent. By the end of the 1990s, slot machine winnings accounted for 71 per cent of the total casino win.[331]

The rebound year of 1992 was a pivotal point for the rise of slots as a source of profits for Atlantic City casinos. With expanded space for slots, gross operating profit rose across the board – averaging 10.3 per cent among all the casinos. Simultaneously, the slot machine percent win rose from around 62 per cent to approximately 66 per cent of the total casino win – the biggest one-year rise in this category in the entire casino era. Resorts, Tropicana and Trump Plaza also reversed years of slow or even declining revenue growth with a new emphasis on slots. Resorts's slots win percentage leapt up to 66 per cent from 59 per cent in 1990, while Tropicana's increased by 10 percentage points in the same span to 73 per cent of total revenue. Meanwhile table game 'win' declined substantially in almost all the casinos between 1990 and 1992. Tropicana's 1992 table game 'win' was $82.7 million, down from $100.4 million in 1990. In 1992 Showboat's table game 'win' was $72.6 million, about 21 per cent less than its $91.7 million table game 'win' of 1990. Atlantic City's upswing had everything to do with an increasing reliance on slot machines, with the casinos benefiting tremendously by the legislative change to increase the amount of casino floor space devoted to slot machines.[332]

The new popularity of slot machines was based on a variety of factors, including innovative machines with progressive jackpots and flashing lights, and new games that were very appealing to players. The success of video poker also propelled the slots sector to new heights. In 1993, Harrah's executive Alyce Parker described the appeal that her company was benefiting from:

> There is an interaction with slots now that wasn't there in the past ... You would simply put your money in and pull a handle or push a button. But

technology has changed all that and the customer has decisions to make now. People like that. When you are playing the video poker games you have to know something about the game, but if you make a mistake, no one knows but you. You don't have to worry about the person on your left or right. You can also play the slots at your own speed so there is a real comfort zone.[333]

Harrah's CEO Phil Satre elaborated on the new emphasis on slot machines and the common-sense regulations that reflected customer demand. Satre noted that his business strategy was very 'demand driven', that Harrah's listened to its guests who told them what they wanted. Harrah's met the demand for more slots, regardless of a restrictive regulatory climate for the early years of the casino era:

> If you look at the decade of the '80s, and what happened in that decade, you saw slots as a growing part of the business. I think table games have and will continue to be basically flat to declining in some areas, but I think they are an essential part of the gaming experience. But basically, regulations should not dictate what your product should be- your customer should.[334]

Between 1991 and 1993, the three Trump casinos led the industry in the drive back towards financial viability, between them accounting for approximately 30 per cent of total revenue by 1993. In 1991, new Trump CEO Nicholas Ribis (former lead counsel) implemented a fresh management team in each casino and began treating them each as separate, competitive entities. Each casino focused on different priorities and initiatives to create separate and lucrative niches and to improve their individual profit margins. For example, at Trump Castle, president Robert Wagner retooled the casino by placing more slot machines and video poker machines around, and making the entire casino floor more comfortable, while reducing total employment from 3,300 to 2,700 employees. By 1992, under Wagner, the Castle had completed its shift from an opulent property designed to appeal to high-end players to more middle- and low-brow casino customers, with video poker and a marketing programme that put it in direct competition for the middle of the gaming market targeted by Harrah's. The Trump Plaza began to phase out expensive junkets and high-end comps, now deemed not very profitable and widened its overall appeal. At the Trump Taj Mahal, new president Dennis Gomes implemented a total management overhaul that broke down each component of the casino to determine its maximum appeal to customer demand, from the buffets to the billboards along the Atlantic City Expressway. Another Wynn protégé, Gomes, brought a personalized, hands-on approach to management of the casino not unlike the strategy that had worked well at the Golden Nugget in the 1980s. Gomes's approach relied on the direct involvement of every employee to support the overall focus of the new Taj and to instill direction in each department: 'to establish an environment where the employees knew what they were working toward'. Gomes was also effective in relaxing the environment at the Trump Taj Mahal and significantly improving employee morale through a friendly, casual manner with employees.[335]

Also key to the Trump revival was the agile financial manoeuvring that allowed the Trump casinos to continually leverage themselves to appease NJCCC regulators and keep the doors open. Trump did it again in 1992 with another 'pre-packaged bankruptcy' and new agreements with bondholders, possible due to a good relationship with creditors who recognized inherent value in the Trump casinos. Trump's ability to successfully leverage the casinos was connected to his New York real estate transactions – selling off 49 per cent of the Plaza Hotel in New York to Citibank freed up $300 million that the organization used to satisfy bondholders in the casinos. In this case, Trump's personal ownership of the casinos worked well, facilitating the group's flexibility to use a combination of creative debt arrangements, personal charisma and effective management to solidify the Trump Organization's powerful position within the industry. In 1992, Whelan commented on Trump's meaning to the casino community:

> Donald understands that the gaming industry turns on personality. Steve Wynn understands that, as well. When Trump runs ads that promote himself and his properties, he's promoting Atlantic City at the same time ... It's analogous to being the quarterback of a football team: When things are going well he gets too much credit, and when things are not going so well, he gets too much blame. I think that happened when things started to go sour in Atlantic City. Some of the problems were of his own doing, others had more to do with outside marketing forces.[336]

Another bold move by the Trump group symbolized its industry leadership in the early 1990s. In 1992, the Trump Plaza became the first casino to expand its casino floor space with a commitment to build a new hotel tower. The move paid off well, with the casino vaulting from a 15.7 per cent decline in casino 'win' to a 12.4 per cent increase in one year – a full 5 per cent over the industry average.[337]

The Trump group also took advantage of the new regulatory climate by opening up a large poker room in 1993 at the Taj Mahal. With its new authority, the Commission approved poker, a departure from all previous table games offered in Atlantic City casinos because it pitted players against each other, rather than against the casino. The Taj's new poker room was not the only one in town – Resorts and Bally's (among others) also moved quickly to bring in poker revenue – but the Taj quickly became the largest by far. In 1994, it generated over $16 million in revenues, quadrupling its closest competitors and almost half of the entire amount of revenue generated by all of the city's poker rooms. By the end of the 1990s, the Taj's poker revenues were at $20 million a year, or about 55 per cent of the total poker revenue for Atlantic City.[338]

A Trump Taj Mahal poker room manager described the impact of poker on the casino's dealers in the early 1990s:

And no one knew what poker was, no one had any experience in poker. It just was not a game from Atlantic City. So the company put up posters, said anyone who would like to transfer to the poker department may put in their application and then we'll review it.

The Trump Taj Mahal's management imported staff from California to gear up the casino for poker:

And this group came here as management to run the poker room ... Well, they came here, they taught us the game, we opened up the poker room. All the dealers were from EVS, and from housekeeping, from the restaurants, and – they put up posters around, anybody who would like to go to the poker, we're going to give you free training, we're going to give you this, we're going to give you that. So all these people came from all these different departments and went to this free training, in an effort to get a better job. And then that's what happened. The room opened up, and we had all the management from California.[339]

The move towards poker also had something to do with new competition from Foxwoods. The Connecticut casino had recently opened an 8,500 square foot poker room and was holding Wednesday evening poker tournaments. In response, the Taj Mahal's poker room opened at 26,000 square feet, while Showboat, Resorts and others all opened both poker rooms and racetrack simulcasting rooms. Simulcasting never did pay off much for any of the casinos in the 1990s, its annual revenue topping off at just over $2 million from 1997 to 1999 for Bally's, the largest simulcast operation in the city.[340]

Harrah's continued to operate as a successful casino in the marina district and used its Atlantic City success as a platform for expansion around the nation. The business's ability to tap into national gaming demand was directly related to its skill, particularly in the 1980s, in developing a casino product focused almost entirely on middle-market gamblers. Harrah's 1980s success created a model for the company's 1990s expansion and eventual rise as the largest casino gaming firm in the world in the 2000s. By 1993, Promus (Harrah's newly spun-off corporate parent) had casinos operating in New Orleans and was actively developing casinos in Biloxi and Tunica County, Mississippi, Illinois. In addition, Harrah's was looking to expand internationally to Australia and New Zealand and had launched a ten-year plan to dramatically expand nationally and internationally, funded with Atlantic City revenues. In its expansion, Harrah's executives looked back towards the successful 'Better People' marketing campaign it launched in 1985 focusing on customer service and employee morale.[341]

Caesar's was another casino that rebounded from recession well in the early 1990s. In the grand tradition of Atlantic City casinos, Caesar's construction of a new parking garage was major news in an industry where parking availability and convenience had played a key role in earlier successes like Harrah's. Opened in

1990, the new garage featured an overpass over Pacific Avenue and was a massive project that architects adorned with Roman towers at the corners and pediments throughout. Caesar's ballyhooed its new garage, calling it 'Aesthetically unique' and 'Designed to create a unique embellishment to the Atlantic City skyline'. It was an expensive, well-crafted strategy approach to meet Atlantic City's car-driving clientele, but were Roman columns on a parking garage enough to bring in new customers? [342] Probably not – so Caesar's tied the garage opening to a major new initiative with slot machines, designed to emphasize its Atlantic City reputation for the higher end of the gambling market. Caesar's went after 'dollar and premium slot players' via direct marketing campaigns in lieu of bus programs. The $44 million garage was integral to a new marketing program, according to Caesar's World chairman Henry Gluck in 1991, along with the overall health of the industry. Guck emphasized his support for twenty-four-hour gaming and the expansion of the casino floor space allotted for slot machines. Caesar's rebound from the 1990 crisis was significant in 1991 and 1992. The garage investment appeared to be paying off as total revenue for the casino increased by 5.1 per cent in 1991 (the industry average was -0.1 per cent) and 6.4 per cent in 1992 (industry average was 7.2 per cent).[343]

The Showboat casino also rebounded from a difficult period with a shift in marketing that focused on increasing slots revenue to improve its bottom line. Showboat's management tried to emulate its Las Vegas formula when it opened in 1987 by creating a casino and bowling centre that would specifically appeal to casino employees as a revenue generator. But the bowling centre was a casualty of the city's dysfunction, because unlike Showboat's Vegas employees, the Atlantic City workers wanted to go home to their suburban bedroom communities as soon as they left their shifts, not being permitted to gamble in the city. Showboat shut down the bowling alley after a few years, caught the slots fever in the early 1990s and turned around its declining casino revenue growth dramatically by 1992, when its casino revenue rose to $258.6 million from $239.8 million in 1991. In addition, Showboat unveiled a $53 million expansion to follow the Taj's lead with a themed casino, with the casino floor and entire property recreated to represent a never-ending New Orleans Mardi Gras celebration. Showboat's revenue growth rebounded from consecutive years of 3–4 per cent revenue decline (1990 and 1991) to a 7.8 per cent increase in 1992, beginning a long run that at one point would top off at a 15.5 per cent revenue increase in 1995 (post-expansion), the second highest growth rate increase recorded by any Atlantic City casino in the 1990s. Similar to the Trump operations, key management decisions made a big difference. For Showboat, the crucial decision was to decrease the slots 'hold' (percent of gamblers' money held by the casino) from about 13 per cent to about 9 per cent. In 1992, the casino's slot machine 'win' growth rate jumped to 12.7 per cent over 5.3 per cent from the previous year and its slots revenue of $185.1 million was approximately 72 per cent of its total casino 'win', well over the 65.7

per cent industry average. CEO Frank Modica explained Showboat's strategy for slots success by noting the importance of making customers feel gratified and of not putting them off too quickly with massive losses. It was a simple philosophy, but vital to the early 1990s transformation in Atlantic City:

> When they go to a casino where their money lasts only half as long, they don't think about percentages. They just know they don't like the place, that they don't feel lucky there.[344]

The recovery of the early 1990s took place as the casinos took advantage of deregulation and made important strategic decisions. The industry also benefited from successful confluence of political compromise, energy and will that led to the beginning of construction on a new convention centre, after years of planning and political wrangling that had stalled the project for a decade. State and local governments and CRDA finally reached a deal to begin work on the project, estimated to cost $256 million and to take three years to build. In addition, the deal included the construction of thousands of new casino hotel rooms to be filled by the anticipated convention bookings.[345]

The Convention Center's emergence from blueprints to building really began in the late 1980s when an increasing number of officials and casino people began to perceive it as a solution for the problems of that time. In 1988, the Atlantic City Convention and Visitors Bureau publicly announced the loss of two major union conventions for which Atlantic City had been in the running. National groups of postal workers and firefighters rejected the city for St Louis and Vancouver respectively. Though the reasons for losing these conventions probably went beyond the lack of a convention facility, the loss helped to highlight a relative weakness of the city in the competition for lucrative conventioneers. In late 1988, the Atlantic County Improvement Authority (ACIA) finally settled on a land transaction with Bacharach Village to acquire the last parcel of land at the foot of the Atlantic City Expressway for the Convention Center. The deal culminated a years-long process that included the condemnation of the property and very different estimates of the land's value, similar to the gulf between the different valuations of Great Island, the future site of Atlantic City High School. Yet, rather than battle a casino, this time public officials battled the real estate firm that ran the project and began the process of relocating residents, in a scene to be played out (with some variation) in the North East Inlet neighborhood a year later. Whether it was for a public building, housing project or via real estate speculation, residential reshuffling was an important feature of the casino era in the 1980s.[346]

Land acquisition and clearing was a big step towards construction, but it did almost nothing to solve the biggest obstacle facing the project: its anticipated quarter-billion dollar price tag for completion and estimated $10–20 million annual operations cost. In 1989, the venture's high cost helped make it controversial as the ACIA forged ahead with assistance from Senator Gormley. By mid-1989, Gormley had become the Convention Center's major champion at the state level and it was he who then proposed a legislative package to fund it. The package included a new tax on comps, something the industry adamantly opposed at a time when CANJ president Carver regularly decried the amount of taxes the industry already paid out. Carver spoke sharply for Trump and other executives by claiming that the 'industry has a limit on the amount of new public money it can generate'. He also considered the situation 'ironic', given concern over the casinos' high junk bond debt and called the comps fee 'an additional tax on an industry that is not performing'.[347] Around the same time, a *Casino Journal* article reiterated Carver's position:

> What we've got is yet another tax burden for the already grossly-overtaxed casino industry to fund enormous deficits on a new publicly-funded (with private industry revenues) convention center which many – including us – think is unnecessary in Atlantic City wherever it is built, and absolutely counter-productive where it is proposed'.

The article also pointed out that the city would have over 600,000 square feet of meeting space when the Trump Taj Mahal opened up, more than enough to satisfy demand. *Casino Journal* provided steadfast opposition to the project right up until construction began, repeatedly lamenting it as a 'white elephant', criticizing Gormley for his comp tax proposal and suggesting that the CRDA's $60 million contribution could be better spent elsewhere.[348]

With Florio's election and Perskie's NJCCC appointment, the Convention Center had the important backing it needed for construction to actually begin. In 1991, the the Assembly passed legislation to provide $165 million for the project, to go along with CRDA's commitment. The state's intervention was crucial for the centre to actually get built. Perskie recalled that the project 'only happened when the State of New Jersey, which was the only agency that was going to have the economic and the political muscle to do it, decided to do it'. The state also responded to local inertia by creating a number of new agencies designed to force collaboration with state supervision, including a new 'Atlantic City Convention Center and Visitor's Authority'. Ironically, in 1994, new Governor Christine Todd Whitman presided over the centre's ribbon cutting, despite having opposed state funding for it a few years earlier. James Florio and Steve Perskie, both in attendance, just looked at each other and laughed at the irony of the situation. They were Democratic politicians, who had lost in the state's Republican wave of 1993, but they were on hand to witness a crowning state achievement come to fruition after years of stagnation.[349]

By 1991, resistance to the Convention Center had ebbed as the project attained a certain inevitability. It still presented problems, however, as a potential drain on the casino enterprise, though the prevailing view held that it could only help the industry generate more revenue. In late 1990, Carver acknowledged that despite lots of disagreement, the 'state is determined to build it', but that

> Citywide conventions run in detriment to our business because you can't turn your rooms over the people who are going to make the convention centre work in favour of people who make our casino work.

Carver's argument was basically that conventioneers would be busy convention-eering most of their time, not gambling. As such, they would be taking hotel slots from more serious gamblers, the casinos' preferred visitors for obvious reasons. Mayor Whelan was pivotal in bringing in CRDA support for the project – an approach based on assisting the casino community and emulating Las Vegas via public investment, rather than reacting against it. Whelan's stance echoed that of others like Steve Wynn, who had been saying something similar for years. The casino crisis of the late 1980s and early 1990s had clearly shifted opinion on this point, and Las Vegas had become a positive model of growth and public-private synchronicity. It was no longer perceived of as an organized crime haven, as had often been the case during the casino legalization debate of the seventies. Las Vegas's success was Atlantic City's new ideal, certified by the mayor in 1990, when he noted that the

> Mirage has 3000 hotel rooms, and now there's the Excalibur and other major expansions. With those two investments of convention centre and the airport, they were there so that when the economy was ready – bang! – they were ready for the explosion.

However, others within the community voiced support for the Convention Center as momentum for it picked up, including Local 54 president Roy Silbert. In a rare appearance on the pages of *Casino Journal*, the union leader called it a pressing concern for the health of the community. By contrast, only two of five casino executives interviewed at the same time as Silbert also voiced support for the Convention Center.[350]

Within a year of the deal to secure its funding, the Convention Center spurred major casino expansion. Soon, many of the casinos would follow the Trump lead by adding casino floor space quickly, with a commitment to increased hotel capacity in the future, in an ingenious way around the original *CCA* restrictions. In 1992, Caesar's, TropWorld, Showboat, and Harrah's all announced hotel expansion plans, this time with a new feature: CRDA funding. Having achieved some success with state deregulation, the casinos now sought a change in the CRDA's use of their proceeds, so that the agency would more directly support the industry through city improvements and casino projects, as opposed to housing. To some extent, new CRDA chief Nick Amato was on board. For Amato, 'Housing, in and of itself', was not satisfactory as CRDA also needed to 'create an atmosphere that makes the business community happy'. In 1992, the consensus solution was to steer money towards new hotel projects that would allow the casinos to also expand operations. Meanwhile, a regulatory change gave the industry a voting slot on CRDA, in addition to allowing more local input. In 1993, the Commission added to the momentum for expansion when it allowed casinos to increase their casino square footage beyond the *CCA*-mandated 60,000 square feet by planning new hotel rooms, ostensibly for the purposes of accommodating the influx of visitors once the centre opened.[351] Pursuing this retooled strategy, by 1996 CRDA contributed $175 million to an industry-wide $1.54 billion expansion that added sparkling new hotel towers at the Tropicana, Caesar's, Resorts, Trump Plaza, Harrah's and Showboat and new rooms at a number of others. Virtually all of the casinos took advantage of CRDA'a money, combined with the allowance for casino floor expansion, to grow larger in the 1990s.[352]

The CRDA's shift in emphasis also led to new casino support for the Convention Center. Bally's CEO Richard Gillman succinctly summarized the new mood:

> We now have to find a way to build non-casino rooms. We have to clean up the city.

Donald Trump also welcomed the new CRDA focus, and was clear on his distaste for CRDA's former priorities:

> Those funds have been wasted over the past ten years. Those funds have been absolutely worthless. I mean, they are using them to build low-income housing in an area that already has a tremendous amount of low-income housing.

Instead, Trump wanted more funds for beautification of entrances and other features to attract and maintain visitors to build the casinos' business. It was a less direct way to support the workforce – not by providing affordable housing – but by strengthening the industry that employed the workers. Though the CRDA did not give up its housing mission, it was moving in this direction with major investments in city beautification. In 1992, CRDA committed $78 million to the 'Corridor' a proposed three-square entertainment and shopping region linking the Convention Center to the Boardwalk with an elevated walkway, shops and restaurants. CRDA also funded a 'gateway' lighthouse plaza at the foot of the Atlantic City Expressway and the refurbishment of Gardner's Basin, including the construction of a new aquarium.[353]

On paper, the Corridor project was magnificent, as envisioned by its proposed developer. The Maryland-based Rouse Company had previously redeveloped Baltimore's Inner Harbor, and in 1993, CRDA chose it to create the 'Corridor'. The proposal included a link from the Boardwalk to the Convention Center and included man-made lagoons, waterside pavilions with trees, stores and restaurants abound, parks and other entertainment venues. It would also include a sixty-foot lighthouse tower with a park and fountain to go at the beginning of a new 'Grand Boulevard' to begin at the foot of the Atlantic City Expressway. The 1993 news of a Convention Center and Corridor also drew positive national press for Atlantic City, perceived in a *USA Today* article as beginning a major transformation on par with Baltimore's Inner Harbor. CRDA alone committed $70 million, in part to come from a new $2 parking fee. The proposal, however, along with an anchor non-casino hotel for the Convention Center, was estimated to cost $350 million – well over the Convention Center's expected cost.[354] A poster depicting the Corridor called it 'The Gateway to Economic Prosperity' and celebrated the project as a CRDA achievement, championing the agency as 'one of the most unique public agencies for urban redevelopment ever created by government'.[355]

But was it all too much? Through 1993, *Casino Journal* editors continued to lament the costly Convention Center and now opposed the new parking fee for the Corridor project along with a new hotel room tax implemented to support the new projects. As in the 1980s, a state legislature 'mired in provincialism' became a target for not going far enough in supporting the casino industry in the face of direct competition from Foxwoods and other potential competitors east of the Mississippi. The legislature also faced criticism for rejecting a public referendum on sports betting in 1993.[356]

In the early 1990s, the casino industry continued to have a significant impact in the suburban townships and communities surrounding Atlantic City. The Commission's 1993 annual report showed a total of $917.9 million spent on goods and services from Atlantic County out of a total of $1.4 billion spent on New Jersey firms. 1,717 Atlantic County firms did business with the casinos in 1993, out of a total 4,093 New Jersey companies that were also casino vendors. Outside of the tremendous job creation that produced over $900 million in annual wages in 1993, the casinos created a tremendous amount of volume in local business from car dealers to florists to cleaners and food providers. In 1989, approximately 72 per cent of 43,250 casino employees also lived in either Atlantic City or Atlantic County at this time, again indicating the significant impact of the casinos on the local economy. In 1989 alone, the industry generated $3 billion in expenditures throughout southern New Jersey, with 80 per cent of this money spent in Atlantic County.[357]

The economic impacts were felt most strongly in the bedroom communities around Atlantic County. The county's population grew by 15.6 per cent to 224,327 between 1980 and 1990, and kept increasing into the early 1990s. While Atlantic City actually lost population (7.3 per cent) in the 1980s, Atlantic County's population growth rate tripled that of New Jersey, with the larger municipalities like Egg Harbor Township, Galloway and Hamilton adding thousands. The population of Galloway township increased by 91.6 per cent in the 1980s and Hamilton's rose by 68.6 per cent. The county's growth focused especially on a few townships due to restrictions on development in the Pinelands. Early in the casino era, community planners working with the Pinelands Commission designated certain places 'Regional Growth Areas'. Consequently, these townships grew at a much more accelerated rate in ensuing years. By 1991, new housing construction in Atlantic Count slowed a little from the torrid pace of the 1980s, slipping to a low of approximately 500 permits in 1992, compared to 3,971 new permits in 1987. Despite the growth, Regional Growth Area townships continued to experience a steady wave of development in the early 1990s, with the big three (Hamilton, Galloway and Egg Harbor Township) accounting for over 60 per cent of new homes.[358]

By the early 1990s, the regional economic impact of the casino industry was clear throughout Atlantic County. In Absecon township (adjacent to Atlantic City), job growth increased by 20 per cent in 1990, with 4,958 jobs, though this total fell down to 4,041 in 1992. Yet, Absecon's population only increased 1.5 per cent in the same period. In a 1993 report, Absecon planners were cautiously optimistic about the future, noting that 'the regional economy is intimately linked to the casino industry' and that future 'growth in Atlantic County will be dependent on the successful expansion of the Convention Center'. Absecon planners had good reason to think positively about the industry's power to effect economic change, with a wealth of new jobs created and an average household income having risen quickly over a decade, though it still lagged behind the state average. In 1989 Atlantic County's average income was $41,448 compare to New Jersey's $52,241. The local unemployment rate remained higher than the state average as well in the early 1990s, hovering around 8.3 per cent compared to New Jersey's 6.8 per cent, a smaller discrepancy (by 0.3 per cent) than 1980. Absecon planners attributed the higher unemployment to 'seasonal influences' and pointed out that the rate of private sector job growth between 1981 and 1990 was 45.9 per cent in Atlantic County – more than double the state's rate of 21.1 per cent.[359] For many young people growing up in the Atlantic City suburbs, the casinos had become an income magnet by the early 1990s. Nanette Stuart, who worked as a Pleasantville guidance counselor recalled that 'a lot of students would say that they were going to go to school and college, but in actuality, they ended up working at the casino'.[360]

By 1991, the considerable growth in the suburbs had become a key point of pride for casino boosters such as the Greater Atlantic City Chamber of Commerce. The Chamber reported on the incredible regional impact on the industry – an estimated $6.5 billion in total expenditures and $1 billion in direct wages and salaries paid to the 73 per cent of the casino workforce that lived in Atlantic County. Major suburban projects attributed to this casino wealth effect included the Hamilton Mall (1,500 jobs) and the Atlantic City International Airport expansion (phase I – $59 million). Meanwhile, county real estate valuations increased 758 per cent between 1976 and 1991, with the cumulative county real estate total at approximately $16 billion in 1991, compared to $1.8 billion in 1976. Self-serving as it might have been ('For All We Do – The Winner is … You!'), the Chamber's brochure accurately reflected the massive economic impact of the industry on the region at this point.[361]

Yet, as business and job prospects surged, so did traffic problems in Atlantic County. Between 1978 and 1993, the number of cars tracked on White Horse Pike (Rt. 30) and Delilah Road in Egg Harbor Township approximately doubled, from 12,327,000 in 1978 to 24,966,000 in 1993. In 2005, Egg Harbor Township's mayor commented on the increased traffic:

> People who are used to getting around the mainland quickly no longer can get around as quickly as they'd like to. People are sitting through two or three lights, starting to feel the impact of it.

In second phase maturity, the casino era branched out well into the county and beyond, creating business opportunity yet also changing the lives of county residents. Their once sleepy three-month resort community had become a noisy, busy booming place by the early 1990s. Economic opportunities were everywhere, as were the social costs of the industry, such as congestion. By 1993, the casino industry accounted for approximately 75 per cent of the county's entire economy.[362]

As 1994 began, there was good justification for casino optimism. The major regulatory obstacles of the casino era's early years were gone and the industry had got through a significant crisis caused by the economic stagnation and market saturation that came together to hurt the industry from 1988 and 1991. The economy was now on an upswing and casino investors like Steve Wynn were beginning to reassess their negative judgments of the late 1980s about the industry's prospects. Yet, in 1993 casino revenue growth also slowed to an average 1.3 per cent, down from the rebound 7.2 per cent growth in 1992. The decreased growth reflected Foxwoods' success in the northeastern gaming market, but also assured that the new competition-inspired state attitude towards the casinos would continue into the 1990s with positive effect. Meanwhile, slot machine profits grew at a 4.8 per cent rate in 1993 despite the overall slowdown in total revenues. Only a few years removed from multiple casino bankruptcies and the Trump Taj Mahal crisis, the casino industry was much better poised to face competition in the rapidly developing American casino era.[363]

5 CASINO MAGNETS: NEW IMMIGRANTS AND ATLANTIC CITY OPPORTUNITY

Hurricane Katrina devastated much of the northern Gulf of Mexico coast in August 2005, including the casino city of Biloxi, Mississippi. A few days after the hurricane, city residents were still struggling with devastation but a few small businesses began to reopen. One of these was the International Food Mart, owned by Imelda Duvane. The store catered to Filipino casino workers and featured items such as sardines in tomato sauce, coconut gel and duck eggs dyed fuchsia, supposedly good for the libido. Like Atlantic City, Biloxi's casinos had attracted a diverse set of employees who established their own unique communities amidst the golden economic opportunities.[364]

By the late 1990s, the ethnic communities and diverse residents of greater Atlantic City were not exactly out of the sight lines of casino visitors. Collectively, immigrants had become a major force in the labour-intensive casino industry of Atlantic City; by then, they predominated as table dealers, slot machine attendants, cashiers, valets, waiters, busboys, cleaners, cooks and room service attendants. Yet, ethnic diversity and global sensibility were hardly associated with Atlantic City. Most casino customers hardly noticed who was cashing their slots vouchers or bringing them drinks to accompany their buffet meals, though some may have noticed the increasing numbers of immigrants working in the casinos or in the stores alongside Atlantic Avenue. The immigrants who populated the casino industry in Atlantic City were hidden in plain sight from the millions of casino patrons, yet they contributed powerfully to the remaking of the old resort town into a dynamic, diverse and thriving American casino community.

The new immigration of Atlantic City's casino era actually replicated the earlier experience of earlier generations in the region. Between 1880 and 1920, there was a strong wave of immigration to the city and, by the early twentieth century, it was extensively populated by foreign immigrants: Jewish, Italian and Irish primarily. By about 1910, the Ducktown neighbourhood (around Atlantic and Arctic Avenues in the middle part of the city) had become an immigrant enclave for multitudes of Italians who migrated to the region. They came after a 1906 strike in which black hotel waiters tried to gain higher pay but ended up with no jobs, finding themselves themselves blacklisted. In the span of a few decades, the area became an Italian cultural enclave, complete with festivals and thousands of summer visitors from south Philadelphia. Soon, much of the city was thick with working-class immigrants and their familiar ethnic businesses. There were Italian delis selling cappicola hoagies in Ducktown, kosher markets in the south Inlet appealing to Jewish migrants, and pubs and local restaurants everywhere. Like the immigrants of the casino era, the previous immigrants often came to Atlantic City after making a go at American life elsewhere, but they found the resort town a better place to work and forge comfortably familiar communities. Many of the Irish became involved in construction after building one of the main nineteenth-century railroads, connecting Atlantic City to New York and Philadelphia. Between 1920 and 1950, a huge influx of African-Americans came to town, creating the predominately black 'Northside' neighbourhood beyond Atlantic Avenue, with Adriatic and Arctic avenues running through it. They lived in a culture of deep segregation and municipal neglect as city officials focused mainly below Atlantic Avenue with pools, parks, development, and planning. Yet, like the earlier European migrants and the casino era immigrants, they developed a vibrant and close-knit society within the region.[365]

By the beginning of the casino era, the communities created earlier in the twentieth century were largely gone. The city's tourism lifeline had long since frayed as the grand Boardwalk hotels had collapsed. Most of the older immigrant families decamped to the suburbs and young people with prospects left the region for opportunity. Ducktown remained an Italian community, but, from the 1960s, began to close itself off from years of decay and the increasing social anxiety that came with higher crime and poverty. As historian Bryant Simon noted,

> Atlantic City stopped being a place where people lived their lives on the street and on their porches. Many families retreated behind lace curtains, barred windows, and double-locked doors, and then out to the suburbs.[366]

By 1981 (three years into the casino era), the once-diverse and thriving neighbourhoods around the Inlet had deteriorated into depressing slums, with much of the land empty and some of it controlled by casino speculators. The Latino population of the southeast Inlet was mainly poor, but was often employed in kitchen jobs in the new casinos. Meanwhile, plans to create a 'Spanish commercial district' along Atlantic Avenue fell apart when the city's interest faded and the Department of Housing and Urban Development did not come through with a $30 million grant for the project. William DeJesus, director of the Latin Organization of Atlantic City blamed the casinos for his community's plight, and commented to a reporter that

We believe in God, not gold. This fight is God against the casinos. If God wants us here, the casinos will have to look for more money to get us.[367]

While DeJesus's concern for Atlantic City's Latino community made sense, his blame was misplaced. Actually, the casinos came in and provided work for local residents, albeit with overly strict requirements (see previous chapters). The new jobs made a significant difference, according to J. David Alcantara, a Latino community leader, who recalled the early casino era:

> With only a high school degree, you can get a job as a casino dealer, at that time, full-time. Now it's only part-time, for the most part, with no medical coverage until three months, I think. And you could end up, in that time, making $30,000 a year. Now that's 1979, 1980. Thirty-thousand dollars then was like $50,000, $60,000 now. And you could live very well on that. You could live very well on that. And a lot of people did very well that way.[368]

People began migrating to the Atlantic City region in the early 1980s from all around the world to realize their versions of the American dream by working in the new casinos. By the beginning of the twenty-first century, the communities they had built had changed the culture of Atlantic City and southern New Jersey by infusing the region with ethnic folkways from around the world, but especially east Asia, south Asia, South and Central America. On the surface, Atlantic City's new immigrant communities appeared very similar to other American immigrant communities, such as those one might find in Queens (New York City), Los Angeles, Montgomery County, Maryland or Miami, Florida. Yet, what made the casino community an exceptional place for immigrants to settle and thrive was relatively simple: the casinos offered stable employment with excellent medical benefits, regardless of English language ability.

In the early 1990s, the increasing diversity of the region (city and county) became important local news. A 1991 *Atlantic City Press* article suggested that people were coming from various east Asian countries for economic opportunities related to the casinos: as Taiwanese-American Jimmy Yin said, 'I saw the gambling; I saw I could do some business'. The *Press* also reported on the burgeoning number of small operations such as dry cleaners and restaurants spawned by casino business. It commented on the strong family connections that immigrants to Atlantic City (and elsewhere) established –spouses, children, siblings coming to join networks of families and friends.[369] This continued a pattern of network building established earlier in the region, during the first few years of casino operations in Atlantic City.[370]

In 1993, another reporter wrote about

> a new wave of immigrants from lands far and wide with cultures as diverse as their language who are peppering the city with an exotic spice and flair

– making their mark on its history and changing its schools, businesses and neighborhoods.

By then, the Atlantic City public schools included students who spoke thirty-five different native languages and were increasing enrollment in English-as-a-second-language classes by about 17 per cent per year. School enrollment figures for Vietnamese, Polish and Hispanic students all increased significantly in the early 1990s, as did the ethnic diversity of private schools, such as Our Lady of the Star of the Sea Catholic school. One community professional noted that

> A lot come for the casino industry ... It's the land of opportunity, to get ahead, get a job, make some money.[371]

In a 2003 interview, Atlantic City priest Joseph Pham discussed the attraction of the casino community for his congregants:

> the casino environment down here ... advantage down here have good pay for them, don't need to go to college get a degree but still get higher pay down here, no experience, no degrees, have higher pay [that is] why most Vietnamese are here.[372]

For many immigrants, the casino community contrasted sharply with other areas of the country that offered less reliable employment, usually without benefits. Consequently, Atlantic City became very attractive to immigrants already working difficult jobs for low pay, and for immigrants around the world seeking a new life in the US. Pham elaborated:

> old people, they don't speak any word of English, but they still can have a job down here. They can't find a job anywhere else except down here, the casino. They can be a janitor. They don't have to speak English ... they have medical benefits in the casino. People speak English can be dealers, people who don't speak English can do another job, like housekeeping ... so that's why. Because you know, really, they hire everyone. It doesn't matter, speak English well or not speak English well, they still have position for these people.[373]

Family connections were crucial to the construction of new immigrant communities in Atlantic City's casino era. In a 2002 interview, Hasumati Patel (originally from Gujarat, India) noted that she left New York for Atlantic City in 1999 in part because 'one cousin and two brothers are here'.[374] Another Indian immigrant came to Atlantic City in 1995 mainly to live with his daughter and her family, who ran a small grocery.[375] Pham remarked that in the early 1990s, the few existing Vietnamese families tried hard to 'to build a community' and 'called whoever they knew' to come to the region for the casino opportunities.[376] A major motivation for the family outreach may have been the employee shortage faced by the casino industry in 1990 with the opening of the Trump Taj Mahal (see Chapter 4).

These family outreach efforts worked very well. Beginning in the early 1990s, immigrants flooded into Atlantic City for the economic promise that seemed to emanate. In 2003, community social worker Marta Lopez suggested that Latinos began coming to Atlantic City 'from many places because they know casinos pay a good salary'. Lopez continued: 'here they [are] starting with a good salary'.[377]

The casinos offered improved chances for an economically prosperous, and self-sufficient American life, apparently more accessible to newcomers of limited skills and means there than in other places. A Haitian casino employee, Jean Baptiste Noel, reiterated this point:

> [The] good part in Atlantic City is when you find a job ... since you got a job ... you can take care of yourself, so you can be out of trouble you can buy anything you want ... you can do anything that you want since you have a job ... you can do your own way the way you want to.[378]

Similarly, a Nicaraguan interview subject reported that he moved to Atlantic City from Miami in 1988. Though employed near Miami in a packaging factory, he migrated to the casino community on the advice of a friend who said 'come [to] Atlantic City: Atlantic City a lot of work more pay'. His response was simple and direct: 'OK, I go'.[379] One Cambodian-American business owner (and former casino dealer) remembered that when she came to the region in the early 1980s, she found it 'easier finding a job than other cities and [she could] make more money than other cities with casino work'.[380]

Along with better wages came substantial benefits. In the absence of comprehensive government assistance, health care became very expensive for immigrants without reliable government support or an employer to pay for it. In conjunction with Local 54, the casinos provided jobs that often included benefits such as health insurance, despite a lack of English proficiency. A Haitian immigrant pointed out that

> life in Atlantic City is not an easy life it is a good life & I like it, life is expensive. If ... I don't have insurance and the medication for me can cost me $100 for only one medication.[381]

A Bangladeshi-American casino worker suggested that the health care provided to the casino employees

> is good because [this is a] union job everybody has insurance health care plan.[382]

Both the Latino and Asian populations of Atlantic City and County grew at a terrific pace in the 1980s and 1990s. Between 1990 and 2000 the proportion of city residents with Asian backgrounds more than doubled to 4,237, or 10.5 per cent of Atlantic City's population, up from 978, or approximately 1 per cent of the city's population in 1980. Atlantic City's Latino population also increased dramatically in the casino era, growing from 15.3 per cent to 24.9 per cent of the city's population between 1990 and 2000.[383]

Closer scrutiny of the population data showed that specific ethnic communities grew dramatically in the 1990s. For example, the 1990 census for Atlantic County listed 736 Vietnamese residents compared to 2,248 Vietnamese residents in 2000: an increase of 205 per cent. Likewise, the number of Asian Indian residents increased from 753 to 3,371 in the same span, a 348 per cent rise. Another remarkable gain took shape in the census category of 'Other Hispanic or Latino', which would include those from Central America, South America and the Caribbean. The 1990 census showed an increase of 176 per cent of people from these regions, almost double the overall increase of Latinos in Atlantic County. These census data indicate that more than one in three (over 35 per cent) living in Atlantic City identified themselves as Asian, Pacific Islander or Latino in the 2000 census. In the late 1990s, Atlantic County planners projected the Latino population to keep growing, to the extent that Latinos would make up by approximately 16 per cent of the population by 2010.[384]

The casinos were powerful engines of economic sustenance for the immigrants of Atlantic City. A 1998 study showed that casino employees were disproportionately immigrants, as reflected in Atlantic County census data. Asian and Pacific Islander employees made up 13.3 per cent of total casino employment, while Hispanic employees amounted to 17.4 per cent of the total. Both these numbers were significantly higher than the proportion of these groups in Atlantic County (5.1 per cent and 12.2 per cent respectively). In particular, the numbers demonstrated a substantial reliance on Asian employees for the casinos. This trend just continued into the 2000s. In 2005, approximately 50 per cent of the Trump Taj Mahal's poker dealers were immigrants, according to the Taj's poker room manager.[385]

The data clearly demonstrate the significantly higher profile and presence of both Asians and Latinos in Atlantic City in recent years and also reflect the extent to which the casinos valued immigrant employees. In 1991, the Sands sent recruiters to Little Havana in Miami to find employees for its back-of-the-room positions. One Colombian immigrant and then-Miami resident found employment via the Sands's recruitment office in Miami after working there as an airport courier and (formerly) a merchant marine operating out of Venezuela. The Sands put him up in a hotel for fifteen days and helped him find an apartment as he settled in to Atlantic City. Eventually, he worked as a waiter at Sands's Brighton Steak House before moving on to Resorts and the Taj Mahal.[386] By the mid-1990s, casino executives had begun to prize immigrant employees from Asia and to some extent, mountainous areas of South America for their strong work ethic.

Executives also perceived certain advantages to hiring immigrants such as lower salary requirements and a willingness to work long hard hours: they complained less and seemed more appreciative for the work. Also cited was the notion that many immigrant employees lived in extended families and therefore had fewer childcare needs.[387]

In 2005, a long-time Atlantic City resident recalled how the casinos spurred familial expansion in the Latino community:

> And it's one of the reasons why the Latino community grew, because once you give enough [jobs], they'll invite their friends, relatives, cousins, brothers and other people to come to the Atlantic City area to live.[388]

In 1993 Dominican immigrant Limbert Reynosa reported success finding a job and a suitable apartment in Atlantic City, allowing him bring his family to stay, after a three-month search period in which he stayed with his wife's relatives. Reynosa's dream included a rise from poverty and his hopeless prospects in Santo Domingo.

Within the greater casino community, numerous ethnic communities emerged and thrived by offering support to newcomers and assistance once fellow countrymen have arrived in the region. By 2003, this migration had transformed particular neighbourhoods in a dramatic fashion, and led to new and enlightening encounters between the old and new residents. One neighbourhood called Lower Chelsea became the epicentre of the new wave of immigrants, though their influx caused some fear amongst earlier residents:

> My neighbors just on my block are Indian, Pakistani, Vietnamese, Chinese, Asian, Spanish, German, Italian. Our biggest problem ... we went house to house, because people were starting to just get locked in, some of the older, German families and the Italian families. People are also afraid of what they don't understand.[389]

The increasing numbers of Asian immigrants in the community paralleled a casino outreach initiative towards Asian customers. By the mid-1990s, the casinos had many bus programmes in place to bring in Chinese-Americans and other immigrants from New York. At one point, Bally's Grand officials estimated that 80 per cent of their customers from midnight to 8:00 a.m. were of Asian descent.

Other casinos appealed to this niche by offering shows, festivals and restaurants specifically geared towards their Chinese and Vietnamese-American patrons. Anecdotal evidence from the casino floor suggested that the casinos' Asian gamblers also preferred Asian dealers at the tables. To meet the late-night Asian-American gamblers' demand, casinos like Bally's Grand also brought in new Chinese and Korean hosts and hostesses. They also offered more games for this new clientele, including Pai Gow Poker, baccarat and mini-baccarat and re-arranged floor plans. In 1998, a *Press* reporter walked into a laundromat on Chelsea's main drag, Ventnor Avenue, and reported the following survey of patrons by the patron, an African-American : 'Where are you from?' 'Vietnam' 'Peru' 'India' 'El Salvador'.[390]

The brief exchange above summarizes well the cultural tone of Lower Chelsea by the late 1990s. The immigrants came for opportunity, to find their American dream, and unexpectedly brought Atlantic City an international, cosmopolitan quality. In Chelsea Heights (across the Albany Avenue bridge), long-time residents noticed the changes in their neighbourhood, formerly known as 'Chelsea Whites' – a name that simply did not apply in the late 1990s following the influx of new immigrants.[391] An essay in the 1999 Atlantic City High School yearbook observed that

> looking closely at groups of friends having fun at a social event, you can see just how diverse ACHS really is. One group was made up of Chinese, Indian, Vietnamese, Puerto Rican, Caucasian, African American and Pakistani – all friends and all blind to the old stereotype that they should not be friends.[392]

By the late 1990s, new immigrants had transformed whole neighbourhoods of Atlantic City. In Chelsea and Lower Chelsea (adjacent to Ventnor), the streets were lively with Asian-owned stores and businesses catering to a community growing with every census projection. Many of the new businesses were Vietnamese-owned, and included a wide variety of boutiques and services geared to Chinese, Vietnamese and Cambodian customers. Meanwhile, Asian-Americans continued to find satisfactory jobs in the casinos, as reported by thirty-three-year old Vietnamese immigrant Chung Nguyen. In a 1997 interview, Nguyen pointed out that he had 'a good job with good benefits' and that of his friends, 'Some are undereducated and lack skills, but they still have a job in a casino and can make good money'. Similarly, fifty-seven-year-old Lisa Lin in 2001 reported success after coming to Atlantic City from Taiwan in 1983. At first she struggled to learn English while working under poor conditions at a Chinese restaurant. But she took classes to learn English and eventually found a job at the Tropicana Casino, where she eventually rose to become pit manager of Asian games (Pai Gow poker, etc.).[393]

Lin's upwardly mobile casino career represented a common experience. A community social worker detailed this phenomenon:

> know many who start working as housekeeping and now are doing dealer. As soon as they learn English [they] go to casino school and become dealers ... make like 500–600 a week so many people do that, many Hispanics dealing.[394]

The move from an entry-level position to a dealer job became a common way of rising in the casino industry, and a typical path taken by many Asian and Latino immigrants. Indian immigrant Chhitubhai Patel spoke of the need to 'use your brain' once in the casino to advance into positions as slot attendants or dealers, better jobs possible with a combination of experience and English language skills. Patel also had an Indian acquaintance who advanced to a desk-bound computer job from an entry-level floor position at sixty-five, using skills he developed while working at the casino.[395] Conversely, the relative stability of an entry-level position without the need for adequate English or much room for upward mobility also proved attractive to at least one oral history narrator, Hasmati Patel, who commented that 'my job is not tension'. Patel's job as public area janitor was easy to complete and walk away from, something she appreciated.[396]

Another fairly commonplace path involved the establishment of small businesses after beginning in the casinos. Such was the odyssey of Hai-Lee Lim, a Cambodian native who arrived in Atlantic City via New York City. With little professional or technological skills, he took an entry-level job at the Golden Nugget in the early 1980s, but quickly trained to be a dealer and earned his gaming licence. From savings gained from that job, he opened a store specializing in Asian foods. Lim's experience was similar to that of many Asian-Americans between 1984 and 1988, who advanced quickly from entry-level jobs in cleaning or food service, and then moved to higher-paying jobs on the casino floor. An Indian-American commented that many Indians he knew worked in the casino to save money to enter the hotel business, a practice especially popular with the Patel community in the US.[397] Immigrant casino workers often used savings from those jobs in addition to family networks to build stable businesses. Such was the case for one beauty salon owner of Dominican and Haitian descent. Mayra Momperousse, who opened her salon on lower Atlantic Avenue in the heart of the city's immigrant community, just a block north of the sprawling Tropicana casino and retail complex. She moved from New York in the mid-1990s to connect with her mother, brother and sister. Each of them had stable casino jobs, such as cleaner in the Showboat casino and dealer at the Sands. From there, she worked in a salon until able to utilize savings and family support to open her own salon in 2001. It thrived and by 2005 she enjoyed the ethnic mix of her neighbourhood, along with the steady clientele of casino employees.[398]

The language barrier faced by immigrants traditionally seeking to succeed in the US was not a huge problem in the casino community. Firstly, the casinos were willing to hire non-English speakers for many jobs, including cleaners, kitchen workers and food attendants, and secondly, there were opportunities to learn English at work. A Bangladeshi immigrant pointed out that

> if I speak good English if then I can get a better job, a cashier or something like this. If I speak not good English, then I can get some kind of job like dishwasher or cleaning the room.[399]

English skills acquired in India as students helped an Indian-American couple move directly into jobs as Bally's cashiers after coming from India to Atlantic City in 2002.[400] The casinos assisted non-English speaking employees by offering classes in English-as-a-Second Language, and by paying them hourly wages to take the courses. Indian-American Chhitubhai Patel took one of these classes early in his casino career at the Tropicana and described the experience in 2002:

> You go to ESL class, casino give ESL class ... On job you go there. I go to ESL class, $6.50 pay for 1 hour, for ESL class.[401]

All casino employees and others interviewed for this study highlighted health insurance as an important factor in the positive assessment of the casino jobs in Atlantic City.[402] One housekeeping employee drew a sharp contrast between casino and non-casino jobs based solely on health insurance:

> more people come in here because here is benefits, medical benefits, insurance, medical insurance – you working in store, in motel: no benefit, therefore because more people work in casino. My wife no working in casino, I am working in casino I have insurance.[403]

The insurance benefits enjoyed by these casino employees had a lot to do with the successful ability of Local 54, the Hotel and Restaurants Employees Union. In 2002, a union official noted that members needed only work a 112-hour month in order to qualify for full benefits that did not require premium payments from union members (though co-pays were sometimes required). This contrasted with non-union employees (such as dealers) who paid partial premiums via their paychecks. In response to a question about health care, Honduras native Carlos Flores noted that his health care was 'very good because of Local 54'.[404]

Local 54 also developed programmes to assist members with immigration forms and casino licence applications. At the beginning of the twenty-first century, Local 54 created two additional member services' positions specifically to help the flood of Asian and Latino immigrants coming to work in the casinos. After 2000, the union also became more involved in supporting undocumented immigrants and in manoeuvring through the long and complex processes of naturalization and temporary work permits. These efforts were enhanced as a consequence of stricter enforcement and supervision by federal authorities following the 11 September 2001 terrorist attacks.[405]

In 1998, the NJCCC reported that the casino community's attractiveness to immigrants had become a significant point of pride, although it also cited it as a partial explanation for the continued high rate of unemployment in Atlantic City:

> Although the unemployment rate is lower today than before casinos arrived in Atlantic City, it remains high due, in part, to the fact that the large number of jobs has made the Atlantic City a magnet for people seeking employment, particularly from Asian, Central American and South American countries.[406]

One reason for the positive experiences of many immigrants in Atlantic City was underlined by National Gambling Impact Study (NGIS) Commission in 1999. The NGIS commission found that the 'real income' of casino employees in Atlantic City rose while it decreased for service workers in other parts of New Jersey and around the Untied States. In addition, the NGIS group discovered that Atlantic City's casino employees were much more likely to have health insurance for their families than other service workers (by almost twice the rate). The commission rightfully attributed this success to unionization, noting that the predominance of unionized casinos in large 'destination resorts' (i.e. Las Vegas and Atlantic City) led to 'more and better quality jobs' than found in other casinos (i.e. smaller commercial casinos and tribal casinos).[407]

Sometimes, the immigrant experience in Atlantic City involved more hardship, as was the case with Eduardo, a Peruvian accountant and undocumented immigrant who spent a year working as a housekeeper and food runner in two casinos. Eduardo ran into problems in his professional pursuit:

> What I long for is to develop my career, but my English is poor and it requires good English.

He was biding his time before returning to Peru.[408] Another problem that faced immigrants in the casino era was the pull of the casinos themselves: the temptation to gamble away earnings. One Asian-American estimated that as many as 50 per cent of her Asian acquaintances had suffered due to a gambling problem. Another narrator spoke of losing a lot of money, including 150 quarters at one point in the casinos, before he really understood what was happening to him.[409]

The inability of families to maintain continuity and support for children, given the demands of casino employment and parents working different shifts, also caused problems for immigrants who came to Atlantic City. In one observer's words:

> You have a father working one shift, the mother working another shift, there's no adult supervision most of the time. You have children raising children, and it's a cycle.

Another immigrant noted a similar pattern with her customers and acquaintances and lamented herself she time she had missed with her three children over the years, due to the demands of her work (mainly in a store).

Furthermore, inflated housing costs continued to be a problem for some and led to overcrowding, particularly amongst Latino immigrants, with some recalling police action and resistance in severe cases.[410] In the early 1980s, the real estate crisis led to a steep decline in the city's older Hispanic population. As well, promised worker housing units did not become reality for the city until the 1990s when casino investment in affordable urban real estate finally occurred through the state's CRDA.[411] Nevertheless, by the early 2000s, many Asian and Latino immigrants had pushed out into the suburbs, beginning to transform neighbourhoods and shopping centres in towns like Northfield and Pleasantville. By 2004, there were specific real estate agents catering to Latino and Vietnamese clients. They appealed to homebuyers like Idelsa and Jose Rodriquez, immigrants from the Dominican Republic who came to the region from the Bronx and worked for years at Caesar's and the Atlantic City Hilton.[412]

Nowhere is the spirit of renewal and change for American opportunity more evident than in the experience of the thousands of Vietnamese-Americans and other southeast Asians who have come to Atlantic City since the early 1980s. The 'kinship network'-building established during the first few years of casino operations in Atlantic City has continued to the present.[413] One narrator noted that:

> The Vietnamese [are] family oriented, have good opportunity ... for family friends call people around to come down, really have connection, family connection if I know my friend are in Philadelphia Or California, I call over here: 'good opportunity for good job, make higher pay ... that's why every year you see population increase and increase.[414]

Another Vietnamese-American newcomer to Atlantic City described the economic experience in positive terms, as the fulfillment of opportunity for people who otherwise had little. A lower-rung casino job may have only paid $30,000 annually in 2005, but the fringe benefits made it a good deal for thousands of immigrants. In an age of astronomical medical costs, this was crucial for the successful relationship between the immigrant workforce and the casino industry. A narrator pointed out that

> you go to the hospital once, and you owe for the rest of your life perhaps. Or you can spend $20,000, $30,000 for a two-day hospital stay. No problem. See? And that's where your saving all these years goes. But with these benefits, it is really a benefit. There is 401K matching plans. It's really amazing here, what the casinos give and offer to their employees.[415]

In part, the Vietnamese coming to Atlantic City looked towards family for support in the migration process. Family connections were even more important for latter arrivals who did not have the same benefits as war refugees of the 1970s and 1980s, like the Orderly Departure Program (1979) and the Humanitarian Operation Program (1989).[416] A Cambodian-American explained:

> Most of them right now, they have their family. Their relatives sponsor them. And then since they came, right now the city don't help them, like the welfare, any more. And they have to find their own job ... Not like before, I came and I came like a refugee. So the government, they support you, give you some welfare or something like that. Help you to find a job. They had somebody to come to help you. But right now only your relative [needs] to sponsor you and they respond for your relative, the family ... and they don't depend on the government anymore. You can't depend on that anymore.[417]

Another narrator spoke of the Vietnamese community in Atlantic City as a means for support

> There is no formal association here. Vietnamese people, when they come here, money's very important for their livelihood. So they need to get employment right away. And a lot of time the language is the barrier.[418]

The Vietnamese community grew vibrant and active in the 1990s. By the beginning of the 2000s, there were numerous salons, food markets and video stores that were run by and appealed specifically to these immigrants. A walk through Chelsea brought out the flavour of this community, as did a visit to the parish of Our Lady Star of the Sea Church, a church with three distinct masses every Sunday: in Spanish, Vietnamese and English. The Vietnamese-American casino community was organized around hard work and the economic chances afforded by the casino industry. Families' divergent schedules, that rarely allowed both parents the opportunity to remain home with the children, had the consequence of limiting recreational opportunities, as one narrator explained:

> And because of the environment here – the casino opens 24 hours a day, seven days a week. And holidays, it's demanded that they work. Really, they have to work the holidays, and that makes it very, very difficult for family life. The family dynamic is not there. The nurturing, the policing of the children. The child does whatever he or she wants, because the parent's not there. The parent goes to work and comes home and want to go to sleep because they're tired.[419]

In 2005, an immigrant discussed the desire to create a more cohesive Vietnamese-American community in greater Atlantic City:

> And right now, I mean, Atlantic City, they got the open forum in the Vietnam community, but because right now we don't have a strong people, I mean, do about leaders right now. I think that in the future they have an open forum for the Vietnam community in Atlantic City. So we have a window of why

talking about it and the community in Atlantic City. We do ... what we call the working in the casino different time take off, some day take off, we cannot make total attempt. That's very, very hard to make a good community in here. But when we have – I think that we are, I mean, love of my country, love of my community, and we are support for somebody if they have a time and make the good community with them in the city right now. And the city has been very, very happy about it, make a Vietnam community right now.[420]

The Vietnamese community had a strong will to come together in the casino era, to create a new regional identity for Atlantic City. Yet, there were also particular difficulties inherent in that prospect due to the casino environment. For many of the immigrants, establishing a local community was difficult due to the labour demands of the casinos, which required a round-the-clock workforce.

In 2003, the city's Office of Multi-Cultural Affairs created a new 'Quick Guide' to city services in three languages: English, Spanish and Vietnamese. By 2002, the Atlantic City police and fire departments were trying hard to increase their diversity with outreach efforts in the public schools, and by creating police and fire cadet programmes.[421]

Another immigrant community formed in Atlantic City in the casino era consisted of Indian-Americans, including an especially a tight-knit group from Gujarat, India – a state on India's west coast. The Gujarat community was very successful in Atlantic City's casino era, with members working and often moving up in casino environments, as reported by one narrator who commented that 'many of my Gujarat state people all working in casino floor, cashier and slots attendants all business jobs'. The Gujarati Indians utilized similar support networks as the Vietnamese to maintain a vibrant cultural life, explained another member of the Gujarati community, with 'everybody ... taking good care of the community activities'.[422]

Latino immigrants were also a major force in the success of the casino community. Building on a base of older Puerto Rican and Dominican communities, immigrants from the Caribbean, Central and South America contributed to a wave of regional migration and cultural expansion in the region, beginning in the mid-1980s. By 2001 they had formed various small communities bound by Latino characteristics, yet often separate on the basis of national origins.

When asked why Latino immigrants chose Atlantic City as a destination over other areas of large immigrant communities like New York or Los Angeles, a Latino union official replied in 2003:

Atlantic City is more like home. People feel comfortable in here. They come to get a job and everybody have their own network with community. It's easier for you to get – for instance, you get a job in the casino. You know with six months you have established wages. You know exactly how much you're making next year if you keep your job and you have a good job. You know how much you – You can predict how much you going to make in five years.

So you have more reason to settle. I believe people want to settle down. Like, be able to know what can afford in the next couple years. They don't have – you have a permanent job.[423]

The casinos provided stability through employment that worked very well for many Latino immigrants who appreciated jobs with good benefits, despite their low pay. This was the case for one Columbian migrant who came to the region with her much older husband and worked as a restaurant server before training to be a casino dealer. She eventually took another position as a real estate assistant for a firm focused on immigrants in the region. With her income, she could afford a suburban home (Egg Harbor Township) and in 2005 she marvelled at her daughter's school's tolerance of diversity.[424] A community social worker described a common path in 2003:

> Most of those people that have a salary, they used to move out of Atlantic City. They move to Egg Harbor Township ... they move to they move to Ventnor, because they consider that it is better for their kids.[425]

One criticism offered by a number of narrators interviewed was that the casinos were not especially humane employers. A former casino employee and Colombian community leader related a long story of casino restaurant managers using employees to hide their illegal activities and then blaming relatively quiescent immigrants when facing pressure from senior management. Another oral history narrator commented on the dismissal of his wife for staying home with an ill child and the supposed trouble she had finding a casino job consequently after lodging a grievance:

> They told her, don't call back, because you're terminated. You've been out for so long that your position has been covered by someone else. So we don't care about the child, you're not here, you're fired. So when she went to apply for benefits, unemployment benefits, they originally – they denied them, and they kept denying them for three months, until finally she had a hearing and she won. And this was after she was working for the industry for four and a half years.[426]

The immigrant communities of Atlantic City created American lives in the casino era through determined efforts to take advantage of the available opportunities. From one perspective, the immigrants interviewed for this project expressed a notable desire to assimilate via their acceptance of American standards of success: being able to buy a house, own a business, improve life for their children. Yet, outside work they prospered in ethnic enclaves and through the accumulation of 'social capital' via niche businesses, churches, professional services and agencies. The new ethnic communities fit a strong pattern of assimilation via simultaneous cultural retention: they facilitated success on American terms, yet did not try to transform their members entirely into Americans. For Asian immigrants, for example, the role of women and men remained far from equal: in a few oral history interviews involving married couples, the husband often spoke for and directed a clearly subordinate wife.[427] A Columbian narrator elaborated on a local soccer league modelled on an international soccer competition (Atlantic City's own World Cup). A number of narrators for the project had limited English skills, even after years living in the region and working for the casino industry. Recent ethnologists have described similar patterns of assimilation and retention for Mexican immigrants working in rural Illinois slaughterhouses and the Vietnamese-American neighbourhood of Versailles in pre-Katrina New Orleans.[428]

Central and South Americans became much more prominent in Atlantic City as a component of the American Latino community. The success of the various Central American ethnic conclaves in Atlantic City affirmed one recent study that determined

> by the early 1990s migrant networks linking Central Americans in the US to their communities and neighborhoods of origin were well established.

The new Latinos of Atlantic City have successfully utilized the major casino union Local 54, a group that has been reaching out to immigrant workers for two decades. The union has also taken a pro-active approach with regard to providing English-language training and assistance with immigration paperwork.[429]

Above all, the immigrants in the Atlantic City gaming industry largely created independent and productive lives. For most, that translated into decent, steady jobs, with health benefits and the chance to assimilate and progress in American society. For some, this also means home ownership (a feat accomplished by a majority of Vietnamese immigrants for example within 5 years) and a high degree of social independence.[430] The lives created by these Atlantic City immigrants also included the ability to maintain distinct ethnic characteristics and community ties. Thus, narrators talked about the myriad Hispanic and Asian-owned businesses that catered primarily to immigrants that have sprung up around Atlantic City and its surrounding communities (such as Ventnor city) in recent years. Professional mobility within the casino setting was a high point of immigrant life in the early casino era. In 2002, an Indian-American migrant to Atlantic City talked proudly about seeing his friends and countrymen from Gujarat, India progress in the casino hierarchy: 'Many of my Gujarat state people all working in casino floor, cashier and slots attendants all business jobs'.[431]

Like all immigrants, the American lives created in Atlantic City also included no small amount of concern for future generations. There is some evidence that immigrants working in Atlantic City were better able to pursue dreams of higher education: 31 per cent of casino employees from the Asian sub-continent were already graduate students, compared to 30 per cent of employees with European descent. Yet, others saw problems. Father Pham identified the lack of ambition for a college degree as a significant concern for Vietnamese parents who saw their children choose relatively high-paying casino jobs upon high school graduation in lieu of college or university attendance. [432] Yet the very dilemma can be seen as a luxury – distinctly not a characteristic of life in the Asian nations that the immigrants came from.

The social benefits of the industry have been significant for Atlantic City immigrants in the casino era. The growth of vibrant, immigrant communities and the ability of immigrants to sustain a good living (especially since 1990) help dispel the oft-repeated notion that the casinos have been altogether disastrous for the region and its people.[433] None of the negative portrayals of the casino era in Atlantic City even refer to the immigrant experience. These portrayals tended to view the casinos as predatory and their social benefits minimal or non-exist-ent, even comparing the casinos to devices used by a 'Third World country' to exploit resources and people.[434] The immigrant experience in the casino era was heartening, if not altogether comforting. The casinos offered a difficult existence for many of their front-end employees. Yet, this did not seem to bother most of the immigrants in the community who were variously escaping from totalitarian regimes in southeast Asia, political oppression in Nicaragua, religious violence between Hindus and Muslims in India, or desperate poverty and turmoil in Haiti.[435] Generally, they made it in America by American standards, yet included conscious and determined efforts to retain their non-American cultures.[436]

Thirty years into the casino era, the living standards for many of the newer immigrants remained lower than New Jersey or national averages, taking into account factors like home ownership. Yet, a 2006 casino employee survey demon-strated that, on average, immigrants working in the Atlantic City casino industry were more content with their employment than others. When asked whether they wanted a 'spouse or close relative working in the gaming industry', 68 per cent of Pacific Rim Asian-American employees and 61 per cent of Asian sub-continent employees responded affirmatively. As well, 56 per cent of Latino employees said yes to the question. While the immigrant employees may have understood the question as an economic choice, the data demonstrated a fairly high degree of sat-isfaction, especially compared to people of European and African backgrounds, who reported affirmatively at lower rates: 45 per cent and 46 per cent respec-tively.[437]

6 BIG VISIONS: EXPANSION, CONSOLIDATION AND THE GREAT TUNNEL-CONNECTOR WAR OF THE 1990S

By 1996, the CRDA had a lot to report. Over the previous decade, its 1.25 per cent casino 'win' proceeds had allowed it to fund a variety of projects in and around Atlantic City. Controversial at times, the CRDA had become a bulwark of expansion by the mid-1990s and had become a central player in the city's accelerated rebuilding programme. The CRDA's support for the new hotel towers sprouting up around town symbolized the new symbiosis between the casino industry, local and state government. They were the physical outcome of the philosophical sea change that occurred in the early 1990s, leading to an explosive synergy between casino executives, state legislators and local officials. As a state agency with voting local and casino representatives, the CRDA was the perfect entity to focus different casino community perspectives to support the original casino mission: Atlantic City's revitalization. Nineteen years into the experiment, redevelopment was all over the place – a huge new Convention Center under construction along with a 'gateway' park and lighthouse, new houses all over the uptown Inlet neighbourhood, a new aquarium and retail area under development at Gardner's basin, and a supermarket-anchored plaza in the heart of the city's retail district on Atlantic Avenue. Then there were the new, glistening hotel towers at Caesar's, Harrah's, Trump Plaza and the Tropicana. The CRDA had spent $175 million to help leverage $1.54 billion in casino hotel expansion by 1996, a sometimes controversial investment that had, in fact, been significant in restoring the industry to steady revenue growth.[438]

Meanwhile, the long-lamented city government had launched a massive building campaign in the early 1990s to improve the look and overall functionality of the city. By late 1994, with some CRDA assistance, a new fire and police plaza had been built along with a new Police Athletic League building, the Garden Pier Arts Center, little league baseball fields and the brand new Atlantic City High School. Significantly, a 1994 city government report on the progress included these public works along with the casino expansions underway at Showboat and

Trump Plaza. Linking the private and public developments underscored the new synchronicity between local authorities, state agencies and the casino industry. The public versus private distinction over the greater good of the community blurred a bit in the early 1990s, with some controversy to follow.[439]

The CRDA's hotel expansion was a key expenditure in restoring casino industry health after the difficult period from 1988 to 1991 when the industry seemed on the verge of collapse due to a combination of high junk bond debt, a northeastern recession, a horrible national perception of Atlantic City, political corruption and the costly Trump Taj Mahal. Between 1992 and 1995, the gross operating grew at an average 8.8 per cent, including a 15.1 per cent rate in 1995. Gross profit growth in these years greatly eclipsed the anemic 1.5 per cent average between 1988 and 1991 and actually included two years of declining gross operating profits (1989 and 1990). There was certainly a great disparity between the casinos, but the numbers indicated a healthy industry by 1995 – a blockbuster year in terms of casino profit. In 1995, ten of the twelve casinos reported a double-digit percentage profit growth rate, a considerable difference from 1990, when eight of eleven casinos reported a decline in profits.[440] By the mid-1990s, the casino experience was somewhat different from what it had been a few years earlier. Slot machines now dominated casino floors, and changed the casino environment and community by mandating much increased numbers of slots operators and technicians over table game dealers. In 1995, slots accounted for 68.7 per cent of the total casino win, in sharp contrast to 1988 when slots accounted for 54.6 per cent of the total win and 1981 when slot winnings were 42.8 per cent of the total win for the industry. Between 1992 and 1995, slot machine 'handle' increased an average of 13.8 per cent annually.[441]

On the regulation front, in 1994 new CCC chairman Bradford Smith made clear his intent to continue streamlining the commission for the purposes of aiding the casino business and dealing with a more complex gaming industry. Since the 1990s began, almost twenty states had legalized casinos in some form and the number of publicly-owned gaming corporations had tripled, from 20 to 60. Smith's message infused the popular pro-business, anti-state ethos that helped make Republican Christine Todd Whitman the governor of New Jersey. Smith and the Commission basically continued the agency's streamlining and the casino deregulation championed by Steve Perskie from 1990 to 1993. In 1995, the CCC had 370 full-time employees, down from 567 in 1988 despite the substantial increase in casino square footage. Smith pronounced his operating philosophy in the 1994 annual report in clear terms:

> We must continue to prune away unnecessary regulations, or remove ourselves entirely from areas that are no longer public policy concerns.

From the beginning, Smith actively sought out more capital for the casino industry, even making a point of noting all the investment banks he had meetings with
in 1994. After its transformation, the Commission continued to function as a
regulatory agency while simultaneously operating as a casino booster of sorts
– certainly not its originally-intended role.[442]

The election that made Whitman governor and solidified the Republican hold
in Trenton did not make much of a difference in casino policy. Legislators continued to make it easier for the casinos to run their own operations with another
omnibus deregulation bill signed into law by the governor in early 1995. The new
legislation removed the CCC and the DGE entirely from 'purely business-related'
decisions, including marketing programme pre-approval and job descriptions for
casino employees. It also eliminated all remaining registration requirements for
non-casino floor employees and significantly cleared the path for casino mergers
and acquisitions by removing the three-casino maximum for licensees. In addition, it granted the casino operators new power to determine their own training
requirements. The law provided means for casino floor employees like dealers,
cage workers, security personnel and floor persons to obtain temporary licences.
It created a new class of casino floor employee who would not require a 'key
licence' (requiring a full investigation) but who could still work on the casino
floor. Finally, the act mandated more collaboration between the CCC and the
DGE to prevent duplication of efforts and created a new 'Atlantic City Fund'
with efficiency savings to go to CRDA for local development.[443]

Before getting Whitman's signature, the bill had picked up some controversy
when a few of the casinos objected to the three-casino waiver. That clause was
clearly designed to benefit the Trump group, which was looking to develop the
former Atlantis property into the city's fourth casino. Executives of Caesar's,
Showboat, Sands and Resorts originally opposed the bill for competitive reasons,
but eventually dropped objections for the greater good of its passage. In explain-
ing the change, Caesar's president Peter Boynton noted

> There's too much good in the bill and hard work that's gone into it, and we
> don't' want to be in a position of jeopardizing it.

The stalemate was quickly averted and the casinos were united for the bill, a
marked contrast to the situation a few years earlier when competition and legal
battles characterized the inter-casino relationships more often than not. This was
not the Sands vs. Trump, or CANJ vs. Harrah's – this was the sign of a heady and
bountiful new approach that benefited the casino community.[444]

By the mid-1990s, the CCC's mission had changed substantially from its
primary purpose to maintain integrity in Atlantic City's casino industry and to
prevent organized crime from industry infiltration. Mainly, the commission was
successful in this task, securing a tight system of casino licensure, despite occa-

sional controversies like the 1985 decision not to grant Hilton a licence. This focus was understandable, given the considerable role that organized crime continued to play in the Las Vegas industry well into the 1980s. Las Vegas's casino history is well-documented, with the Flamingo and other early resorts emerging with the help of investment from mobsters like Bugsy Siegal, Meyer Lansky and Frank Costello in the 1940s and 1950s. At the same time casinos were legalized in New Jersey, criminal skimmers and shady 'hidden owners' were making money in the desert at the Stardust, Aladdin and Tropicana casinos among others.[445] As the American casino era achieved critical mass in the corporate, competitive 1990s, the 1970's-style NJCCC became obsolete. Some contemporary critics decried the new focus of the Commission and its CRDA cousin for moving too far away from their original purposes. They disagreed with NJCCC decisions that allowed for ATMs on the casino floor and twenty-four-hour gaming, for example, and even perceived the industry's mid-decade boom as creating 'more opportunities [for people] to lose their money'. Some locals complained about CRDA's new priorities like the Corridor project and other CRDA-supported projects designed to beautify the city and expand the casino industry.[446]

But CRDA and NJCCC critics who disagreed with the agencies' new priorities were short-sighted. They misunderstood the reality that Atlantic City's casinos needed to evolve to meet the competitive challenges around them and expand a market that appeared saturated just a few years earlier. Atlantic City's casino business had to become more business-like, and the state and local officials responded to understandable requests for more authority for those who knew their industry best. Allowing a casino executive a CRDA vote did not jeopardize its mission: rather it helped the agency stay relevant and promoted the greater purpose of expanding the industry, which brought ever-increasing revenues to the region, in the form of wages, profits, small and large business proceeds. Likewise, the legislation to ease access to credit and cash in the casinos was a smart business move that helped the industry.

Smart management was also an important factor in the industry's resurgence and nowhere was this more apparent than the Taj Mahal. By 1994, the Taj finally had stable leadership under Dennis Gomes who successfully steered the Trump behemoth by bringing an air of informality to the gilded surroundings and raising employee morale. Of course, no casino was better at this than Harrah's – which had essentially been using the strategy since 1980 to build a very successful operation. In 1994, Harrah's kept up its marketing campaign along these lines, the extension of its 'Better People' campaign in the 1980s. One Harrah's advertisement in *Casino Journal* highlighted long-time dealer Tom Woodruff, 'an expert with people' who trained his fellow dealers, pit bosses and supervisors in excellent customer service.[447]

Also in the mid-1990s, more momentum was building up towards marina development as the industry's fortunes improved. As such, a separate sensibility emerged that the current and future marina casinos needed to counter their geographic isolation from the Boardwalk by working in concert to a greater degree than before. In 1994, new Trump Castle CEO Nick Niglio announced a recent agreement between Harrah's and the Castle to improve the corridor leading to the marina district, which included a shared billboard on the Atlantic City Expressway. Joint marketing to promote the marina casinos was a new approach and remarkable given the usually intense competition between casinos. Even better, by 1995 the CRDA provided funding for the project as part of its larger 'Corridor' commitment.[448]

Optimism for development in Atlantic City permeated a 1995 Salomon Brothers investment prospectus. The report highlighted the recent deregulatory legislation as an example of the resort's new circumstances. It invited potential investors to re-think investment in Atlantic City, that the industry 'deserves a second look – and we think that you might be pleasantly surprised at what you find'. Salomon celebrated the 'breath of fresh air' along the Boardwalk in sharp contrast to the bad old eighties when 'anxiety and distrust abounded' and casino customers were neglected in the ongoing battles. Yet, Saloman's positive outlook relied on more than rosy statements of new harmony in Atlantic City. The prospectus also used recent financial statistics to show that the Atlantic City casinos surpassed Las Vegas's 'High-Revenue Strip Properties' by 25 per cent in casino revenue, yet trailed Vegas by 20 per cent in total revenues. The disparity in total revenue was due to the western city's success as a 'destination resort' while Atlantic City continued to rely on day-trippers, albeit increasingly these were more profitable visitors who drove themselves as opposed to bus tourists. Despite this, by 1994, profit margins for the two casino communities were the closest they had been in a decade, within a few points of each other.[449]

So what made Atlantic City worthy of a 'second look' if it still lagged behind Las Vegas in visitor appeal? Addressing this question was difficult given that the number of visitors had actually declined to 31.3 million in 1994, down from a peak of 33.1 million visitors in 1988. However, the overall visitor decline was due to the decrease in charter bus programmes, down 40 per cent in seven years, from 14.2 million in 1988 to 8.3 million in 1994. This was actually a good thing for the casinos as chartered and fully-comped bus visitors had long ago proven to be not worth their expense. By contrast, self-driving visitors increased in the same span, from 17.2 million visitors in 1988 to 21.8 million in 1994. The increasing number of more lucrative car-borne casino customers appealed to Salomon along with hotel occupancy rates at approximately 90 per cent, akin to Las Vegas. This rate was about 5 to 10 per cent higher than the occupancy rates for most of the 1980s, and a major plus for the firm as overnight visitors accounted for a casino 'win' approximately three to three and half times that of day-trippers. The Salomon report also dealt with the biggest red flag of all for potential investors: casino debt. By 1995, most of the casinos had gone through debt restructurings to reduce their high-rate junk bond obligations of the 1980s. Yet, they remained highly-leveraged to the tune of 80 to 85 per cent of capital structure, compared to 50 to 55 per cent for Nevada casinos. Salomon's reconciled this with their positive forecast by noting that 'most' of the Atlantic City casinos were actually joint Nevada–New Jersey operations and that casino operators typically loaded up their corporate debt on their Jersey properties to reduce their nine per cent state tax obligations (actually nine and a quarter per cent) on the casino win. This was compared to zero state income taxes on Nevada casinos.[450]

The prospectus also highlighted the recent development in the city as a great sign for the casino business. The CRDA's new projects represented a 'major shift in the spending priorities' of the agency, now focused on city beautification and substantive public works projects. The Salomon analysts were especially positive about the major public works projects underway, including an expansion of the Atlantic City airport. A contentious issue throughout the 1980s, the state had finally come through with an $11.3 million to buy the airport from the city in 1991, put it under the South Jersey Transportation Authority's authority and began an expansion project soon thereafter. Like the Convention Center, lack of progress on the airport had come to symbolize the stalemate of the 1980s. Now it represented the successful state–local coordination of the 1990s. The coordinating council chaired by Whelan was a primary force behind the airport's expansion.[451] Salomon's analysis also celebrated CRDA's recent hotel projects, developed in line with the Convention Center to add over two thousand new casino hotel rooms in time for the Center opening in 1997. The analysts admired the scope and vision of the project:

> To stimulate the development of lodging capacity to coincide with the 1997 opening of the new Convention Center, the CRDA has been authorized to allocate funds in support of hotel room development. This change represents the first time that CRDA funds have been authorized for use directly within casino/hotel complexes. It also is indicative of the growing spirit of cooperation and partnership between the state and industry in Atlantic City. Continued development of quality overnight accommodations, coupled with current beautification efforts, may enhance the appeal of Atlantic City and begin to modify negative customer perceptions.[452]

Salomon's positive outlook was a sharp rebuke to those who decried the CRDA's new emphasis on urban beautification and casino development over housing development.[453] To some extent, critics had a point – millions of CRDA funds were now going to hotel expansion projects that might have otherwise been used to develop more city homes. But this also missed the larger view that the casino community was a broad-based regional entity that employed thousands and provided billions of dollars in the form of wages and in the form of goods and services to contractors. The CRDA's new focus shored up the investment the city made in gaming, and only partially supported the casino hotel towers. By the mid-1990s, there was no going back on that investment and not much else for the local economy if casinos failed, as they appeared to be doing just five years earlier. Having a voting casino representative and local authority on CRDA's board made sense and the decisions reflected the local, regional priority to maintain the health of the industry via redeveloping the city in a broad sense. What would be the point of more houses, if there was no economy to support them?

Despite the powerful support of the mayor and the CRDA and despite the fact that the plans were already drawn up, the Corridor project ran into a fatal roadblock in early 1995. Bally's Chairman and CRDA board member Arthur Goldberg basically killed further consideration of the project when he lashed out at Rouse for not consulting him on use of Bally's property, called Monopoly Square, after the famous board game. At a CRDA meeting, Goldberg called the plan 'too heavily retailed' and opined that 'I don't think we'll add one person to our visitor base with this plan'. The Bally's chairman opened up a split within the CRDA and was at odds with Whelan and others who promoted the project in addition to a non-casino hotel alongside the new Convention Center. Whelan expressed disappointment, but the project went down when CRDA rejected further consideration of Rouse's plan. In addition to Goldberg's specific problems with Monopoly Square, Corridor opponents never warmed to Rouse's planned overhaul of Boardwalk Hall (the old Convention Center), complete with new skyboxes, the world's largest indoor wave pool and exploding volcano. The city and the CRDA continued to plan development for the blocks adjoining the new Convention Center and Pacific Avenue, but the grand plan was dead by the end of 1995.[454] In 1995, the Casino industry was ready for a lighthouse with laser show, but not an indoor wave pool.

In addition to Rouse's Corridor proposal, another development that ran into controversy in the 1990s was the Forest City Ratner project. Forest City was a highlight of Mayor Whelan's plan to develop the long-vacant lots controlled by the city known as the 'Uptown Renewal tract', along the Boardwalk just above (or east) of the Showboat casino. Locals called the region 'Pauline's Praire' in reference to a city planner from the 1960s. The Forest City plan included a sports centre, a roller rink, movie theatre and twenty-seven acres of retail establishments, but no casino. To some extent, it was modelled after Las Vegas's Fremont Street Experience, as a venture designed to present a commercial and secure section of Boardwalk to appeal to tourists. Fremont opened controversially in 1995 as a private–public space developed by a handful of the city's casinos and the Las Vegas Convention and Visitor Authority. Originally proposed with the city's thirteenth casino, Forest City drew the opposition of the CANJ because the city planned to subsidize part of it with a bond offering. When the planners dropped the casino but kept the retail and entertainment feature, Showboat's management objected on the basis that it did not include a casino. Showboat eventually relented when executive Howard Wolfe explained that he would prefer a casino, but the retail establishment/complex worked because 'Anything next to us will help'. Forest City's project never did get built, however, after MGM Grand bought much of the property and then focused on other ventures around town.[455]

Wrangling over the Corridor and Forest City projects exposed latent tension amongst the major players of redevelopment. Disagreements over the scope, details and control of major redevelopment continued to impact Atlantic City's expansion into the late 1990s. While these disagreements never caused a 1980s-style stalemate, they demonstrated a persistent identity of particular interests within the new unity of purpose. Officials like Whelan and Lorenzo Langford, a leading city councilman wanted something done and pressed ahead for development. In reference to the dying projects, Whelan commented that now was a 'time for action', not 'reflection' and Langford questioned the joint authority of the projects:

> I'm growing very weary of the disputes over the corridor project. We should be in charge, and it would get done.

In particular, Langford – a former dealer and Trump Taj Mahal pit boss– noted that not all was harmonious in the casino community, despite the achievements of the nineties. In the context of the Corridor debate, Langford talked about a 'disgruntled faction' that had

> been promised the bounty of the casino industry that has not materialized. I'm concerned that this new drive for casino development will not produce the employment opportunities that these people deserve.

Claridge president Bob Rennaissen effectively put the situation into perspective for the casino industry and its future by connecting the public interest and private investment:

> The investment community believes their money is wasted when the public sector does not support private development, and when gaming heats up once again in other areas, the money will dry up.[456]

Changing the physical reality of Atlantic City in the 1990s involved more than new public structures, affordable new houses and shining new hotel towers. In the early 1990s, the Whelan administration also made a point of demolishing decayed older buildings. According to Whelan, his planning director Ken Platt brought a refreshingly simple approach to redevelopment after years of complex studies and plans that never amounted to much improvement. During his second interview for the job, Platt suggested tossing them out the window, declaring that instead the city should just 'knock down buildings and plant trees'. From 1990 to 1995, that was exactly what the city did – controversially clearing away hundreds of older structures, but also taking away places used for crime as part of a successful effort to dramatically reduce street crime under Whelan. The demolition programme contributed to the positive outlook for investment as did the 'Special Improvement District' – a downtown business district that included a major swath of the Boardwalk. The district involved decorative street lights, benches, gazebos, information kiosks and new Boardwalk sweepers. It was a city-run project jointly funded by CRDA and local businesses by a special charge.[457]

Momentum for new casinos increased when the industry had its best year ever in 1995, even edging out the Las Vegas's strip in casino 'win', at $3.7 billion to Vegas's $3.6 billion. Total revenue grew at an average 8.3 per cent over 1994 to $4.6 billion in 1995, the highest percentage growth increase since 1987. Gross operating profits increased by a huge 15.1 per cent average in 1995 to $1 billion – the highest ever increase from the time the casino era began. All this growth took place with no new casinos. The positive investment forecasts appeared to be exactly right. While a recovering northeastern economy probably had something to do with the boom, the 1995 deregulation bill which allowed for slot machine expansion was also responsible. In fact, the slot machine 'win' averaged 12 per cent higher than 1994 for total winnings of $2.6 billion. The higher total 'win' was despite the fact that the 'slot machine win', or percentage of slots wagers that the casinos held, dropped to 8.5 per cent – down from 10.6 per cent in 1990. The casinos were actually giving more money back in the form of slots winnings while dramatically increasing their total take from slot machines. The slots were looser than ever and so was the revenue. It really was all about volume in the slots in Atlantic City in the 1990s.[458]

The marina district's future as a casino zone appeared brighter in 1995 following casino legislation signed early in the year. Steve Wynn and the Mirage had maintained a fourteen-acre parcel of property in the area next to the Trump Castle for over a decade. Wynn's frustration with Atlantic City and the state's regulatory system had prevented his re-entry into the city's casino industry for years, but after the deregulatory legislation of the early 1990s and the omnibus 1995 bill, he was ready to jump back in. On a fervent mission to restyle Atlantic City in the image of Las Vegas, Mayor Whelan personally pitched Wynn at a University of Pennsylvania board meeting to re-invest in the city. A city-owned property and landfill known as the Huron North Redevelopment Area (called the 'H-Tract') stood next to Wynn's parcel. With the city improving along with the industry's fortunes, now was the time to build new casinos, thought Whelan, with full backing from the CCC, the CRDA and even the South Jersey Transit Authority (SJTA). Anticipating the interest in late 1994, Mirage actually had environmental testing done on the H-tract to ensure its viability for development.[459]

To make things easier for Mirage to develop, the city basically gave the 168-acre H-Tract to Mirage in 1995 in return for a commitment to clean up the site and develop the property into a casino (or two or three casinos) that would eventually employ 2,000 city residents. Yet, that was not quite enough for Wynn to come back. So, he successfully negotiated a deal with the city and state via the SJTA for a 'Brigantine Tunnel-Connector' to lead directly from the end of the Atlantic City expressway to the H-Tract, where up to four new casinos were planned at one point. The Mirage deal also included new legislation for casinos to receive reimbursement for environmental clean-up efforts on sites they owned. In addition, the Mirage deal spurred a wave of new development plans across the community, such that by the end of 1995, close to $4 billion in capital investment looked to be coming to Atlantic City. After years of flirting with a return, now Wynn intended to steer Atlantic City in the direction of Las Vegas, which boomed in the 1990s with the opening of luxurious themed resorts, beginning with the Golden Nugget's Mirage in 1989. He put together a development partnership with Circus Circus and Boyd Gaming after failing to convince enough Connecticut legislators to break the Foxwoods monopoly and allow a Mirage casino in Bridgeport, Conneticut. The Mirage announcement also propelled other casinos to move forward with expansion projects (some long-delayed), spurred by the new competitive pressure. Wynn's proposed marina project was designed to bring some Vegas flash to the style to Atlantic City, a casino resort he considered to be 'a grey experience' for visitors. At this point, Mirage also appeared to have support from other casino operators for its marina casino, including the Trump group. In 1995, Trump himself even welcomed Wynn, suggesting at one point that his return was a harbinger of positive change and a healthy business climate in Atlantic City.[460]

Wynn and the Mirage eventually got the tunnel connector built, in exchange for coming back to Atlantic City with other casino developers in tow. The tunnel-connector project was a massive undertaking with a novel approach, in that the Mirage would essentially partner with the state to get it built, but immediately the project ran into trouble. Was this a sweetheart deal for Mirage at public expense and at the expense of the other casinos? The tunnel deal quickly destroyed any good feelings between the Trump and Wynn camps, something Trump Castle president and CANJ president Robert Wagner made very clear in 1996 when he became the point man of the Trump Organization's public and political assault on the plan. Wagner had just overseen a collaborative landscape project with Harrah's at the entrance to the marina district. Now he suggested that the existing thoroughfares were perfectly adequate to handle the increased traffic. Wagner also objected to the high cost and argued that state and city authorities favoured Mirage over the older Atlantic City casinos. The tunnel battle also created unlikely allies as the debate surrounding the Mirage deal played out on the Atlantic City council, consisting of Boardwalk casino owners and inner city politicians. In the midst of the local discussion, a group called the 'Neighborhood Preservation Coalition' formed to rally community support against the deal.

As with the Corridor project, Lorenzo Langford spoke up for his constituents, including Westside residents who lived right in the path of the new roadway. He lashed out at Wynn and the Mirage and promised to hold out for many years, 'even if one homeowner refuses to sell'. This was a key skirmish in a long political war between Whelan and Langford that included three mayoral elections (1994, 1998, 2001). Whelan sought to defuse Langford's opposition by pointing out that most city residents wanted the project and that the northeastern Inlet project had caused far more disruption in the neighbourhood, along with a new police building on Iowa Avenue. Whelan sounded the by-now common theme identified with his administration: that the work would benefit the entire city and region by supporting casino expansion. Meanwhile, Mirage's executives were not waiting for the political battle to play out. In fact, they actively joined the campaign, at one point even venturing into the community and showing residents the project blueprints, after which effort Mirage development director Skip Bronson declared that 80 per cent of residents supported the plan. Bronson also went further to underline the showdown between Mirage and Trump by suggesting that other Boardwalk operators just do what Trump tells them, that they did not really know the details of the project. True or not, this probably was not the best political move on Mirage's part for getting through City Council, though it was not a deal-breaker.[461]

Trump lobbied hard to prevent the Mirage–H-Tract deal to no avail. At one point he reportedly spoke to each member of the City Council and threatened to pursue tax reductions to 'destroy' Atlantic City. His full-blown effort to block the deal actually ended up in front of DGE director Thomas Auriemma, who ruled that Trump's rhetoric was hyperbole and took no action. Aligned with Trump and on the wrong side of the Council's 6–3 vote for the project, Langford turned the tables on the escalating battle between the two casino magnates:

> They [DGE] should be more concerned with the people who talked to Steve Wynn. Wynn had a lot more to gain than Donald Trump. People were going to Wynn's house.

After their financial rebound following the near-disaster of the early 1990s, the Trump Organization may have had some competitive justification for attempting to block the deal. The group went public in 1995, and stock prices went up quickly before declining for most of the 1990s. In early 1996, Trump, Inc. impressed Wall Street analysts, including Marvin Roffman whom Trump had previously had fired from an earlier position for being negative at the time of the Taj's opening. Now Roffman recommended Trump stock as a good buy. In 1995, all three Trump casinos showed a profit and the company appeared to be in solid shape as the Trump World's Fair casino was set to open in the former Playboy-Atlantis property. Despite his efforts to block the city's deal with Mirage, Trump himself extravagantly publicized the planned expansion as a sign of Atlantic City's success and future prospects. Trump also directed his considerable rhetorical energies against fast-expanding tribal gaming by continuing to make a case that non-Indians were the ones really benefiting from the tribal casinos. He separated the Atlantic City and Las Vegas gaming industries and justified his non-participation in the American Gaming Association (AGA) by calling AGA president Frank Fahrenkopf, Jr. a 'Las Vegas guy' and suggesting 'Vegas and Atlantic City have never been together. Until perhaps now with everyone else coming in.'[462]

The Mirage deal added to an already considerable casino industry buzz as casino executives and their controlling corporations looked towards Atlantic City for new or expanded opportunities. Within six months of City Council's Mirage deal, ITT (Caesar's new parent company) announced a $500 million expansion and looked to grow its Atlantic City operations in partnership with Planet Hollywood. Hilton Hotels reached a deal to buy Bally's Entertainment for $3 billion and installed Bally's chairman (Arthur Goldberg) as the new president of Hilton Gaming. Meanwhile, Harrah's was busy constructing a huge new hotel tower and Bally's Wild, Wild West casino was under construction in old Monopoly Square, where the Corridor was once planned to end. MGM Grand had also begun preliminary work to develop a casino on the Uptown Renewal tract above Showboat. Ironically, Mirage's successful deal to develop the II-tract made it harder to get the tunnel-connector built because the deal itself made the casino community so attractive for other casino developers. According to one industry analyst, public subsidies no longer made sense given the huge demand without governmental help. He therefore advised the state not to help out Mirage any more by funding the connector.[463]

At the state level, Governor Whitman had a major choice in 1996 with ramifications for her 1997 re-election campaign. She could either lend her personal support to the Mirage/tunnel project to forge a legislative deal for its funding or she could listen to Donald Trump, among many in Atlantic City's casino community, who were lobbying to kill the deal. Trump publicly declared that Atlantic City was already 'bursting at the seams' with business and new projects and did not need the Mirage casinos and tunnel. But the momentum was clearly with Wynn and Whitman noted it as such, commenting to the *New York Times* that marina development was inevitable and that the state needed to 'improve transportation within the city' to offset competing casino interests. Yet, the proposal remained on the table well into 1997 as negotiations on the connector-tunnel details slowed. Meanwhile, state officials infuriated Wynn and the Mirage team by consulting the Trump Organization with the plans. At one point, negotiations almost broke down when a state negotiator wanted to change the plans by adding new ramps and traffic lights. The Mirage side objected to one traffic light, saying it would cause traffic jams near their casino. The Trump-approved state response was traffic parity – the light was acceptable so that Mirage would suffer from the same traffic jams as other casinos. The traffic light stand-off lasted three weeks before the light was removed from the plans, but not before it escalated tension between the two sides and solidified Mirage's exasperation with Whitman's chief negotiator, an outgoing transportation commissioner. At one point, the drawn-out negotiations caused Wynn to question his own judgment that things really had changed enough in New Jersey. Meanwhile, some northern New Jersey communities also objected to the plan on the grounds that it was wrong for money to come out of the state's Transportation Fund for an out-of-state casino operator. A few mayors from North Jersey even sued to stop the project before losing in court in late 1997.[464]

Not surprisingly, Whitman decided in favour of Wynn and the tunnel seemed on its way to construction in 1997 after a deal was struck in the Assembly to free up funding, The legislative deal ratcheted up Wall Street's confidence in both Wynn's Mirage and Atlantic City. But soon after, Trump took legal action against the project, arguing that it was a misuse of CRDA funding. Despite the court action, the CRDA, the SJTA and Atlantic City all proceeded towards the project and by the end of 1997, CRDA had committed $55 million to the project, now estimated to cost $400 million, including the widening of the Atlantic City expressway leading to the connector roadway. Mirage committed to another $110 million for its construction, but also benefited from a bill put through by Senator Gormley to enable the company to recoup the environmental costs of cleaning up the old city dump it had acquired in 1995 from the city for a promise – about $30 million.[465]

The state legislature debated the tunnel-connector in 1997 as part of a discussion to raise the spending cap of the New Jersey Transportation Trust Fund by $200 million to fund the project and assorted others across the state. New transportation commissioner John Haley argued mainly on the economic merits of the project – that it was a huge benefit to the region and 'one of the most important projects that the Department is undertaking in the last decade'. Haley projected 86,000 construction jobs and 16,500 new permanent jobs with H-Tract development. On this point Senate committee chair Andrew Ciesla pressed Haley: how could he guarantee legislators that the state would benefit from its investment? Ciesla's questioning also honed in on the novel approach to the project's development involving the state's partnership with Mirage:

> Do we have any assurance that the projects that we're going to build here, and I'm specifically talking about the contributions that we'll be making to a private developer for the tunnel project, that we're going to get a return on that investment?

Ciesla signalled his wariness over the relationship between one private developer and the state:

My concern is that we're taking public dollars and we're allowing a private individual to build projects with the private dollars and the Transportation Trust Fund is public money. I'm hoping that all of the procurements that are made relative to the expenditure of those funds can follow the public bidding statutes so that our New Jersey corporations can, in fact, bid and be awarded certain projects, and I'm getting the feeling that may not be the case.[466]

Throughout the hearing, the commissioner characterized the venture as a partnership between New Jersey and the Mirage for the mutual benefit of both entities. He received solid support at one point from a South Jersey legislator (Nicholas Asselta) who argued against a proposed pre-construction 'exploration':

those 16,000-plus jobs would have to wait, and I could, quite frankly, tell every member on this Committee that our area, our region, can't wait for these 16,000 jobs. We have the highest unemployment rate in the whole State.

In fact, to many of the legislators and people testifying at the hearing, the bill was best framed as an economic bill – a jobs programme of sorts – for South Jersey, in the long tradition of the casino era when casinos were brought in to create jobs and economic opportunity for local residents. A whole of host of advocates at the hearing chimed in for the bill, including a constructions union official (Local 472, Heavy and General Construction Laborers' Union, AFL-CIO), Ed Kline resident of Brigantine (a former assemblyman), and Gloria Soto of the Coalition for New Jersey Jobs Now. Soto's group included the state AFL-CIO and Chamber of Commerce. She testified to the

mutual interest between the public sector, the business community, and labor in moving forward with transportation projects that move our economy forward and create work and good jobs.

The mayor's office also sent a representative to the hearing and he summed up the prevailing argument in the blunt successful style that had worked repeatedly for Whelan's redevelopment efforts throughout the 1990s:

The economic impact, quite frankly, jobs, jobs, jobs, and taxes.[467]

The bill's opponents were also present at the hearing, though quite out-numbered. Advocates for Hilton Hotels and the Trump group showed up to testify, though the main opposition strategy had already shifted to the courts. By April 1997, momentum was clearly with the project, given Mirage's public relations campaign, the mayor's role, Senator Gormley's backing, the governor's support, and the appealing economic arguments surrounding it. But the Trump and Hilton advocates tried hard to play on the logistical and fiscal sensibilities of the legislators. The two Trump reps included a former New Jersey state treasurer (Clifford

Goldman) who argued that the deal favoured Mirage by ceding much control over the project and the right to pull out if the state did not come through in various ways. Goldman also objected to the real cost of the project, pointing out that Mirage only committed to a $55 million investment in the tunnel connector, meaning that the SJTA would have to finance via bond issuances. Goldman attempted to sow doubt in the committee that New Jersey taxpayers would eventually benefit from the project by charging that

> there is a significant risk in this project that this money will go out and, for one reason or another, at different stages in the project, the project will not be completed.

The Hilton advocate (Hazel Frank Gluck of the GluckShaw Group) used drama when she read from a recent letter from Arthur Goldberg to Whelan declaring that Hilton was ready to work a deal to purchase the H-Tract with no expensive public improvements required:

> As you know, Hilton Hotels has publicly stated its interest in purchasing the H-Tract and proceeding with substantial development including casino, retail, entertainment, and hotel rooms without the need for public subsidy, free land, and the reimbursement of remediation costs. Further, Hilton will not require extensive, time-consuming, disruptive, and unnecessary tunnels or other roadway improvements in order to proceed with its development of the H-Tract. Therefore, I would like to meet with you.

Gluck then framed her testimony in the context of the then-hot casino marketplace, in which companies like Hilton were increasingly prepared to invest heavily in the future of the casino community:

> With the merger or the takeover – whatever the proper terminology is – Hilton, obviously, now has the wherewithal because they are a player and can do it as a result of acquiring Bally's.[468]

Hilton Hotels' position at the hearing demonstrated the powerful new financial dynamic at work in Atlantic City, and the entire casino industry of the late 1990s: casino consolidation. The Mirage deal and all its ramifications showed that the new power players in the casino marketplace were those able to successfully merge and act as a block. In some ways, this was nothing new. After all, Donald Trump had realized some of the advantages of consolidation in the 1980s, yet was hampered by the Taj Mahal's difficult beginning and the long-term junk bond debt that continued to impact his casinos through the 1990s, despite various restructurings and Trump taking his casino business public in 1995. Mirage was a consolidated operation using its powerful capital position to usher in a new age of consolidation. At the deal's outset, Mirage held $1.1 billion of shareholder equity, with only $292 million of debt to go with a $1 billion credit line. With the H-tract deal, Wynn was about to reverse his 1987 Golden Nugget move back to Las Vegas. This time, he was set to plow the Vegas proceeds into an Atlantic City deal, just as he had plowed Atlantic City winnings into the Mirage's construction in the late 1980s. By the mid-1990s, Mirage had brought more than flashy new Las Vegas casinos to the relatively staid Atlantic City marketplace. It also brought a more sophisticated, higher-stakes corporate approach from the west with bigger stakes, bigger potential and national integration aided by the 1995 elimination of the 3-casino limit for one licensee. The city's existing casino executives were faced with a new reality: stay viable through consolidation or fade away into obscurity and isolation. This consolidation ethos would drive Atlantic City's casino era well into the first decade of the twenty-first century.

The Mirage deal with the city of Atlantic City for the H-Tract also spelled an end to the existing CANJ. In late 1996, a letter on CANJ stationary went to the legislature officially opposing Mirage's deal for the H-Tract. The problem was that four out of ten casino representatives of the CANJ had not authorized such a letter, nor was there any discussion over the matter before the letter went out. Four casinos subsequently dropped out of the association in protest (Caesar's, Harrah's, the Sands and Tropicana) and the group officially ceased operations a few months later. The split that broke up the CANJ highlighted the significant industry fall-out from the anti-Mirage stance taken by the Trump and Bally's casinos, and the extent that the city's decision (supported by the state bill to reimburse Mirage for site clean-up) was controversial within the casino industry. Led by the outspoken Tom Carver, CANJ was a loud and powerful group on behalf of the casinos throughout the 1980s, even if it did not always keep every casino to the same agenda. It pushed hard for regulation reform and publicized the substantial economic impact of the casino industry in south Jersey. From one perspective, CANJ had outlived its usefulness by 1996, by which time it had realized most of its agenda, with massive regulatory reform, a streamlined CCC, twenty-four-hour gaming, the CRDA's shift in emphasis and an improving urban setting for the industry.[469]

The CANJ's 1996 demise also left some open questions on the future of the casino industry, and contributed to a generalized break-down of casino unity in the increasingly competitive gaming industry. The group was revived in 1998 with a new structure in which each casino company had a vote. The new format reduced the influence of the bigger operators like Trump.

Though the CANJ's downfall was a sign of divisiveness in the casino industry, the casino community came together in 1997 with the opening of the long-delayed Convention Center. Though he may not have played a slot machine or taken a hit at a blackjack table, Winnie the Pooh made a high-profile appearance in Atlantic City in 1997, the highlight of the three-day grand opening of the new Convention Center. Along with a Dixieland band, jazz, a Civil War re-enactment and General 'Stormin'" Norman Schwarzkopf, the city commemorated the huge new building at the foot of the Atlantic City Expressway. 'Come Celebrate the Renaissance!' shouted an event brochure directed at local residents. Hosting the event, the ACCVA proudly proclaimed all of the recent projects meant to turn Atlantic City into a destination resort: including the new 'Grand Boulevard' entranceway and a cleaner Boardwalk. The Convention Center opened at an especially optimistic time for the resort town, with six new casinos on the horizon, including a short-lived ITT-Planet Hollywood casino proposal next to the Sands, three Mirage projects for the H-Tract, MGM Grand's Uptown Renewal tract casino and a Sun International project. While only one of these actually made it from blueprint to building (the Borgata), in 1997 there was plenty of reason to think that they would collectively transform the community within the next few years. By then, the political synergy achieved in the early 1990s had also led to a $17.1 million renovation to Atlantic City International Airport, now under the SJTA. As well, a new bus terminal was scheduled to open in 1998 and a New Jersey Transit railroad line that would operate regularly between Atlantic City and Philadelphia. No wonder ACCVA's marketers called it a 'Renaissance' – the mid-1990s was a time for major improvements easily recognizable by visitors and residents.[470]

The centre's opening even included Miss America – Tara Dawn Holland, who was quite impressed. She had reason to be: it was an impressive structure, if stark and somewhat isolated in its location at the time. The length of six football fields, it opened with 610,000 square feet of meeting and exhibition space and was the eleventh largest convention centre in the nation at the time. With all temporary walls removed, it could open to 500,000 square feet – the biggest such space in the entire Northeast. To demonstrate its high-tech capabilities during the grand opening, Governor Whitman held a video conference with high school students in Jersey City and Newark. ACCVA promoters called it the most technologically-capable convention centre around, with 275 miles of fiber optics cable and internet connections throughout. It was adjacent to the refurbished railroad station and to a new non-casino hotel, the Atlantic City Sheraton. According to the executive director, the convention had some 290 conventions and trade shows already booked a decade in advance.[471] The Convention Center's festive grand opening also represented a conclusion (of sorts) to the contentious history of the project. For years, many casino insiders called it a 'white elephant', an unnecessary project that might actually cut into the industry's success by replacing casino convention space with public convention space. Casino critics of the project were later joined by some local representatives who objected to the destruction of some local housing and use of eminent domain to get it done. But now, city councilman Ernest Coursey (who represented the district) called it a 'beautiful building' and said 'we look forward to it'. But he remained wary that the city was going too far to accommodate tourists at the possible expense of locals. When the venue opened, Coursey expressed his sincere, yet historically-laden wish that

> Atlantic City residents who remain will be treated just as well as the conventioneers and tourists we are attracting.

Earlier, when construction was well underway, Langford had similarly expressed opposition to the project in the context of the city's deal with the Mirage. During the debate over the tunnel-connector, Langford commented that

> If they had just expanded the Convention Center across Pacific Ave or put it on 'Pauline's Prairie' up in the Inlet, we could have saved the taxpayers more than $600 million because we wouldn't have needed the corridor or tunnel project.[472]

The Convention Center's opening was the most celebrated non-casino event of the casino era, though it really meant everything for the casino community. Five years earlier, the centre had sparked the expansion boom in the city's drive for more hotel rooms. This in turn drove the revised CRDA policy that allowed the casinos to utilize redevelopment funds for their own expansion. Since 1992, the casinos had added a number of hotel towers and more were already underway. Meanwhile, the commission (via its new jurisdiction) allowed the casinos to expand their casino square footage, and vastly increase the amount of floor space they could devote towards increasingly lucrative slot machines. The finished Convention Center was more than a building. It was a symbol of the casino era in Atlantic City and the progress of the 1990s.[473] Within a year, the Convention Center likely increased paying fares on New Jersey Transit's Atlantic City Rail Line by 26.7 per cent (123,893 passengers). Yet, as the 1990s drew to a close, the Convention Center's long-term ability to expand Atlantic City's visitor base remained questionable.[474]

In 1997, as the legislature approved the financial package for the project (now called the Atlantic City-Brigantine Connector), the legal battle took off with suits and counter-suits flying about, with close to a dozen filed before the dust finally settled on the roadway's construction in 2001. Trump picked up allies in their anti-Mirage efforts, including the Westside residents whose homes were now slated for demolition, the city politicians who represented them (like Langford) and other Boardwalk casino executives, such as Hilton's Goldberg. As always, Trump himself took on a high-profile role in the process, at one point blasting the project as a 'private driveway' leading up to Mirage's proposed Le Jardin Palais casino, to be built on the H-Tract. Meanwhile, Westside residents were in court trying to prevent nine houses from demolition on Horace Bryant Jr. Drive. Supported by the Trump group, in 1996 they filed an unsuccessful lawsuit to prevent the project, maintaining legal action until eventually they reached a buy-out deal with Mirage. A federal judge finally dismissed the homeowners' lawsuit in early 1998. One of the affected residents was Pierre Hollingsworth. In 1997, Hollingsworth used the occasion of testimony to the National Gaming

Study Commission to argue that project supporters disregarded the inner-city residents of the Westside, as urban planners had in the 1960s with new highways that cut through and destroyed neighbourhoods. Hollingsworth and a group of other homeowners went to court to block and stall the project for a year, before finally selling out for $200,000 apiece, double the market value for their homes in some cases. Hollingsworth's resentment towards Wynn remained strong eight years after his testimony to the NGIS commission:

> They were able to convince some people on that block to sell for $200,000, and they sold. Wherein, had they stuck together, each one of them would have got a minimum of half a mil. Just no question about it. He [Wynn] sold Governor Whitman a bill of goods and everything.

The Mirage executives, Whelan and their allies simply could not win over Westside residents, who believed the tunnel-connector project to be steamrolling through their neighbourhood because they were 'disposable' in the eyes of the authorities and casinos.[475]

Mirage's tunnel-connector deal may have played a pivotal role in changing the broader direction of Atlantic City's casino industry. But it did not do much to change the old perception that the casinos were unfairly treating the community's African-Americans. Lillian E. Bryant, retired city worker and descendent of her street's namesake had a huge billboard outside her house that read 'NO TUNNEL'. She and her eight-six-year old mother held out as long as possible, but they were overwhelmed by a combination of public and private forces that moved Atlantic City steadily closer towards becoming a 'destination resort' – now attainable via the Mirage project. The Bryant's desire to hold fast to their Westside house was rooted in their claim to personal and community history. Ironically, so was the momentum that led to the project in the first place. Like the Bryants, officials like Whitman moved the tunnel-connector along in order to finally reconnect Atlantic City's casino present with its resort past. The re-creation of a 'destination resort' remained the ultimate goal for planners and continued motivation for expansion and development in 1997.[476]

In late 1998, prominent dignitaries assembled near the new Convention Center and Atlantic City Expressway for a ribbon-cutting ceremony to officially begin construction on the tunnel-connector. The governor's office declared that it would generate 6,000 construction jobs alone, and 47,000 more jobs in the local economy via three new casinos. Whitman's office also noted Mirage's commitment to reserving 30 per cent of the expected 7,200 Le Jardin jobs to Atlantic City residents. It had taken over three years to get to this point, but now there was optimism that the project would finally begin and the city would have its long-promised transformation. Steve Wynn was amongst those who shovelled the first lumps of earth while a brass quintet played. Trump himself was temporarily defeated, but certainly not ready to concede:

They would've come without having to give away hundreds of millions of dollars. It could've been much better for Atlantic City. They would've come without the free land, without the cleanup money, without the subsidies.[477]

Despite the late 1998 groundbreaking, the legal conflict had yet to resolve itself. Trump's suit to block CRDA from funding the project was still in the court system, as was a 1997 Mirage suit levelled against Trump and Hilton Hotels for anti-competitive practices, including 'litigation and lobbying activities' to prevent Mirage's project from moving forward. In 1999, the New Jersey Supreme Court rejected Trump's long-standing suit against the tunnel's funding mechanism with a sweeping judgment that upheld the CRDA's right to fund the tunnel. A few days later, Mirage issued an angry press release, referring directly to Trump as pernicious, hypocritical, reckless and a loser, that betrayed how intense, personal and divisive the battle had become,.[478]

In its losing battle to block CRDA funding for the Connector, the Trump group argued that the project actually violated the basis of the 1976 constitutional referendum for legalization. Trump's lawyers explained that the referendum mandated casino proceeds to be slotted only for programmes to benefit senior citizens and the disabled, the main beneficiaries of the Casino Revenue Fund. So, the Trump action was really a sweeping argument against the CRDA itself, and all of its redevelopment efforts – some of which had directly benefited the Trump casinos via support for additional hotel rooms.[479]

The Trump position, if upheld, would have been a huge blow to the progress of the 1990s, not because it would have stopped the tunnel-connector project. That project alone (along with Mirage's casino proposal) was a gamble from the beginning as to whether the public investment would pay off for the region's residents. But a pro-Trump ruling may also have been a death knell to the massive CRDA-backed housing programme, which had transformed the Inlet area, and to all of its city projects that had obviously been successful in changing the investment prospects for the casino industry. To some extent, the case was consistent with a long-held position by some in the casino community that the casino 'win' was never meant to fund redevelopment projects. It dated back to the late 1980s when some (such as the *Casino Journal* editors) opposed the CRDA's housing mission as a wrong-headed interpretation of the 'redevelopment' mandate for Atlantic City written into the 1977 *CCA*. Opponents at that time also argued that the *CCA*'s original reinvestment mandate (two per cent of casino win) was for reinvestment in the casino properties themselves and that CRDA was selling out to state and local governments to make up for their own shortcomings. Opposition to the CRDA in the 1980s also came from disagreements over its housing priorities (Harrah's northeastern Inlet project) and the desire to create a better business climate for the industry of the time.[480]

Whatever Trump's motives, there was no question that his cause had the support of many Atlantic City residents who had been similarly rebuffed by the courts. A few days before the Trump group definitively lost in the state's highest court, a group of ninety-two city homeowners also lost their case in federal court. Led by lead plaintiff Epps Running Deer, the residents had also tried to block the connector, using health concerns as one key point. An SJTA spokesman applauded the ruling and noted that 'the SJTA and our partners have consistently been found to have proceeded properly'. Meanwhile, the Wall Street community showed its skepticism for the tunnel-connector with 'lukewarm' ratings for the 1999 transportation bonds issued to provide $220 million for the project. Moody's and Standard and Poor's both rated the bonds at the 'B' level over concerns about the high level of debt incurred by the transportation agency. The legal showdown over the tunnel-connector finally ended in 2000 when the SJTA and the Trump group agreed to add an extra ramp that connected the new casino with the existing Trump Marina to make it much easier for patrons to travel between the two casinos.[481]

During the tunnel-connector's construction, the city and the Mirage tried hard to ameliorate the impact on local residents in the path of the new road. In 1999, a vaguely-attributed *Community Connection Bulletin* appeared on the street to address 'Questions frequently asked by residents and the right answers'. The *Bulletin*'s intent was to inform, and it did so, but by its very existence it also betrayed the suspicion built up in over the years in the community, surrounding the project:

'Q-Some say residents will not get information about all construction activities that will affect their daily lives. Is this true?'

Of course, the *Bulletin*'s answer was that the rumour had no merit and that the community would receive plenty of detailed information on the project via the bulletin, a *Community Connection* newsletter and the local news media.[482]

The Atlantic City–Brigantine Connector finally opened on 27 July 2001 with a grand ceremony in which people walked the length of the tunnel. To no one's surprise, the opening was delayed four days due to a tunnel communications system failure, a fitting way to begin given its delay-filled past. Its first traveller was Joseph Haney, who cruised through in his Toyota 4-Runner and reminisced to a reporter that he was also the first person to have been ejected from an Atlantic City casino, he having been thrown out of Resorts on opening day in 1978 for playing a slot machine at the age of seventeen. One year later, 18,000–20,000 vehicles travelled through the tunnel daily, after a dip to 11,000 following the 11 September attacks. After the Borgata opened in 2003, the 2.3-mile roadway had about 25,000 vehicles per day, as tracked by the SJTA – higher than the 14,000–17,000 vehicles expected annually in 2001.[483]

While the tunnel-connector was under construction between 1998 and 2001, the H-Tract casino project and the prospects for the town's gaming industry were undergoing significant changes. Now, there were only solid plans for one casino in the Marina district, after a series of manoeuvres that eventually left only Mirage and Boyd Gaming working together as partners. In 1998, Mirage tried to force both Boyd and Circus Circus off the project after claiming that neither was willing to support the tunnel-connector. Eventually Circus Circus pulled out of the project, leaving Mirage and Boyd to develop a one billion dollar mega-casino known as the Borgata, modelled after a Tuscan villa, to ultimately employ 3,000 people. Meanwhile, other casino developers continued to prospect in Atlantic City, including Sun International and MGM Grand. Sol Kerzner (a.k.a. 'the Sun King') of Sun International had successfully opened the Mohegan Sun in Connecticut in 1996 and now looked to acquire Resorts International in Atlantic City. Between 1996 and 1999, the older casinos continued to add hotel rooms and expand their casino floors, in line with expansion plans hatched in the early 1990s to meet the expected demand from the new Convention Center's 1997 opening. The resort community edged ever closer to the consensus 20,000 hotel rooms necessary to be a premium convention destination, yet was still approximately 8,000 rooms short in 1999, but with over 7,000 planned in upcoming projects. Where once had been planned a public 'Monopoly Plaza' via the Corridor project, Bally's quasi-public 'Wild, Wild West' casino opened in 1997, complete with an entire Boardwalk block that looked something like an old Warner Brothers' cartoon version of a western town and played country music on its outdoor speakers. Venturing into the casino from the Boardwalk, patrons experienced an animatronic version of a nineteenth century gold prospector and an old-fashioned looking railroad that ran partially along the casino's interior wall. Bally's Wild Wild West casino was the closest thing to a new casino in Atlantic City since the Taj Mahal's 1990 opening, and was celebrated with much fanfare. Its western theme was quirky and fun, and demonstrated the continued adoption of Las Vegas-style development in Atlantic City, as themed casinos virtually defined the explosive growth in Las Vegas of the era. It also connected directly to Caesar's via a send floor walkway – a physical precursor to a coming merger between the two Atlantic City giants. [484]

In the mid-1990s, major retail and tourist-based operators invested close to $1 billion along the Boardwalk. New projects included a Planet Hollywood at Caesar's and the Sands's planned 'Hollywood Studio Store'. A Rainforest Café opened at Trump Plaza and a Ripley's 'Believe it or Not' museum opened on the Boardwalk. Caesar's president Mark Juliano attributed the new investment climate to the Mirage deal, claiming that

> it woke the town up a little bit. The message to operators like myself is 'Make sure you're running things right' and if not, do something about it. [485]

The late 1990s were also notable for the industry's immersion into a broader context of corporate mergers and manoeuvres. In 1996, Hilton Hotels bought Bally's and in 1998 the company spun off Park Place Entertainment for its casino operations, which now included Bally's and the Atlantic City Hilton. In addition, Starwood Hotels and Resorts acquired ITT, Caesar's parent company. Along with the eternal notion of creating a 'destination resort', consolidation was the new mantra for success in Atlantic City. Without the three-casino limit, there appeared to be only very minimal restrictions on expansion, though there was still a required NJCCC review for new licences and for each new merger. Early 1990s deregulation set the legal tenor for the high-level financial activity, now more focused on broader concerns about competitive balance than the personal integrity of casino personnel and mob-free operations. However, long-term debt problems continued to weigh down the industry, most notably in the case of the Trump group. The company went public in 1995, but remained mired in $1.8 billion in debt, even after numerous restructurings that freed up capital for expansion through the 1990s but also restricted the ability of Trump to compete in the increasingly higher stakes corporate environment of the late 1990s. Within eighteen months of its initial public offering, Trump Hotel and Casino Inc. stock had also dropped below its original price of $14, despite the broader gains of the stock market and gaming industry over the same span. Financially, the Trump Organization still had not recovered from the Taj Mahal's expense and at one point in 1998, Trump offered his company up for a buy-out, although he had no takers. Trump ended the year unable to perform another re-structuring – this time on Trump Marina's $315 million high-interest bonds.[486]

One of the more important industry mergers of the consolidation era took place in 1998 when Harrah's acquired the Showboat casino. With the move, Harrah's almost doubled its revenue operations in Atlantic City and set up a Boardwalk operation to complement its highly successful Marina property. After expanding with a new tower and all-round improvements in the late 1990s, Harrah's was in full expansion mode, acquiring properties and developing casinos from Mississippi to Illinois to California and Iowa. Harrah's Showboat acquisition made huge sense from a marketing perspective. Like Harrah's, Showboat had also developed a strong, loyal customer base in the 1990s after letting go of its unsuccessful casino/bowling strategy begun in the late 1980s. Both properties focused on direct marketing and building up loyal customers, and the merger enabled Harrah's to add almost 2 million customers to its 10 million customer database. Harrah's CEO Phil Satre pointed out that the Showboat acquisition was a natural because of Harrah's community-oriented approach to the gaming business:

> We were looking for an acquisition that fit our strategy. We are a loyalty-intensive, marketing-based company. We identify markets throughout the

U.S., go there and establish relationships and leverage those relationships at our other properties around the country.[487]

Harrah's acquisition of Showboat was not just an Atlantic City merger. Harrah's also acquired new properties in Chicagoland and Las Vegas. The expanded operation allowed it to implement an expanded Total Gold players' club – something akin to a frequent flyer card for casino gamblers. The company began to aggressively 'cross-market' its properties via direct mail promotions, promoting a 'seamless' service experience. Harrah's challenge in Atlantic City was to maintain Showboat's unique qualities (such as its 'Mardi Gras' atmosphere) while implementing its customer-friendly approach with the company's focus on establishing good employee relations and loyalty. By the end of the 1990s, Harrah's 'seamless' marketing programme had achieved considerable success through an effective loyalty programme. Harrah's invested in research that indicated a player's typical Harrah's loss amounted to 36 cents of every dollar, with the remainder going to other casinos. Through area consolidation and cross-marketing programmes in Atlantic City and Chicagoland, the company increased its share of a typical player's loss to 42 cents on the dollar – which increased its cash flow by approximately $120 million annually. Within a few years of the Showboat deal, Harrah's Chicagoland casinos quickly became huge feeders to both its Las Vegas and Atlantic City properties. Harrah's executives developed the gaming industry's players clubs so that they worked like an airline's frequent flyer programme, maximizing customer loyalty in competitive markets. Knowing that gamblers typically gambled in multiple casinos, their strategy relied on increasing the numbers of Harrah's casinos to retain the customers. Customers could maximize their comped rewards by gambling at Harrah's properties the same way frequent flyers maximized their mileage rewards by focusing on one or two airlines. Harrah's did not invent players clubs, but it certainly improved on them in the late 1990s and early 2000s as it added properties around the country. Harrah's expansion strategy utilized its 'Total Rewards' program to move customers around to their own properties (within one locality or across the country). Harrah's extensive data analysis programme allowed for increasingly sophisticated direct marketing and customer retention. Within a few years, Harrah's used a three-tiered system (gold, platinum, diamond 'Total Rewards' cards) to build greater customer loyalty and an extensive database. Database analysis from card use contributed to every strategic decision, from facility investment to customer service and the type of amenities offered at each casino.[488]

By the end of the 1990s, Harrah's integrated programme of customer service, players' club, corporate style and employee relations had positioned it to take off in the gaming industry. The Atlantic City job market for casino employees was still tight in the late 1990s, and the programme gave Harrah's an edge in attracting the best employees. They ranked the casino highest on surveys that measured morale, indicated by prospects for advancement, job security, treatment of supervisors and a generous retirement and vacation packages. Like no casino before, Harrah's effectively nationalized its employee management programmes to allow local property managers to focus on hiring and training workers specific to their locales. In Atlantic City, Harrah's actively promoted its player's club to maintain particular market niches for both Harrah's Marina and the Showboat. It specifically targeted older, budget gamblers at Showboat and more sophisticated higher-end slots players at Harrah's. In Las Vegas, it presented the Rio (acquired in 1999) to young, hip gamblers of the type that Tropicana and Borgata would soon go after in Atlantic City. Meanwhile, corporate headquarters favoured a streamlined, non-hierarchical system with a lot of communications and employee feedback loops. Pressure was great, however, on employees at every level to increase Harrah's share of every gambler's wallet throughout the operations. To some extent, this constant pressure to maximize efficiency undercut employee morale at the service-level ranks.[489]

Harrah's successful strategy catapulted it to the top of the Atlantic City casino marketplace and the national gaming industry in the early 2000s. Its programme also mirrored Golden Nugget's successful formula of the 1980s by focusing on employee satisfaction and the effective use of a players' club, something Steve Wynn basically pioneered in Atlantic City with his programme modelled on the old green stamps. Yet, the two operations also went after different segments of the casino market – different routes to success. The legendary (though short-lived) Golden Nugget made its mark by bringing in entertainers like Frank Sinatra, creating a luxurious aura to attract, retain and entertain high rollers. Throughout its history in Atlantic City, Harrah's always emphasized casino gaming as an affordable recreational outlet for middle Americans that cut across ethnic, age, gender and class lines. Always central to Harrah's Atlantic City success was CEO Phil Satre, who began his career at Harrah's in Reno in the mid 1970s as a lawyer for company founder Bill Harrah. After Harrah died in 1978, Satre quickly impressed the new CEO and Chairman (Mead Dixon) and Dixon tagged him to lead the company's foray into Atlantic City in the late 1970s. Satre outlined his gaming philosophy in a 1993 speech:

> People who come to a casino come for entertainment ... a form of entertainment with several unique qualities – interaction, excitement, and accessibility. Money ... and the shot to win more money ... is 'the medium'. But clearly, the message is entertainment. A friend of mine tells me that the opening of casinos in Atlantic City has added five years to his mother's life. Alone in New Jersey and nearly 80 years old after her husband and lifelong companion died, this lady and her friends travel to Atlantic City once a week for the interaction, enjoyment and excitement playing in a casino provides them ... These trips are not about getting rich. They are about friends having fun and enjoying time together in an environment of celebration.[490]

Following the Showboat acquisition, the opening of new hotel towers, casino space additions, an expanded and acclaimed $15 million 'FantaSea' seafood buffet, and the benefits wrought by national expansion of the late 1990s, Harrah's vaulted ahead of the other Atlantic City properties in terms of profitability. Between 2000 and 2004, Harrah's Marina and Showboat were the two most profitable casinos in Atlantic City, despite Showboat taking a considerable hit from the 11 September slowdown due to its reliance on bus customers from New York City. Over this five-year span, Harrah's Marina's annual gross operating profit margin averaged 38.8 per cent and Showboat's 31.1 per cent. Overall, the Atlantic City casino industry average gross operating proft margin was 25.8 per cent. In 2002, Showboat's operating profit rose 23.7 per cent from 2001 to 2002. In addition to Harrah's and Showboat, the consolidated Park Place Entertainment casinos (Bally's and Caesar's) also did well in these years – both averaging about 30 per cent in profit margin.[491]

In the late 1990s, Harrah's slowly and quietly built a casino empire while Donald Trump and Steve Wynn fought over the tunnel-connector and the Borgata project slowly developed. By 2003, Harrah's operated twenty-six properties across the US, including casinos on Native American lands and midwestern and Mississippi riverboat and Gulf coast casinos. Harrah's geographic distribution allowed it to maximize 'cross-market play', making $1 billion in 2002 on customers who gambled outside their home regions. CEO Gary Loveman's 2002 statement to stockholders made it clear that there was no end in sight for Harrah's expansion wave. He reported on 'large budget deficits' and the reality of 'border states where taxes from legalized casino gaming have helped fill treasuries' to demonstrate potentially new opportunities in Maryland, New York, Pennsylvania and Rhode Island. Loveman made clear that Harrah's investors understood his corporate vision: 'Rest assured that we're actively pursuing such opportunities'. The buying spree was not over and the Atlantic City casino community would find out soon what that meant for Harrah's and the local gaming industry.[492]

7 NEW STYLINGS: FINANCE, RETAIL AND CHALLENGES AT THE TURN OF THE CENTURY

After a few years of dizzying events, deals, projects, suits and counter-suits, the twentieth anniversary year of Resorts's 1978 opening provided a good opportunity for reflection. What had the legalization gamble wrought for the casino community in the two decades since gamblers literally swamped the one legal casino on the east coast? Early in 1998, the community had a chance to document the positive stories of the casino era when the National Gaming Impact Study Commission came to town. The NGIS commission included anti-gambling, 'Focus on the Family' leader James Dobson and Kay James, NGIS Chairperson and Dobson's associate on the 'Focus on the Family' board. To his chagrin, Dobson listened to numerous stories of the casinos' positive impacts on various individuals: city officials, casino managers and rank-and-file employees. At one point during the hearings, Dobson, who probably based his perception of Atlantic City on the negative national publicity of the 1980s, became agitated because so much testimony was positive – something he found incredible. He attacked New Jersey Senator Robert Torricelli for advocating for the casinos and complained that

> We need more balance in the presentations. We make these site visits to hear the pros and cons. There must be problems that need to be addressed, but we're not hearing them. We need to hear from both sides.

As the Commission pulled out of town, Congressman Frank LoBiondo remarked that

> The commission tried to dig up dirt. They made several visits to Atlantic City to find witnesses who they thought would spin this in a bad light. They weren't successful because that's not the story, [if it was] they would have found plenty of negatives.[493]

Even if there were problems, in 1998 the commission could not easily point to Atlantic City as a community that needed some kind of federal regulation or taxation, as many who testified believed was the commission's goal. The NGIS group stayed at the Flagship – a non-casino Boardwalk suite hotel – and received guided tours of the community, listened to local officials, casino executives, a representative of the Atlantic City Rescue Mission and others from the community. Especially prominent on the witness stand were rank-and-file members of HERE Local 54, the service employees union so prominent in the casino community for the entire era. Local 54 showed up in force at the Convention Center's hearing room wearing matching orange tee-shirts. The union members occasionally cheered each other's remarks which prompted a scolding from the chair, who condescendingly claimed that the applause delayed the proceedings. Local 54's membership, approximately 15,000 casino employees at the time, represented the guts of every casino's operations. They spoke as bartenders, porters, cooks, cocktail waitresses and banquet servers. But mostly they spoke as proud members of a community and a lifestyle that needed defence, as they perceived it, in the wake of federal scrutiny.

There were some elements of production to the testimony, and some whose responses seemed scripted to glorify their union in particular. But largely they were honest, earnest statements that encapsulated the mainly positive impact of the casinos on thousands of working people in the region. The NGIS hearing highlighted the significant role of Local 54 in conjunction with the casino industry as co-guarantors of individual prosperity. For example, Atlantic City Hilton waitress Frances Brevin described her eighteen-year career at the casino as a sharp contrast to her pre-casino employment, in which she got by with meagre wages and non-existent benefits. In her casino career, she received 'a fair wage and terrific benefits'. William Maguire, bartender, described his status in simple terms as 'good job and good life' and the community as rife 'with jobs, good jobs'. Cindy Armstrong, a Harrah's cocktail waitress, proclaimed herself very satisfied with the industry and painted a poignant image of the difference between her Atlantic City and her father's Atlantic City. Whereas her father – a union pipe fitter – had to travel far and wide for gainful employment, Armstrong and her husband (a Trump Marina bartender) could work alternate shifts, had substantial time for their family and enough money to afford a new house. Likewise, Ira Shtab, a cook at the Sands, described his casino position as a vast improvement from his former North Jersey job that provided no benefits and left him with thousands in medical bills after a newborn child's death. In Atlantic City, his 'salary doubled', he had medical benefits, and he and his dealer wife lived a decent life that included a 401 K plan. Tara Mains, an Atlantic City Hilton cocktail server, reviewed her casino career, one that began at Resorts in 1978, took her to the Playboy casino as a Playboy bunny and led her to the Atlantic City Hilton after a city job simply did not pay well enough. In Mains's view, these experiences and those of others like her demonstrated that the casino industry 'brought a lot of hope to town'.[494]

Throughout the testimony, a number of Local 54 members described their experiences as an American dream achieved. For some, this involved getting children into college. Bartender Bill Barry proudly discussed his daughter, the Richard Stockton State College graduate, and his son at John Jay College in New York. Others spoke of owning a house or forging a 'stable way of life' via casino employment. To some, prosperity and success in the casino community had everything to do with maintaining family ties. This was the case for Cindy Armstrong's husband (Kevin Armstrong) who lauded the casinos for employing himself and seven siblings, so they could 'stay close as a family' by remaining in South Jersey. Jerry Breeden, a bartender at Caesar's, spoke about his father, who went from being a usually-unemployed electrician in the pre-casino years to someone constantly employed into the 1990s. Breeden also related his own family story: in 1979 Caesar's hired his grandfather, brother and cousin when he was hired. He, like others, defined their casino-powered American dreams in terms of material success, home ownership and family stability. Sydney Meadows of Showboat expressed his satisfaction with the casinos for improving the resort's profile.[495]

The stories of the Local 54 rank and file were designed for a specific purpose – to present the industry and its community impact in a positive light. Nevertheless, the cocktail waitresses, food servers, cooks and bartenders who trekked over to the Convention Center in their orange shirts drew a clear picture of American success in the casino era. In effect, they spoke for the tens of thousands of blue-collar residents who had found a modest but certain prosperity where only bleak prospects had existed before. Importantly, they defined their personal achievements within the framework of community achievement. Living in places like Pleasantville, Northfield, Ventnor, Egg Harbor Township, Hamilton and Galloway, their comfortable lives could easily be missed by the visitors who made beelines for the casinos, often passing through the bleakest areas of Atlantic City. But their lives, the lives of those who reaped the benefits of casino wealth, form a more significant part of the casino-era story than those of the relatively few who did not reap similar benefits.

The casino employees testifying to potentially sceptical commissioners understood the casino dream to be broader than any individual success story. They tried hard to get this across, in some cases highlighting community achievement. Frances Brevin used her time to highlight the tangible benefits of suburban life in Northfield that the casino made possible, like the new $17 million elementary school, 'new shopping centers' and 'new homes'. Brevin also made a significant verbal slip when she told the commission that her employment benefits included a paid vacation, 'something I never received in the private sector'. Why would Bevin imply that her casino employment was in the public sector when her casino employers were so clearly private and for-profit? Her mistake was quite under-standable given the reality of the casino era and the industry's evolution since the 1970s. From the beginning, the Atlantic City casino industry had a power-ful public purpose. The casinos were quasi-public organizations fully integrated with the public apparatus of state and local government. To be sure the private business of the casinos (a $5 billion annual industry by 1998) drove the culture. But at every step public entities like the NJCCC, or the City of Atlantic City or the CRDA monitored, expanded, controlled, directed and collaborated with the industry. These unique partnerships and regulatory mechanisms impacted employees and local residents to such a degree that one can easily understand how a career food server at the Atlantic City Hilton could perceive her employer as separate from 'the private sector'.[496]

Two decades of gaming had, in fact, brought benefits and economic oppor-tunity to thousands of South Jerseyites and others. Between 1978 and 1996, the eight per cent on casino gross revenues raised $3.46 billion for the CRF. CRF money was dedicated to assisting the state's elderly and disabled residents. In the fiscal year 1996, the CRF gave $173.3 million for the Pharmaceutical Assistance to the Aged and Disabled programme. CRF support also included millions for a 'Lifeline' programme to offset high utility bills. In 1998, the casinos paid out $1.06 billion in salaries and wages to their employees – approximately 78 per cent of whom lived in Atlantic County. Close to one third of Atlantic City residents (approximately 11,000) worked in the casinos, along with thousands of people from surrounding counties like Cape May, Camden, Cumberland, Ocean and Gloucester. In 1997, these surrounding counties (outside Atlantic) employed 20 per cent of the casino workforce. Twenty years into the casino era, the industry was a huge component of the South Jersey economy, well beyond the boundaries of Atlantic County. According to a 1995 Rowan University study, the industry also created 1.09 jobs for every direct casino job, pumping another billion dollars into the local economy. The economy created a population boom in the region. Although population in Atlantic City actually declined from around 41,200 in 1980 to 38,361 in 1996, Atlantic County's population increased from 189,012 to 235,447 in the same period – a growth rate of over 24 per cent.[497]

What kind of jobs were these, in terms of compensation? One common com-plaint about the casinos was that the jobs created were largely low-wage and not viable enough for subsistence.[498] In reality, by 1998 the casinos provided mostly solid jobs that were overwhelmingly full-time (91 per cent) and that paid fairly well with tips, especially if benefits were factored in. Unionized or not (and deal-ers were not), full-time casino employees received health benefits, retirement plans, disability pay, vacation time and free meals while working. 56 per cent of all employees made between $20,000 and $40,000 – a percentage that increased to 81 per cent when the range expanded to $15,000 to $50,000. These wages should also be considered in the context of a largely un-educated casino workforce. Of all casino employees, a mere 15 per cent had a four-year college degree in 1998 and over half (approximately 52 per cent) had only a high school education or less. Without much education, one could still make a solid, stable income with benefits in the Atlantic City casino era. 95 per cent of Atlantic City's unionized casino employees earned pension benefits compared to just 45 per cent of private-sector workers nationwide. Twice as many unionized casino employees had family health insurance than similar workers across New Jersey and the United States.[499]

Despite all the jobs, Atlantic City unemployment was still at 12.7 per cent in 1997, and overall county unemployment was slightly higher than New Jersey at 5.7 per cent, compared to the state's 3.8 per cent in 2000. Though somewhat lower than two adjacent rural counties (Cape May and Cumberland), Atlantic County's rate probably reflected the city's persistent social problems. The job losses described in an economic bulletin were possibly short-term and layoffs, as opposed to the persistent long-term unemployment of the casino era. Despite the year-round casino operations, there was still a seasonal component to the region's unemployment, with the rate fluctuating by as much as 3 points between seasons.[500] Atlantic City continued to lag behind the region economically well into the first decade of the twenty-first century. In 2003, only about 5 per cent of the 10,500 city residents who worked in the city were 'key' employees (supervisors or higher), and close to 70 per cent of city residents were renters. No wonder that Eleanor May, a senior citizen and veteran casino housekeeper, commented to a reporter that 'Whatever the casinos bring in is for them. It doesn't come across Atlantic Avenue'. Yet, the casino impact on May's own family was substantial – all three of her daughters worked for casinos with good jobs on the casino floor or in their computer operations.[501]

At a Garden Pier dinner sometime around the turn of the century, a writer briefly discussed his book project with Jim Whelan. Whelan seemed concerned that the upcoming story would in fact, be another 'tale of two cities' about Atlantic City.[502] Whelan's apprehension made sense because this had become a powerful literary theme for discussing Atlantic City in the casino era during his reign as mayor, from 1990 to 2001.[503] It was also a notion heard in some of the oral history research conducted for this book, particularly as a guiding theme to explain the persistence of inner-city problems like poverty and street crime, despite the billions in new wealth created along the Boardwalk and in the marina district. The tunnel-connector project added to this, with the largely African-American residents of the central Westside neighbourhood perceiving that they were 'disposable'. In 1998, a Westsider remarked to a reporter that the casinos 'turned our streets into speedways.'[504]

But just how accurately does this describe Atlantic City's casino era? The purposeful Dickensian allusion evokes a picture of crass, un-feeling capitalism – inhumane in a classic sense. While the theme may have had just a little basis in truth during the difficult early years,[505] a more substantive review of the historical material and anecdotal evidence suggests that the 'tale of two cites' theme was more of a mythical framework, largely inaccurate in describing the casino impact on the region as a whole (Atlantic City's population was down to about 16 per cent of the combined city and Atlantic County population by the late 1990s). A more accurate regional perspective would also factor in the casino impact in much of South Jersey, including Cape May, Cumberland and Camden counties.

The crime spike of the 1970s and early 1980s had also done much to further the 'two cities' theme, to the detriment of inner-city residents. But in the 1990s, one could hardly make that case as crime dropped substantially across the city at a higher rate than at national or state level. Between 1990 and 1996, the city's overall visitor-adjusted crime index dropped by 34.3 per cent, significantly more drastic than the state drop (20.4 per cent) or the national decrease (12.5 per cent), The visitor-adjusted index for violent crime dropped even more – by 39.2 per cent, compared to 12.7 per cent and 12.3 per cent for the state and nation respectively. In 2000, a city government newsletter proudly proclaimed that 'Crime is down FIFTY PERCENT!' Aside from the broader national decrease in crime, city authorities were justifiably boastful of this accomplishment and attributed it to a focus on community policing, more beat cops, police accessibility, special operations targeting tough neighbourhoods, a bonus for officers who lived in the city, and a bicycle patrol.[506]

The perception of a lack of opportunity for the city's African-American community may be rooted in high black inner-city unemployment, but did not accurately reflect the substantial affirmative action and minority contracting policies that the industry had had in place for decades. Via the NJCCC, the casinos actually set goals for minority employment in nine specific job categories. By the mid-1990s, all the casinos had met these goals in eight of the nine categories, though some categories, such as 'Craftspersons' (c. 17 per cent minority) and 'Technicians' (c. 21 per cent minority), had not made much progress or even slipped a bit. Yet, by 1997, half of all casino employees were minorities: 17 per cent were Hispanic employees, 19 per cent were black and 11 per cent were Asian.[507] These numbers were actually in greater proportion to comparable numbers of minorities in the region, as measured by census data for Atlantic County from 1990 and 2000. If casino employment were measured in terms of minority proportions in Atlantic City alone, then these numbers would probably be lower than the population at large. However, that would be an unfair measurement, given the regional scope of the industry and the reality that 75 per cent of all employees lived outside Atlantic City.

The overly strict licensure requirements probably did hold back a significant portion of the city population until the early 1990s when they were substantially loosened. However, the new opportunities created by the casino industry for the local population were an important story and thousands benefited from them through the years. For a twenty-year-anniversary newspaper article, fifty-seven-year old Cornelius Cyrus reflected on his own positive experience in the casino era. Cyrus was a security guard at Harrah's, born and raised in Atlantic City. He recalled the difficulty 'getting a job from Labor Day to Memorial Day' in the pre-casino era, but remembered that the city's tourist industry offered up many hotel jobs in the summer. For a while, he operated elevators at the old Dennis and Traymore hotels. When the pre-casino tourist industry 'really failed', he took low-paying industrial or retail jobs when he could find them – stretching aluminum or pressing clothes – until even those jobs dried up. In 1986, he found work at Harrah's and his fortunes changed – his version of the American dream achieved.[508] In 2003, the opportunities continued to flow to city residents with some motivation and initiative. Such was the case for twenty-year old Jose Rivera, barber at an Atlantic Avenue salon who also earned $19.75 an hour as a Navy-trained computer technician for Caesar's.[509]

Opportunities for minorities in the casinos received a boost from the NJCCC in the early 1990s. In 1992, the commission took action to ensure greater opportunity in the casino era by creating a special directory of minority/women-owned business enterprises (M/WBE) that could do business with the casinos. Also in 1992, the NJCCC held a hearing to specifically examine the issue of M/WBE contracting and heard from a variety of sources that the casinos needed to do a better job supporting it, as only around half of the casinos met 5 or 10 per cent goals in 1991.[510] In 1993, the Commission implemented a new programme that allowed each casino to develop Equal Employment / Business Opportunity Plans designed to address areas where they were not meeting minority requirements by job category or contractual employment. By 1993, the industry had made some progress in this area, in fact increasing the total volume of MBE contracting dollars to $42.5 million, 4.49 per cent of the total amount for MBE's, up from $14.3 million or 1.7 per cent in 1988. In 1992, Pierre Hollingsworth acknowledged the casinos' improving record on minority hiring as well, important praise coming from a usually fierce critic on this particular issue. Despite the progress, the industry still remained under the overall CCA statute that 15 per cent of contracting should be from M/WBE, at 12.2 per cent of purchasing in 1993.[511]

During a 1992 hearing on M/WBE, an interesting exchange took place between Kaleem Shabazz, advisory committee chairman and NJCCC commissioner Frank 'Pat' Dodd over the commission's role in minority contracting. Shabazz suggested that the casinos' affirmative action officers faced subtle pressure from management not to act too aggressively and that the officers complied to preserve their jobs. His solution was for the officers to become NJCCC employees to guarantee their independence. Commissioner Dodd disagreed with this approach, not wanting public officials to have such an impact on contracting or hiring decisions.[512] The exchange between Shabazz and Dodd displayed a natural conflict between the deregulatory shift of the era and the state's original mission of urban revitalization. Shabazz understood the commission's role as an agency that should directly intervene in the business operations of the casinos, in this case for minority contracting. Dodd's response symbolized the changing times as the NJCCC moved away from intervening in the business of the casinos, newly understanding its mission as to support the casinos in their business decisions.

The commission's approach to affirmative action shifted the emphasis on quota counting to collaboration with the casinos, and all casinos in fact improved their minority hiring between 1992 and 1995 between 1 and 7 per cent per job category. Meanwhile, M/WBE purchasing really took off across the industry in the same period, jumping to 26.6 per cent of the total, or $243.1 million in 1995. MBE purchasing increased to 11.6 per cent of the total in 1995, a major leap from the 1–2 per cent levels of the late 1980s. NJCCC commissioner Jeannine LaRue attributed the shift to a familiar justification – far greater collaboration between the industry and its regulators:

> The panic of meeting quotas is gone. People don't want you in their face, pointing a finger, saying that you'd better hire women and minorities. The message from the commission is that we are concerned with the programme itself, and the casinos cooperative effort reach goals. Once we took the adversarial environment out of the issue of affirmative action, everybody agreed there should be a level playing field.

The commission's affirmative action chief suggested that the relationship between the casinos and NJCCC on affirmative action moved 'from cellar to flying sky high in the sky'. How did this happen? Mainly, by renewed outreach and recruitment programmes. For example, Harrah's used minority search firms, national searches and an undergraduate intern programme to reach its goals. Trump Castle implemented a 'career enrichment program' to bring selected lower-paid workers into a higher income bracket, above $35,000 annually. At Claridge, Laura Monaghan benefited from acceptance into a 'Quality Track' programme that targeted women and minorities for promotion to supervisor positions. She utilized the programme to move from gift shop clerk to professional development specialist at the casino. Bally's Grand executive director of bus marketing Vicki Tilton spoke of her success moving up the ladder: 'There are numerous opportunities for woman and minorities in the gaming industry'. Sherryl Lynn Blackwell of the Sands worked her way up from front desk agent to transportation assistant manager between 1983 and 1995. Yet she subtly noted a prejudice that would be impossible for any NJCCC programme to eradicate: 'Perhaps the greatest obstacle a black female faces in climbing the corporate ladder is the perception your supervisors have of you and your capabilities'. The increased emphasis on M/BWE purchasing did have some complications for the existing network of casino suppliers however. When the NJCCC created the new M/BWE directory and began to heavily promote its use, some of the existing contractors were very much put off. Stories about the system's abuse in the early also became commonplace as some licensed contractors apparently just transferred ownership to wives or other female relatives as a way of qualifying as a WBE.[513]

Ultimately, the issue of the casinos' impact on the urban minority populations was never easily resolved in the mind of the community. In fact, the casino industry had done wonders to provide economic opportunity to a depressed local population, by way of jobs and business that simply did not exist before. But it certainly did not eradicate the pockets of deep poverty and urban decay that continued to plague Atlantic City into the new millennium.[514] Meanwhile, the long and bitter battle over the tunnel-connector only served to emphasize perceptions of unfairness and inequity in the casino era. In fact, this perception played a crucial role in the 2001 mayoral race that brought the second African-American to the mayor's office – city councilman and former pit boss Lorenzo Langford.

Contrary, however, to the perception that some in the inner city, and millions of Atlantic City visitors, shared about the casino era, urban dysfunction and poverty were not the prevailing realities of its first thirty years. In fact, the economic story of the casino era is much more of a suburban and regional story about South Jersey. The suburban communities were the main repositories of all those gambling losses and the casino industry dominated the economy throughout the region. By 1993, approximately 75 per cent of the Atlantic County economy was dependent upon the casinos according to one county analysis. Besides the twelve casinos, there were only four institutions that employed over 1,000 people in Atlantic County in 2000: three hospitals and Richard Stockton College. As the casino industry continued its revenue expansion in the 1990, places like Brigantine and Egg Harbor Township really took off. By 1997, employment in the four-county southern Jersey economic region (Atlantic, Cape May, Cumberland, Salem) had risen to its highest level ever – with 5,000 new non-farm jobs added. Bedroom communities pushed farther and farther out into the region surrounding Atlantic City as the construction and housing blitz that hit Atlantic County in the 1980s now extended to Cape May and Cumberland. In 1997, Cumberland's non-residential construction activity grew by 161 per cent while Cape May grew at 50 per cent, well above the state's 25 per cent growth level. Between 1980 and 2000, Cape May County's population increased by 25 per cent, while Ocean County's population (to the north) was one of the fastest growing in the state by 2000. In the prosperous 1990s, one could barely find a more dynamic economy than South Jersey's greater casino region.[515]

Atlantic County development remained restricted in much of the county throughout the casino era due to Pinelands conservation. After passing the Pinelands Protections Act in 1979, the New Jersey legislature developed and adopted the New Jersey Comprehensive Management Plan (CMP). The CMP took effect in 1981 and put vast acreage of Pinelands forest under state management. Pinelands preservation was well-intended for environmental reasons, yet collided with the booming reality of casino-related development in the 1980s and 1990s. Placing half the county (west of the Garden State Parkway) essentially off-limits to large sub-divisions was bound to spur resistance from township authorities, and that was exactly what happened. Officials in the growth-targeted townships resented the uneven development concentrated in their areas. A former Egg Harbor Township mayor (James 'Sonny' McCullough) looked back on the state's mandate and the local controversy that ensured:

> So they decided they were going to take the three big townships that were around Atlantic City and designate them as the high growth municipalities. And they said to the municipalities – and Egg Harbor Township being the largest – they said you will create a master plan that will call for 33,000 additional homes in half your county. Well, every governing body fought forever.

Under Mayor McCullough, Egg Harbor Township held out from compliance with the Pinelands restrictions until 1993. Despite the restrictions, by 2000 growth was shifting ever westward into the more rural parts of townships like Galloway and Hamilton, in a 'second wave' of development via the casino economy. New building permits slowed considerably in the 1990s, declining by two-thirds from the levels of the 1980s, yet growth was still concentrated in the big three townships: Egg Harbor Township, Galloway and Hamilton.[516]

In the years following casino legalization, the Atlantic County population increased at a very rapid rate – around 1.6 per cent annually between 1980 and 1990. In the 1990s, the county's population growth was half that of the 1980s – 0.8 per cent, but still vibrant and much higher than the state's population increase in the same period. Between 1990 and 2000, Atlantic County's population grew by 9.2 per cent to 244,900 compared to New Jersey's 6 per cent growth in the decade. Also in the 1990s, many of the new housing developments around the county required shopping centres, and these sprung up in places like Somers Point, Absecon, Brigantine, Hammonton and Hamilton Township. These added to the Hamilton Mall and English Creek shopping centres built in the 1980s. By 1997, national chains like Fuddruckers, Lonestar, Applebee's and Outback were 'feeding the newly resurgent casino-based economy', according to one restaurant analyst. The positive restaurant marketplace in the suburbs was in stark contrast to the situation in Atlantic City, where the casinos effectively retained their gambling visitors' meal money as well as their gaming money. Despite this, venues like Rainforest Café and Planet Hollywood also opened along the Boardwalk in the late 1990s.[517]

The real regional impact of the casino industry in greater Atlantic City was on the small business community of South Jersey. All around Atlantic county and surrounding areas, local businesspeople adjusted, moved and often prospered by catering to the casinos directly, or to their legions of employees that lived in the townships. Pasquale DiPalma Jr, a men's clothier, took advantage of the industry's reach to open a branch of the family business Italian Dimension in Northfield. Initially, the DiPalmas were not uplifted by the casinos. DiPalma noted, 'they could have sent them [high rollers] over in a limousine' to his store, rather than outfitting them within the casinos. But the casino employees – not the customers – eventually proved to be the key for Italian Dimension, DiPalma noted that his Northfield store was 'where the [casino] people, and especially the higher-level executives live'. The sponsors of a 1998 anniversary magazine demonstrated the comprehensive economic impact of the casinos on the community. They included a florist, building contractors, an advertising studio, a public relations firm, chauffeurs, lorry drivers and a 'theatrical and stage employees' union. Sixteen years into the casino era (1994), 6,014 small businesses existed in Atlantic County – up from 4,236 in 1977. This 42 per cent increase far exceeded the county's population increase in the same time span. A 1999 city study estimated the creation of 1.82 indirect jobs for every direct job created by a large-scale casino (such as the Trump Taj Mahal, or then-planned Le Jardin Palais). The study also estimated $250 million in annual goods and purchases for such a casino, helping to explain the broad-based public support for the big casino projects on the table at the time.[518] The owner of one women's apparel chain originally had shops in both Tropicana and Showboat, but eventually closed them and opened up a store in expanding Margate, down the shore. The shop owner, Ira Zelden, reflected on the business experience for a 2000 New York Times article: 'You can't get them in a cocktail dress when they come in a nylon jogging suit'. In contrast, Christine Brown actually moved her videotaping business from Egg Harbor Township to the Ocean One Mall in Atlantic City and found her casino-related business quadruple.[519]

The ripple effect of casino wealth was felt, for example, in the Atlantic County legal community. In 2003, 600 lawyers practised in the county, compared to 150 in 1975. Most of these lawyers represented small business people and according to the local bar association president, 'Neither they, nor their clients, would be here without the casino industry'. The same was true for a whole legion of professionals who worked in service industries and who filled the jobs created with casino revenue. They were electricians, plumbers, accountants – many directly employed by the casinos, others in unions and firms contracted by the casinos, or with casino employees as customers.[520] Harry Hasson, who in the mid-1970s had struggled to maintain a one-shop, two-person operation, had expanded to five shops and overt thirty employees by the 1990s. It was a remarkable story of business growth. Without casinos, the family business begun in the 1920s would probably have folded by 1980.[521]

Throughout the casino era, casino spending on goods and services steadily rose and helped float the regional economy, along with the billions paid out directly in salaries and wages. In 1999, the casinos spent $810.9 million on goods and services in Atlantic County alone, out of a total $1.48 billion paid out to New Jersey firms for goods and services and $2.31 billion paid out in total to vendors supporting the casinos. In 1999, Cape May County firms benefited from $17.2 million in casino spending, while rural Cumberland businesses brought in $7.4 million via the casinos. In 1999, the casino's financial reach into South Jersey was broader than it was in 1989, as proximate counties Cape May, Gloucester, Ocean, Cumberland and Camden all increased their percentages of casino business substantially. In 2003, approximately 14 per cent of licensed casino employees (6,283 people) lived in these surrounding counties.[522]

Though crime in Atlantic County also increased in the 1980s, it never was close to the high levels in Atlantic City. It decreased during the 1990s, falling faster than the state's overall decline during the decade. In terms of violent crime, the county rate was higher than the state's rate, though appeared to decline slightly as the state levelled off in the early 1990s. Of course, Atlantic City is in Atlantic County, so the city's sharp reduction probably impacted the county's numbers. Between 1995 and 2000, violent crime in Atlantic County decreased from about 10 per 1,000 persons to 5 per 1,000 – a 50 per cent drop that was more significant than the state's 37 per cent drop in the same time span. In 2000, eighteen out of twenty-three cities and townships in the county actually had crime indexes lower than the state's 34.2 crimes per 1,000 people. The townships included the fastest growing, large areas of Egg Harbor Township and Galloway. As with Atlantic City, there is no conclusive data linking crime to the casino impact on Atlantic County. Despite perceptions, even the NGIS could not establish a link between casinos and community crime.[523]

In other indicators of community risk, Atlantic County often fared higher than the state average during the casino era, though often within a few percentage points. For example, the 1990 census showed that approximately 13.2 per cent of children in the county lived in poverty compared to the state average of 11.3 per cent. Also in 1990, approximately 9.5 per cent of county residents used food stamps compared to 7.2 per cent of New Jerseyites as a whole. In addition, county divorce rates and domestic violence rates were among the highest in the state. In 2000, there were approximately twenty domestic violence incidents for every 1,000 Atlantic County residents, more than twice the state average. Cumberland and Cape May counties were also high in this area. Atlantic County also had one of the lower rates of college education in New Jersey in 2000, at 18.6 per cent for adults over 25, significantly lower than the state average of 29.8 per cent. While this rate had increased from 2.2 per cent in 1990, it had gone up far less than the state's overall increase of 4.9 per cent. Yet, Atlantic County also halved its high school dropout rate in the 1990s, while the state's reduction was somewhat less.[524] Low educational attainment probably had something to do with casino opportunities, as a former Pleasantville guidance counselor observed:

You see a lot of them when you go to the casinos to work, or you see a lot of them around in the region, shopping somewhere, with their casino uniforms on. They seem to be more focused on working in the casino [than going to college].[525]

In other community risk factors like drug and alcohol abuse, adolescent aliena-tion and AIDS cases, Atlantic County typically fared in the bottom half of the state's counties. The greater Atlantic City region's generally low rating on most social indicators of community well-being is partially explained by the commu-nity problems in Atlantic City. The city was still the largest area of the county in 2000 with a population of 40,517 – close to 9,000 more people than the next highest area, Galloway Township. In many ways, the city's poor showing in areas like unemployment continued to weigh down the county. For example, fourteen out of twenty-three cities and townships in Atlantic County were actually within one percentage point of the 2000 state unemployment rate of 3.6 per cent, includ-ing Galloway, Egg Harbor and Hamilton townships.[526]

Compulsive gambling and the problems that stemmed from it drove up indicators of social pathology in greater Atlantic City during the casino era. It is hard to quantify the percentage of problem and compulsive gamblers in the general population. The NGIS Commission found that that anywhere from 1.7 per cent to 7.3 per cent of gamblers are compulsive gamblers, or at least problem gamblers. Gambling addicts and problem gamblers can cause a ripple effect of troubles for themselves, their families and their communities. In 2001, for exam-ple, bankruptcy filings from Atlantic City were twice as high as both state and national averages. As well, problems associated with pathological gambling were more acute amongst young people in Atlantic City after the casinos opened.[527] Throughout the first thirty years of the casino era, underage gambling remained an issue, though in the 1990s the casinos and the DGE confronted the problem more directly. In 1994, casino security prevented 142,844 young people from entering the casino and escorted 10,815 young people from casinos. In 2000, 53,862 did not make it inside the casinos while 34,817 were escorted from the casinos. In 1999, NJCCC Chair James Hurley testified in Trenton that of the 30,000 plus underage people annually ejected from casinos, 'fewer than 500 are actually found gambling, but casinos know that we take this issue very seriously'. In 2001, the state legislature passed an act creating a 'Self-Exclusion Program' for compulsive gamblers to have themselves legally banned from casinos.[528]

In the 1980s, Steve Perskie spoke to a local seventh-grade class where he found out how the casinos were making an impression on young people in the com-munity:

So I say to them, OK, who's got an idea for a bill that you want to become a law? Let's take that idea and we'll see how it works. So raise your hand, give me an idea. And kid raises his hand and he says, lower the gambling age to

16. And it was like he hit me with a hammer. So I said OK, and then when I took that idea and I showed them how it would become a law, but I deliberately left about 10 or 15 minutes at the end and once we got it into law I said OK. I said now let's have a conversation. I said why is that a good idea? You could pay for college. You could buy a car. You can live at — Now if you think all these 20 years later that this conversation didn't bother me, imagine why it's 20 years later that I can remember every word of it. I said, let me ask you a question. I said, did any of you notice in this morning's newspaper – you know the casinos were terrific. Every time somebody would go in and win a jackpot, a $990,000 jackpot, their picture would be on the front page of the newspaper. So I said to Ben, did you see the story in the paper this morning where this lady from Brooklyn won a million and a half dollars? I remember seeing it. I said who'd she win that from? And maybe she won it from Harrah's, she'd won it from Resorts, and I kept taking my hit and finally tried to explain to them who she won the money from.[529]

As the 1990s came to a close, the climate was still positive for the casino industry. The tunnel-connector was finally being built, construction on the Borgata was imminent, the Convention Center was beginning to increase convention business, and the city even had a new minor-league baseball team called the Atlantic City Surf playing in a new, CRDA-funded stadium on Albany Avenue (the Sandcastle). Nine years of the Whelan administration had changed the relationship between the casino industry and city government for the better. Meanwhile, the casinos increased their share of local property taxes to 80 per cent in 1998, up from 62 per cent in 1984. From a business perspective, many of the casinos were operating more smoothly and more leanly than before. For example, Showboat had reduced its full-time gaming employees by almost 20 per cent between 1995 and 1998, while showing a significant increase in gaming revenues and profitability – a 14.7 per cent growth increase in gross operating profit in 1998. After a brief, but dramatic dip in growth in 1996 after a record-breaking 1995, the overall gross operating profit increased at an average of 6.8 per cent between 1997 and 1999. Total and net revenues climbed in the same span between 2 and 3 per cent on average, although the corporate shuffling of the period had begun to weed out smaller or less well-capitalized casinos. For instance, the Sands casino remained a poor performer, entering into bankruptcy in 1998, and actually declining in net revenue to $246.8 million in 1999, compared to $256.3 million in 1997. The Claridge was another increasingly isolated, smaller operation not competing well in the consolidation era – dropping from $177.4 million total revenue in 1997 to $173.6 million in 1999. Resorts, Trump Plaza and Trump Taj Mahal also appeared to be losing ground in the overall marketplace, with declining revenues at a time of overall increase across the casino industry in Atlantic City. By contrast, Caesar's increased its net revenue from $401.2 million in 1997 to $493.9 million in 1999. Similarly, Bally's grew its net revenue at a fast pace in the same period, from $456.3 million in 1997 to $545.6 million 1999. Las Vegas-based Aztar Corporation's Tropicana also registered a sizeable increase in net revenue in these years, from $371.7 million in 1997 to $398.5 million in 1999. Harrah's net revenue jumped from $323 million in 1997 to $382.8 million in 1997 – an 18.5 per cent rise in two years.[530]

In the late 1990s, many casinos also became more efficient as they relied more on full-time employees and consequently increased their average 'win' per employee. In 1998, Trump Taj Mahal earned $101,342 per full-time employee, up from $87,113 in 1995. In 1998, Showboat earned $114,346 per full-time employee compared to $92,230 in 1995. Harrah's increased its 'win' by 6.7 per cent between 1995 and 1998, to $106,184 in 1998. According to a close industry observer, the greater efficiency was probably tied to the casinos' increasing emphasis on slot machines, which were less 'labor intensive than tables' and to the fact that all the casinos had been 'searching for economies of scale and trying to make it with fewer bodies'. Almost all the casinos increased the proportion of casino floor space devoted to slot machines (slots density) in the late 1990s. From 1996 to 1998, Atlantic City Hilton (formerly Bally's Grand) increased from 54.8 per cent to 60.6 per cent, Showboat from 64.5 per cent to 82.08 per cent, Trump Plaza from 67.5 per cent to 81.4 per cent and Caesar's from 53.5 per cent to 72.6. Meanwhile the Sands bucked the trend by reducing slots density to 57.4 per cent in 1998, from 66.7 per cent in 1996, and also ended up in bankruptcy court in 1999. Meanwhile, some data also indicated that the resort had progressed a little towards its 'destination' ideal. In 1998, with a few hundred less annual visitors from 1997 (approximately 33.5 million), the casino actually paid over $2 million more in luxury taxes to the city, suggesting growth in non-gaming revenue. Hotel occupancy tax revenues were also on the rise in the late 1990s, again indicating some success in the long-standing goal to reclaim the community's identity as a destination resort.[531]

The contrasting fortunes of the various casinos in the late 1990s appeared to prove the 1995 *Casino Journal* prediction that the casinos needed to look for deeper pockets (i.e. corporate partners and parents) for expansion. By then, national competition and the Las Vegas boom had already transformed the American casino era, and casino insiders hungered more for deeper 'tourism infrastructure – the hotels, other entertainment attractions, transportation facilities' necessary for them to attain deeper market attraction and retain customers.[532] Between 1995 and 1999, the more successful casinos in Atlantic City accomplished success by expanding their gaming and hotel facilities. Meanwhile, the city (via the CRDA) added to the non-casino entertainment features a minor-league baseball stadium, a new 'Grand Boulevard' entrance from the Atlantic City Expressway, Gardner's Basin, a new aquarium and a cleaner and safer Boardwalk. Yet, the extent to which these facilities attracted new casino patrons was never clear – unto themselves, did they bring Atlantic City to that ever-elusive goal of once again becoming a 'destination resort'? There is really not much evidence that they ever had that effect, yet they may have improved the quality of life for local residents.

The casinos themselves essentially increased their revenue base and grew more successful via expansion and creativity – having been spurred into action by Foxwoods' and Mirage's success and the threat of legalized gaming on the east coast. Much less restricted, they grew in ways necessary for survival, and this meant expansion, if you could afford it. By 2000, the casino community had benefited from $3.2 billion capital investment since 1989, approximately doubling the original investment of the first decade of the casino era (which included the exorbitant Taj Mahal). From 1978 to 2000, the casinos invested about $6.8 billion into Atlantic City. So Bally's added Wild, Wild West, Harrah's built a $20 million new buffet restaurant, and Caesar's built a grandiose, Romanesque lobby. All saw their business rise dramatically and the industry added about 7,000 jobs in these years – to 47,366 total employment in 1999, despite no additional casino coming online. By contrast, the Trump casinos were somewhat held back due to the company's heavy debt load. Claridge, Resorts and Sands remained stalled in place due to a lack of capital investment coming from corporate entities, with both Claridge and the Sands filing for bankruptcy in 1999. At one point, Sun International did invest $50 million in renovations to Resorts, but Sun sold off Resorts to Colony Capital in 2001 without ever committing to more substantial improvements.[533] The message was even more clear in 2000 than it had been in 1995 – casinos needed to merge, grow, consolidate and expand to survive in the ever more competitive marketplace. Atlantic City's successful casinos created their own version of a destination resort to fit the reality of the casino era, and their niche within it. The ones that could afford it essentially made themselves into fulfilling destinations by the beginning of the twenty-first century. The old resort town was once again becoming a 'destination resort', albeit not the one that many had originally envisioned. But it was successful and continued to bring prosperity to the region, prosperity that had been severely threatened just a few years earlier.

In early 1999, a very significant acquisition took place when Park Place Entertainment, Inc. (PPE) purchased Caesar's World from Starwood Resorts for $3 billion in cash and created the largest casino company in the world. This brought up issues of industry concentration, dealt with by the Commission in hearings during the year. The CCC finally approved of the deal at the end of 1999. The merger meant that Park Place would soon control approximately 30.4 per cent of the $5.04 billion Atlantic City gaming market, as measured by 1999 total revenue figures. But the CCC could hardly rule against the Park Place–Caesar's merger given that Trump Hotels and Casino Resorts already controlled 28 per cent of the local gaming market (using 1999 total revenue figures) and had been a formidable, concentrated industry block for almost a decade. The commission also had to weigh its decision in the context of the looming Mirage and MGM Grand projects, soon to bring in the biggest Las Vegas casino firms.[534]

Engineered by PPE CEO Arthur Goldberg and Hilton CEO Stephen Bollenbach, the PPE–Caesar's merger reflected the nationalization of the casino era, a trend often spearheaded in the 1990s by the more successful Atlantic City operations like Harrah's and Park Place. The merger also gave PPE and Goldberg leverage to strike a deal in 2000 with the St Regis Mohawk Indians to develop the former Kutsher's Catskill resort into a casino in upstate New York. The PPE–Caesar's merger was also the capstone deal and final great achievement for Arthur Goldberg, who died young, at fifty-eight in late 2000. In 2000, PPE sought to add to its middle-Boardwalk casino empire by initiating a long process to acquire the struggling Claridge. In 2001, the regulators finally approved the deal after finding that it would 'not result in undue in economic concentration' and PPE's market share grew ever larger.[535]

The late 1990s success even had good tidings for the long vacant Uptown Urban Renewal Tract (above Showboat) – a symbol to many over the years for everything the casinos did not bring to the community. The tract was under the authority of the Atlantic City Housing and Redevelopment Agency (ACHRA). The housing agency approved development by Forest City Ratner into a shopping, retail and entertainment complex sans casino but the plan fell through and the land just sat vacant, as it had since the early 1980s when speculators first cleared out old houses in hopes of selling out to a casino developer. After its initial interest in the investment boom spurred by Mirage in 1996, MGM Grand slowly acquired property and parcels in the tract independently and from Showboat, so that it eventually owned 95 per cent of the 40-acre property. Yet Forest City retained development rights for years and, as late as 1999, an Atlantic City 'Developer's Package' detailed the long-stalled proposal to develop the area as a retail and entertainment complex including a movie theatre, roller rink and 24,000-square foot food court. Land speculators owning key parcels in the tract also proved to be difficult and caused various delays by tying the project up in the courts. In 2005, a city housing official recalled the delays:

> even when MGM had to acquire just 20 or so parcels, the process was very long, the holdouts – there were a couple holdouts demanding exorbitant, exorbitant prices.[536]

By 2000, an MGM Grand casino for Atlantic City appeared much closer, having finally concluded its land purchase from Showboat and benefiting from a City Council eminent domain decision in 1997. In early 2000, the City Council unanimously approved a casino development deal with MGM Grand that included a future project to create direct access to the new casino via Arctic Avenue. Much had yet to be done, but the deal was a short-lived triumph for city officials who had been trying to develop the Uptown tract for a decade. The slowly-progress-ing Mirage project, however, played into MGM's difficulty when Langford and another councilman sought to delay approval, commenting 'once bitten, twice shy' with regard to MGM's proposal. Though unsuccessful, it was an ominous move that betrayed the political fallout that came from the long, often torturous process to develop the Borgata and its companion roadway.[537]

Just when everything appeared to be in place with the MGM's deal, a bombshell hit the casino community in early 2000. After his five-year flirtation with Atlantic City, Steve Wynn reached an agreement to sell Mirage Resorts, Inc. to MGM Grand for $4.4 billion, and personally made $500 million on the deal. The creation of MGM Mirage was the biggest transaction in casino history and, for Atlantic City, it meant Wynn's latest exit from the scene. Wynn's long Atlantic City history that began with the Golden Nugget's 1980 opening appeared at a close, to the lament of many casino workers who never forgot his employee-friendly style and who had been looking forward to his return. Among other things, Wynn had long been remembered for giving his supervisors new cars after an especially good year at the Golden Nugget. 'Is he really leaving?' an anonymous casino employee queried the news desk of the Press of Atlantic City: 'There are a couple of us here who wanted to go over there ... I guess that idea is history'.[538]

Mirage's move demonstrated how much the industry had progressed with large mergers since Wynn struck Mirage's original deal with the city in 1995. The Mirage and tunnel-connector affair had often seemed a very personal matter between Whelan, Whitman, Langford, Wynn, Trump, Goldberg, et. al. In fact, the MGM–Mirage merger illustrated the main constant of the casino era: that business decisions drove everything. This, like all Wynn's decisions, was a calculated business move and a good one for himself and for Mirage. Just as in 1987, when he worked a great deal to sell off the Atlantic City Golden Nugget to Bally's, Wynn showed his acumen for the casino industry. Similarly, just as the Bally's deal was seen by many as a loss for the Atlantic City casino community at that time, this too was also seen as negative for the casino community. But in the 1980s, Wynn left a considerable positive legacy for Atlantic City's community by way of innovative customer loyalty programmes and the development of a whole slew of talented executives who went on to emulate Golden Nugget's success in other casinos after he left. In 2000, he was leaving again, and again he was leaving the community a positive legacy, even if it was a little uncertain at the time. By the time he sold out to MGM, Wynn's Atlantic City projects were underway and not reversible. The city was in the midst of a major, positive transformation that had something (if not everything) to do with Mirage's bold, expensive and dedicated efforts to develop the H-Tract and provide direct access to it from the Atlantic City Expressway. Even Donald Trump sounded wistful at the news of Wynn's deal, commenting to a reporter that he and his industry rival were 'friends again' and 'I think it's a loss for the industry not having him'. By this time, the political and legal battles over Wynn's grand initiative had mainly played out. Of course, the Borgata's eventual impact on the community and the ultimate utility of the tunnel-connector on the community were as yet unknown in 2000. But even then they represented the essence of the community's reach for its American dream: a gambit, to be sure, but one with a goal and rooted in the hopefulness that permeated the Atlantic City community throughout the casino era.[539]

Naturally, the people of Atlantic City immediately wondered what was to become of the major casino projects along the Boardwalk and in the H-Tract with the formation of MGM Mirage. Casino insiders speculated that the new firm would probably not pursue both casinos simultaneously. In fact, within a few months MGM Mirage did back off its Boardwalk project to focus on building the Borgata with Boyd Gaming. Much hope existed that the large, opulent resort would attract new investment in Atlantic City to tap into the relatively un-tapped, vast mid-Atlantic gaming market. By one calculation, net casino revenue for the Atlantic City casinos had actually declined in five years as a percent of mid-Atlantic personal income from 0.297 per cent in 1995 to 0.266 per cent in 2000 (approximately $500 million). This 'wealth gap' – where casino revenues did not keep up with growth in discretionary spending – provided hope, now in the form of the Borgata project. In the ever-optimistic casino era, this 'wealth gap' presented an opportunity and yet another reason to seek out investment in the casino community. Even as the Uptown renewal tract project appeared to be stalled again, things were looking up, based on an analysis that gaming demand was increasing.[540]

Mixed community sentiment over the Mirage/tunnel-connector project and city support for casino projects came to a political boil during the 2001 mayoral election between incumbent Jim Whelan and challenger Lorenzo Langford. Langford's 2001 victory came via an updated election process that reflected a successful 2000 referendum (pushed by Langford and allies) to bring partisan identification to the mayoral candidates. Langford then defeated Whelan in the first ever mayoral primary for the Democratic spot, then again in the general election as Whelan ran as an independent, like he had before in his three victories. Langford became a city councilman in 1992 after a thirteen-year casino career spent mainly on gaming floors as a dealer, pit boss and floor supervisor for Caesar's, Playboy, Atlantis and the Trump Taj Mahal. Langford had gained a high political profile in Atlantic City for his opposition to the Mirage, MGM and tunnel-connector projects. He also ran for mayor twice before, losing to Whelan in 1994 and 1998. In his campaigns and council role, he became well known in the region as a voice for the inner city residents, particularly those who felt powerless and victimized by the casino industry and its political allies. In 1998, Langford and his supporters culminated a two-year recall campaign against Whelan that began shortly after the city's deal with Mirage. Though unsuccessful, the recall campaign and election demonstrated the power of casino critics and others who felt that local officials were too cosy with casino management. Langford won approximately 40 per cent of the vote in the losing effort.[541]

In 2001, Langford defeated Whelan by a close margin decided by absentee ballots, at least some of which were cast by homeless Boardwalk residents registered by the Langford campaign. In winning the election, Langford also had the support of many in the local Democratic party apparatus as he was the party's candidate as opposed to the independent Whelan. After Whelan conceded that he would come up short in the absentee count, Langford commented on the meaning of his election:

> The visitors are important and the casinos are our lifeblood. But its time to return this city to the neighborhoods and to our people.

Though not overtly anti-casino, Langford had often campaigned by accusing Whelan of being too personally close to casino interests, though remained vague on exactly how he would do things differently. Eleven years of Mayor Whelan probably played some role in Langford's victory, as voters looked for a change.[542]

After the election, casino executives sounded political and cautiously optimistic –Tim Wilmott of Harrah's remarked that 'We can only hope the relationship going forward is as productive as it was with Mayor Whelan'. Langford commented that he would have an 'open door' policy for the casinos, but that in general he viewed casino development as 'market-driven', and that the city government had a minimal role in supporting the industry. At the outset of his mayoralty, he looked towards the state to support both the casino industry and the city. If any of the casino companies appeared to be in better shape with a Langford administration, it was the Trump group. Langford and the Trump people had also become de facto allies in the residential battles against Mirage to stop the tunnel-connector. Trump CEO Nicholas Ribis knew Langford from the new mayor's time at the Taj and expressed confidence that Langford would be able to 'deal with the industry' as things came up.[543]

For the *Press of Atlantic City*, the 2001 election result was a triumph of the 'have nots' over the 'haves' of Atlantic City's casino era. A *Press* editorial placed the election in the context of the 'tale of two cities' theme by suggesting that Langford won by appealing to 'those who were simply left behind' in the casino era, such as the 10 per cent unemployed. To the *Press* editorialist, in 2001 both sides still viewed each other with 'general distrust' and mutual 'animosity', so the newspaper called on Langford to reach out to both sides for appointments and commissions and not to act drastically for change as mayor.[544]

But the 'haves' and 'have nots' interpretation was a false dichotomy for understanding the casino community in 2001. While Langford capitalized on popular dissatisfaction with casino development within Atlantic City, it certainly did not demonstrate that a wide section of the community had not benefited from the casinos or were somehow against them. In fact, viewed in regional context, the few thousand Langford voters and supporters were quite small compared to the approximately 250,000-plus Atlantic County population. Casino employees populated neighbourhoods all over the region and mainly, they benefited from the industry. Over 41 per cent of the region's jobs were casino-related: an estimated 75,000 out of the 181,000 existing jobs in Atlantic and Cape May counties in 2002.[545] Langford's election however, did prove that the perception of casino alienation remained high in the city itself, even as the many of city's neighbourhoods showed real signs of renewal. Indeed, Langford's victory was possible, maybe even inevitable, 'in a city where many still feel that they can only view casinos through a glass wall', as casino industry analyst Michael Pollack understood it.[546] Meanwhile, casino outreach programmes like the Sands's, and Borgata's commitment to hiring city residents reflected the reality of the new casino community and the opportunities they had created for locals.

The terrorist attacks of 11 September 2001 had an instantaneous impact on the Atlantic City casino industry, just as they affected tourist destinations around the world. With little controversy, all the casinos remained open as they dealt with issues such as New York City guests stranded from home and employees with urgent issues that required scheduling flexibility. The casinos operated continuously, but little changes were apparent, such as an increase in police presence for public areas (mandated by New Jersey's governor), including casinos. Harrah's held a blood drive in their ballrooms in the days following 11 September and the Tropicana postponed its scheduled 'Chicken Challenge', a game in which players could try to defeat a live chicken playing tic-tac-toe in hopes of winning $10,000. Tropicana's management decided that the game was just too frivolous in the context of national mourning. Casino management braced for a major slowdown with flight restrictions in place. Atlantic City was far less impacted by flight restrictions than Las Vegas, though chartered bus trips were hit hard in the aftermath of the attacks. Coach USA, a major charter bus company between New York and Atlantic City, found its business dramatically hampered by tunnel and bridge closures. A week after the attacks, discussion in Atlantic City focused on the economic impact of the attacks on the community: i.e. to what extent would terrorism fears impact casino trips? Business fell off for the casinos during the first week after the attacks by about 10 per cent. Meanwhile some casinos began to rethink improvements and renovations plans, such as PPE's $50 million Hilton expansion, postponed until the next board meeting. PPE also shelved a planned $12 million renovation to Caesar's façade.[547]

However, major casino and community expansion projects remained on track despite the 11 September attacks. Construction on the Borgata hummed along with little interruption, as did a $225 million Tropicana expansion set to open in 2004 as 'the Quarter'. Resorts and Harrah's continued work on new hotel towers with measured hope that the attacks were only a temporary problem. According to an MGM-Mirage spokesman, the business impact presented 'short-term challenges' but the outlook for Atlantic City was still positive. The company continued as a partner with Boyd Gaming on the Borgata and persisted in exploring casino development on its uptown property. By the end of September, cautious optimism for Atlantic City's casino community was the rule because of people like Helen and Joe Nicita of Staten Island, New York. The Nicitas strolled the Boardwalk peacefully in late September on a bus tour of the east coast, unfazed by terrorists. They were happy to be in Atlantic City, a place where they did not have to fly to like Florida or Hawaii, places they would not go after 9/11 for fear of flying. The SJTA reported that auto traffic was actually up 3.8 per cent over September 2000 for Atlantic City despite a 4.6 per cent decline between 11 September and 16 September. PPE reported hotel occupancy rates in its Atlantic City resorts at 90 per cent – significantly higher than for the company's Las Vegas hotels. Ironically, Atlantic City's lower national profile than Las Vegas worked in its favour following the 9/11 attacks, because it was not dependent on air travellers. One local official also attributed the industry's ability to maintain its customers to the nature of the gaming experience itself: the concentration required for table games and the 'hypnotic' quality of playing the slots provided escapes, pulling people in.[548]

In the months after 9/11, early predictions of near-doom for the Atlantic City casino industry proved to be clearly exaggerated. Local 54 president Bob McDevitt summed up the town's good fortune by way of its regional focus, calling the casino car traffic 'our salvation'. While Las Vegas casinos laid off almost 15,000 employees after 9/11, the Atlantic City casinos held employment steady. As costly non-gaming attractions in Nevada took a big hit, the Atlantic City casinos were not similarly affected as there simply were not many costly non-gaming attractions to not spend money on. As well, Las Vegas's heavier reliance on international high rollers reduced its 'win' rate, as these players significantly cut back their gambling in the desert town for fear of being stranded by another attack. Remarkably, the Atlantic City casino industry actually increased its fourth quarter profits for 2001 by almost 25 per cent over 2000. For the year, the industry increased total gross revenue and casino win, though by less than a percentage point for both measures. The slight increase occurred despite a tough September in which luxury tax collection fell by 48 per cent. As Americans curtailed their air travel and sent the airline industry into a tailspin following the attacks, more and more cars kept cruising down the Atlantic City Expressway. In 2001, the SJTA reported over 54 million tolls collected on the highway, almost four million more tolls from the previous year.[549]

As quasi-public entities, casino security forces and involved law enforcement remained on high alert for quite some time after the 11 September attacks and the anthrax terrorism of late 2001. In the cultural climate of fear that characterized the immediate aftermath, Trump Plaza mailroom employees acted quickly when they received an ominous letter in late 2002. An anonymous individual claimed to have overheard some men talking about a planned chemical and biological attack on an Atlantic City casino via air conditioning vents. Within a few hours, authorities discovered that every casino had received a similar letter. Each letter requested $20,000 or $25,000, included a bank account number and e-mail address, along with a rather hopeful request to 'NOT GIVE MY INFORMATION TO ANYONE INCLUDING LAW ENFORCEMENT'. Of course, the casinos turned to federal law enforcement right away. With the help of Bally's, the FBI then contacted the letter-writer via e-mail, and identified him as a laid-off Ohio food salesman who had recently lost a few thousand dollars at a riverboat casino at Lawrenceberg, Indiana, on the Ohio River. Far from being a terrorist (or even much of an extortionist), the salesman eventually pleaded guilty to a charge involving the use of the mail system for fraud and received probation. Letters and extortion attempts from angry, aggrieved or otherwise unstable patrons were relatively commonplace in the casino era, but usually dismissed out of hand by busy casino officials. However, the post-9/11 legal and cultural atmosphere meant that these threats would now receive more scrutiny and quicker action.[550]

After 9/11, authorities focused on money laundering as part of the greater security threat to the nation. In fact, criminal money laundering via the Atlantic City casinos had received scrutiny a few years earlier when Governor Whitman authorized her Attorney General to specifically investigate the issue. That led to the establishment of a special commission to explore the issue by the state. In early 2001, a federal anti-drug agency reported that street gangs like the Bloods and Latin Kings regularly laundered proceeds from marijuana, cocaine and heroin sales in North Jersey with help from so-called 'corrupt casino employees'. The federal report may have been related to a 1998 case in which four casino hosts at Resorts, Showboat and Bally's were charged with aiding a drug gang by laundering $400,000 through their casinos. The Resorts and Bally's employees eventually pleaded guilty, but charges were eventually dismissed against the two Showboat hosts when a federal jury agreed that they had been entrapped. The case also raised legitimate questions about the ability of employees like casino hosts to do their jobs without occasionally abetting a money launderer. Casino hosts were employed specifically to help high rollers gamble large amounts of cash, so how could they apply too much scrutiny to these gamblers without defeating their whole purpose?[551]

After 9/11, the legal focus on casinos and money laundering understandably shifted from drug-dealers to terrorists. Consequently, the federal Treasury Department implemented new regulations that impacted the ways casinos could do business. In 2003, the Treasury created 'Operation Green Quest' to follow the terrorist money. 'Green Quest' included representatives from the Financial Crime Enforcement Network and eventually imposed regulations that required casinos to submit something called a secret Suspicious Activities Report by Casinos (SARC) for almost any gambler with a $5,000 cash transaction. It was a burdensome new regulation and the casinos were barred from reporting SARC filings to their subjects. SARCs differed from the existing Cash Transaction Reports (CTRs) that were already required whenever there was a casino cash transaction involving $10,000 because of their secrecy. CTR's required two forms of identification from the patrons, hence were obviously not kept secret. Gambling law expert J. Nelson Rose critiqued the new regulations in the climate of post-9/11 paranoia by pointing out that casinos were much more likely to be terrorist targets than sites for financial crimes. Rose joked that 'Congress and the federal bureaucracy are now seeing terrorist threats under every bridge and inside every slot machine'.[552]

The election of Democratic Governor James McGreevey in 2001 led to fresh leadership of the NJCCC. New Commission Chair Linda Kassekert's message in the 2002 annual report sounded an optimistic note for the casino community as she noted that 'there are almost 3,500 rooms under construction at the Borgata, Showboat, Resorts, and the Tropicana' and that there was 'a massive infusion of new investment going on right now – not only in hotel rooms, but also in retail and commercial space and other attractions'. Kassekert's allusion to 'retail and commercial space' was a direct reference to 'the Walk' (an outlet mall situated between the Convention Center and Pacific Avenue), Tropicana's 'the Quarter', and Pier at Caesar's. Construction for all three was underway by then, and collectively they were designed to bring a Las Vegas-style entertainment and shopping aura to Atlantic City. Creating a broader non-gambling resort was also the goal of the new McGreevey administration. His transition team sought to make Atlantic City more of a family resort than an exclusively gambling destination. Ever hopeful, McGreevey's planners wanted to increase the average length of stay, and with that increase, bring in more general revenue. Langford's election victory also appeared to have brought a new state-level focus to the perceived dichotomy between casino wealth and urban poverty in the community. In early 2002, McGreevey staffers reviewed the scope and function of all the major casino-related agencies to 'balance the interests of Atlantic City residents with everyone else so no one has to sacrifice'.[553]

At the beginning of the 2000s, the renewed drive for a diversified destination resort featured pro-casino legislation similar to the deregulation acts of the 1990s. A Gormley-backed law passed that was designed to save developers significant tax revenues by providing a rebate on sales taxes for new construction, that credited the casinos for hotel room occupancy taxes and that capped sales taxes at $2.5 million for new entertainment and retail complexes. The new act dovetailed well with the Walk and Quarter projects, and included the extension of CRDA commitments by five years to thirty-five years. Paul Rubeli, Chairman of Tropicana parent Aztar, attributed his company's $225 million investment in the Quarter to the new legislation and Donald Trump called it 'spectacular' for Atlantic City, with its promise to facilitate new entertainment and retail complexes Significantly, the bill also modified the complicated formula that distributed CRDA funds in Atlantic City and across the state. In adding five more years to CRDA obligations, the bill increased the distribution of the funds across the state. In the first three years of CRDA obligation, Atlantic City received 100 per cent of CRDA funds, but only 20 per cent by the twenty-first to the twenty-fifth year, with other regions of the state getting the rest. Officials in Cumberland County supported the bill in hopes of using CRDA money to build a world-class motor speedway. In 2002, the state continued to refine the CCA, with a modification that removed some advertising restrictions, quickened the pace for internal reviews and allowed cocktail waitresses to be more explicit in offering free alcoholic drinks to gamblers. It also granted the Commission more flexibility on regulating hotel room requirements.[554]

The political tide turned against the casino industry in 2003 when McGreevey pushed through a new tax measure on the casinos. McGreevey's plan involved raising new revenue by taxing comps, increasing the CRF tax to 10 per cent and imposing a new 7 per cent tax on hotel rooms on top of the local luxury taxes already paid by hotel guests at the casinos. Pursued for two years, McGreevey's plan gained traction in early 2003 with the state facing a $5 billion budget deficit. After 2002, when revenue only grew 2.5 per cent, the casinos instantly put up a wall of opposition to the proposal, based on concerns that it would cost the industry $200 million and drive away casino investors who would soon have other investment options around the mid-Atlantic. Trump Chief Operating Officer Mark Brown responded in disbelief at the administration's proposal with a comment that could easily have come directly from a casino official in the 1980s: 'Why would anybody want to come in and invest when things like this constantly are brought up? It's like they keep saying, "How can we get money out of you?"' CANJ president and Aztar president Dennis Gomes suggested the governor's plan would slow expansion, lead to job cuts and possibly push weaker casinos out of business. Gomes noted that the state would end up having higher taxes on less revenue via lost business, as customers rebelled against the comp tax and business slowed as a result of the expansion slowdown. After an all-night session to pass a budget before 1 July, legislators agreed on a compromise via casino taxes to raise $90 million more from the industry. The compromise put in place the comp tax, but kept the CRF tax at eight per cent and included higher hotel and parking fees. In an ominous political manoeuvre, McGreevey began to implement plans to shut down the casinos without a budget agreement by making sure state gaming regulators would not report to work, thereby forcing the casinos to close, according to state law. It was a tough tactic that may have helped push through the deal, with the Borgata's grand opening scheduled for 2 July. It also foreshadowed the budget debate of 2006, in which the casinos were forced to close for three days, the first such shutdown in the history of the casino era. The contretemps between the legislature and the casinos demonstrated again the extent to which the casino industry of New Jersey was tied to the public sector and governmental oversight, this time to the detriment of the industry.[555]

If the McGreevey administration wanted to shift the focus of the Atlantic City visitor experience away from gambling, then it was ironic that the biggest event that occurred in the community during McGreevey's abbreviated term was a casino opening. After years of publicity, Boyd Gaming and MGM-Mirage opened its enormous Tuscan-styled casino, the Borgata, in July 2003 with a low-key opening night involving a star from the *Sopranos* television show and lots of plasma television screens. It opened at midnight specifically to avoid an overwhelming crush of visitors, as Boyd had recently experienced at the grand opening of its Delta Downs racino in Louisiana. Boyd invited McGreevey, despite recent attacks by the governor on the casinos, including lambasting casino executives at a recent labour rally outside Caesar's for excessive bonuses at the expense of the rank and file. The billion-dollar Borgata was a masterful, sleek, tasteful structure with a looming gold tower and purple-neon letters across its top. Its position in the Marina district set it apart from the Boardwalk skyline, but also had the effect of making it visible and distinct from almost every part of the city and especially prominent as one drove into town on the Atlantic City Expressway. The new casino opened with less casino square footage than the Trump Taj Mahal, Bally's, Harrah's and the Tropicana, but CEO Robert Boughner was not just selling the gaming experience. The Borgata had a 50,000 square foot spa and 14,000 bottle 'wine room', glass sculptures and artful paintings. The whole focus was to bring in more upscale visitors to gamble, drink, play and relax in luxury as they might in Las Vegas. A common interpretation for the new casino was that it was something like a combination of Las Vegas's upscale Bellagio and Mandalay Bay casinos. A casino-produced magazine called *Borgata Style* emphasized sensuality and proclaimed that 'Suddenly, Five Senses Just Don't Seem like Enough'. The glossy publication featured nightspots, restaurants, and the resort's features like like Spa Toccare, where 'tensions melt. Knots disappear. And a new you emerges just in time to wave buh-bye to your worldly cares'.[556]

The Borgata's opening was vaguely reminiscent of the Trump Taj Mahal's, though much more subdued. The Taj's opening was driven by Donald Trump's personal star power as much as anything. It also represented something relatively new for 1990: a big, expensive, showy theme-casino resort. The multiple openings of luxurious theme casinos in Las Vegas in the 1990s detracted from the Borgata's novelty, though it certainly was a major moment for the Atlantic City casino community. Since Steve Wynn had sold out his interest, there was no comparable star identification. But the Taj Mahal and the Borgata shared a powerful, challenging aura of expectations. In the works for seven years before it opened, the Borgata had come to represent Atlantic City's future, perhaps even more powerfully than the Taj had years earlier. Unlike the poorly-planned and unfortunately-timed white elephant that Trump acquired from Resorts International, the Borgata was a genuine Las Vegas enterprise. For the previous four years, people in the community had been looking forward to its opening as the long-delayed moment when Atlantic City would really join Las Vegas as a destination resort where people came for days rather then hours. The Borgata could succeed where the Taj had failed to re-invent the town's image and purpose and to finally restore the nostalgic pride that some residents still had in their community as a glamorous, popular destination. Like always in Atlantic City's casino era, hope played a major role in the city's collective drive and self-identity.

Optimism for the Borgata's potential to transform Atlantic City stemmed in part from the perception that it would be easier to succeed in the age of deregulation. In stark contrast to the earlier casinos, the Borgata opened in a fresh climate, one in which it would not be 'hamstrung' by earlier, stultifying regulations. While it was under construction, analysts expected it to add thousands of new jobs and to help bring new visitors to Atlantic City. Michael Pollock anticipated that it would raise the overall quality and attractiveness of the industry. Related to the Borgata or not, the industry was certainly in full expansion mode at the beginning of the twenty-first century. Again, the deep capital pockets of multi-casino entities like PPE (which acquired the Claridge in 2001), Aztar, and Harrah's helped launch the new century of the casino era. Like Tropicana with 'The Quarter' and PPE with the Pier at Caesar's, Harrah's dove into the new marketplace with an $80 million expansion for an opulent new hotel tower and expensive new restaurants. Harrah's also invested in a new hotel tower for the Showboat and permanently knocked down the pins in its bowling alley in exchange for $17 million worth of new restaurant space. Even Resorts began a 500-room hotel tower to keep up. Under new president Audrey Oswell and Colony Capital's oversight, Resorts had recently begun to climb out of its long doldrums and frenetic, failed rejuvenation under Sun International to increase revenue and efficiency by 2001. In total, between 2001 and 2003, the other casinos and development companies invested approximately $700 million in this latest wave of renovation and re-invention that characterized the early Borgata era (2001–3).[557]

As the Borgata's opening drew closer, expectations continued to rise. Was its predecessor the Taj Mahal, or perhaps Resorts? Could it dramatically transform the casino community like Resorts did in Atlantic City in 1978, or as the Mirage did in Las Vegas in 1989? By the beginning of 2003, the town was alive with the sounds of cranes, tractors and workers. From the Tropicana at the Boardwalk's west end to the farthest stretches of the Marina district, the optimism was powerful. Much hope rested on the Borgata's ability to 'help build the Atlantic City brand' just as casinos and racinos in New York and Pennsylvania were gaining political support. Locally, the new casino was also expected to enhance the casino industry's ability to compete with other entertainment venues. Gaming analysts remained bullish on the overall market in the Northeast, buoyed by the runaway success of Foxwoods and the Mohegan Sun in Connecticut. By the end of 2004, Atlantic City had 16,000 premium hotel rooms, up from 12,000 just a few years earlier.[558]

By the time the Borgata opened in mid-2003, the financial markets that controlled the gaming industry in the consolidation age clearly expressed enthusiasm and optimism for the companies involved in the town's new ventures. Between 1999 and 2003, Boyd Gaming stock more than tripled, from $5 to $17 a share, while MGM Mirage went up from $15 to $34 per share. Similarly, Tropicana parent Aztar's stock went from $5 to $16 in the same period, while Harrah's stock doubled in value to approximately $40 in July 2003. On the downside, PPE was relatively flat in the same period and Trump Hotels and Casino Resorts Inc.'s stock fell drastically from around $7 to approximately $2 per share. The gaming investment market clearly favoured the companies that took substantial risks on non-gaming ventures between 1999 and 2003, in pursuit of so-called 'Atlantic City rejectors' (northeastern casino visitors who rejected Atlantic City). The Borgata, in particular, focused its marketing strategy on these 'rejectors' who now flocked to Mohegan Sun or Foxwoods for gambling and weekend entertainment. Yet, Atlantic City's reputation, gained two decades before, still impacted its prospects, even if the business and urban environment had changed considerably. A *Barron's* analyst noted that

> One thing Borgata is trying to change is Atlantic City's image as a depressed, crime-ridden place. To many in the east, the city's low-brow reputation is only reinforced by the elderly slot players arriving by the busload, enticed by the $15 of gambling money that casinos typically offer as incentive.

The Borgata's effort to inject a new style to Atlantic City stood in contrast to the Trump casinos, which had never quite recovered from the massive debt and crisis of the Taj Mahal's construction and disappointing debut year. In 2003, the company had little capital to invest in improvements, with a debt load of $1.9 billion next to a meager $50 million market valuation. Moreover, the Trump group never really benefited via national expansion as had Harrah's and PPE through expansion to Mississippi and riverboat sites around the Midwest. While the *Barron's* analyst was positive on other Atlantic City stocks, he called Trump 'the diciest' because its market value was a mere 'sliver of equity atop a mountain of debt'. Though the other gaming firms were also highly-leveraged, their market valuations were considerably better, allowing them to more easily improve and expand. For example, Harrah's carried $3.3 billion in debt in 2003, yet also had a $4.7 billion market value. It could easily fund its continued drive towards expansion, soon to become the largest gaming company in the world.[559]

In 2005, the newly-renamed Trump Entertainment Resorts, Inc. went through yet another financial reorganization and was able to convince the regulators that it was still a viable operator. Trump's latest reorganization freed up millions for investment, and by the end of 2006, the company managed to refurbish most of its hotel rooms and began construction on a new 800-room hotel tower for the Trump Taj Mahal. Mark Juliano, (Trump's new chief operating officer) sounded the new Atlantic City mantra in 2006 and showed the extent to which the Trump group was trying to embrace the Borgata solution:

> Atlantic City can attract younger people. They are coming, and not just for the gambling, but for everything, whether for shows or clubs, hotels or spas. If you offer the right product at the right price points, that's competitive with what can be found in New York or Philadelphia, people will come.

In the mid-2000s, the Trump properties also took advantage of Donald Trump's renewed celebrity as star of the popular television show *The Apprentice*. The Trump casinos held various gaming promotions, contests and marketed many *Apprentice* items at the casino gift shops. In 2006, the Trump Taj Mahal showed some signs of recovery, growing its net revenue by 5.2 per cent, over the industry average of 4 per cent, but the Trump Plaza and Trump Marina continued to lag behind the local gaming industry, as measured by net revenue growth. Of all the Atlantic City properties, the Trump casinos entered the hyper-competitive late 2000s in a vulnerable state with racinos and slots casinos going online in Pennsylvania (where the Trump group lost its bid for a Philadelphia property in 2006) and greater New York City.[560]

The challenge of the Atlantic City casinos was to raise the amount spent per visitor on non-gambling pursuits, only about one-tenth the amount that each Las Vegas visitor spent. Gambling revenues were approximately equal between Atlantic City and Las Vegas at the time, but Vegas tourists spent about $120 away from the table games and slot machines, compared to only approximately $12 per visitor in Atlantic City. It still seemed daunting, even with the hubbub and activity of recent years. Aztar CEO Paul Rubeli remarked that the problem with Atlantic City was that 'after you're done gambling, there's absolutely nothing to do'. Whether mere perception or reality, overcoming this notion was the major challenge of the 2000s, just as overcoming the city's unsafe and decrepit image had been the big challenge of the 1990s. Before the Borgata opened, a Deutsche Bank gaming analyst estimated that overnight visitors spent approximately $350 a day versus $150 for a day tripper and $50–60 for a bus patron. The Borgata's debut and the CRDA-funded project to refurbish the old convention centre also helped to improve entertainment in town. The new 'Boardwalk Hall' attracted Cher, Paul McCartney, Britney Spears, Fleetwood Mac, Christina Aguilera and Justin Timberlake. Aside from the projects under construction, the struggling Sands actually jumped in most noticeably right away, with a big new lounge called

Swingers in the middle of its casino floor. Swingers emphasized the casino's Rat Pack theme and highlighted dancers who would come off platforms, dance and interact with patrons. The Sands's new approach, like the Borgata's, was to appeal to younger people coming in for fun and sensual entertainment. Trump Marina also responded to the challenge as it lined up popular young bands like the Love Puppies, added a 'Hooters' restaurant and began holding bikini contests. A Philadelphia reporter interviewed a handful of Sands's patrons in their sixties and seventies and found a mix of incredulity and acceptance over the new emphasis on youth and hipness. Sixty-five-year old Rhode Islander Richard Hemond understood the new marketing approach well from his generation's perspective:

> All young ladies? The old guys will get a good thing out of it. The retirees. They'll get them all wound up to spend their money in the slot machine.

After all the effort, Trump Marina's average patron age dropped about five years – from fifty-five to fifty.[561]

From the beginning, Boyd Gaming's approach to its casino was to establish a strong mix of local and imported talent, and to make a positive community impression on Atlantic City. Boughner's early management staff included a mix of executives brought in from Boyd's other areas, local talent like Caesar's senior vice-president Paul Tjoumakaris and an information technology specialist from Disneyland. In 2000, Boyd sought to fulfill Wynn's original promise to help city residents and established the Atlantic City Jobs and Opportunities Programme – a $2 million investment to specifically train people and develop skills for casino employment for the Borgata and other casinos. The jobs programme opened up shop in the commercial hub of downtown Atlantic City, right on Atlantic Avenue. Boyd also brought a flattened, less hierarchical management style based entirely on running one successful casino to Atlantic City. Along with its new style and community commitment, this made it very attractive to Atlantic City veteran Tjoumakaris. In a 2005 interview he described the pull:

> It [the Borgata] was built well-designed, and the culture that I am working with, which is a Boyd culture, even though MGM owns 50 per cent, the Boyd kind of managing style portrays through. I'm very pleased the way we look at the community, the way we actually spend money for the community.[562]

Tjoumakaris, who had been at the Atlantic City Caesar's for over 20 years, appreciated the contrast between the Borgata's style and the recent impact of corporate expansion of the management culture of the casino community:

> And so I was able to, because of my experiences, to bring something that I wanted to always do but I could not because of the capital, because of corporate issues, meaning that when Bally's came in and bought Caesar's before Harrah's did, they were dictating some things from corporate where you were

just part of the bigger picture, instead of you being the big picture. Here, the emphasis is this is the picture. What do we need and how do we improve? So I had an opportunity that I couldn't have in another property that was evolving the way it did, with consolidation and the capital that exists and so on.[563]

The Borgata's corporate culture was in fact, so appealing to casino workers that it was already the 'employer of choice' by the time it opened in mid-2003. Boyd emphasized its democratic ethos and business focus by keeping its top executives in small offices right alongside the convention planners and purposefully leaving off job titles from executive business cards. Employee perks included internet access, high-level employee lounges, a deluxe cafeteria (in the Steve Wynn tradition) and a special company store for employees.[564]

The Borgata's first month was not as stupendous as the Taj Mahal's first month in 1990, but it did establish a 'solid foundation' in the words of CEO Boughner. It grew gross gambling revenue by 4.4 per cent over July 2002 in Atlantic City – not enough to grow market share to lift all the other casinos. Specifically, the Borgata's marina neighbours fared poorly in the month with Trump Marina actually declining its slot revenue by 18 per cent from the previous year. Harrah's also reported a sharp decline for the month, which prompted its senior vice-president to comment that he was 'a little surprised' that Harrah's was not lifted by more people in the marina district and to speculate that heavy road traffic in the area may have discouraged some patrons. Trump officials also blamed their lower-than-expected revenues on road issues because the promised ramp connecting the Trump Marina with the Borgata was still not complete. Meanwhile, gaming analysts were largely unimpressed by the Borgata's opening because, in total, the eleven casinos in existence the previous year (Claridge merged with Bally's) declined in revenue by 6.8 per cent. In its first month, the Borgata grew the overall market, but initially not enough to live up to its promise to uplift the town.[565]

By the end of 2004, revenues demonstrated that in fact, in its first eighteen months of operation, the Borgata had not grown the overall casino market in Atlantic City. However, it had increased the number of total visitor hours and increased the overall casino win per visitor by $2. Yet, the industry had been increasing its average win steadily per casino since the mid-1990s, from $113.69 in 1995 to $143.80 in 2003. Meanwhile, the average length of stay per visit had edged up in recent years, to 13.99 hours in 2004, versus 12.61 hours per stay in 1999. Even the 'wealth gap' shrank after the Borgata opened, meaning the amount of mid-Atlantic disposable income spent in Atlantic City edged up slightly in the Borgata's first year.[566] By the end of 2004, however, the numbers on the Borgata's impact showed its growth effect was more limited than anticipated before it opened. In 2004, the casinos only experienced a negligible rate of visit growth, from 33.19 million visits in 2002 to 33.23 million visits in 2004. In fact, the total number of visit-trips in 2006 (34.5 million) was about the same that it was in 1998 (34.3 million). Yet, the percentage of visitors coming to town by car was also growing, boding well for the casinos as car-borne visitors were bigger spenders than bus passengers. In 2006, approximately 79.8 per cent of visitors to Atlantic City came by car, compared to 67.6 per cent in 1996 and just 54.7 per cent in 1986. The decision to scale back the major bus programmes in the late 1980s and early 1990s stuck in the later casino era.[567]

In its first full year of operations, the Borgata led a slight industry shift away from slot machines with a strategy that involved the heavy use of table games for casino revenue. In 2004, the casino won $217 million on table games, $60 million more than the next casino (Bally's Atlantic City). With only 11.3 per cent of the city's tables, the Borgata pulled in 18 per cent of the table revenue. The Borgata's strategy involved reaching out to table games players, who had been treated 'like second class citizens' in the slots era, according to executive Jim Rigot. The Borgata's emphasis on table games jibed with its marketing programme for younger players, who enjoyed the social aspect of the gaming experience. So the casino put a bar (B Bar) in the middle of the casino floor, surrounded by table games to generate excitement for gambling. Soon, Harrah's and the Tropicana followed suit. Resorts International pushed its table games as component with its own strategy to capture younger, hip gamblers by adding Nikki Beach and a Gallagher's Steak House. Harrah's executive Phil Juliano commented that

> The table player is now a social animal willing to take risks, and that skews younger. The market growth is synonymous with the demographic of the 21- to 40-year old that is growing in the market. That type of player is a risk-taker, unlike most slot players.[568]

Yet, the early Borgata era was characterized by greater profitability and efficiency within a few years, even if it was selective by company. Along with Tropicana's 'The Quarter' (which opened in late 2004), the Borgata also began to transform the industry by generating increasing proceeds from non-gambling sources, as had been the intent from its inception in bringing a Las Vegas-style experience to the South Jersey shore. In 2005, A Baltimore-based writer told her local audience that 'ultra-cool outdoor cafes, open-air boutiques, and upscale marketplaces' had replaced the ticky-tacky shops of the past and that 'Today, strolling along the boardwalk [sic] is something you will actually want to do'. Between 2003 and 2006, total industry revenue grew by an average of 5.3 per cent annually, almost double the average rate of annual inflation (2.9 per cent) in the same period. Total revenue even increased by 8.2 per cent in 2004, when seven of twelve casinos were hit by a month-long strike by Local 54. In 2006, the industry generated approximately $6.53 billion in annual revenue, up from $5.5 billion in 2003 and $5.2 billion in 2006. In 2000, net non-gaming revenue accounted for just 8.4 per cent of net revenue, compared to 10.7 per cent in 2006. It was still much lower than

Las Vegas (where almost half of proceeds came from non-gambling activities), the Borgata and the Tropicana had clearly moved the bar in this direction – each topping 17 per cent of net revenue for non-gambling in 2006. By 2007, the Borgata's non-gambling revenue was close to 35 per cent, very high for Atlantic City, but still somewhat below the Las Vegas Strip's 59 per cent average. Yet, an industry split also emerged along these lines, with the PPE/Caesar's casinos generally at or about the same percentage of non-gaming revenue they had been in 2000.

Caesar's became even more reliant on gaming revenue, actually increasing its casino revenue as a percentage of total revenue by about 3 per cent to 82.2 per cent in 2006. The Harrah's operations – mainly Harrah's and Showboat from 2000 to 2005 – especially felt the impact of their new hotel towers and restaurants in the non-gaming areas. In 2006, Showboat's gaming revenue was only 79.3 per cent of total revenue, down from 84.2 per cent in 2000. The Trump casinos remained about the same between 2000 and 2006 on casinos revenue as a percentage of total revenue. Resorts also edged down slightly on its percentage of gaming revenue, having also opened the gleaming white and gold art deco 'Rendezvous Tower' tower in 2004. In 2005, Resorts joined the wave of Boardwalk casinos with beach bars by opening Nikki Beach, an upscale pleasure parcel with Roman sofas and private cabanas for two. Nikki Beach fit the mood of the time, as the Borgata and other casinos sought to redefine their market to include younger, free-wheeling visitors. Nikki Beach's owner noticed the new climate in Atlantic City, which he attributed to the Borgata, 'which gave us all the [guts] to come here'. Unfortunately for seaside hedonists, Nikki Beach only lasted one summer on the Jersey shore.[569]

With corporate consolidation and capital investment, casino profitability swung wildly in the 2000s. For example, Tropicana's first full year operating 'The Quarter' in 2005 garnered a 46.9 per cent rise in gross operating profits to $121.1 million over $82.4 million in 2004. In 2004, Aztar was still building 'The Quarter' and much of the Tropicana property was physically impacted by the massive new retail/bar/restaurant complex, hotel tower and garage rising on two whole city blocks between Atlantic and Pacific avenues. For the industry, profit rates rose 4.5 per cent on average annually between 2002 and 2006 and actually improved over the growth rate of the late 1990s. Gross operating profits margin statistics compiled by the NJCCC demonstrated that the consolidated Atlantic City casino industry did quite well in these years. Between 2002 and 2006, the industry averaged 27 per cent annually for gross operating profits margin, with two of the three Trump casinos even managing a margin over 20 per cent in these years. Not surprisingly (given its profitable history), the Harrah's casinos were especially efficient – with both Harrah's and Showboat easily outperforming the industry – by as much as 10 and 15 per cent in some years. For its first year, the Borgata's margin was also higher than average – dipping only to 30.7 per cent in 2006, but still above the 26.9 per cent industry average for that year. Tropicana's margin was usually at or above the average margin as well. The Borgata continued its astounding performance in 2006 by topping over $1 billion in total revenue ($1.01 billion), a first for any Atlantic City casino for one year. It also maintained a high profit margin – 30.7 per cent – over the industry's 26.9 per cent average. Approximately 73 per cent of the Borgata's casino revenue was from gambling sources, well below the industry's 79 per cent average.[570]

The casino business became more efficient in the early 2000s through a major feature of consolidation: workforce reduction. Despite the addition of the Borgata, the total number of casino employees in the industry actually decreased slightly between 2001 and 2004, from 45,592 in 2001 to 45,501 in 2004. The entire industry payroll increased by just two per cent in these years to $1.12 billion in 2004, from $1.10 billion in 2001. The Trump group was especially aggressive in cutting workforce, reducing its total number of employees by 22 per cent to 10,206 in 2004 spread between its three casinos. The Sands – barely hanging on by 2004 – reduced its workforce by a third in four years, from 3,005 in 2001 to 2,095 in 2004. The Sands's demise took place despite its 2000 purchase by financier Carl Icahn and a renovation that included the 'Swinger's Lounge' and the addition of the adjacent Madison House hotel to its property. Sold to Pinnacle Entertainment in 2006, the Atlantic City Sands spent its last few years trying to appeal to the local and down-market clientele, with limited success. Aside from the Borgata and Tropicana, the rest of the casinos all downsized their workforces about 10–12 per cent between 2001 and 2004.[571] In 2005, Caesar's slots cashier Selina Jahan described her brief casino career, which included a 2004 layoff, and the difficulties she faced trying to regain casino employment in the downsized industry:

> I was doing the slot cashiering job in Taj Mahal Casino, in one year, and they used to pay $8.50, the starting pay per hour. And I worked there one year ... save money, and then I thought, if I get better chance, I'll change to better job. Then I come back to Caesar's 2001 and it has some tips money. Same hourly salary, but little bit extra tips. So it was a little help for us family, because he has too much credit card bills and mortgage, everything. So it was very helping us. Until 2004, where I was doing the same job. 2004, they gave me lay off. Now I am in home ... I'm trying to get a job, but nobody hiring right now. I try all the casinos. They keep the applications, say OK, we're going to call you back later, but they never call. I keep putting application at the casinos, and I'm waiting, waiting, waiting. They just told us 23 peoples ... they call us and everybody's in the office room and told us our business is very slow and we're going to give you – you have been laid off.[572]

A casino insider described a brutal form of reduction that took place through the casino era when business slowed:

Their MO is to bring somebody in, and that person, whoever it is, comes in and they cut bodies. You know what I mean? Someone at the top. They'll bring someone into top, that person comes in, they have no strings attached, and they come in, they look at everything and then they'll say give me bodies. They'll go to my boss and they'll say, give me bodies. Then my boss will come to me and he'll say give me bodies. I just need bodies. So what we do, we get out the evaluations, see who's got the bad scores ... and who's got the bad attendance and we come up with a criteria, property-wide, and then we deliver the bad news. We're sorry but [we have to] let you go.[573]

Various personnel issues led to a major crisis in the community in 2004, when Local 54 members struck seven of city's casinos as negotiations broke down over a new contract. The strike involved about 10,000 Local 54 workers, who held a sit-in at the base of the Atlantic City Expressway, marched along Pacific Avenue and kept up a steady drumbeat on the Boardwalk for a month for $200 and $300 a week while the casino industry kept going. On the Boardwalk near Caesar's, Local 54 members banged everything from 'sauce pans to cookie cans to picket signs to plain-old drums' and five-gallon plastic buckets commonly used to hold pickles. The strike hit Bally's, Resorts, Harrah's, Caesar's, the Atlantic City Hilton, Tropicana and Showboat while sparing the Borgata, Trump casinos and the Sands – all of which were in the midst of three-year contracts. The union eventually won most of their requests for higher wages and greater employer health insurance contributions but conceded the biggest point of contention: the length of the union–casino contract. The union did not win any concession on another casino subleasing to restaurants, typically non-unionized. In concert with the national union leadership (UNITE), Local 54's leaders wanted a new three-year deal to coincide with the contract of the 60,000-plus Las Vegas's Culinary Union Local 226. This could theoretically have enhanced their unified power by connecting to their counterparts out west. Union leaders and their supporters like Democratic Senator Jon Corzine framed the conflict as a struggle between the local working people and the large corporate entities of the consolidated era. The 2004 strike reflected labour fallout from the age of mergers and acquisitions – as consolidation took place at the corporate level, the lowest paid workers also fought for consolidation to maximize their bargaining power. As one union leader put it during the strike, 'The companies are getting bigger, and we need to be more unified and together in bargaining'. But in 2004, the seven Atlantic City casinos held fast on this key point – the main one that drove the conflict. Local 54's rank and file eventually had most of their benefits extended through 2009, but their future was unclear as the age of casino consolidation rolled on and equity-based buyouts impacted the industry beginning in 2006.[574]

Despite the strike, the casino industry maintained its strong pace in 2004, on its way to an 8.2 per cent increase in total revenue for the year, led by the Borgata. Two of the struck casinos (Resorts and Tropicana) even increased revenue during the strike, despite a major radio and newspaper advertising campaign by the union to keep people out of them. The union also ran advertisements in Philadelphia and New York encouraging gamblers to visit the non-struck casinos before deciding to warn people away altogether. The non-struck casinos did quite well – the Borgata continued a very successful year with a 40 per cent increase in revenue over October 2003 and all three Trump casinos showed double-digit increases over the year earlier. Total industry revenue for October 2004 was $388.1 million, approximately 2 per cent over the total for October 2003. As a local reporter wryly noted, the strike was 'bad for business. It was also good for business'. Local 54's 2004 strike lasted a month, while its 1986 action lasted just one day. Yet, the 2004 strike was arguably less disruptive to the industry's long-term prospects than the 1986 action, because there was very little violence or sensationalized chaos this time. Solidly on the side of the strikers, Mayor Langford addressed a crowd alongside Jesse Jackson and thanked the strikers for making his work easier by conducting orderly protests.[575]

Even as the casinos grew more efficient with their workforce, spending on external vendors rose to $2.98 billion in 2004 from $2.28 billion in 2001, a 31 per cent increase. The numbers suggested that the casinos were hiring fewer employees, but not generating less revenue for registered entrepreneurs. Yet, the increased revenue was not necessarily staying local this time. The percentage of business going to New Jersey vendors actually declined by about 10 per cent from 75.9 per cent ($1.73 billion) in 2001 to 65.3 per cent ($1.95 billion) in 2004. Where was the money going? In these years, Pennsylvania business increased their share of Atlantic City's casino business from 6 per cent in 2001 to 10 per cent in 2004 and 'All Other States' increased from 12.4 per cent in 2001 to 21.5 per cent in 2004.[576] The shift away from New Jersey businesses may have reflected the Nevada connections of the Borgata, Tropicana and Harrah's – the operators with the most significant and expensive capital projects in these years. Aside from the relatively tiny Sands and the three Trump casinos, all the Atlantic City casinos had become increasingly tied to national and international corporate trends since the late 1990s.

Moreover, casino operators maintained the wave of physical expansion and infrastructure improvements into the mid-2000s. Capital costs rose every year from 2000 to 2006. A few years after the Borgata's grand opening, Boyd Gaming began construction on a new hotel tower and in 2006 alone pumped $255.5 million into its property. Likewise, Harrah's began construction on another new tower and overall property makeover costing $166.4 million. Harrah's also invested close to $116 million in 2004 and 2005, adding a tower and new House of Blues casino at Showboat. After yet another bankruptcy and debt reconstruction in 2005, the Trump group invested $63.8 million in the Taj Mahal for a long-overdue interior renovation and for construction to begin on a new diamond-shaped tower between the Taj and Showboat. From 2000 to 2006, gaming companies and their financial backers sunk $3.3 billion into the Atlantic City casino industry. In 2006, Pinnacle entertainment purchased the Sands, shut it down and planned a $1.5 billion casino for the property. The expansion wave begun in the mid-1990s with Mirage's H-Tract deal effectively continued for an entire decade, at least.[577] The opening of the Borgata, the Walk and the Quarter may not have brought in many new visitors initially, but they did begin to transform Atlantic City within the regional community. The Quarter's restaurants and comfortable décor along with the Walk's familiar outlets have attracted suburban and urban residents back into the city's centre. Whether shopping at a Polo or Banana Republic outlet, eating at PF Chang's, or clubbing in the various bars of the Quarter, there was now more to do than gamble. The Quarter also began to re-create the city's role as social hub of the regional community, as opposed to the pariah it was in the 1980s.[578]

The age of consolidation reached a climax of sorts in 2005 when the NJCCC approved a $9.4 billion deal in which Harrah's Entertainment Inc. acquired Caesar's Entertainment, Inc (formerly PPE). The merger made Harrah's the biggest casino company in the world, and capped its 1990s strategy to expand and create shareholder wealth on par with no other gaming firm. In 2004, the company was the only gaming or hospitality company to make the Dow Jones Sustainability World Index of the top 300 global companies for long-term shareholder value. In fact, Harrah's made the index four years in a row, beginning in 2001. Begun with an offer in 2004, Harrah's move followed its 2003 purchase of Horseshoe Gaming, which gave the company the top casino in Tunica County, Mississippi. At the same time, Harrah's also forged an agreement with ESPN to expand the World Series of Poker tournaments to its casinos around the US, including Atlantic City.[579]

But would the merger give the consolidated Harrah's too much market power in Atlantic City? In a move reminiscent of the 1980s, a DGE operative tried to convince the commission that Harrah's concentration would allow it to roll over its competitors with no state restraints. But it was fruitless and counter-productive for the commission to break into the market process at this point, and Chair Kassekert recognized this reality. Armed with a market analysis, Kassekert boldly pronounced that

> I am convinced that today's Atlantic City casino market is vigorously competitive and dynamic, despite the industry trend toward consolidation.

Her statement was emblematic of the extent the commission had demonstrated confidence in the industry to make its own decisions for business reasons since the beginning of the deregulation wave in the early 1990s and dropping of the three-casino ownership limit. After adding the Caesar's casinos, Harrah's had about 41 per cent of the market share of the $6.53 billion industry, compared to approximately 20 per cent for the Trump casinos (down by ten per-cent from fifteen years earlier) and 15 per cent for the Borgata. To lessen regulatory concerns over market concentration, Harrah's sold off Caesar's Atlantic City Hilton to Colony Capital quickly after the merger and increased Colony's market share to approximately 11 per cent of the industry with the Atlantic City Hilton and Resorts International. The Tropicana alone had about 9 per cent of the Atlantic City market share, growing its total revenue by 25 per cent (or approximately $119 million) in 2005 with 'the Quarter' open all year. In the first full year following the big merger (2006), all four of the Harrah's casinos had strong gross operating profits margins, with Harrah's itself the leader at 37.4 per cent and Bally's on the lower end with 30.2 per cent, but still about 3 per cent over the average for the industry.[580]

Harrah's acquisition of Caesar's also represented the merger of two very different casino cultures. In twenty-five years, Harrah's developed a strong reputation as a somewhat plain, low-brow gaming house, a pioneer in the reliance of slot machines and in its direct marketing towards its primarily working class and middling clientele. By contrast, in twenty-six years, the Atlantic City Caesar's had developed just the opposite reputation, as a high-end resort, more upscale than other casinos. In reaction to the news, Harrah's loyal customers (some enjoying $24-a-night-rooms), called Caesar's 'gaudy' among other things and harped at its reputation for hotshots. Meanwhile, a few Caesar's denizens were incredulous at the thought of being enticed to go to Harrah's marina casino, which might as well have been a foreign nation. One Caesar's loyalist fondly recalled the personal service she had received from an employee who had taken her by the arm and escorted her around after she became lost on the casino floor once. For employees, the concerns were different of course. While Local 54 president McDevitt saw no reason to be concerned about his workers' jobs, higher-level managers had every reason to be alarmed: their positions were far from guaranteed with Harrah's management. The Harrah's expansion paralleled another huge merger in the greater casino industry in 2005, when MGM Mirage bought the Mandalay Resort Group, owner of Excalibur, Luxor and Mandalay Bay casinos in Las Vegas, for $7.9 billion.[581]

Two years shy of its thirty-year anniversary, the Atlantic City casino community faced a new and substantial challenge arising from a leveraged buy-out of Harrah's. In late 2006, two private equity firms bought the Harrah's group, suddenly shifting the largest, most successful casino company in the world to private ownership. CEO Gary Loveman and Harrah's senior management essentially sold their company to Apollo Management and Texas Pacific for $17.1 billion in equity, one of the biggest leveraged buy-outs in history. With the buy-out, Harrah's leveraged debt jumped by close to $10 billion, and the gaming industry was rife with rumours and speculation that management would try to cut back by selling off casinos like the Showboat and Las Vegas's Rio.

Just after announcing the deal, Loveman presented to key employees that the deal and Harrah's high debt load would likely rein in its expansion prospects in favour of debt reduction. Soon after reaching the buy-out deal, Harrah's looked to sell-off some of its vast real estate holdings to lower its debt, calling its expansion plans into question even more. Six months after the deal was announced, Harrah's was still planning its $700 million 'Margaritaville' casino in Biloxi. However, it also appeared to be cutting back on casino prospects in Asia, where casino gaming was really taking off in Macau and Singapore. Some analysts pointed out that Harrah's highly-leveraged circumstance could put it at a severe disadvantage to less debt-laden competitors like Boyd Gaming. Boyd and others in a better capital position (like Colony Capital) could capitalize on any cutback of Harrah's 'Total Rewards' comps system, or other promotions, by themselves adding promotions to gain new business or simply reducing current programmes now deemed unnecessary for the marketplace. The full human and competitive impact of the deal on Atlantic City's casino community would take a few years to materialize. Key issues included the possibility that Harrah's would sell off one or more of its casino properties in Atlantic City and the question of the private firm's impact on the staffing and administration of the four Harrah's Atlantic City properties.[582]

In 2006, the casino community also took a hit when the casinos were shut down for three days in July following a legislative impasse over the state budget. Democratic Governor Corzine tried to push through a one percent sales tax hike to close a $1.1 billion budget deficit, but was rebuffed by the Democratic majority in both branches of the legislature who stood firm. Under state law, the casinos could not operate without CCC staff on premises, who were laid off along with tens of thousands of state employees. As a result the casinos were forced to close, thereby furloughing over 45,000 employees for the duration of the shutdown, which lasted three days before they reached an agreement. For the first time since the casinos went to twenty-four-hour gaming in 1992, the gambling shut down; the casinos lost millions of dollars in revenue while casino employees stayed home. Despite the resolution, the resentment lasted at least a year and played a role in the 2007 state elections. Local 54 President Bob McDevitt posted an open letter to his employees on the shutdown and the local assembly races taking place, promising that the union would vent their anger at the ballot box:

> They are all up for re-election next year and it's time that they be called on their intellectual dishonesty and plain old disloyalty.

McDevitt urged Local 54 employees (approximately 16,000 in number) to vote against legislators who blocked Corzine's tax proposal, decrying the Assembly Democrats' 'maniacal assault on their own Governor' as a 'tragic mistake'. He singled out Jim Whelan (elected to the Assembly in 2005 and a state senate candidate in 2007) and others for standing on 'twisted principle' while casino workers lost work. McDevitt's letter appeared in both English and Spanish and remained on the union's website well into 2007. It demonstrated the union's sharp political strategy – since the late 1990s, it had played a major role in state legislative issues affecting the casinos.[583]

Ironically, the state shutdown may also have helped the casino industry by increasing its profile around the US and the world. The main news that most Americans got from the shutdown was that the casinos closed. Trump Taj Mahal's communications director did forty phone interviews with media outlets from Washington DC to Boston. Television coverage of the fallout in Atlantic City included shots of the busy Walk, Boardwalk and other non-gaming sites in lieu of the quiet casino floors. The shutdown may also have generated enough sympathy and support for the casinos around New Jersey to head off a long-threatened initiative to install Video Lottery Terminals at the state's racetracks, a move long opposed by the CANJ.[584]

In the first two months of 2007, Atlantic City gaming revenue was down by 4 per cent and slots revenue down by 8 per cent from 2006. Seven of eleven casinos showed lower revenue from a year earlier, and casino analyst Michael Pollock predicted that 2007 would likely be the first year in the casino era where revenues declined from the previous year. Part of the problem was the loss of the Sands, closed in November by Pinnacle Entertainment as Pinnacle began planning its new $1.5 billion casino. In the meantime, many of the Philadelphia region's slots players were heading to the new Philadelphia Park racino and the Chester Harrah's, just south of Philadelphia. Significantly, three of four casinos actually raised their table games revenue in the early part of the year. Also significantly, both the Borgata and Caesar's were up in revenue early in 2007 – the two casinos that probably had the most upscale reputation and were more table-games-focused than the other property. At least one gaming analyst attributed Caesar's success to the opening of the Pier at Caesar's, bringing the old casino closer to the new Atlantic City style pioneered by the Borgata.[585]

8 ATLANTIC CITY AND THE AMERICAN CASINO ERA

Atlantic City's casino experience is crucial for understanding the expansion of casino gaming across the United States between 1990 and 2007. The casino era in South Jersey wrought wealth and opportunity where very little existed before. Consequently, it represented a model of sorts for the new casino communities around the country, including tribal casinos, neo-riverboat casinos and the thriving casino communities in Mississippi. But the Atlantic City experience also demonstrated that simply opening casinos in a community was no guarantee of success, renewal or stability, despite the almost-certain money that flowed where none or little did before. The Atlantic City experience also provided an exceptional example of a careful relationship forged between local and state governments, local residents and the gaming industry, such that all would eventually achieve their major goals. Yet it took close to fifteen years for Atlantic City to achieve a moderately successfully government–industry partnership, and to some residents at least (albeit a minority), it never was very satisfactory.

The notion of casino gaming on Indian reservations took off in the 1980s when various tribes began offering high-stakes bingo games to raise desperately needed money for their impoverished people. This was not 'urban reevelopment' (the catch phrase of Atlantic City's casino era), but something like an attempt at tribal revitalization. Tribes like the Seminoles of Florida, the Cherokee of North Carolina and the Yaqui of Arizona sought to replicate the achievement of the Boardwalk denizens who won the 1976 state referendum that legalized Atlantic City's casinos. They looked towards gambling to improve their tribes economically just as Atlantic City and New Jersey had sought 'urban redevelopment'. By 1983, approximately fifty of these bingo halls were open around the country, catering to middle-American weekend gamblers who competed for big stakes. In 1984, the Otoe Missouri tribe of northeast Oklahoma opened a 6,000-seat bingo hall and began offering games for close to $400,000 in prizes in one weekend. Meanwhile, the Reagan administration promoted the new gambling halls and all Indian gambling operations by pushing tribal financial independence, reducing

Indian appropriations and even offering start-up funding for new bingo joints. In 1987, the Supreme Court upheld the legality of the bingo halls and poker rooms in a California case (California versus Cabazon Band of Mission Indians). In 1988, the federal government promoted the new gaming ventures even further by passing the Indian Gaming Regulatory Act, which provided a temporary federal regulatory mechanism to oversee the existing gambling halls (by 1988, bingo was supplemented by poker and lotteries) and to allow for casino games. Spurred originally by South Jersey, the American casino era was about to surge forward. Within a decade, the vast majority of Americans would live within a few driving hours of casinos.[586]

One day in 1992, insurance worker Cherry Catania from East Hartford looked out at the new Foxwoods casino in Ledyard, Connecticut on the casino's opening day. She admired the new venue for its big skylights and bay windows that surveyed the classic New England countryside in the southeastern corner of the state. Patrons gambled amidst an atrium, a waterfall and a wigwam diorama. They played roulette and blackjack and other table games while enjoying the subtle, open elegance of Foxwoods, amidst views of old stone walls built by hearty yeoman farmers three centuries earlier. The hard-working and retired day-trippers who flocked to Foxwoods on its first day immediately noticed a difference between it and the casinos they typically frequented down the Atlantic coast. Unlike the Atlantic City casinos, Foxwoods embraced and even celebrated its exterior environment with the windows, cultural theme and open atmosphere. Draftsman Bruce Milardo noticed the obvious care that the casino's Mashantucket Pequot owners had placed in creating a welcoming environment. Milardo observed that 'In Atlantic City, you're enclosed, and sometimes you have to get out. In here you can stay as long as the money lasts'. Also by way of contrast, Catania remarked that Foxwoods was instantly more appealing to women because it felt automatically safer. 'In Atlantic City', she said, 'a woman is afraid to walk outside at night'.[587]

The colonial English settlers who settled Connecticut's coast and river valleys with neat, productive farms and church-centred communities also displaced many thousands of Native Americans from their homes in a series of violent struggles in the seventeenth century. Now some of the ancestors of those same Native Americans had come back to resettle the region for the sake of commerce. The commercial dynamo of a country that those early New Englanders helped to create now afforded an opportunity for their original adversaries to make their own version of an American dream in the casino era. This time, the Indians were the newcomers, of sorts, having recently reorganized and unified for the purpose of winning tribal recognition for that most American of pursuits: making money.

The opening of Foxwoods Casino Resort in 1992 was a monumental event in the casino era. Foxwoods opened as a tribal casino operated by the Mashantucket Pequot Tribal Nation of eastern Connecticut. The Pequots became the first tribe to both effectively capitalize on the 1988 law allowing tribal casino gaming and to develop a casino large enough to compete with the big players of the casino industry. It was perfectly situated between New York City and Boston, a naturally large market of casino gamblers that formerly had no place but Atlantic City to drive to and gamble. In the 1970s, tribe member Richard 'Skip' Hayward led a successful drive to have the Pequots officially recognized by the federal government as a tribe. By doing so, he began to implement his plans to enrich the tribe and with it, the economy of southeast Connecticut. As early as 1980, he was able to convince a local boat draftsman to quit his job and join the tribe, promising that one day they would all drive Lincolns. In 1986, he persuaded the tribal council to open a high-stakes bingo hall that sat 2,100 people. After the passage of the Indian Gaming Act in 1988, the tribe sought to open a full-scale casino but ran into trouble because no local bank would put up the $60 million needed to build and open the property. Eventually, a Malaysian developer stepped in with the capital and Foxwoods was born. Within three years, the Pequots went from offering a regular bingo game to Foxwoods.[588]

From the very beginning, Foxwoods had strong connections to Atlantic City, even as it emerged as the town's only east coast competition and quickly cut into casino proceeds on the Jersey shore. Led by Hayward, the Pequots smartly brought in casino industry veterans with Atlantic City and Las Vegas experience, including G. Michael 'Mickey' Brown as president of their newly-created Gaming Commission. Brown was a lawyer, former casino regulator and casino consultant in New Jersey who had overseen the licensing of the first seven casinos and who had earlier gained a high profile prosecuting organized crime figures. Brown quickly brought in Al Luciani to be chief operating officer. Luciani was a former Golden Nugget and Resorts International executive who had been mentored by Steve Wynn. Brown and Luciani represented the business and government realms of the Atlantic City casino industry. They also represented the Pequots' early commitment to creating a successful casino that could effectively manoeuvre within the Connecticut and Native American legal systems. With Brown, the Pequots also had a seasoned regulator and someone with good contacts on Wall Street. His financial connections proved very helpful in the deal struck between the Malaysian gaming firm Genting Berhard and its Chinese-Malaysian chairman Lim Goh Tong for $60 million to build the casino.[589]

Together, Brown and Luciani set about creating a casino in rural Connecticut using the experience and knowledge they had gained in Atlantic City. In addition, they brought in numerous Atlantic City casino professionals – supervisors and dealers – to run Foxwoods' gaming tables. Luciani focused on hiring seasoned professionals to stop schemers taking advantage of rookie dealers. Luciani also counselled Hayward and the Pequot tribal Council to create Foxwoods in the manner of Atlantic City casinos, with no windows or clocks and with 'seductive casino colors'. But he was overruled quickly by Hayward, who envisioned the new casino as fully integrated and open to the pristine forest environment around it. But Luciani was instrumental in bringing the Pequots a basic understanding of the gaming business, communicating how a casino made its money over the long haul and reliance upon the law of averages, as well as the powerful tendency of gamblers to play through winning streaks until the casino typically made back its loss and then some. But he was not a Pequot, and this is ultimately what made his Foxwoods tenure short-lived. A significant difference between Foxwoods and the Atlantic City industry stemmed from the former's tribal leadership and restoration mission. Foxwoods's dual purpose (firstly, to make money and secondly, to re-build the Mashantucket Pequots) meant that Luciani found himself the target of resentful Pequots. Within a few months of the 1992 opening, a 'Narragansett' Pequot faction emerged as an opposition force to Skip Hayward, Luciani and the outsiders they spuriously cast as the 'Atlantic City crowd'. Soon, Luciani was forced out by the Naragansetts faction – a Rhode Island-based group that seriously chafed at Hayward's leadership and their perception that they were receiving second-class treatment via lesser jobs at Foxwoods. Luciani left for New Jersey after an incident involving gift store theft by the gift store manager (a member of the tribe) in which the manager drew on her background to undermine Luciani by appealing over his head to the council. His departure exposed the familial trait of Foxwoods, something quite foreign in the intensely corporate Atlantic City industry, with the possible exception of Steve Wynn's Golden Nugget of the early 1980s. Mickey Brown took over Foxwoods's operations after Luciani resigned.[590]

Like Resorts's 1978 Boardwalk debut, Foxwoods's opening provided a needed economic boost to regional residents. Southeast Connecticut's economic circumstances in the early 1990s were rather poor, if not quite as downtrodden as South Jersey in the 1970s. The ending of the Cold War and subsequent defence cutbacks meant that the region's nuclear submarine programme was in serious jeopardy. New London-based General Dynamics had just announced the layoff of 2,200 workers from its submarine works and the whole plant had an uncertain future. In 1992, a Reuters reporter labelled the region 'economically ravaged'. By the time it opened, Foxwoods employed 2,300 workers – on a par with the smaller casinos in Atlantic City. A few days before its official opening, the local Chamber of Commerce president lauded the casino for providing a 'very good shot in the arm'. The northeast recession that had depressed Atlantic City for a few years also hit Connecticut hard. Between 1989 and 1992, the state lost some 155,800 jobs in the defence industry, mainly centred around the ship and submarine works of its coast. Close to 30,000 people applied for Foxwoods first positions, gearing up towards opening day in 1992. Like Atlantic City, the depressed southeastern region of Connecticut had become a glaring spot of poverty in an otherwise prosperous state. Just as Atlantic City's casino developers had construction obstacles in the form of older structures and items in the way, so did the Foxwoods developers. However, the Foxwoods structures were somewhat older. Some 250 archeological sites were uncovered during construction and the tribe worked around them, pursuant to its dual mission of economic and tribal renaissance. Brown and his Pequot bosses quickly recognized that the casino needed to bring in slot machines to make a dent in the northeastern gaming market, and set about attaining that goal right away. Upon opening, however, Foxwoods was limited by state law to offering table games.[591]

In early 1993, Pequot tribal leaders struck a deal with Connecticut Governor Lowell Weicker to offer slot machines in exchange for $100 million to the state for the first year and 25 per cent of slots revenue annually thereafter, for as long as the Pequots retained an exclusive right to have slots in the state. The deal was significant because it represented a rapprochement between the tribe and the governor, who had formerly litigated to prevent Foxwoods from opening. It was also a novel approach to the new casino's public benefice to the people of Connecticut, beyond the jobs and new wealth brought into the region. It was a substitute way of gaining revenue from the tribe, which was formally exempt from regular taxation, quite unlike the Atlantic City casinos. The governor's office called the programme 'Pilot' for 'payment in lieu of taxes' and quickly began to broadcast the benefits of the payment. Like New Jersey's CRF, the Pequot 'Pilot' funded public programmes to benefit state residents. However, it differed from the New Jersey programme in its flexibility. Where the CRF had to be directed towards programmes that benefited only senior citizens and disabled Jerseyites, 'Pilot' moneys could go to almost anything in the public interest. So, the money helped put more cops on the street in high-crime cities and went directly to shore up tax revenues and budget cuts in every town across the stat, with particular emphasis on the poorest cities. Bigger cities like New London, Hartford, New Haven and Bridgeport received most of the money to help shore up their budgets. The state used the casino revenue to help reduce the sting of budget cuts that reduced road repair funds, public school transportation and welfare benefits.[592]

Where the Connecticut and New Jersey models differed most was in regulation. This was the key difference between the Atlantic City model and many of the tribal casinos that opened around the United States in the 1990s. Connecticut's approach was to basically benefit from casino revenue, while Foxwoods and later, the Mohegan Sun, were regulated by a comparably smaller federal agency created with the 1988 act. The system left each state to develop unique arrangements with the Native American casinos, and Connecticut came up with a system based not so much on state regulation, but steady revenue flow. The Pequots effectively utilized their federal standing as a sovereign nation and carefully cultivated political relationships to develop an exceptional independence and powerful presence in Connecticut. Rather than integrate within the existing community, the Pequots created their own powerful and dynamic new community. As such, they avoided much of the practical problems that beset the Atlantic City community in the 1980s. Within two years after slots came to Ledyard, Foxwoods had earned over $800 million in total revenues and had a $242 million payroll. By the end of the

1990s, the Pequots and their Atlantic City-based management team had created a regional business that provided 9,500 benefits-paying jobs that averaged $35,000 in annual compensation. In addition, the casino created approximately 20,000 more jobs in New London County, adding close to $500 million in the cumulative regional payroll.[593]

The Pequots' venture was noteworthy for its self-sustenance and the substantial efforts to improve its community. In addition to the casino, the tribe created and funded its own police and fire departments, modernized the local water and sewer systems and paid for local road maintenance. Between 1992 and 1996, the tribe also donated close to $30 million to various local and state charities, including the Special Olympics, Mystic Aquarium, Hartford Ballet, and the Ledyard Mavericks girl's softball team. The Pequots also donated $10 million towards the construction of the Smithsonian's American Indian Museum. Without a legal mandate other than the 1993 revenue guarantee, the Foxwoods ownership and management actually had to work harder than their Atlantic City predecessors to create community goodwill, to justify their stunning new riches and to secure their political standing in the state.[594]

Connecticut's venture into tribal casinos also impacted the Atlantic City gaming industry by helping to shift Steve Wynn's attention back to town in the early 1990s. Just as Foxwoods opened and quickly demonstrated the huge potential of the regional demand for gaming, Wynn conducted an extensive lobbying campaign directed at the Connecticut legislature to legalize slots (beyond Foxwoods) and to allow Mirage to develop mega-casino resorts in Bridgeport and Hartford. Soon after the state's attorney general certified the Weicker–Pequot deal in early 1993, Wynn went before the legislature and promised that Mirage could easily outdo Foxwoods by guaranteeing $140 million annually for Connecticut's treasury via traditional taxation (property, liquor, hotel room, corporate, income) and an additional 8–10 per cent gaming tax, à la New Jersey. At one point, he even flew a group of key legislators to Las Vegas, where they ate lobster cordon rouge at a Mirage-held University of Nevada event, listened to Elizabeth Dole, and hobnobbed with attractive hostesses who wore nametags that included Connecticut towns. But alas, Wynn's efforts were for naught and Weicker successfully argued that he wanted to prevent the state from creating another Atlantic City (where he would not bring his dog) by creating a free-wheeling casino marketplace. Throughout 1993, the slots revenue rolled into Foxwoods and the Pequots landed Frank Sinatra to open a new theatre. Meanwhile, Wynn persisted with a big push to convince the legislature to allow his casino to open in severely depressed Bridgeport. The Mirage aggressively sought clearance by dropping their effort to legalize slots and by guaranteeing that 75 per cent of the construction work would be done by Connecticut contractors. Mirage also promised to hire 20 per cent of the workforce from Connecticut's welfare rolls. Wynn hoped to open a casino and then lobby for slots legalization – a reversal of strategy from the previous year's campaign, but also unsuccessful. The Mirage's attempt to enter the Pequot's market also spurred the tribe to act to expand Indian casino gaming by reaching out to the Mohegans, a nearby tribe that had federal recognition and therefore had the sovereignty status required to operate a casino.[595]

As was the case with New England gamblers now heading to a supposedly safer Foxwoods, Atlantic City's negative image played a large role in political decisions on gaming. Meanwhile, Wynn and the Mirage's management began to refocus on Atlantic City, where the regulatory environment had changed considerably since Golden Nugget sold out to Bally's in 1987. By 1994, the legislature in Trenton had moved to allow twenty-four-hour gaming. One of Wynn's most significant and long-standing grievances with New Jersey had been finally addressed along with the host of pro-industry reforms implemented between 1990 and 1994 (see Chapter 6). When Wynn gave up on the Nutmeg state, the competitive loss turned into a win for Atlantic City's gaming industry, by freeing up the casino prodigy to direct his considerable energies there. The gain was soon realized by the huge influx of positive analyses and investment capital that characterized the resort town's successful period of the mid-1990s and Mirage's marina project.

The Mohegan Sun finally opened its doors in 1996 after a convoluted journey involving the Pequots, Mohegans, Wynn, two governors and the state legislature. In 1994, Mickey Brown and Skip Hayward negotiated a deal with the Mohegans to build a casino near Foxwoods (Uncasville, CT) in partnership with the South African Sun International casino development firm led by Sol Kerzner of Sun City fame. In negotiations with the outgoing Weicker, the Mohegans struck the same slots revenue deal for the state that the Pequots had struck. The arrangement was good as long as Connecticut continued to disallow non-Indian casinos. It looked great to the incoming governor (John Rowland), given the immense success of Foxwoods – which had quickly surpassed the $100 million mark in slots revenues for the state and revived the economy of its surrounding community. It went through, but not before Brown, Hayward and Rowland almost derailed all goodwill between the Mohegans and Pequots by forging a deal to build a new casino in Bridgeport – a move that the Mohegan band viewed as a double-cross because of its potential to take away their New York customers. The legislature killed the deal in late 1995 and Bridgeport never got its casino. By the end of 1996, the Mohegan Sun and Foxwoods directly employed almost 16,000 people, approximately one-third of the total employed by the Atlantic City casinos. Foxwoods was already spending hundreds of millions of dollars on a new convention centre and hotel expansion. Total annual revenues for the two casinos already approached $1.5 billion, almost half that of the 13 Atlantic City casinos. Together, the two casinos had dramatically changed the economic fortunes of the region, just as Resorts and the early Atlantic City casinos had done between 1978 and 1981.[596]

By 2000, Foxwoods and Mohegan Sun had become the first and second largest casinos in the world, each with annual revenues of over $1 billion. The fast growth came at a cost – a five-fold increase in traffic on local roads, for example – just as it had in Atlantic City, but the big money bankrolled a huge new museum and research centre. They created approximately 41,000 direct and indirect jobs for the region, approximately 2.4 per cent of all jobs in Connecticut, and generated $1.9 billion in personal income for their employees. In eight years of operations, Foxwoods alone had contributed over $1 billion in revenues that were distributed to 193 towns around Connecticut. A decade after Foxwoods opened, the Connecticut economy had improved remarkably and the state had recovered from its severe recession to become a remarkably successful and prosperous place. Both the Pequots and Mohegans also invested heavily in local infrastructure that benefited both their casinos and local residents. By 2002, the two casinos combined to contribute over $400 million to Connecticut's treasury annually. They did this without the political showdown and inter-casino conflict that had beset Atlantic City industry during the great tunnel-connector war. In 2006, the two casinos had a combined payroll of $838 million and spent about $700 million locally on goods and services. The ripple effect was tangible, if not always easy to quantify. For example, a dentist in a nearby town like Groton could have as much as a fifth of his practice accounted for by the casino trade. They also contributed to a local housing crunch and to a demand for more English-as-a-second language classes and interpreters locally. In 2006, the two casinos planned to spend close to $1.5 billion in expansion and improvement projects on their properties through 2010.[597]

While Connecticut did not create anything comparable to New Jersey's CRDA, the tribes themselves contributed heavily to the physical redevelopment of the region through direct investment in various projects. In 2003, the Pequots invested $19 million in the Mercantile Exchange – an office building in depressed downtown Norwich. The building was the first new office building to rise in downtown Norwich in decades and underscored the tribe's community mission. Similarly, Mohegan Sun directly contributed $35 million to the state for improvements to public roads and the highway near the casino in 2002.[598]

Without formal taxes and a separate development agency, Connecticut's casino tribes and the state managed to accomplish similar outcomes by way of local development. Yet again, the model established by Atlantic City was essentially borne out and the purposes of those involved in each region were consistent. Both in Atlantic City and southeast Connecticut, the casino interests needed to be especially pro-active in both facilitating regional improvements and promoting themselves as public entities.

The early efforts on the part of the Pequots and Mohegans to support the state's treasury and local infrastructure without a formal regulatory system and without formal taxation had roots in the Atlantic City experience. They similarly managed to avoid organized crime infiltration through their process of exclusive tribal control in accord with the corporate accountability necessary for their financial backers and partners (Genting Berhard and Sun International). The parallel had much to do with the knowledge gained in New Jersey by Mickey Brown, Al Luciani and others who certainly understood Atlantic City's casino-era experience. They applied that experience towards their new employers in a wide array of areas, but especially important was their expertise in gaming regulation, law enforcement, local relations and gaming operations. Early in the process, Brown informed Hayward that the locals may have accepted the bingo hall, but they would soon come to hate the tribe when it opened its casinos. So, presentation became the first job: ensuring that Ledyard residents would accept the new venture as it began to take shape in the early 1990s.[599]

In the first fifteen years of tribal gaming in Connecticut, there was plenty of controversy over the real origins of the tribes, local concerns over the ever-expanding casinos buying up too much property and increased traffic congestion. But mainly, Foxwoods and the Mohegan Sun received acclaim both in the gaming industry and from state residents for their sheer economic impact and incredible success. At a 2002 Las Vegas gaming conference, Foxwoods and Mohegan Sun executives were in high demand and were sought out for expertise on marketing and appeal to Asian players. Apparently, Foxwoods was not doing anything much different to the measures Atlantic City casinos had pioneered in the late 1990s: adding noodle bars, clustering Asian games together and arranging special golf outings for their Asian customers. Yet, by then, Foxwoods was running close to seventy-five buses a day from the Chinatowns of New York and Boston, at a time when the Atlantic City casinos were steadily decreasing their bused-in players. By 2002, it was netting $65 million per month on slots alone, having, like its prosperous neighbour, fully realized its geographic advantage. After completing an $800 million expansion in 2003, the Mohegan Sun became a very profitable casino, as measured by revenue per square foot at $3,600 per square foot over its huge 291,000 square foot casino (huge by Atlantic City standards). According to gaming analysts, Mohegan Sun overtook Las Vegas's Bellagio in 2003 on the profitability scale and had built a huge gaming empire very quickly. But its management was hungry for greater efficiency and higher profits, and to achieve these, the casino added popular nickel slot machines and created an Asian-themed mini-casino within the larger operation. Chief financial officer Jeff Hartmann lauded his Mohegan bosses for giving the casino managers broad leeway to run the gaming operations.[600]

The Connecticut casinos' acuity in adapting to customer demand, their effective marketing and their tribal, streamlined bureaucracy were reminiscent of Atlantic City's Harrah's operation. There was no direct link between Harrah's of Atlantic City and the two tribes, but there were certainly some business parallels. Harrah's, Foxwoods and Mohegan Sun had become the leading casino operations in the northeast with a similar, focused agenda that emphasized customized marketing, and a relentless appeal to mid-level gamblers such as Chinatown bus riders. Harrah's had originally pioneered the heavy reliance on slot machines in the 1980s and now Foxwoods and the Mohegan Sun were creating gaming behemoths that similarly focused on creating the highest efficiency and volume operations for profitable purposes. Harrah's and the tribal casinos also shared an affinity for message and purpose. The two Native American operations were remarkably committed to commemorating their unique cultures and viewed the casinos as extensions of those identities. By the end of the 1990s, Harrah's had also created a unique corporate and social identity within the gaming industry. Along the way, it had become a much-loved employer and community benefactor in Atlantic City. Its support for the Northeast Inlet project along with its employee-friendly policies and flat, interactive management system paid great dividends for the company. In 2001, Harrah's national management defined its corporate identity with its three-pronged 'Code of Commitment'. Harrah's 'Code' simply formalized its long-standing approach to gaming success by focusing on guests, employees and the community. This formula essentially catapulted it to the top of the commercial gaming world by 2005, when it bought out Caesar's (see Chapter 7).[601]

In creating the Connecticut casinos' gaming empire, there was a lot of conflict and tribal infighting (particularly between the Pequots and Narragansetts who ran Foxwoods), but just as Harrah's had done in Atlantic City, these disputes helped to build the casinos' reputations as cultural and social entities,. Their community benefice (most of it voluntary) served the same purpose and undoubtedly contributed to their success. The positive reputations gained by the two casinos also helped them stave off competitors. In 2002, both Connecticut senators actually sought a federal moratorium on recognizing any more tribes in the state – a protective move for the two existing casinos. The Connecticut authorities never did open up the state to commercial competition. The reputations also helped to mute the impact of a group called the Connecticut Alliance against Casino Expansion that actively opposed casino expansion plans and related projects. The 'Alliance' was led by Jeff Benedict, who wrote a scathing, controversial book about the Pequots that was published in 2001. But by then, it was much too late to hold back the tribal casinos as they reached new industry heights.[602]

Casino expansion was also a phenomenon in the American South during the 1990s. In 1995, singer Johnny Cash stepped on the stage at Sam's Town Hotel and Gambling Hall of Tunica County, Mississippi to a packed house. At the time,

Sam's Town thrived on the banks of the river, where nothing but an old dirt road formerly existed on the Mississippi river about forty miles south of Memphis. Linda Ross, who relied on her blackjack dealer job, and casino cashier Angela Jones understood how dramatically the casinos had injected economic life into the region: 'It was dead', Jones said of her home county, 'But gambling saved us'. Between 1993 and 1995, ten casinos went up in a county formerly know for not much other than being 'the most southern place' on earth, replete with cotton plantations, sharecroppers, open sewers, shacks, trailers and deep, deep rural poverty. Within three years, the county's annual budget went up 600 per cent, from $3 million to $18 million thanks to a 4 per cent local tax on casino revenues. Consequently, a group of black teachers and parents successfully fought for 12 per cent of the casino tax revenue to go to the county public schools (they wanted 20 per cent), which had been the worst in Mississippi and which were rejected by almost all the white parents. In a few years, the welfare and food stamp rolls dropped dramatically as Tunicans found solid employment where no opportunity previously existed outside of farm labour. Memphis-based contractor Jack Henning could hardly believe the change, as he gambled in the new casinos: 'Boy, you shoulda seen this place before. People cannot believe it. Tunica was nothing. I mean, if you drove down these roads at night, nothing but stars and sky'. To the sure chagrin of local star-watchers, by 1995 casinos around the county now lit up the sky. Within a few years of Mississippi's 1990 law allowing floating casinos, Bally's, Harrah's and the Sheraton all had operating casinos in Tunica and more were on the way, along the state's Gulf of Mexico coast and in Vicksburg (further south along the river). While gaming improved formerly depressed areas of southeastern New England in the 1990s, it brought parts of Mississippi back from economic death and social stagnation.[603]

As was the case with the Atlantic City casino industry, the Mississippi casinos that opened in the 1990s had a long history behind them. Gambling in Mississippi first took off in the 1820s when Natchez became a scene of drinking, with 'gambling houses' and 'brothels' available for travellers passing through on steamboats. Gambling on cockfights, billiards, horse racing, and card games like poker and Faro was commonplace in Mississippi for much of the nineteenth century, even after a mob of Vicksburg citizens caught up in the fervour of religious revival hung five riverboat gamblers in 1835. Later, Biloxi and the Gulf coast became a popular resort region with baths and hotels after the Civil War. In the 1920s, enterprising locals built a resort on a small island near Biloxi called the Isle of Caprice, opened a casino there and began to rake in money from gambling. After Prohibition ended in 1933, Biloxi and Gulfport became hotbeds of gambling with slot machines everywhere and the state benefited by taxing them, even while maintaining an official stance against gambling. For example, a 1 cent slot machine had a $50 assessment, a five-cent machine, $100. Many of the area's hotels, clubs and pubs were by then operating casinos in backrooms. At one point after World

War II, airman from the local Keeler Air Force Base spent close to $500,000 of their collective $4 million monthly payroll (12.5 per cent) in illegal honky tonk gambling joints near the base. The Kefauver commission investigations of the early 1950s slowed the casino trade along the Gulf Coast by knocking out a lot of the backroom casinos. In the 1960s, a moralistic anti-gambling governor and hurricane Camille (1969) also took a toll on the region's gambling operations, but never wiped them out. A $22 million post-Camille urban renewal project did not include the gambling halls destroyed by the storm and the area struggled financially through the 1980s, despite an influx of Vietnamese immigrants who came for the fishing opportunities. When the state legalized riverboats and mandated that each county had to approve casinos via referendum, Gulf residents approved them. Soon, the first casino opened – the aptly named Isle of Capri – and longtime Biloxians saw their community come full circle.[604]

In both Atlantic City and Biloxi, modern casinos emerged partially as a restoration of historical identity. Both areas, as vacation spots for their respective regions, had a long tradition of gambling. In each, the gambling was not quite legal, but had been so rampant that it helped to define them – especially to the locals who benefited from the income left behind by the players. In mid-twentieth century Atlantic City, people played poker and blackjack in the 500 Club back room with Dean Martin singing up front. In Biloxi, they played the five-cent 'gambling machines' in beach joints along Highway 90 while listening to Hank Williams, Sr. The historical context of gambling informed the late twentieth-century campaigns that led to legal gambling in each. Along with economic factors, it certainly played a role in gambling's local acceptance, even if both legalization efforts attracted opponents who tried hard to prevent the arrival of modern casinos.

In Mississippi, there was also a political campaign to legalize casinos, though it was conducted in the legislature, as opposed to the state-wide referendum campaign that occurred in New Jersey. Inspired by the recent legalization of riverboat gambling in Iowa, Mississippi legislators from the Gulf coast and Mississippi river delta counties formed a coalition to pass a similar measure. The southern advocates for legalization echoed New Jersey's earlier casino proponents by emphasizing the local economic gains to be had with the new casinos. Like Atlantic City, communities around the state looked to gaming as a solution to revive business. In 1998, Biloxi mayor A. J. Holloway told the NGIS commission how dire the town's economy was in the 1980s, pre-legalization:

> Our decline began in the 80's when the bottom fell out of the oil industry in Louisiana and Texas. We lost a large section of the tourist trade from our area. We had hotels in bankruptcy. They could not pay their water bills. The golfers, who we depended on to visit us each winter, were finding better accommodations in other places. We were a tourist town with no tourists. Nine years ago, I was a member of the city council and I could tell

you firsthand this was a disaster for city government. The declining tax revenue meant we were six to nine months behind paying our bills. We were barely meeting the city payroll. We were having to borrow money on next year's property taxes to pay this year's bills. Then we'd have to turn right back around and pay off the loan with the taxes we collected in January and February. City employees took 10 percent pay cuts and city services suffered as our roads and infrastructure began to crumble.[605]

The story was similar along Mississippi's coast and delta towns, places like Vicksburg and Tunica County. But still, legislators wanted to ensure local residents maintained control over their casino futures, so the legalization bill that passed in 1990 mandated that each county would have to approve the casinos. Hence one argument put forth to gain state-wide legislative support was that casinos would probably only affect a few areas – that it was not a bill to bring casinos all over the state. After the state bill passed, the real politics of Mississippi gaming took place at the county level with local referendums. Here, Mississippi's legalization diverged, demonstrating the extent to which casino gaming was much more of a local concern in the southern state than it was in New Jersey. The legalization referendum, regulatory process, CRDA and the tunnel-connector project all demonstrated that Atlantic City's casino industry was always a state-level initiative and concern.. Sometimes, gaming firms invested substantial dollars in the Mississippi local campaigns, and even took opposite positions to protect earlier investments. In 1996, Harrah's understandably sought to protect its heavy casino investment in Tunica County by supporting gaming opponents in nearby DeSoto County (just below Memphis). The Mississippi case put the key decisions into a more directly democratic process, but also opened up ugly battles between communities in competition with each other over gaming revenue. Yet, Mississipians (like New Jerseyites) voted for their casinos and for basically the same reasons. In both places, gaming supporters overrode anti-gaming forces like Christian crusaders with powerful economic arguments. Ultimately, casinos began and prospered in both states through a popular democratic process.[606]

While Connecticut's regulatory hands were somewhat tied by tribal sovereignty and the 1988 Indian Gambling Act, state regulation of Mississippi's casinos was an open question with the 1990 legalization of riverboat casinos. Would Mississippi's regulatory mechanism emulate New Jersey's tight and relatively restrictive system or Nevada's looser regulatory format? Like both states, the Mississippi legislature created a state-wide agency to make key decisions with regard to casino licensing, but generally emulated the Nevada system via the establishment of the Mississippi Gaming Commission. In 1997, the commission's executive director (Paul Harvey) explained the perception of difference that drove the decision:

We're patterned after Nevada, which is different from the New Jersey model. We're a free enterprise state. We don't limit licenses and the bottom line is, if you come to us and you've got a problem, we'll help you with that problem ... I think that we've got the confidence of the industry that we're not going to get adversarial with casinos.

The perception of New Jersey's anti-casino regulatory climate drove the legislature's 1990 decision to adapt Nevada's regulatory model over the garden state's scheme. A Mississippi legislature sub-committee drafted a bill that was designed to specifically avoid regulations which may have sounded good on paper, but that served less well to attract gaming companies or to maintain a healthy casino industry. Looking at Iowa's recent and ill-fated experiment with its riverboats, they specifically avoided minimum and maximum loss-per-bet limits and a progressively rising tax system (to 20 per cent). In sharp contrast to New Jersey's 1977 *CCA* (as it existed in 1990), the politicians specifically declined to limit the number of licences a casino operator could hold, minimized background checks and fees, did not restrict gaming hours and included only an eight per cent state tax, with each casino county also receiving the right to also impose a four per cent local tax. The one substantive restriction that set Mississippi apart from Nevada was the limitation that casinos could only operate on the state's waterways – and originally that included a stipulation that gaming could only take place on boats that were 'underway'. The 'underway' clause would have ensured that new operations be smaller, traveling operations – actual paddlewheel steamboats cutting up and down Big River or along the Gulf coast. But the term 'underway' never made it into the final bill, thus ensuring that the casinos could be stationary along the shore, which made it much easier to develop large properties with hotels and multiple restaurants. In 2005, the waterway restriction proved shortsighted when the storm surge from hurricane Katrina broke the moorings of casino barges in Biloxi-Gulfport, sending them inland and increasing overall destruction when some came down on top of land-based structures.[607]

Mississippi's deliberate decision to create an industry-friendly climate for its new casinos paid off remarkably in the dynamic growth of its casinos in the highly competitive 1990s. Despite the rapid spread of tribal casinos and riverboat casinos around the country, by the late 1990s Tunica County and the Gulf coast emerged as concentrated rivals to Atlantic City and Las Vegas as gaming destinations. Like Atlantic City, the casinos proved to be tremendous revenue generators and engines of economic growth within a few years of their debut. Unlike Atlantic City, the Mississippi casino industry emerged without a regional monopoly on the trade. Casino players could easily go up the river to St Louis or over to Louisiana, but the state created a powerful regional casino niche with the development of specific casino communities in designated areas. By 1996, there were twenty-nine operating casinos in the state, and tax revenues skyrocketed where they existed. Between 1992 and 1996, the city of Gulfport increased its tax revenue by $7.78 million, distributed mainly to the public schools and for public safety. In the same span, Biloxi's eight casinos generated approximately $19.1 million in extra local tax revenues that also went primarily to the schools and police. With just one casino (Casino Magic), Bay St Louis' revenue gains were smaller, but they still allowed the town to reduce its property taxes by 85 per cent and accounted for sales tax revenues 100 per cent higher than they had been just four years earlier. Five years after the 1992 opening of the Isle of Capri in Biloxi (named after its Prohibition era predecessor), the industry racked up close to $2 billion annually in revenues. Meanwhile, the Mirage committed $600 million to the construction of Beau Rivage, a 1,400-room casino resort.[608]

The state's casino-friendly atmosphere stood in remarkable contrast to New Jersey in the 1980s, where the casino industry leaders and editorial writers regularly blasted the state for its supposed anti-casino stance (Chapters 3 and 4). In Mississippi, casino insiders were pleased that their public officials understood that gaming was a lucrative business that created economic opportunity unto itself and that tax rates needed to be reasonable for the businesses to succeed. In 1996, a general manager at Sam's Town Hotel and Gambling Hall in Tunica County lauded the state for creating a lucrative environment for the casinos, with fair guidelines 'where investors come in and build more than just a place where there's slots and table games'. By contrast, the Mississippi casinos prospered next to New Orleans's failed Harrah's Jazz, which suffered under a 28 per cent tax rate. In 1997, Biloxi's Grand Casino had 110,000 square feet of gaming space – just a few thousand feet under the Trump Taj Mahal. The recently-opened Tunica Grand was the third-largest casino in the nation, behind Foxwoods and Las Vegas' MGM Grand.[609]

By 1998, the national gaming industry was clearly poised southward, with the anticipated opening of Beau Rivage set to create a 'Las Vegas of the South'. In addition to the Mirage, major operators like Bally's and Harrah's were invested in the Gulf coast and in Tunica County. Meanwhile, Mississippi's total casino square footage had surpassed Atlantic City's. Just as it had done successfully in Las Vegas, Mirage sought to create the Beau Rivage as an entertainment experience for its visitors with a spa, golf course, and numerous things to do and places to eat. In 1998, Mirage senior vice president Barry Shier commented that 'none of this conversation is about gaming' and that Mirage's strategy was to utilize 'non-gaming amenities to expand the Coast market from 250–500 miles'. While there certainly was a buzz and positive outlook for Atlantic City's casinos in the late 1990s, Mississippi's casino industry boomed at a much faster pace. Between February 1997 and February 1998, Mississippi total gross revenues increased at a 10 per cent clip, while Atlantic City's actually fell by 0.7 per cent.[610] By 1997, the Mississippi casinos had already been through a few cycles, and seven had closed in Tunica County alone. But statewide, they had created 33,000 jobs and dramatically altered the economic landscape of the state, as one analyst noted: 'there is no doubt that casino gaming has lifted Mississippi out of economic doldrums'. By 2000, the industry was generating nearly $3 billion annually in gross revenues.[611]

A 2000 study completed at the University of Southern Mississippi assessed the state's impressive casino industry at the turn of the century. By then, the casinos employed approximately 40,000 people directly, with $800 million paid out in wages and salaries in fiscal year 2000. Like Atlantic County in the 1980s, residential and commercial construction took off in the counties surrounding Biloxi and Gulfport in the 1990s. In Gulfport alone there were 97 commercial building permits issued, worth $5.2 million in 1990, compared to 358 permits, worth $182.1 million, issued in 1998. Retail sales growth rose at an approximate average of 12 per cent annually in the coastal counties between 1991 and 1998, about double the state's average. The Mississippi casinos spent about $4 billion on construction between 1992 and 1999. As was the case in South Jersey, millions of new visitors put a tremendous strain on existing roads – leading to a widening of Highway 90 along the coast and traffic volumes approximately double in seven years between 1990 and 1997 for roads near the major casino centres of the state. By 1999, casino success led to somewhat severe labour shortages in Tunica and the Gulf Coast, with unemployment hovering at 2.8 per cent in Harrison County (Biloxi and Gulfport) – well below that state's average of 5.6 per cent unemployment for 2000. By 1998, the industry produced approximately $300 million in tax revenue to the state, approximately 10 per cent of Mississippi's entire budget.[612]

In Tunica County, the casino impact was dramatic and extensive, especially given the county's pre-casino circumstances. This was a place that Jesse Jackson called 'America's Ethiopia' in 1985. By 1998, Mississippi's 'Ethiopia' was no longer desperately poor. 'Everything has changed' testified Tunica's mayor to the NGIS commission in 1998 and the county administrator read off a litany of social improvements funded by casino revenues. These included a youth recreation programme and new facility, an outreach programme for at-risk teens, new emergency communications equipment, new fire trucks, a twenty-four-hour medical clinic, water and sewer improvements, road infrastructure and a summer youth jobs counselor and programme. The county was operating at virtually full-employment, though the labour situation was complicated by the fact that so many of its poor, rural residents had neither skills nor transportation to be effective casino employees.[613]

Tunica's casino beginnings did not always happen easily for the environment or the industry. In a number of cases, the law requiring that the casinos be 'floating' on water connected to the river caused substantial wetlands destruction and demanded careful work from the US Army Corps of Engineers and US Fish and Wildlife Service. Some casinos satisfied the legal requirement simply by running a pipe from the Mississippi into a special lagoon dug to float a casino barge. Meanwhile, a variety of casinos opened quickly (between 1993 and 1995) in newly dug ditches, in paddlewheel riverboats, or on bends in the river along old steamboat landings. But the wild, relatively unregulated environment and geographic chaos caused much industry turmoil in a highly competitive environment. After a few years, the area where the Tunica casinos began had become a 'casino ghost town' as other operators moved in closer to Memphis, thus drawing all the business. By 1995, this area – called 'Mhoon Landing' was desolate, despite the road investments and improvements made by the casinos trying to improve access to the remote site. Meanwhile, aggressive competition drove out operators like Treasure Bay Tunica, driven into bankruptcy when it decided not to join a casino coalition that shared a common parking lot in an area called Casino Center. The alliance then built a fence to block it off from other patrons and soon Treasure Bay was history. Between 1992 and 1997, six of the fifteen casinos that opened in Tunica either closed or moved. The lack of permanence caused the Mississippi Gaming Commission to take action by insisting that new casinos spend 25 per cent of their original investment on 'permanent' structures (like hotels). Despite the volatility, the Tunica casino industry expanded steadily, added hotels and built an entertainment centre with over 6,000 hotel rooms in 2000 from a starting point of twenty motel rooms in 1992. Harrah's two-casino early investment in Tunica helped anchor the industry and expand it further. Harrah's consolidated its two Tunica casinos into one large operation in 1997.[614]

By almost every measure, the quality of life for Tunica residents rose dramatically in the early years of its casino era. Families needing food stamp subsidies dropped from 51.2 per cent to 30.8 per cent within a few years and the county's per capita income rose to being the second-highest of Mississippi's Delta counties by 1996. By the end of the 1990s Tunica 'had been transformed from one of the poorest counties in the Mississippi Delta region to a comparatively prosperous one', using mean income level and decreasing poverty rates as a standard. Yet, economic improvements did not completely change Tunica's fortunes. By 2006, it still had a poverty rate double that of the state (26.6 per cent). The situation was not as desperate as it had been before, but local elites still controlled the economy and political structure. To some extent the predominately rural poor simply changed from being 'unemployed poor' to 'working poor', though many now had health and retirement benefits that kept them off the public dole. In 2002, one resident commented to a reporter on the turnabout: 'Older people up in age, like their 60's, they've got jobs, jobs nobody thought a black person would get'. The legacy of Jim Crow apartheid, sharecropping and racially-exclusive politics continued well into the new millennium, despite the economic gains advanced by the casino industry. Similar to the Atlantic City experience, there remained a hardcore and multi-generational poverty that the casinos did not eradicate, even as they advanced Tunica economically. The number of jobs in Tunica far exceeded the local workforce, suggesting that a lot of the new casino wealth flowed out to people living in surrounding counties and in the greater Memphis area. By national standards, poverty was still high in Tunica of the late 1990s, though it was certainly not as extreme as it had been before 1992.[615]

As was the case with many impoverished residents of Atlantic City during the 1980s, the poorest residents of Tunica County noticed that the casinos did not instantly transform their lives. With ten casinos operational in 1997 and pumping new revenue into the county treasury, Tunica's public schools still fell far short of providing a quality education to its students, though there were some signs of slow improvement. In 1996, one high school celebrated the fact that its first junior class passed the state's eighth-grade functional literacy exam. A local resident declared that 'Tunica is its own little inner city ... Right in the middle of nowhere'. In 1997, casino revenue was helping to build a $1 million library and science lab for one high school, a new elementary school, and was funding classroom renovations all over the district. But the deeply-rooted poverty and history of regional segregation tended to block progress despite the physical improvements. In addition, the long history of a segregated educational system (despite 1954's Brown versus Board of Education) now helped to maintain a wall between the county's largely black impoverished core and the increasingly white and diverse regional residents who came for casino opportunities. In 1997, a local teacher recalled an incident from the mid-1990s that implied resistance to social change, despite Tunica county's new casino riches:

> A few years ago, several of her eighth grade students in the public junior high school asked if they could go to the private academy to watch the baseball practice. 'I said I wish you could. They really have some good talent', Sturgill said. 'And they said, 'You know, Miss Sturgill, we really don't understand why we couldn't play a game against them. It'd be fun. We read about them in the paper all the time and they read about us'. And I said that would probably be one of the greatest things for Tunica County that could ever happen'. Sturgill said she mentioned the conversation to the coaches at both schools. Nothing happened.

Yet, the casino demand created hope for the public schools, mainly because of pressures that were applied by the casino operators, who 'merely want a literate work force and good public schools for their employees' kids'.[616]

By 2002, new apartment buildings had replaced the old shacks along Sugar Ditch in the town of Tunica (the county seat), but many townspeople felt left out of the casino prosperity and some still lived in shacks. Others could not afford the cars needed to transport them to casino jobs. Interviewed outside a liquor store in 2002, one woman lamented the lack of a hospital for locals and her $6.68 per hour floor job at the Horseshoe Casino. Most of the jobs available for Tunica town residents paid less than $10 an hour, a problem exacerbated by the exceedingly low local literacy rate. According to the 2000 census, 40 per cent of the country's adults over twenty-five lacked high school diplomas. Yet, casino jobs with some benefits were better than welfare – something a local nun recognized as an improvement over the pre-casino era: 'It would not have been my choice of what came in', she said, but 'It's [the casino industry] been so helpful that I see no problem'.[617]

The industry's phenomenal growth between 1992 and 2004 had placed it third behind Nevada and New Jersey in terms of annual gaming revenue. The coastal casinos alone brought in half a million dollars a day in direct tax revenues for the state. In 2005, hurricane Katrina's destructive surge pushed a number of the casino barges in Biloxi right over US 90 and further inland. The storm surge floated the President Casino right across the highway and landed it on top of a Holiday Inn close to a mile from its berth. Water inundated MGM-Mirage's Beau Rivage up to its third floor. As the recovery began, the industry benefited from a quick legislative reform that allowed the casinos to rebuild on land as far as 800 feet from the shoreline. Even after Katrina, placing casinos on Mississippi land was too much for anti-gambling groups like the Mississippi Baptist Convention, but they fell short of blocking the reform.[618]

The big operations with casinos on the Gulf Coast wasted no time in rebuilding (Harrah's, Boyd Gaming, MGM Mirage) and within two years, the casinos had substantially returned to revive the industry and local economy. By mid-2007, nine of the twelve coastal casinos closed by Katrina were back in business, and three more were reborn as larger, land-based operations, such as the 100,000 square foot Island View in Gulfport – formerly the barge-based Copa Casino until wrecked by the hurricane. Helped by state reform and federal tax incentives to rebuild, the renovated or brand new casinos were the sole reason for the region's economic recovery from devastation. By reopening, their workforces returned and so did the demand for local restaurants and other businesses. With their ready access to insurance moneys and other capital, the casinos really steered the rebuilding of the region. In 2007, Biloxi Mayor A.J. Holloway called them 'the engine driving this train' and commented to a reporter that the casino income was allowing the coast to recover faster than if there were no casinos. To some extent, the same was true for New Orleans as well. The casinos benefited as other businesses and entertainment venues had not reopened two years after the storm. As of the end of July 2007, Harrah's New Orleans casino was on track for a record-breaking year. However, Louisiana's casinos remained legally tied to water, thus putting them at a severe competitive disadvantage to Mississippi's after the new regulations went into effect. Five months into 2007, the state's casinos were on a pace to earn over $3 billion in casino gross revenues for the year– a total that would exceed the $2.78 billion figure for 2004, the last full year before Katrina. With fewer tourists than before Katrina, the Gulf Coast casinos still brought in more revenue, with bigger, glitzier properties that facilitated longer stays from less gamblers. They also appealed strongly to local gamblers like Craig Williams, an Amtrak worker who frequented New Orleans casinos 'because there's really nothing else to do'. Even with 30 per cent fewer visitors, the Biloxi-Gulfport casinos still made more in gaming revenues as some properties upgraded into full resorts from previously limited operations. By July 2007, the pre-Katrina Imperial Palace had transformed itself from a 'low-rent gambling hall' to a full casino hotel with spa, good restaurants, a nightclub, a new VIP check-in area and a high-stakes gaming area for high rollers.[619]

The coming of casinos to Mississippi had a lot of parallels to the Atlantic City experience. Despite their initially different approaches to a regulatory system, both states realized tremendous economic growth and tax revenues with the casino industry in place and with a similar state tax rate on gaming revenues (9.25 per cent for New Jersey including CRDA obligations, 8 per cent for Mississippi). In both places, the casino industry grew remarkably within a few years in the absence of nearby competition and with the investment of major industry players. Just as Caesar's, Bally's, and Harrah's quickly poured money into the Atlantic City market between 1978 and 1985, major casino companies poured investment capital into Mississippi in the 1990s. Mirage's Beau Rivage in Biloxi and Harrah's consolidated operation in Tunica (sold to Colony Capital in 2004 as part of Harrah's purchase of Caesar's) were developmental milestones and powerful votes of confidence in the regional casino market. From a pure business perspective, the fast growth of the Atlantic City market in its first seven years provided a good business model for developing relatively un-tapped gaming demand for Mississippi.

Locally, there were also relevant comparisons. At one level, there were high expectations for the casino industry to rejuvenate economies. Atlantic City, Tunica County and Biloxi-Gulfport were all economically depressed regions with minimal or failing commerce before casinos came. In each place, the casinos transformed the local community dramatically – mainly by bringing in thousands of direct jobs and millions, even billions of dollars worth of contracts to local providers of goods and services. Another parallel came in the form of disappointed expectations and the persistence of poverty amidst wealth, such as the parallel between Atlantic City's hardcore urban poor and Tunica County's rural poor. Both experiences proved that casinos could not automatically create middle-class enclaves out of extremely blighted areas, nor could they eradicate multi-generational poverty, personal and socio-political dysfunction.[620] Atlantic City's corrupt political system was still powerful eleven years after Resorts opened in 1978, while Tunica's racially-exclusive political structure also persisted over a decade its first casino began operations fifteen years later.[621] However, one could hardly miss the new local benefits of casino revenue, filtered directly to Tunica via its local 4 per cent casino tax and to Atlantic City through the CRDA. High school students in both places, for example, benefited via new technology and new classroom space. In both Mississippi and New Jersey, casino revenue also directly improved physical infrastructure (such as US route 90 on the Gulf Coast and the Boardwalk in Atlantic City) that benefited both the casino industry and the local population. Less tangibly, the casino era in Mississippi's two largest casino communities and in Atlantic City had everything to do with hope. In the mid-1970s on the crumbling South Jersey shore, amidst the dusty cotton fields of the Mississippi Delta in the early 1990s and along the wrecked post-Katrina Gulf Coast in the mid-2000s, the casino industry brought hope for survival, hope for revival and hope for the future.

Like New Jersey and Mississippi, the state of Pennsylvania also turned towards casino gaming to help bolster the economic fortunes of its residents, but mainly through taxation as opposed to the development of a major casino industry within its borders. After years of political and legal wrangling, Pennsylvania finally legalized slots machines at designated racetracks and stand-alone operations in 2004. Driven by Democratic governor Ed Rendell, Pennsylvania's push to legalize slot machines had everything to do with the state's revenues. Specifically, Rendell began his efforts to reduce Pennsylvania property taxes after becoming governor in 2003. By mid-2004, he had succeeded in bringing a legalization bill before the Pennsylvania General Assembly that allowed for fourteen separate gaming outlets around the state that would have an estimated 61,000 slot machines. The Assembly passed the slots bill in 2004 with a total 55 per cent tax on total gross revenues attached, a move that underlined the extent to which the keystone state's venture into casino gaming was a public programme to reduce property taxes, go towards a special fund for the horse racing industry, provide local revenues (four per cent, and even offset the city of Philadelphia's wage tax. The large number of slot machines would make Pennsylvania the second-largest casino gaming state after Nevada and, from the view of the bill's supporters, bring in $1 billion plus in new revenue to the state treasury.[622]

Like the 1977 *CCA* that cleared the New Jersey legislature, Pennsylvania's new bill was meant to bolster the state's racing industry in addition to helping residents with their economic obligations:

> the authorization of limited gaming is intended to provide a significant source of new revenue to the commonwealth to support property tax relief, wage tax reduction, economic development opportunities and other similar incentives.

The bill provided 45 per cent of revenue to casino operators, 34 per cent for the state (where the property tax relief was to come from), 9 per cent for the horse racing industry, 5 per cent for a new fund for 'Gaming, Economic Development and Tourism Fund', and 4 per cent for counties and municipalities where the new slots parlors and racinos would be located. It also provided $60 million for the Pittsburgh Development Fund. It also set up a seven-member Gaming Control Board (GCB) to determine licensure, collect revenues and otherwise make sure the new operators adhered to Pennsylvania law. To some extent, the debate that preceded passage of the bill reflected New Jersey's, with concerns expressed over organized crime and again over replicating Las Vegas in Pennsylvania. Even after two decades of success and the virtual eradication of organized crime from Las Vegas' industry in the 1980s, Republican Paul Clymer of Bucks County still commented that 'I fear that we'll become Las Vegas East'. Governor Rendell sought to allay these worries by appointing people to the GCB with law enforcement backgrounds and specific experience in investigating organized crime. Sounding a lot like backers of New Jersey's bill twenty-seven years earlier, he proclaimed that 'I am bound and determined that organized crime will not get a foothold in Pennsylvania' via the new gaming operations. Casino opponents also objected to a provision in the slots bill that allowed Pennsylvania government officials to hold up to 1 per cent of a gaming company's ownership, similar to a measure adopted by New Jersey.[623]

The Pennsylvania slots bill also included a measure to limit multiple ownership of the new gaming properties. The gaming bill also restricted licensed operators from owning more than 33 per cent of another facility when they already owned 100 per cent of the first facility. By adopting this rule, the Pennsylvania General Assembly demonstrated its intent that Pennsylvania would essentially move in the opposite direction from that of Atlantic City in recent years, and away from the natural casino marketplace. It was reminiscent of New Jersey's original three-casino limitation, and in sharp contrast to both Atlantic City (since 1995) and Mississippi. The restriction did not make much sense in terms of allowing the industry to expand according to the free gaming market, but it certainly signalled that the Pennsylvania casinos were coming online with tight state regulation. The restriction also underscored the fundamental basis of the Pennsylvania casinos: public revenue over private commerce. The overall adoption of the New Jersey model would probably bring some stability to the Pennsylvania casinos, in addition to the integrity spurred by licensing all casino suppliers (including non-gaming businesses) as a bulwark against organized crime involvement. But the high taxation-'Christmas Tree' model (with presents for everyone) along with the market restrictions were not especially conducive to casino expansion. In Pennsylvania, however, that seemed to be the point. Like the New Jersey designers of the *CCA*, the actors behind the keystone state slots envisioned only public benefits via tax revenue as opposed to the expansion of a new gaming business.[624]

There was a certain irony to Pennsylvania's efforts to steer organized crime away from its new slots parlors and racinos when it was the Philadelphia mafia that had tried to infiltrate New Jersey's casino industry in the late 1970s and early 1980s. At that time, organized crime already had quite a 'foothold' in and around Philadelphia but was mainly repulsed via New Jersey's restrictive process that in the 1980s even denied casino licence applications for simple associations with suspected mob figures, not direct mob involvement. The concern also demonstrated the persistence of an aura surrounding the casino industry despite three decades of corporatization, international expansion, and the industry's evolution into a high-stakes financial operation closely tied to the Wall Street equity markets. By 2004, it was virtually impossible for the organized crime to infiltrate the casino industry given that stockholders and modern, MBA-equipped executives ran the companies, but the spectre had not gone away. If nothing else, it could still be used to rally opposition to the industry's expansion and also represented a misperception of the extent to which south Philadelphia mobsters had actually benefited from the Atlantic City casinos. If anything, the casino industry in Atlantic City contributed largely to the Philadelphia mob's decline, as mobsters fought over a slice of casino-related business that was largely illusory.[625]

After costly legal battles and a particularly well-organized anti-casino effort in Philadelphia, three racinos opened in Pennsylvania in 2006. The state reserved two more casino sites for downtown Philadelphia despite a strident effort by a group called Casino Free Philadelphia that took their objections and desire to hold a local referendum on the city's casinos to the Pennsylvania Supreme Court, where they lost. Reflecting its expansion efforts, Harrah's actually owned one of the three sites: Harrah's Chester Downs in Chester County, Pennsylvania. Two other Atlantic City operations (Trump and Pinnacle) both applied for a Philadelphia site, but lost, in part, due to GCB concerns about Atlantic City operations competing for resources and the companies shifting their customers down to the ocean. The 2007 winners for the two Philadelphia casinos included Foxwoods Resorts, another coup for the Connecticut operation. In 2006, Mohegan Sun became the first operator in Pennsylvania, opening the doors to its no-frills gambling hall at Pocono Downs in Wilkes Barre.[626]

For the Atlantic City gaming industry, the impact of Pennsylvania slots came quickly. One winter Sunday in early 2007 at the Philadelphia Park Casino, Ron Thomas played two $5 'Double Diamond' slot machines simultaneously and wondered why he and his wife should ever return to Atlantic City when they could do 'exactly what we can do here?' By the middle of 2007, there were strong indications that Pennsylvania gaming was cutting into Atlantic City's casino revenues, thus reversing the positive trend that continued through 2006, despite the shutdown and despite Borgata's continuing success. In early 2007, the Atlantic City casino industry was also hit with a partial ban on smoking and a new spike in gas prices. Casino revenue was down for five of the first six months of the year and gaming analysts at firms like Spectrum Gaming Group and Bear Stearns pointed directly at Pennsylvania, though remained bullish on Atlantic City continuing the success of 2003–6 by taking advantage of its coastal location.[627]

Just how dire were the effects of the Pennsylvania incursion into the Atlantic City customer base? After the first six months of 2007, casino gross revenue was down approximately 4 per cent ($102 million) from the same period of 2006. Yet, the year-to-year loss was much less than the casino revenues pulled in by the three open slots parlours in eastern Pennsylvania during the same period. Philadelphia Park, Harrah's Chester Downs and the Mohegan Sun collectively brought in about $350 million in the same period – close to three and a half times the amount that Atlantic City was down. Did this represent additional gaming revenue that would have gone to Atlantic City, or did these revenues come from new slots players attracted to nearby casinos? These new players might never make it to a casino on the Boardwalk or in the marina. Yet, as slots revenue declined in the first six months of 2007, overall table games revenue increased by 2.9 per cent to $706.5 million. The total Atlantic City numbers should also be considered in light of the Sands's closing in November 2006.[628]

With less than a year of such local competition, the impact of Pennsylvania gaming on the Atlantic City casino industry is not yet clear. Significantly, in the first half of 2007 both Borgata and Caesar's (where the Pier at Caesar's recently opened) bucked the overall decline in casino revenues. Borgata's casino 'win' actually increased 5.4 per cent and Caesar's increased its casinos 'win' and Caesar's was up 11.1 per cent. As the Atlantic City casino industry prepares to celebrate its thirtieth anniversary in 2008, its future and long-desired re-birth as a destination resort could actually have more to do with non-gaming attractions than gambling itself.

The Atlantic City casino era has been a success for the people of the coastal South Jersey region, for the state of New Jersey and for the gaming firms based there. Yet, the story of the local casino era is barely known to most people who live outside the region, who may visit a casino only occasionally, or not at all. To many Americans, Atlantic City's image is frozen in the mid-1980s, when the city went through its rough period and the national press seized upon Boardwalk decay, the crime spike and continued poverty to declare the casino experiment a failure. This misleading perception often characterized other states' debates over casino legalization well into the 2000s. In Maryland, an ailing horse racing industry, periodic state budget deficits, casinos and racinos in surrounding states ratcheted up the prospects of legalizing casino-style gaming in 2007. Gaming opponents often cited Atlantic City to try to prevent slot machines from coming to town. In Ocean City, Maryland the business community decided to rally against slot machines coming to the state and, in 2007, the local tourism commission at a meeting voted to oppose their arrival, the commissioners concluding that in Atlantic City, 'although the casinos brought booming hotels and business, it left the surrounding areas in squalor'.[629] A post on an internet bulletin board about Maryland slots summed up an oft-heard perception about bringing slot machines to Ocean Downs, a harness race track outside Ocean City: 'So get your money CARPETBAGGERS, hire more police to handle the calls and reports that come along with the gambling. Then change the city's name to Atlantic City South'.[630]

EPILOGUE

Walking the famed Boardwalk on a gorgeous summer evening in 2007, the liveliness and diversity of attractions was impossible to miss. Above the now-shuttered Sands's 'People Mover' moving sidewalk, a brilliant purple billboard implored Boardwalk denizens to wait a few years for the Pinnacle casino to open, and indicated that the advertisement was approved by the mislabelled 'New Jersey Gaming Commission'. At the Boardwalk junction of Trump Plaza and Caesar's, a young rock band filmed a video. The souvenir stands, hot dog counters, pizza joints, fortune-telling stands and garish clothes stores did brisk business, as they always did on warm summer nights. Yet, now some of them looked different than they had ten years earlier, when I had first experienced Atlantic City: their canvas awnings had been replaced by stucco and brick facades with cupolas on their roofs, a CRDA sign here and there taking credit for the improvements. Parts of the Boardwalk were in the midst of a major facelift and it seemed poised, even eager for a more radical makeover. Now, the Pier at Caesar's was open, and walking through it one experienced something very different from the Boardwalk. The Pier had smooth, glowing aisles, elegant restaurants and lounges upstairs, a coordinated music-light show, and a multi-layered candy store teeming with families designing customized candy bars and learning about candy through the ages. The Pier opened in 2006, no less opulent than advertised, though two years behind schedule. Was this the new Atlantic City? Would the candy store still be here in five years, or would it go the way of so many non-gaming establishments that have come and gone during Atlantic City's casino era? Was this another Planet Hollywood or Ocean One Mall (its geographic ancestor), or would it last, would it remain commercially viable in the casino town? Would new stores like 'IT'SUGAR' or the Banana Republic outlet in the Walk, cool nightclubs and Borgata style, finally transform the casino community into the long-desired 'destination resort?'

As always, the Atlantic City casino community is in a state of flux, heading towards the second decade of the twenty-first century. After three decades, the casino era has wrought great wealth, but also plenty of problems. The casino industry faced major, unprecedented pressure with the 2006 opening of two racinos and a slots parlour in eastern Pennsylvania, with the fourteen gaming halls soon to come online in Pennsylvania. Gaming revenue – casino 'win' – was already down 4 per cent for the first six months of 2007, and New York's nascent slots industry provided more competitive pressures than there had been before. Could the Atlantic City casino community sustain itself as the mid-Atlantic and northeastern gaming industry took off?

When the Sands shut down in late 2006 after Pinnacle's acquisition, it was a sad but inevitable moment for Atlantic City's casino era. In many ways, the Sands symbolized a long-faded time of smaller, more personalized gaming. It closed after a last ditch effort to compete with its bigger and well-funded rivals by recalling the Rat Pack era, when Frank Sinatra, Dean Martin and Sammy Davis Jr first made Las Vegas a hip place to party. But a new bar and the Rat Pack aura was not enough to bring in new players and it had been unprofitable for years before owner Carl Icahn sold out to Pinnacle. The eighty-something Grinaldis of Staten Island, New York sounded wistful, but ever optimistic about the future: 'We're going to miss the Sands ... Unless we win at the Claridge'.[631]

The Sands's closure was personally sad for me. Though I am not much of a gambler, I sometimes wandered through the Sands during my five years of research for this book, enjoying a drink at the 'Swingers' bar, and (very) occasionally playing blackjack at one of the few $5 tables left in the city. I liked the retro ambience and also benefited from the various programmes it implemented in its efforts to survive, like free self-parking. But when I compared the Sands's cool, cosy atmosphere to the new style of the Quarter or the comfortable chic of the Borgata, I realized that it simply was not enough to bring in new people who had choices about where to spend a couple of days. I also noticed that I was almost always younger most of its patrons by a few decades – something not so apparent in a Quarter restaurant or anywhere in the Borgata.

Other unprecedented factors also led to questions about the casino community's future. For example, how would Harrah's buy-out by two private equity firms impact the casino community? When that buy-out occurred in late 2006, 40 per cent of the Atlantic City casino industry now fell under control of a non-gaming entity. The purchase recalled Starwood hotels' brief ownership of Caesar's in the 1990s, but at least Starwood was in the hospitality business. While the capital infusion could promote growth, the deal raised significant red flags, such as one that appeared in *Michael Pollack's Gaming Industry Observer*:

> Casinos, in our view, are best operated by gaming companies – a recognition that gaming is a knowledge-intensive industry, as much as it is a capital-intensive one.

Would the new ownership retain experienced and visionary gaming executives like Gary Loveman and Tim Wilmott? The *Observer* summed up the new reality and concern for the community:

At Harrah's, for instance, casinos are the company's raison d'etre; casinos in a private equity firm are simply one collection of assets in a larger-portfolio.

The Harrah's buy-out faced regulatory scrutiny by the NJCCC in 2007, though there was no real doubt that the commissioners would approve it. One positive sign for Atlantic City actually came from another casino community in 2007, when Harrah's announced plans to forge ahead with a planned $700 million 'Margaritaville' casino in Biloxi, as a joint project with Jimmy Buffet. Within a few months of its purchase, Harrah's put a hold on a $3 billion planned renovation of Caesar's, Bally's and Showboat that included a 1,000-room hotel tower on top of the new Caesar's garage.[632]

Corporate actions also caused considerable angst in the community when the hospitality firm Columbia Sussex acquired the Tropicana from Aztar Corporation in 2006 in a $2.75 billion transaction. Within a year, the Kentucky-based company changed its name to Tropicana, but also shocked many in the community and drew the unified wrath of politicians, union officials and others when it laid off approximately 1,000 Tropicana employees. By summer 2007, Tropicana had lost 15 per cent of its 2006 workforce, from room cleaners to slots supervisors. The Tropicana layoffs came just months after the loss of 2,000 casino employees' jobs when the Sands closed, leading Local 54's president Bob McDevitt to comment that the casino's restrooms might rival the city's bus station for cleanliness. At one point, the Commission actually intervened over concerns that the company's slot technician cuts might cause the Tropicana to fall below a minimum mandated threshold to uphold the integrity of slots operations. Assemblyman James Whelan (Atlantic City's former mayor) called for a state labour department investigation. The situation led to the firing of Tropicana president Fred Buro (reportedly for complaining about the cuts and condition of the property) and a scathing *Press of Atlantic City* editorial. *Press* editors accused the Columbia of violating the spirit of the *CCA* and urged the commission to consider all their options in a pending licensure hearing:

> Is the slash-and-burn business model being used by Columbia Sussex Corp., a privately held Kentucky company that took over the Tropicana Casino and Resort in January, good for Atlantic City, the region and the state?[633]

For its part, Columbia Sussex's president (William Yung III) argued that the cuts were only necessary to bring the company in line with more efficient operators like Harrah's and highlighted a $25 million infrastructure investment as important for the company's future. He blamed Aztar for 'some of the most inflated payroll ratios in the industry' and sought to assure people in the community that the Tropicana's new owner was making a sincere effort to grow the casino's business for long-term security. Still, McDevitt vowed to oppose the company's application for a permanent gaming license and a Deutsche Bank analyst cautioned that the company needed to do more than cost-cutting to compete in Atlantic City. The Tropicana's financial prospects grew even murkier when Columbia Sussex abruptly halted a highly-leveraged $2.5 billion makeover project for the Las Vegas Tropicana following the credit crisis that jolted the American financial sector in August 2007. By the middle of 2007, Tropicana's casino revenue was down 7 per cent from 2006.[634]

Tropicana's travails may turn out to be a short-term phenomenon and in a few years the casino might return to stability and efficiency. Alternatively, they may represent beginning of a trip down the same road to Atlantic City oblivion already trodden by the Atlantis and the Sands casinos. Either way, the casino's 2007 bloodletting or efficiency initiative (choose your label) was an effective reminder that big business serves the cause of commerce first and community second. Thirty years into the experiment, the casinos were nothing if they were not big businesses. To the *Press of Atlantic City* editors, this reality was difficult to accept, tied as they appeared to be to the original community concept that went along with legalization in the 1970s. But talk about the 'unique role' of casinos in the garden state had a nostalgic ring to it in 2007, with local casino executives in pitched battle to retain market share. In fact, the reality of the casino business meant that the community concept had already been losing ground for two decades. In the 1990s, a new generation of public officials recognized that the casinos' ultimate benefit to the greater Atlantic City community came via the billions of dollars they wrought, that spread throughout the economy in the form of wages, tips, contracts, profits, and multiplier-effect jobs. They also reacted to the threat to Atlantic City's east coast casino monopoly that came with the opening of Foxwoods and the Mississippi casinos. With Indian gaming rising from a $10 billion annual business to a $23 billion annual business from 1999 to 2005, Atlantic City's commercial operators along the Boardwalk and Marina district understood the need to maximize revenue while keeping down costs. And that was before a single player slid a $20 bill into a shiny new Pennsylvania slot machine. The new Tropicana management clearly blundered with its ham-handed personnel actions in 2007, possibly inflicting damage to its own prospects that would be too far to overcome. The management of Columbia Sussex arrived in Atlantic City casino community with little apparent understanding of its culture and has paid a political and public relations price for that managerial deficiency.[635]

One of the benefits of the new casino era has been the opening of many great ethnic restaurants around town. So it was that on a recent trip, after enjoying my dinner at a Vietnamese restaurant on Atlantic Avenue, I noticed a posting on the wall alerting Caesar's dealers (many Asian-Americans among them) that a vote was set to take place on joining the United Auto Workers (UAW). The dealers were spurred by market factors, wage and personnel concerns and a national outreach campaign by the United Auto Workers to unionize casino workers around the country. In 2007, casino dealers began voting to join the UAW, beginning with Caesar's. The Caesar's vote passed, and a few months later, the dealers (now represented by the UAW) began negotiations for the first ever collective bargaining agreement for casino dealers in Atlantic City. Following Caesar's vote, dealers at Trump Plaza also voted to unionize, as did dealers at Bally's and Tropicana. Bally's dealers passed the union vote by a strong majority, 628 to 255, while Tropicana dealers voted to approve by 80 per cent. However, dealers at both the Atlantic City Hilton and Trump Marina rejected the UAW vote. The issue ratcheted up quickly with the casinos and unions both charging unfair interference in the process as the votes proceeded. In July 2007, the NJCCC approved live testing for electronic versions of roulette and poker, the first step towards bringing the machines online in the casinos. By then, both Pennsylvania and Delaware slots parlors offered electronic blackjack, and the commission began the testing process in light of the newly-competitive environment. UAW's unionization drive continued through 2007, and also included Foxwoods in Connecticut and a casino in Evansville, Indiana.[636]

The future of the Trump casinos was also ambiguous thirty years into Atlantic City's casino era. The company re-structured again in 2005 to bring itself out of bankruptcy and freed up approximately $500 million for improvements. The 2005 restructuring also cost Trump his controlling share of the company. Trump Entertainment Resorts went on the auction block in 2007. But there were no takers, so the company announced that it would shift strategy again and redouble its efforts to rebuild market share in Atlantic City's casino marketplace. These included a diamond-shaped, 768-room tower at Trump Taj Mahal and a commitment to the NJCCC that the company was financially sound, despite its abysmally-performing stock and continued debt problems. Between 1995 and 2007, an overall casino stock index increased 268 per cent while Trump stock actually fell by 93 per cent. By 2006, the Trump market share in Atlantic City was down to 20 per cent of total revenue – an 8 per cent drop since 1999. The Trump casinos were all over 80 per cent in gaming revenue as a percentage of total revenue. Meanwhile, two of the capital-starved Trump casinos (Trump Plaza and Trump Marina) performed worse than the industry average in 2007 – with the marina down 7.7 per cent in casino win. Of all the Atlantic City properties, the Trump casinos appeared to be in the weakest position to sustain themselves in the new climate of competition with Pennsylvania and New York operators. A Bear Stearns analysis had ominous words both about the Trump prospects and the casino industry:

> [the failure to sell] speaks to the fundamental problems inherent in Trump's properties at present and the difficult operating environment in Atlantic City.[637]

Whatever happens to the Trump casinos in the future, the Trump legacy of the first thirty years of the Atlantic City casino era is a remarkable story. From one perspective, Trump's personal flamboyance, boldness and risk-taking helped saved the industry in the late 1980s when he bought out the Taj Mahal. At the time, the huge, hulking, expensive disaster on the Boardwalk threatened to bring down Resorts International and it had become unfortunately symbolic of early casino-era mistakes. Trump's investment in the project helped revive the east end of the Boardwalk and eventually led to thousands of additional jobs. It also briefly raised Atlantic City's profile in the international gaming community and the Trump group provided tens of thousand of residents with a living for years. Yet, its failure to prosper and its exorbitant debt load also led quickly to the financial problems that contributed to the Trump group's stagnation for most of the 1990s and 2000s. Trump admitted that the casinos had been good for him personally in a 2004 interview:

> The casinos have always been a great deal for me. How much have I made off the casinos? Off the record, a lot. I put a lot of debt on them and I took the money out and I bought a lot of real estate in New York. So I'm very happy at the way things worked out.[638]

Yet, the very deals that made Donald Trump money to invest in New York real estate were not always so great for Trump casino contractors, bondholders or stockholders. In the late 2000s, the Trump casinos persisted in the same corporate environment and competitive atmosphere as all the other casinos. Market conditions and the business climate were all that mattered anymore and these would dictate the company's future in Atlantic City.

Despite the Sands's closure, Trump's problems, Harrah's uncertainty and the Tropicana layoffs, the outlook was actually quite bright for the casino industry's future in the late 2000s. Before the credit crisis hit American markets in mid-2007, close to $10 billion of casino investment was on the table for projects up and down the Boardwalk. Pinnacle moved ahead with its $1.5–2 billion project by beginning demolition of the Sands property to make way for construction on its new casino, planned to take about four years. Meanwhile, Revel Entertainment – former Trump executive Kevin DeSanctis – was ready to develop the Boardwalk parcel above Showboat, now owned by investment bank Morgan Stanley. In 2007, it began to develop plans for a $2 billon casino to finally bring the rest of barren Pauline's Praire into the casino era. Colony Capital's Atlantic City Hilton also planned a $1 billion expansion to keep up with its competitors. As well, MGM Mirage announced a $4.5 billion mixed casino and condominium development on land it still held in the marina district. Boyd Gaming's president (Bill Boyd) was quick to credit his company's casino for all the new investment:

> When we first began in this market, Atlantic City was viewed as a one-dimensional, gaming-only destination ... Today Atlantic City is viewed widely as an entertainment destination with a wider variety than ever in its history.[639]

Meanwhile, a new group of investors that included a former Caesar's executive and a CRDA official planned a small casino on a Boardwalk parcel to the west of the Atlantic City Hilton, on the site of the old Atlantic City High School where a parking lot now stood. The Borgata and Harrah's pushed forward with their new towers, both to include sumptuous spas, luxurious towers, and many new upscale restaurants and shops. Harrah's new spa ('Red Door') was planned to include twenty-four treatment rooms and an indoor pool, while Borgata's new tower ('The Water Club at Borgata') would be oriented around its new 36,000 square foot spa and pool center. It will have four swimming pools, 18,000 square feet of meeting space, 800 rooms, but apparently, not add one more square foot of gaming space to the casino.[640]

Bill Boyd's assessment had an obvious bias to it, but the evidence to back his assertion was rather clear. Along with the Quarter, the successful Borgata had gone a long way towards attracting new capital to Atlantic City's casino industry by demonstrating that non-gaming attractions could be profitable, and what could separate Atlantic City from its new regional competitors if not destination resorts like Las Vegas had successfully developed in the 1990s? Gaming specialists always seemed quick to note that, while Atlantic City and Las Vegas were relatively close in annual gaming revenues, Las Vegas operators raked in much more revenue than the Atlantic City casinos in non-gaming attractions.

The investment buzz and optimism that characterized the nascent post-Borgata era can be compared to the similar atmosphere in the mid-1990s surrounding the Mirage's H-Tract deal. Investor interest stayed strong through the late 1990s, until the local casino industry slowed down a bit after Mohegan Sun's spectacular success and as the tunnel-connector war raged. The MGM merger with Mirage, along with Steve Wynn's renewed focus on Las Vegas (and new casino horizons in Asia), meant that, besides improvements by existing operators, new investors stayed away until the Borgata's success appeared to bring them back in the mid-2000s. There were, however, key differences between the mid-1990s and mid-2000s. Firstly, the gaming industry itself had changed considerably. In 1997, nine companies ran twelve individual casinos. In 2007, Atlantic City still had eleven casinos, but now they were run by only five operators and, except for Trump, all the casino operators were national or multi-national operators. As the consolidated casino industry vaults into the future, virtually all casino decisions that impact Atlantic City will be consequent to the national or international gaming marketplace. What started as a project by locals to revive their economic prospects has lost much of its local focus through a natural, commercial process. Secondly, the contentious legal and political climate surrounding the Mirage and tunnel-connector deal has changed considerably. Potential casino developers appeared to have little concern that city politics, grassroots community organization or state legislative opposition would block their projects. As Steve Perskie stated in 2005:

by and large the kinds of titanic, really basic philosophical and political struggles that marked my time in that respect are gone and not to come back. I think you've now got a city government that better understands its role. I think you've got a state government that basically has said we put our chips on the table in the early 1990s and there's no way we can take them off.[641]

A main difference between Atlantic City's casino era of the 1990s and 2000s was the presence of Steve Wynn. Wynn's dynamic, energetic persona has been central to both Atlantic City's casino era and the entire international gaming industry sine the 1970s. Would the promising, challenging Atlantic City gaming marketplace once again entice Wynn and his new company (Wynn Resorts Ltd.) to roll the dice on the Jersey shore? In 2006, rumors briefly surfaced that Wynn and Trump were putting together a deal to remake Trump Plaza into a mega-casino resort, but nothing came of it. Then, the city government decided to close its little-used municipal airport, Bader Field. Bader Field was located on a 140-acre piece of bayfront property on the city's western side, not far from the Tropicana and just off the Atlantic City Expressway, almost adjacent to the Sandcastle, the CRDA-funded minor league baseball stadium built in the late 1990s. The prospect of the developing the property was enough to refocus Wynn on Atlantic City. In the 1980s, he had hoped to develop Great Island for casinos before the school board and city latched on to it as the site for the new high school. Like the Great Island prospect before, the Bader Field site had great potential in Wynn's eyes for a project he envisioned as 'Wynn Atlantic City'. By Autumn 2007, he had already met with Governor Corzine to talk about a Wynn Resorts casino for Atlantic City and made public his interest in the Bader Field site: 'If we have the property, I'll build the hotel' he commented to a reporter in July 2007'.[642]

Mark Twain once noted that 'History does not repeat itself, but it rhymes.'[643] Perhaps Steve Wynn will rhyme historically by working another special deal with the city and state for the Bader Field property. Maybe the deal will include public support for access improvements à la the Brigantine Connector and renovation reimbursement that the state granted Mirage for cleaning up the toxic H-Tract. However, not everyone in the casino community shared Wynn's enthusiasm for the new project. Again, opposition arose quickly from an industry rival. This time, Pinnacle's CEO and Chairman John Lee spoke out against the idea and threatened to pull out of its Boardwalk project on the basis that Wynn was trying to unfairly use his political influence to land Bader Field. The response from the Wynn team was sharp:

> Pinnacle's efforts should be directed at creating their own successful venture rather than trying to stop others from developing projects in Atlantic City ... If Pinnacle Entertainment is afraid of competition, Wynn Resorts Ltd. would be willing to buy their Boardwalk site at their cost and they can then leave and try to control competition somewhere else.

The Wynn statement also made reference to Atlantic City's recent past and crediting Mirage with Atlantic City's recent success:

> For a period of more than four years, beginning in 1995, Mirage Resorts fought to redevelop the Marina District. During that time, a number of casino operators on the Boardwalk claimed that if the property was developed it would be the end of life as we know it for Atlantic City.

As of this book's publication, there has been no definitive development plan established for Bader Field and it is unclear whether the city will even rezone it for gaming. So far, Donald Trump has stayed out of the fray.[644]

Yet, there was certainly no end to conflict in the casino community as the Borgata era unfolded. Another bitterly-contentious mayoral race took place in 2005, resulting in Lorenzo Langford becoming a one-term mayor and fellow Democrat Bob Levy (a Whelan ally and chief lifeguard) taking power. Local 54's leadership backed Langford, who stood behind the union in the 2004 strike. Members walked the city streets and handed out placards on primary day supporting Langford and urging voters to 'Elect Real Democrats'. In return, Levy supporters parked a huge inflatable rat in front of the Sovereign Avenue union hall. It was a vicious-looking reminder of the political fights that have often absorbed the city since it transitioned from a commission government in 1982. As before, bitter resentment hung over the city's politics following the election and official corruption became an issue again with the 2006 conviction of City Council president Craig Calloway on federal extortion charges for accepting $36,000 in bribes from a local contractor.[645]

Aside from the peculiarities of Atlantic City politics, the casino era has unfolded as a regional phenomenon much more than an urban story. Though I was based in Atlantic City throughout my research years, I spent a considerable time in Atlantic County and around South Jersey learning how the casino industry had affected life in the region. From Vineland to Pleasantville, Egg Harbor Township to Margate, the casinos quickly became central to many aspects of life. In 2007, casinos employed approximately 36,000 residents of Atlantic County and 73 per cent of them lived outside Atlantic City. Two county townships alone (Egg Harbor Township and Galloway) accounted for 25 per cent of casino employees, nearly as many casino employees as lived in Atlantic City proper.[646] These communities look like thousands of other prosperous suburbs around the nation, with neat (if uniform) housing developments, strip malls, box stores, chain restaurants and accessible public facilities. For the most part, they have good public schools and little crime to worry about. In oral history interviews with these suburbanites, I came away with a powerful sense that whatever they felt about the casino industry, they enjoyed the ease of middle-American life outside the city, largely funded by the casino industry. Sitting in her comfortable dining room in a new Egg Harbor Township development, local educator

Nanette Stuart spoke briefly about the difference between living in Atlantic City and Atlantic County:

> you feel more comfortable. You feel more at ease. You have more peace of mind and less stressful. It's a lot less stressful, living out here than it is there.

Stuart taught at an Atlantic City middle school, but lived in a neighbourhood of clean, neat owner-occupied homes, full of casino employees.[647]

Aside from the economic opportunity created by casinos, the state's treasury has benefited tremendously via casino revenue. By the end of 2006, the industry had contributed over $7 billion in taxes via the CRF. By 2006, there were six additional taxes on casino revenue in addition to the 8 per cent of casino 'win' dedicated to the CRF. These included a controversial 4.25 per cent comp tax, a $3 per day parking fee, a $3 per day hotel room tax and a new 8 per cent tax on multi-casino progressive slot revenue.

To be sure, pockets of Atlantic City itself remained beset by urban decay in the late 2000s, deep poverty and the social ills that tend to accompany poverty such as illegal drug use and violence. In 2000, Atlantic City's unemployment rate was 9.9 per cent, almost three times New Jersey's 3.6 per cent. Yet, Atlantic County's unemployment rate was much lower at 5.7 per cent and the bigger townships of the county such as Egg Harbor, Galloway and Hamilton hovered right around the state average.[648] The casinos did not completely eradicate the desperate poverty and economic plight of Atlantic City in the thirty years since Resorts opened, but they certainly brought new wealth and opportunity to a place that otherwise would have remained deeply depressed for years. As well, big sections of the uptown section of the city remain as vacant lots. The sad, empty spaces between houses still serve as reminders of the speculative real estate frenzy that beset the city in the late 1970s and early 1980s.

When the industry really took off in the mid-1990s, social ills like crime decreased dramatically. The CCA's original mission for casinos to accomplish the 'redevelopment' of Atlantic City has been variously interpreted throughout the casino era. Indeed, 'redevelopment' is easy to appreciate when looking at the many CRDA-subsidized homes and clean streets that now fill the Inlet area or absorbing the dynamic, fluid immigrant culture while walking down Ventnor Avenue in the Lower Chelsea neighborhood. 'Redevelopment' comes to mind whilst attending a community picnic with hundreds of Vietnamese-Americans, many of whom arrived in the US as refugees and who now live in their own houses, bought and sustained via casino wages and tips. 'Redevelopment' comes to mind when strolling down the Boardwalk these days. Living in the old Ritz-Carlton hotel (now the Ritz condominiums) next to the Tropicana in 2005, I neither saw nor heard about one major crime taking place on the Boardwalk. Not once did I feel remotely concerned about my safety or for that of my four-year old daughter. It is not pristine or upscale – one can still find an abundance of down-market pizza and Philly cheese steak joints – but it is well lit, heavily patrolled, regularly maintained and increasingly dotted with outdoor cafes and restaurants with diverse cuisines. Some are attached to casinos, some are not. In short, it is the physical and symbolic realization of a revitalized place.

Ultimately, the Atlantic City casino era is a story of hope, redemption, frustration and success. The gamble has paid off by attracting millions more visitors and pumping billions into the local economy, but that payoff came with gut-wrenching conflict, hardship, and an ongoing process of trials and errors. It is still not a destination resort in the manner of Las Vegas, but appears to be closer than ever to that goal. There are no guaranteed strategies for winning at blackjack or playing the slots, and there was never a guarantee that the casino era would succeed. But it has succeeded, and the people who made that success – casino magnates and executives, politicians and public functionaries, casino employees, labor officials, old and new immigrants – have reaped the benefits, even as their northeastern monopoly disappeared in the construction dust kicked up by Foxwoods and the Mohegan Sun. Atlantic City's thirty-year casino odyssey is an exuberant story of human success, ambition, energy, endurance, creativity and the beneficial power of the marketplace in successful partnership with the state. Will the success continue for the next thirty years and beyond? Will the casino industry survive the modern, hyper-competitive gaming environment? If past is prologue, then Atlantic City looks like a good bet for continued success in the American casino era.

NOTES

1. Interview with Russelle Patterson, 19 June 2002, Atlantic City Project Oral History Interviews, MS J. R. Karmel, Heston Room, Atlantic City Free Public Library (ACPOHI).
2. Martin Lizerbram (San Diego, CA), Atlantic City Memory Webpage, http://iloveac. com/memory.php (accessed 7 January 2007).
3. The best literary account of the city's post-World War II decline is B. Simon, *Boardwalk of Dreams: Atlantic City and the Fate of Urban America* (New York: Oxford University Press, 2004).
4. Interview with Daniel Heneghan, 4 and 31 March 2005, ACPOHI.
5. NJCCC, *Annual Report* (1983), p. 12.
6. NJCCC, *Annual Report* (1999), p. 10.
7. Interview with Russelle Patterson, ACPOHI; interview with Daniel Heneghan, ACPOHI; interview with Tom Gitto, 16 June 2005, ACPOHI; interview with Barbara Devlin, 21 June 2002, ACPOHI; D. A. Ritchie, *Doing Oral History: A Practical Guide*, 2nd edn (New York: Oxford University Press, 2003), pp. 36–7.
8. Interview with Russelle Patterson, ACPOHI.
9. Interview with Steve Perskie, 14 May 2005, ACPOHI; interview with Dennis Ricci, 4 and 15 April 2005, ACPOHI.
10. Interview with Pierre Hollingsworth, 30 April 2005, ACPOHI; Simon, *Boardwalk of Dreams*, pp. 17–18.
11. A. Portelli, *The Death of Luigi Trastulli and Other Stories: Form and Meaning in Oral History* (Albany, NY: State University of New York Press, 1991), pp. 50–1; M. Frisch, *A Shared Authority: Essays on the Craft and Meaning of Oral and Public History* (Albany, NY: State University of New York Press, 1991), pp. 12–13.
12. E. Tonkin, *Narrating Our Pasts: The Social Construction of Oral History* (Cambridge: Cambridge University Press, 1992), p. 105.
13. On the powerful connections between memory, social circumstance and oral history, see B. S. Godfrey and J. C. Richardson, 'Loss, Collective Memory and Transcripted Oral Histories', *International Journal of Social Research Methodology*, 7:4 (2004), pp. 143–55.
14. O. Demaris, *The Boardwalk Jungle* (New York: Bantam, 1986); M. Pollack, *Hostage to Fortune: Atlantic City and Casino Gambling* (Princeton, NJ: Center for Analysis of Public Issues, 1987); M Teskea, et al., *A City Revitalized: The Elderly Lose at Monopoly* (Lanham, MD: University Press of America, 1983); R. Goodman, *The Luck Business:*

251

The Devastating Consequences and Broken Promises of America's Gambling Explosion (New York: Simon & Schuster, 1995); T. O'Brien, 'Atlantic City: Resort of Broken Promises', in T. O'Brien, *Bad Bet: The Inside Story of the Glamour, Glitz, and Danger of America's Gambling Industry* (New York: Times Business, 1996), pp. 62–97; G. Sternlieb and J. W. Hughes, *The Atlantic City Gamble* (Cambridge, MA: Harvard University Press, 1983); P. Teske and B. Sur, 'Winners and Losers: Politics, Casino Gambling, and Development in Atlantic City', *Policy Studies Review*, 10:2 (Spring/ Summer 1991), pp. 130–7; M. K. Nelson, 'Casino Gambling in Atlantic City: A Sure Bet For Whom', American Planning Association (APA) 1999 Proceedings, http:// design.asu.edu/apa/proceedings99/Nelson/Nelson.htm (accessed 8 October 2007).

15. J. Wortman, 'Personal Recollections of the New Jersey Gambling "Experiment"' in Atlantic City' and D. Heneghan, 'Economic Impacts of Casino Gaming in Atlantic City', in C. Hsu (ed.), *Legalized Casino Gaming in the United States* (Binghamton, NY: Haworth Hospitality Press, 1999), pp. 25–39 and 113–34.

16. G. Mahan, *The Company that Bought the Boardwalk: A Reporter's Story of Resorts International* (New York: Random House, 1980); R. S. Morrison, *High Stakes to High Risk : The Strange Story of Resorts International and the Taj Mahal* (Ashtabula, OH: Lake Erie Press, 1994); J. Alcamo, *Atlantic City: Behind the Tables* (Grand Rapids, MI, Gollehon,1991); R. L. Snook, *Jackpot! Harrah's Winning Secrets for Customer Loyalty* (Hoboken, NJ: John Wiley & Sons, 2003).

17. Simon, *Boardwalk of Dreams*; H. Rothman, *Neon Metropolis: How Las Vegas Started the Twenty-First Century* (New York: Routledge, 2003); D. G. Schwartz, *Roll the Bones: The History of Gambling* (New York: Gotham, 2006), pp. 427–33; D. G. Schwartz, *Suburban Xanadu: The Casino Resort on the Las Vegas Strip and Beyond* (New York: Routledge, 2003), pp. 176–82.

18. 'Hospitals' Subject File, Heston Room, Atlantic City Free Public Library.

19. NJCCC, *Casino Gambling in New Jersey: A Report to the National Gambling Impact Study Commission* (Atlantic City, NJ: NJCCC, January 1998), p. 24.

20. Simon, *Boardwalk of Dreams*, pp. 132–8; N. Johnson, *Boardwalk Empire: The Birth, High Times, and Corruption of Atlantic City* (Medford, NJ: Plexus Publishing, 2002), pp. 199–200.

21. Interview with Barbara Devlin, ACPOHI.

22. Johnson, *Boardwalk Empire*, p. 176.

23. NJCCC, *Casino Gambling in New Jersey*, p. 7; N. George, 'Will the Gamble Pay Off?', *Black Enterprise* (March 1983), pp. 59–62.

24. Interview with Barbara Devlin, ACPOHI.

25. Interview with Russelle Patterson, ACPOHI.

26. Ibid.

27. Simon, *Boardwalk of Dreams*, pp. 157–8.

28. Interview with David Alcantara, 1 March 2005, ACPOHI.

29. Johnson, *Boardwalk Empire*, p. 113.

30. [Anon.], 'Millions Made by Racketeers', *Press of Atlantic City*, 19 January 1930; S. Schwarz, 'Atlantic City Had a Casino – 81 Years Ago!' *Press of Atlantic City*, 19 August 1979.

31. B. Kershenblatt, 'The Casinos of the Thirties: You Had to Know Uncle Dan', *The Bulletin* (Philadelphia), 23 October 1980.

32. *Press of Atlantic City*, 16 July 1941.
33. Johnson, *Boardwalk Empire*, pp. 133–5.
34. Kershenblatt, 'The Casinos of the Thirties'; Johnson, *Boardwalk Empire*, pp. 109–15.
35. Johnson, *Boardwalk Empire*, pp. 122–3, 134–43.
36. A. Gordon, 'Crime War Waged in Atlantic City', *New York Times*, 16 January 1949.
37. Johnson, *Boardwalk Empire*, pp. 142–6.
38. Johnson, *Boardwalk Empire*, pp. 142–6; Gordon, 'Crime War Waged in Atlantic City'.
39. J. Van Meter, *The Last Good Time: Skinny D'Amato, the Notorious 500 Club, and the Rise and Fall of Atlantic City* (New York: Crown, 2003), pp. 129–30.
40. Gordon, 'Crime War Waged in Atlantic City'.
41. Johnson, *Boardwalk Empire*, pp. 177–8; Simon, *Boardwalk of Dreams*, p. 178.
42. New Jersey General Assembly, *Public Hearing before the Senate and Assembly Judiciary Committees on Senate Concurrent Resolution No. 39 – Proposing a Constitutional Amendment to Permit the Legislature to Authorize the Operation of Gambling Games in Atlantic City and to License and Tax Such Operations*, 19 March 1970 (Trenton, NJ: New Jersey General Assembly, 1970), Heston Room, Atlantic City Free Public Library.
43. Ibid.
44. *Press of Atlantic City*, 9 September 1970; *Press of Atlantic City*, 9 December 1970.
45. New Jersey General Assembly, *Public Hearing before the Senate Judiciary Committee on Senate Concurrent Resolution No. 74 – Proposing to Amend the Constitution of the State of New Jersey to Permit the Legislature to Authorize by Law the Operation of Gambling games in Atlantic City*, 7 April 1971 (Trenton, NJ: New Jersey General Assembly, 1971), Heston Room, Atlantic City Free Public Library.
46. Gambling Study Commission, *Report to the Governor and Legislature*, 5 February 1973 (Trenton, NJ: New Jersey General Assembly, 1973), Heston Room, Atlantic City Free Public Library.
47. Gambing Study Commission, *Public Hearing Before Senate Judiciary and Assembly State Government Committee on Senate Concurrent Resolutions 2011, 2012, & 2013 and Assembly Concurrent Resolutions 2015, 2016, 2017*, 11 April 1973.
48. G. A. D'Amato and V. G. Levi, *Chance of a Lifetime: Nucky Johnson, Skinny D'Amato, and How Atlantic City Became the Naughty Queen of Resorts* (West Creek, NJ, Down the Shore, 2001).
49. J. M. Katz, representative for New Jersey race tracks, in Gambling Study Commission, *Public Hearing before Assembly Judiciary, Law, Public Safety & Defense Committee on Assembly Concurrent Resolution No. 128* [on referendum to amend constitution for gambling] (Trenton, NJ: New Jersey General Assembly 1974), Heston Room, Atlantic City Free Public Library; interview with Daniel Heneghan, ACPOHI.
50. Johnson, *Boardwalk Empire*, p. 183; Simon, *Boardwalk of Dreams*, pp. 176–7.
51. Interview with Steve Perskie, ACPOHI.
52. CRAC, *Help Yourself. Help Atlantic City. Help New Jersey* [brochure] (Atlantic City, NJ, 1976); Gambling Legalization Subject File, Heston Room, ACFPL; interview with Steve Perskie, ACPOHI; conversation between the author and local historian Allen 'Boo' Pergament, 17 August 2007.

53. New Jersey General Assembly, *Public Hearing before Assembly State Government and Federal and Interstate Relations Committee on ACR-126 (which Proposes an Amendment to the Constitution to Permit Gambling Casinos in Atlantic City)* (Trenton, NJ: New Jersey General Assembly, 1976).

54. Interview with Steve Perskie, ACPOHI.

55. New Jersey General Assembly, *Public Hearing before Assembly State Government and Federal and Interstate Relations Committee on ACR-126*.

56. Ibid.

57. Ibid.

58. Atlantic County Chamber of Commerce, *Membership Bulletin*, 1976, Chamber of Commerce Subject File, Heston Room, Atlantic City Free Public Library.

59. Atlantic City Charter Study Commission, *Atlantic City on the Brink of Survival* (Atlantic City, NJ: Atlantic City Charter Study Commission, 1976), pp. 1–3.

60. [Anon.], 'Let's Kill Two Canards', *New Jersey Casino Journal* (March 1995), p. 6; Economic Research Associates, *Impact of Casino Gambling on the Redevelopment Potential of the Uptown Urban Renewal Site and on the Economy of Atlantic City* (Atlantic City, Economic Research Associates, 1976), pp. iii–14.

61. Interview with Barbara Devlin, ACPOHI.

62. Interview with Russelle Patterson, ACPOHI.

63. Interview with Daniel Heneghan, ACPOHI.

64. Atlantic County Chamber of Commerce, *Membership Bulletin*, May 1977.

65. Interview with Daniel Heneghan, ACPOHI; Simon, *Boardwalk of Dreams*, pp. 183–91.

66. New Jersey General Assembly, *Casino Control Act* (Trenton, NJ: New Jersey General Assembly, 1977), p. 1, available online at http://www.state.nj.us/casinos/actreg/act/ (accessed 10 October 2007).

67. Interview with Daniel Heneghan, ACPOHI.

68. New Jersey General Assembly, *Casino Control Act* (1977), p. 53.

69. Ibid., pp. 38, 53–8.

70. Interview with Steve Perskie, ACPOHI.

71. D. P. Rudd, 'Social Impacts of Atlantic City Casino Gaming', in Hsu (ed.), *Legalized Casino Gaming*, pp. 201–20; pp. 213–14.

72. New Jersey General Assembly, *Casino Control Act*; Simon, *Boardwalk of Dreams*, pp. 179–80.

73. Ibid.

74. Interview with Russelle Patterson, ACPOHI.

75. Interview with Barbara Devlin, ACPOHI.

76. New Jersey General Assembly, *Public Hearing before Assembly Legislative Oversight Committee on the Licensing of Casino Employees*, 29 October 1979 (Trenton, NJ: New Jersey General Assembly, 1979).

77. Interview with Barbara Devlin, ACPOHI.

78. Economic Research Associates, *Impact of Casino Gambling*, p. vii–4.

79. New Jersey Department of Labor, *Labor Market Information Review*, October 1978, Atlantic City Labor Area.

80. Schwartz, *Roll the Bones*, pp. 425–6, 429; V. G. Levi, *Atlantic City: 125 Years of Ocean Madness* (Berkeley, CA: Ten Speed Press, 1979), pp. 202–5.

81. New Jersey Department of Labor, *Labor Market Information Review*, October 1978 (Atlantic City Labor Area).
82. NJCCC, *Annual Report* (30 June 1979), p. 3.
83. New Jersey Department of Labor, *Growth Trends Report: Atlantic County, NJ* (Trenton, NJ: New Jersey Labor Department, 4th quarter, 1979).
84. Interview with David Alcantara, ACPOHI.
85. New Jersey Department of Labor, *Atlantic County Wage Survey of Selected Occupations: Casino Versus Noncasino Wages* (Trenton, NJ: New Jersey Department of Labor and Industry, Division of Planning and Research, 1980).
86. Interview with Tom Gitto, ACPOHI.
87. Interview with Barbara Devlin, ACPOHI.
88. NJCCC *Annual Report* (1978); NJCCC *Annual Report* (1979).
89. G. Anastasia, 'Monopoly: The Resorts Game in Atlantic City', *Philadelphia Inquirer*, 16 June 1985.
90. Interview with Daniel Heneghan, ACPOHI.
91. Interview with Dennis Ricci, ACPOHI.
92. Simon, *Boardwalk of Dreams*, pp. 184–5, Pollack, *Hostage to Fortune*, pp. 140–9.
93. [Anon.], 'Gambling Comes to Atlantic City', *Christian Century*, 24 January 1979; J. Rubinstein, 'Casino Gambling in Atlantic City: Issues of Development and Redevelopment', *Annals of the American Academy of Political and Social Science*, 474 (July 1984), pp. 61–71; pp. 64–5.
94. J. McLaughlin, 'The Great Casino Experiment', *New Jersey Monthly* (June 1981), pp. 48–50, 96–100.
95. Interview with Edna Hall, 20 April 2005, ACPOHI; see also Pollack, *Hostage to Fortune*.
96. P. Ross and S. P Haven, 'The Little City That Could', *New York Magazine*, 20 June 1977, pp. 34–40.
97. D. Weinberg, 'The $200 Million Season', *New Jersey Monthly*, March 1979; Schwartz, *Roll the Bones*, pp. 429–30.
98. *Atlantic City Action*, 5 December 1978, p. 1(16).
99. Simon, *Boardwalk of Drams*, pp. 188–90.
100. Interview with Dennis Ricci, ACPOHI.
101. Atlantic County Department of Planning, *1988 Growth Trends* (Atlantic County, New Jersey, 1988).
102. New Jersey Department of Labor, *Growth Trends Report: Atlantic County, NJ* (Trenton, NJ: New Jersey Department of Labor, 4th quarter, 1981).
103. M. Tuthill, 'Is Gambling Good for Business? You bet!' *Nation's Business*, August 1980.
104. Economic Research Associates, *Impact of Casino Gaming*.
105. A. Demetriou, et. al., *The Atlantic City Master Plan* (Office of Angelos C. Demetriou, A.I.A., 1978), pp. 8–10.
106. Ibid., p. 9.
107. Demetriou, 'The Marina Development Plan', in *The Atlantic City Master Plan*.
108. Ibid.
109. *The Herald* (Atlantic City High School Yearbook), 1979 and 1980.
110. NJCCC, Annual Report (1979), p. 8.

111. [Anon.], 'Up With the Downs', *Atlantic City Action*, 10:2 (October 1979); NJCCC, *Casino Gambling in New Jersey*, p. 27.

112. Atlantic City Free Public Library guide: 'Proposed A.C. Casino-Hotels' (as of 5/1/1979), Casinos Subject File, Heston Room, Atlantic City Free Public Library; D. G. Schwartz, 'The Road Not Taken', *Casino Connection*, 3:1 (January 2006), p. 70, available online at http://www.casinoconnectionac.com/articles/The_Road_Not_Taken (accessed 11 October 2007).

113. NJCCC, *Annual Report* (1981), p. 11.

114. ACCHA, *Annual Report* (Atlantic City, NJ: Atlantic City Casino Hotel Association, 1982); Atlantic County Division of Planning, *Growth Trends Report: Atlantic County, NJ* (Atlantic County, NJ: Atlantic County Division of Planning, 4th quarter, 1981).

115. *Atlantic City Action*, 18 December 1980.

116. D. Schwartz, *Jurisdiction Summary: Atlantic City* (Center for Gaming Research, University of Nevada, Las Vegas, 2001–6), available online at http://gaming.unlv.edu/subject/atlanticcity.html (accessed 10 October 2007).

117. NJCCC, *Annual Report* (1982), p. 2.

118. NJCCC, *Annual Report* (1980), pp. 4, 6.

119. Demaris, *Boardwalk Jungle*, pp. 175–6, 196.

120. Ibid., pp. 160–89; NJCCC *Annual Report* (1980), p. 7.

121. Johnson, *Boardwalk Empire*, pp. 210–16; Demaris, *Boardwalk Jungle*, pp. 211–20.

122. Interview with Steve Perskie, ACPOHI

123. Interview with Daniel Heneghan, ACPOHI

124. Ibid.

125. McLaughlin, 'The Great Casino Experiment', pp. 48–50, 96–100.

126. Interview with Paul Tjoumakaris, 18 July 2005, ACPOHI.

127. W. Eadington, 'The Casino Gaming Industry: A Study of Political Economy', *Annals of the American Academy*, 474 (July 1984), pp. 23–35; pp. 29–30.

128. Rubinstein, 'Casino Gambling in Atlantic City', p. 66.

129. NJCCC, *Annual Report* (1982) p. 3; Johnson, *Boardwalk Empire*, pp. 201–205.

130. ACCHA, *Annual Report* (1982), pp. 8–9.

131. ACHHA, *Annual Report* (1983); ACHHA, *Annual Report* (1982), pp. 8–9.

132. ACCHA, *Annual Report* (1983).

133. R. Ochrym, 'Gambling in Atlantic City: The "Grand Vision" Blurs', *National Civic Review*, 72:11 (December 1983), pp. 591–6; Simon, *Boardwalk of Dreams*, p. 180.

134. D. Anderson, 'Who Will Rebuild Atlantic City?', *Atlantic City Magazine* (May 1982), pp. 88–93, 104–6.

135. NJCCC [hearing proceedings] *Housing Obligation of Atlantic City Casinos*, 22 July 1981.

136. Ibid.

137. Ochrym, 'Gambling in Atlantic City', pp. 593–4; the most thorough source on the myriad community problems experienced during the early years of the casino era is Pollack, *Hostage to Fortune*.

138. NJCCC, *Annual Report* (1984), p. 2.

139. Interview with Steve Perskie, ACPOHI.

140. NJCCC, 'Annual Operating Statistics, 1978–1989', available online at http://www.state.nj.us/casinos/financia/histori/ (accessed 10 October 2007). Demaris, *Boardwalk Jungle*, p. 196.

141. Harrah's Entertainment Inc., 'Profile of Competition' [business memo], 'Casinos – General' Subject File, Heston Room, Atlantic City Free Public Library.

142. Interview with Steve Perskie, ACPOHI.

143. Interview with Paul Tjoumakaris, ACPOHI.

144. Interview with Harry Hasson, conducted by the author, 22 March 2007.

145. NJCCC, 'Annual Operating Statistics, 1978–1989'; Johnson, *Boardwalk Empire*, pp. 217–19; Demaris, *Boardwalk Jungle*, pp. 252–3; Schwartz, *History of Gambling*.

146. Interview with Russelle Patterson, ACPOHI.

147. Interview with Luis Guzman, 14 June 2005, ACPOHI.

148. Interview with Paul Tjoumakaris, ACPOHI.

149. New Jersey Department of Commerce and Economic Development, *An Economic Profile of Atlantic County* (Trenton, NJ: New Jersey Department of Commerce, 1982).

150. Interview with Pierre Hollingsworth, ACPOHI.

151. Interview with Barbara Devlin, ACPOHI.

152. Interview with Pierre Hollingsworth, ACPOHI.

153. New Jersey Department of Labor, *Regional Labor Market Review, Atlantic Coastal Region: Atlantic, Cape May, Monmouth and Ocean Counties* (Trenton, NJ: New Jersey Department of Labor, 1984), pp. 11–12.

154. New Jersey Department of Labor, *Growth Trends Report: Atlantic County, NJ* (Trenton, NJ: New Jersey Department of Labor, 4th quarter, 1982).

155. NJ Dept. of Commerce, *An Economic Profile of Atlantic County, New Jersey* (Dept. of Commerce and Economic Development, May 1982), pp. 70–81.

156. B. Lee and J. Chelius, 'Government Regulation of Labor-Management Corruption: The Casino Industry Experience in Atlantic City', *Industrial and Labor Relations Review*, 42:4 (July 1989), pp. 536–48; p. 539; interview with Barbara Devlin, ACPOHI.

157. Lee and Chelius, 'Government Regulation of Labor-Management Corruption', pp. 542–4; NJCCC, *Annual Report* (1983), p. 5.

158. NJCCC, *Annual Report* (1983), pp. 3, 16.

159. *Casino Chronicle*, 25 July 1983.

160. NJCCC, 'Annual Operating Statistics, 1978–1989'.

161. Ibid.

162. Ibid.

163. Interview with Daniel Heneghan, ACPOHI.

164. Interview with Robert Ruffolo, ACPOHI.

165. New Jersey Department of Labor, *Growth Trends Report: Atlantic County, NJ* (Trenton, NJ: New Jersey Department of Labor, 2nd quarter, 1989).

166. M. B. Roffman, 'Casino Gaming in the United States: Las Vegas on a Roll, Atlantic City Trouble Ahead with a Capital 'T', *New Jersey Casino Journal* (June 1988), pp. 30–1; *Casino Chronicle*, 7 April 1985.

167. Simon, *Boardwalk of Dreams*, p. 199.

168. Roffman, 'Casino Gaming'.

169. Ibid; NJCCC, 'Annual Operating Statistics, 1979–1989'.
170. ACCA, *Annual Report* (1985), p. 8.
171. NJCCC, *Annual Report*(s) (1980–6).
172. NJCCC, *Annual Report* (1983), p. 5; NJCCC, *Annual Report* (1984), pp. 2–3; conversation with Barbara Devlin, 17 August 2007; Schwartz, *Roll the Bones*, p. 432; D. G. Schwartz, 'Bunny on the Boardwalk', *Casino Connection*, 3:12 (December 2006), available online at http://www.casinoconnectionac.com/articles/Bunny_on_the_ Boardwalk (accessed 11 October 2007); Demaris, *Boardwalk Jungle*, pp. 274–9.
173. NJCCC, *Annual Report* (December, 1984), p. 2; interview with Daniel Heneghan, ACPOHI.
174. Lee and Chelius, 'Government Regulation of Labor–Management Corruption', pp. 542–6.
175. ACCA, *Annual Report* (1985), p. 9.
176. Ibid.
177. *Casino Chronicle*, 7 May 1984.
178. NJCCC, *Personal and Confidential* [1986 brochure on applying for casino employee licenses], 'Casinos-General' Subject File, Heston Room, Atlantic City Free Public Library.
179. *Casino Chronicle*, 8 July 1985.
180. NJCCC, 'Commissioner's Report', *Annual Report* (1985), pp. 2–4.
181. Interview with Robert Ruffolo, ACPOHI.
182. Snook, *Jackpot!*, pp. 74–6; Johnson, *Boardwalk Empire*, pp. 230–1.
183. G. Blair, *Donald Trump: Master Apprentice* (New York: Simon & Schuster, 2005), pp. 105–12; Johnson, *Boardwalk Empire*, pp. 230–1.
184. *Casino Chronicle*, 24 June 1985; Johnson, *Boardwalk Empire*, pp. 230–233.
185. S. Read, 'Chairman's Report', NJCCC, *Annual Report* (1986), p. 3.
186. Johnson, *Boardwalk Empire*, pp. 231–3.
187. [Anon.], '1987 Year in Review', *New Jersey Casino Journal* (January 1988), pp. 1, 43.
188. Ibid., p. 43; NJCCC, 'Operating Statistics, 1978–1989'.
189. [Anon.], 'DGE Takes on Donald Trump', *New Jersey Casino Journal* (January 1988), p. 54.
190. M. Reifer, 'Justice and the Regulators', *New Jersey Casino Journal* (February 1988), pp. 34–5.
191. D. Heneghan, 'Griffin-Trump Deal Turns Executive Revolving Door', *Press of Atlantic City*, 30 November 1988, p. E1.
192. D. Heneghan, 'Griffin Buys Resorts', *Press of Atlantic City*, 16 November 1988, p. A1.
193. [Anon.], 'Interview with Jack Pratt, Chairman Pratt Hotel Corporation', *New Jersey Casino Journal* (July 1988), pp. 38–41.
194. P. Linsalata, 'Trump Claims Win Over Sands', *Press of Atlantic City*, 21 March 1989, p. A1.
195. M. Reifer, 'Casino Industry Profitability: The Myth and Reality', *New Jersey Casino Journal* (October 1988), pp. 16–18.
196. *Press of Atlantic City*, 8 April 1989.
197. NJCCC, *Annual Report* (1989), pp. 2–5.

198. D. Heneghan, 'Union Has No Place In Atlantis Hearings', *Press of Atlantic City*, 26 March 1989, p. C2.
199. D. Heneghan, 'Atlantis Sold, Trump Will Close Elsinore's Casino', *Press of Atlantic City*, 16 April 1989.
200. Interview with Daniel Heneghan, ACPOHI.
201. M. Reifer, 'Who Really Killed the Atlantis?', *New Jersey Casino Journal* (May 1989), pp. 14–18.
202. [Anon.], 'If We Only Knew Then What We Know Now!' [interview with Brendan Byrne], *New Jersey Casino Journal* (June 1989), pp. 40–6.
203. B. Sless, 'How Serious is the Casinos' Long-Term Debt Problem?', *New Jersey Casino Journal* (May 1989), pp. 26, 39.
204. P. Key, 'Boardwalk Borrowing: Are Casinos Floating Debt Now Only to Founder Later?', *Press of Atlantic City*, 21 May 1989, Marketplace p. 1.
205. NJCCC, 'Operating Statistics, 1978–1989'.
206. Interview with Edna Hall, ACPOHI.
207. Anastasia, 'Monopoly'; Simon, *Boardwalk of Dreams*, pp. 194–6.
208. E. Davis, *Atlantic City Diary: A Century of Memories, 1880–1985* (Atlantic City, NJ: Atlantic City News Agency, 1989), pp. 152–161.
209. P. Yerkes, 'Wheel of Misfortune: Atlantic City, Ten Years Later', *New Jersey Reporter* (October 1986), pp. 15–19, 30.
210. 'How the Casinos Touched our Lives', *Press of Atlantic City*, 19 May 2003.
211. ACCA, *News and Views*, 1:6 (November 1986).
212. *Atlantic City Action*, 8 July 1986.
213. [Anon.], 'Interview with Tom Carver', *New Jersey Casino Journal* (November 1988), pp. 23–35.
214. R. Gillman and T. Carver, 'Chairman and President's Letter', in ACCA, *Annual Report* (1985), p. 3.
215. M. Reifer, 'It's Crunch Time in Fun City', *New Jersey Casino Journal* (May 1986), p. 17.
216. *Casino Chronicle*, 22 September 1986.
217. *Press of Atlantic City*, 17 September 1986, from Stan and Mary Sledek Collection of Sands Casino Memorabilia, Heston Room, Atlantic City Free Public Library.
218. R. P. Frelinghysen, 'What Has Gone Wrong in the Plan?', *New York Times*, 19 October 1986, [New Jersey] p. 26.
219. Letter from Lou DiLaila, held in Scrapbook #1, Stan and Mary Sledek Collection of Sands Casino Memorabilia.
220. D. Russell and L. DiMeo, 'Atlantic City's Bet on Gambling: Who Won What?', *Atlantic City* (January 1987), pp. 29–41, 80; Yerkes, 'Wheel of Misfortune', pp. 15–19, 30.
221. S. Swartz, 'A Bad Risk: Casinos Don't Pay Off In Atlantic City, N.J., "Experiment"', *Wall Street Journal*, 28 March 1986.
222. For example, see O'Brien, *Bad Bet*, p. 73.
223. B. G. Stitt, M. Nichols and D. Giacopassi, 'Does the Presence of Casinos Increase Crime? An Examination of Casino and Control Communities', *Crime & Delinquency*, 49:2 (April 2003), pp. 253–84; Rudd, 'Social Impacts of Atlantic City Casino Gaming', pp. 209–10.

224. Ochrym, 'Gambling in Atlantic City', p. 593.
225. NJCCC, *Casino Gambling in New Jersey*, pp. 55–6; United States and New Jersey crime statistics compiled by FBI Uniform Crime Reports, available online at http://www.disastercenter.com/crime/ (accessed 11 October 2007).
226. Russell and DiMeo, 'Atlantic City's Bet on Gambling', pp. 29–41.
227. Interview with Edna Hall, ACPOHI.
228. M. Reifer, 'Casino Reinvestment Revisited: A Sacrifice of Principle', *New Jersey Casino Journal* (June 1988), p. 19; [Anon.], 'Humpty-Dumpty Rules in Trenton and Ruins Atlantic City' [editorial], *New Jersey Casino Journal* (December 1988), pp. 6–7.
229. P. Rubeli, 'A Bill of Rights for the Atlantic City Casino Industry', *New Jersey Casino Journal* (December 1988), pp. 20–1.
230. P. Painton, 'Boardwalk of Broken Dreams', *Time*, 25 September 1989, pp. 64–9.
231. Interview with Pierre Hollingsworth, ACPOHI.
232. [Anon.], Interview with J.H. Lyles-Belton, *Black Atlantic City* (March/April 1982).
233. [Anon.], 'City vs. Casino is really a Failure to Communicate', *Black News and Events*, 5–18 June 1987.
234. Ibid., July 31–August 13, 1987; interview with Pierre Hollingsworth, ACPOHI.
235. Simon, *Boardwalk of Dreams*, pp. 120–4.
236. NJCCC, *Annual Report* (1987), pp. 10–11.
237. NJCCC, *Annual Report* (1989), p. 7.
238. [Anon.], 'Probe Will Kill', *Black News and Events*, December 1988.
239. K. Shabazz, 'Jackson Came, He Saw and He Conquered', *Black News and Events*, 3–16 June 1988.
240. Simon, *Boardwalk of Dreams*, p. 214; interview with Pierre Hollingsworth, ACPOHI.
241. Interview with Edna Hall, ACPOHI
242. NJCCC, *Annual Report* (1989), p. 7.
243. Interview with Dennis Ricci, ACPOHI.
244. CRDA, *Annual Report* (1986), pp. 1–12.
245. Caesar's Boardwalk Regency, 'Press Release', 28 April 1989, Caesar's, Subject File, Heston Room, Atlantic City Free Public Library.
246. C. Linz and K. Shelly, 'Chelsea Group Wants to Block Inlet Bonding', *Press of Atlantic City*, 30 September 1988, p. B1; [Anon.], 'Why Does It Always Have to Be "We" vs. "Them" in Atlantic City?' [editorial], *Press of Atlantic City*, 16 October 1988, p. D3.
247. C. Linz, 'Inlet Project Passes Another Obstacle', *Press of Atlantic City*, 8 October 1988, p. A1; J. Tanfani and R. Ellis, 'Some Folks Resist Inlet Home Razing', *Press of Atlantic City*, 26 November 1988, p. A1.
248. [Anon.], 'Interview with Phil Satre, President/CEO of Harrah's Gaming Group & Ron Lenczycki, Pres GM of Harrah's Marina', *New Jersey Casino Journal* (January 1989), pp. 19–20, 22–3, 55.
249. M. Reifer, 'CRDA: The Casino Reinvestment Obligation Revisited', *New Jersey Casino Journal* (December 1989), pp. 10–11, 24.
250. Anastasia, 'Monopoly'.
251. [Anon.], 'Visions of a New School', *The Herald* (Atlantic City High School Yearbook, 1988); L. Rehrmann, 'New A.C. High School Planning Continues', *Press of Atlantic City*, 18 October 1988, p. B4.

252. [Anon.], 'Welcome Back, Merv! But be Careful Out There!' [editorial], *New Jersey Casino Journal* (December 1988), pp. 9–10.
253. [Anon.], 'Success After High School, *The Herald* (Atlantic City High School Yearbook, 1988); Oral history interview with James Whelan, 14 April 2005; D. Bontempo, 'The Merchant of Venice', *Casino Connection* 2:4 (April 2005), p. 28, available online at . http://www.casinoconnectionac.com/articles/The_Merchant_of_Venice (accessed 11 October 2007).
254. [Anon.], 'Trump Traits' [editorial], *New Jersey Casino Journal* (February 1989), p. 8; Reifer, 'It's Crunch Time in Fun City', p. 17.
255. [Anon.], 'Interview with Steve Wynn', *New Jersey Casino Journal* (November 1988), pp. 19–20, 48–9, 53–9.
256. Ibid.
257. S. Schwartz, 'Wynn Dumps $110 million Claridge Deal', *Press of Atlantic City*, 26 October 1988, p. A1.
258. [Anon.], 'Interview with Steve Wynn', pp. 19–20, 48–9, 53–9.
259. NJCCC, 'Annual Operating Statistics, 1979–1989'.
260. B. Sless, 'Comps Largest Expense After Salaries', *New Jersey Casino Journal* (September 1988), pp.16–17.
261. Stan and Mary Sledak Collection of Sands Casino Memorabilia (1981–2006).
262. Ibid.
263. R. Gros, 'Junkets: Bang for Your Bucks', *New Jersey Casino Journal* (June 1989), pp. 10–13, 68.
264. Johnson, *Boardwalk Empire*, pp. 237–8.
265. A. Fowler, 'Mayor James Usry Standing Tall in Atlantic City', *Black New Jersey* (June 1987), pp. 1, 3.
266. Johnson, *Boardwalk Empire*, pp. 237–8; interview with James Whelan, 14 April 2005, ACPOHI.
267. J. O'Donnell, *Trumped! The Inside Story of the Real Donald Trump* (New York: Simon & Schuster, 1991), pp. 15, 17, 22, 34, 123, 140–1.
268. Mary and Stan Sledak, 'Fun in The Sands' [unpublished paper], *Stan and Mary Sledak Collection of Sands Casino Memorabilia* (1981–2006); D. Spatz, 'In Hyde and Etess, Casino World Has Lost Two Class Acts', *Press of Atlantic City*, 12 October 1989, p. C6.
269. Mary and Stan Sladek, 'Fun in The Sands'.
270. Rothman, *Neon Metropolis*, pp. 25–7, 45–7; Associated Press, 'Wynn's 30-Story Mirage Shadows Casinos in Las Vegas', *Press of Atlantic City*, 19 November 1989, p. 19, Marketplace p. F1; D. Heneghan, 'Taj Will "Trump" All: Huge Casino Drawing Close to Completion', *Press of Atlantic City*, 3 December 1989; Hengehan, 'Trump Stumps to Boost Taj and City', *Press of Atlantic City*, 1 March 1989, Business p. D1.
271. Rothman, *Neon Metropolis*, pp. 25–47.
272. B. Sless, 'How Serious is the Casinos' Long-Term Debt Problem?', *New Jersey Casino Journal* (May 1989), pp. 26, 39.
273. O'Donnell, *Trumped!*, pp. 232–3.
274. S. Lalli, 'Fantasy becomes reality at Mirage', *New Jersey Casino Journal* (December 1989), pp. 48–52.

275. P. Key, 'Taj Mahal Works Hard for Workforce', *Press of Atlantic* City, 29 November 1989, p. A13; Associated Press, 'Trump Recruits in Gary, A Potential Casino City', *Press of Atlantic* City, 10 December 1989, p. A10.

276. NJCCC, 'Operating Statistics, 1978–1989'; G. M. Slusher, *The Casino Gaming Industry and its Impact on Southern New Jersey* (Atlantic County, NJ: Atlantic County Division of Economic Development, 1991), pp. 23–5.

277. O'Donnell, *Trumped!*, pp. 219–21; NJCCC, 'Annual Operating Statistics, 1978–1989'; Heneghan, 'And Casinos Floated in a Sea of 'Junk', *Press of Atlantic City*, 31 December 1989, p. F1.

278. P. McCoy, 'Senator to Seek a Ban on New Casinos in Atlantic City', *Press of Atlantic City*, 3 October 1989, p. A1.

279. Associated Press, 'Resorts Files its Reorganization Plan', *Press of Atlantic City*, 23 December 1989, p. B4; D. Heneghan, 'Resort's License Renewed Vote Unanimous Despite Troubles', *Press of Atlantic City*, 22 February 1990, p. A1.

280. D. Heneghan, 'Trump Hits Griffin's Plan for Restructuring Resorts', *Press of Atlantic City*, 14 November 1989.

281. C. Linz, 'Trump Shifts Etess to Taj Mahal as Site Work Resumes', *Press of Atlantic City*, 22 December 1988, p. C8; D. Trump, 'Trump Sounds Off', *Press of Atlantic City*, 28 May 1989, p. E1; O'Donnell, *Trumped!*, pp. 225–33.

282. O'Donnell, *Trumped*, pp. 229–31; *Public Hearing before Assembly Independent Authorities Committee: Current and Future Manpower Needs of the Casino Industry, the Availability of Qualified Casino Employees to Meet those Needs and the Impact on the Casino Employees Labor Pool* [hearing transcript] (Trenton, NJ: New Jersey General Assembly, 1990), pp. 1–3, 11–12.

283. J. Froonijian, 'Taj Saps Casino Workers/Hearings Check Labor Shortage', *Press of Atlantic City*, 21 March 1990, p .A1.

284. D. Heneghan, 'Casinos Warn Moonlighting Workers: Claridge, Bally's Park Place: Defectors to Taj Will be Fired', *Press of Atlantic City*, 24 January 1990; [Anon.], 'Executive Forum: Merv Griffin's Resorts' Hotel and Casino: VP Operations Al Luciani', *New Jersey Casino Journal* (January 1990), pp. 10–11.

285. R. Gros, 'The Grass is Greener: Human Resource Departments Face the Taj Mahal Challenge', *New Jersey Casino Journal* (January 1990), pp. 20–2.

286. Interview with Tom Gitto, ACPOHI.

287. D. DiStephan, 'Culture Shock Stuns Foreign Workers Recruited by Trump', *Press of Atlantic City*, 20 March 1990, p. C1; interview with Richard Lopez, 17 May 2005, ACPOHI.

288. D. Vis, 'Publication Predicts Trouble for Trump', *Press of Atlantic City*, 7 February 1990, p. B1; D. Heneghan, 'Taj Will Reshape Market: A.C. Casinos Also Fearful of "Gary Gaming"', *Press of Atlantic City*, 30 January 1990, p. C6; O'Donnell, *Trumped!*, p. 266.

289. *Atlantic City Action*, 8 October 1989.

290. Johnson, *Boardwalk Empire*, pp. 234–5.

291. Simon, *Boardwalk of Dreams*, 202–5; Rothman, *Neon Metropolis*, 44–5.

292. R. Laymon, 'Theme Song: Taj Mahal Borrow's Disney's Theme-Park Techniques', *Press of Atlantic City*, 5 April 1990, p. A15. Simon, *Boardwalk of Dreams*, pp. 202–5.

293. P. Key, '"Destination Marketing" May Have its Day', *Press of Atlantic City*, 28 January 1990, p. BF19; [Anon.], 'Las Vegas, N.J.? Keep it Out There', *Asbury Park Press*, 3 March 1990, p. A8 (via the *Press of Atlantic City*).

294. G. Blair, *The Trumps: Three Generations That Built an Empire* (New York: Simon & Schuster, 2000), pp. 404–5; D. Heneghan and D. Spatz, 'Trump Opens Taj with a Flourish / After Tour Florio Vows to Help City', *Press of Atlantic City* , 6 April 1990.

295. Heneghan, 'Taj Wins $4.9 Million in 6 days/Overall Casino Win up 3.6% for Week', *Press of Atlantic City*, 10 April 1990, p. A1; Heneghan, 'Taj Slots Shut Down Indefinitely/Major Modifications Planned for Casino', *Press of Atlantic City*, 7 April 1990, p. A1; *Atlantic City Action*, May 1990.

296. [Anon.], 'Harrah's Marina: The People Place', *New Jersey Casino Journal* (June 1990), pp. 26–36; D. Spatz, 'Bally's Out to Soften Taj's Effect/Plans Lineup to Pull Customers Its Way', *Press of Atlantic City*, 3 March 1990.

297. D. Heneghan, 'Hundreds Face Layoffs as Casinos Feel the Squeeze', *Press of Atlantic City*, 18 September 1990; D. Heneghan, 'Taj Squeezing Trump, Other Casinos/AC Competition, Bleak Economy Contribute to Weak Win Figures', *Press of Atlantic City*, 5 September 1990; D. Heneghan, 'The Opening of Two Casinos Hikes Revenues in Las Vegas, but New Facility Had No Similar Impact in A.C.', *Press of Atlantic City*, 24 October 1990, p. A1; R. Gros, 'Casinos in Crisis', *New Jersey Casino Journal* (September 1990), pp. 15–30; [Anon.], 'Ed Tracy, Trump's Top Atlantic City Executive: "We Will Survive"', *Press of Atlantic City*, 30 September 1990, p. F1.

298. K. Shelly, '$3.9 Million Taj Tax Check Delivered to Whelan', *Press of Atlantic City*, 6 November 1990, p. B1; D. Bontempo, 'Overlooked Trump Back as Major Player', *Press of Atlantic City*, 7 November 1990, p. E1.

299. D. Heneghan, 'Taj Officials Promise Stability/But CCC Wants to See Proof That Restructuring Will Work', *Press of Atlantic City*, 4 December 1990; D. Heneghan, 'Casinos End Difficult Year With a Little Hope For Better 1991: Opening of Taj Stressed Industry', *Press of Atlantic City*, 27 December 1990, p. C1; Blair, *The Trumps*, pp. 412–25.

300. Interview with James 'Sonny' McCullough, 26 May 2005, ACPOHI.

301. D. Heneghan, 'Trump Opens Taj With a Flourish, After Tour, Florio Vows to Help City', *Press of Atlantic City*, 6 April 1990, p. A1.

302. Interview with James Whelan, 14 April 2005, ACPOHI.

303. *Black New Jersey Magazine*, 4 May 1990; D. DiStephan, 'Whelan Sees "Demoralized" A.C.', *Press of Atlantic City*, 16 April 1990, p. C1.

304. *Black New Jersey Magazine*, Summer 1990.

305. M. Reifer, 'A How-Not-To Guide to State & Local Management of Casino Gaming or How "Moral Opprobrium" can Falsify Facts and Preclude Rational Thought', *New Jersey Casino Journal* (July 1988), pp. 17–19, 82–6.

306. [Anon.], 'A Matter of Semantics?' [editorial], *New Jersey Casino Journal* (February 1990), pp. 23–6; [Anon.], 'Jim Whelan for Mayor: The Fudge Factor', *New Jersey Casino Journal* (May 1990), p. 6.

307. City of Atlantic City, *Atlantic City: Building for Tomorrow* (Atlantic City, NJ: Atlantic City Department of Planning and Development, 1991), p. 5; [Anon.], 'Interview with James Whelan', *New Jersey Casino Journal* (January 1995), pp. 10–13.

308. CANJ, *The 1990s – Promise of a New Decade: 1989 Annual Report* (Atlantic City, NJ: CANJ, 1989), pp. 6–12; D. Heneghan, 'A.C. Casino Industry Struggling, Exec. Says', *Press of Atlantic City*, 2 August 1990, p. A1.

309. [Anon.], 'Interview with Pat Dodd', *New Jersey Casino Journal* (January 1990), pp. 28–33.

310. Interview with James Whelan, ACPOHI.

311. NJCCC, 'Annual Operating Statistics, 1978–1989'.

312. R. Gros, 'Where Have All the Players Gone?', *New Jersey Casino Journal* (July 1990), pp. 32–9.

313. Gros, 'Casinos in Crisis'.

314. NJCCC, *Annual Report* (1989), pp. 2–3; D. Heneghan, 'Casino Commission Cuts Staff, Will Save $1.35 Million', *Press of Atlantic City*, 17 February 1990.

315. Interview with Steve Perskie, ACPOHI.

316. J. Donohue, D. Heneghan and J. Froonjian, 'Casinos, Politicians Hail Perskie Nomination', *Press of Atlantic City*, 23 August 1990.

317. [Anon.], 'Dear Steve ... We've Got a Problem', *New Jersey Casino Journal* (October 1990), pp. 6, 56.

318. Interview with Pierre Hollingsworth, ACPOHI.

319. NJCCC, *Annual Report* (1990), pp. 3–4; NJCCC, *Years of Change 1990–1994: A Report by the New Jersey Casino Control Commission* (Atlantic City, NJ: NJCCC, 1995), pp. 16–19.

320. NJCCC, *Annual Report* (1991), pp. 6–7.

321. [Anon.], Interview with Steve Wynn, *New Jersey Casino Journal* (June 1991), pp. 26–9.

322. NJCCC, *1992 Annual Report – 1977–1992: Years of Progress*, p. 5; NJCCC, *Years of Change, 1990–1994*.

323. [Anon.], 'Up Up and Away in Atlantic City: Interview with Gov. James Florio', *New Jersey Casino Journal* (March 1992), pp. 10–12, 15, 32–3.

324. [Anon.], 'Gormley's Guns', *New Jersey Casino Journal* (May 1992); M. Reifer, 'The Wave of the Future?', *New Jersey Casino Journal* (August 1992), p. 6.

325. [Anon.], 'Bally's Bounces Back: Interview with Richard Gillman', *New Jersey Casino Journal* (August 1992), pp. 11–13; R. Gros, 'Gaming's Greatest Comeback: Donald Trump's Amazing Turnaround' [interview with Donald Trump], *New Jersey Casino Journal* (September 1992), pp. 14–21, 42–3; [Anon.], 'The Year that Was: 1992', *New Jersey Casino Journal* (January 1993), pp. 24–9.

326. Interview with Paul Tjoumakaris, ACPOHI.

327. Ibid.

328. NJCCC, 'Fulfilling the Promise' in *Annual Report* (1993), pp. 2–10.

329. [Anon.], 'The Foxwoods Phenomenon: Does it Threaten Atlantic City?' [interview with Michael 'Mickey' Brown, Foxwoods President and CEO], *New Jersey Casino Journal* (July 1993), pp. 11–12.

330. R. Gros, 'What's Going on in Gaming?' *New Jersey Casino Journal* (November 1992), pp. 10–25.

331. NJCCC, 'Annual Operating Statistics, 1990–1999', available online at http://www.state.nj.us/casinos/financia/histori/ (accessed 10 October 2007).

332. Ibid.

333. R. Gros, M. Epifiano and G. Schnorius, 'Setting the Tables', *New Jersey Casino Journal* (November 1993), pp. 14–17.

334. [Anon.], 'Interview with Phil Satre [CEO Promus]', *New Jersey Casino Journal* (June 1991), pp.14–17, 19.

335. [Anon.], 'The Stabilizer' [interview with Nicholas Ribis, CEO of Trump Hotel and Casino Reports], *New Jersey Casino Journal* (December 1991), pp. 11–14, 42, 56; Gros, 'Gaming's Greatest Comeback'; R. Gros, 'The Heartbeat of the Taj', *New Jersey Casino Journal* (May 1994), pp. 12–13.

336. Gros, 'Gaming's Greatest Comeback'.

337. NJCCC, 'Operating Statistics, 1990–1999'; [Anon.], 'The Year that Was: 1992'.

338. NJCCC, *Annual Report* (1993), p. 8; NJCCC, 'Operating Statistics, 1990–1999'.

339. Interview with Tom Gitto, ACPOHI.

340. D. Bontempo, 'It's No Bluff! Poker Comes to the Atlantic City Boardwalk', *New Jersey Casino Journal* (June 1993), pp. 10–12.

341. [Anon.], 'Leaps and Bounds: How Harrah's Atlantic City Spurred Promus Expansion' [interview with Ron Lenczycki], *New Jersey Casino Journal* (April 1993), pp. 12, 13, 22.

342. Caesar's Casino Hotel, *Fact Sheet* [on its new garage] (1990), Caesar's Subject File, Heston Room, Atlantic City Free Public Library.

343. [Anon.], 'Exclusive Interview: Henry Gluck' [Chair, Caesars World], *New Jersey Casino Journal* (July 1991); NJCCC, 'Operating Statistics, 1990–1999'.

344. R. Gros and G. Fine, 'Continuous Improvement: Showboat's Steady Progress Yields Dynamic Results', *New Jersey Casino Journal* (February 1993).

345. NJCCC, *Annual Report* (1993), pp. 3, 10–11.

346. C. Linz, 'Unions Take Conventions Elsewhere / Cite Dirt, Crime Rate, Lack of Air Connections', *Press of Atlantic City*, 5 October 1988, p. B1; Linz, 'Six Million Cost Reached on Final Tract for Convention Center', *Press of Atlantic City*, 6 October 1988, p. C2.

347. D. Vis, 'Atlantic City's New Convention Hall: An Investment in Debt Casino Owners, State Officials Agree Won't Pay for Itself', *Press of Atlantic City*, 27 August 1989, p. B1; D. Vis, 'Comps Hurt A.C. Quest for New Hall', *Press of Atlantic City*, 22 August 1989, p. A1.

348. M. Reifer, 'A Bad Idea for a Worse Objective', *New Jersey Casino Journal* (October 1989), pp. 24–5.

349. Interview with Steve Perskie, ACPOHI; NJCCC, *Annual Report* (1991), pp. 10–11.

350. [Anon.], 'Interview with Jim Whelan', *New Jersey Casino Journal* (October 1990), pp. 18–22, 60; Gros, 'Casinos in Crisis'.

351. NJCCC, *Years of Change, 1990–1994*, pp. 8–9; R. Gros, 'CRDA's Nick Amato Describes Agency's New Purpose' *New Jersey Casino Journal* (July 1992), pp. 10–11, 22; [Anon.], 'Inside the Industry', *New Jersey Casino Journal* (August 1992), p. 22.

352. CRDA, *The Rebirth of a City: 1996 Annual Report – Casino Reinvestment Development Authority* (Atlantic City, NJ: CRDA, 1997).

353. R. Gros, 'Gaming's Greatest Comeback'; [Anon.], 'Bally's Bounces Back'.

354. CRDA, 'Corridor Approved as New Gateway for Atlantic City: Governor Hails Resort's 'New Front Door' [press release], 1993, Convention Center Subject File,

Heston Room, Atlantic City Free Public Library; G. Sloan, 'Atlantic City Stakes its Future on Rebuilding Plan', *USA Today*, 19 April 1993; Greater Atlantic City Convention and Visitor's Bureau, 'Atlantic City's $1 Billion Renaissance' [press release], 14 December 1993, Convention Center Subject File, Heston Room, Atlantic City Free Public Library.

355. Atlantic City Corridor Project, 'The Gateway to Economic Prosperity' [poster], The Corridor Subject File, Heston Room, Atlantic City Free Public Library.

356. M. Reifer, 'Time for a New Deal', *New Jersey Casino Journal* (August 1993).

357. NJCCC, *Annual Report* (1993), pp. 31–2; CANJ, *1989 Annual Report*, pp. 17; Slusher, *The Casino Gaming Industry*, pp. 1–3.

358. Atlantic County Department of Planning and Economic Development (ACDPED), *Atlantic County Master Plan* (Atlantic City, NJ: Department of Regional Planning and Economic Development, 2000), pp. 16–19, 27–8.

359. J. W. Oldroyd, *Master Plan, City of Absecon* (Pleasantville, NJ: Oldroyd Planning Group, 1993).

360. Interview with Nanette Stuart, 6 June 2005, ACPOHI.

361. Atlantic City Chamber of Commerce, *Gambling's Impact 1976–1990* [brochure] (November 1991).

362. ACDPED, *Atlantic County Master Plan*, pp. 60–1; interview with James McCullough, ACPOHI; Wortman, 'Personal Recollections of the New Jersey Gambling "Experiment" in Atlantic City'; ACOPPED, *Growth Trends: Atlantic County, NJ 1993–1994 Annual Issue* (Atlantic City, NJ: ACOPPED, 1994).

363. NJCCC, 'Operating Statistics 1990–1999'; M. Reifer, 'Atlantic City Under Whitman: Reason to Believe', *New Jersey Casino Journal* (February 1994); M. Reifer and A. Fine, '1993: Year In Review', *New Jersey Casino Journal* (February 1994).

364. A. Tucker, 'Hurricane has Gone, as has Familiar Landscape of Biloxi', *Baltimore Sun*, 2 September 2005.

365. Simon, *Boardwalk of Dreams*, pp. 68–80; Johnson, *Boardwalk Empire*, p. 22; interview with James Whelan, ACPOHI; interview with Edna Hall, ACPOHI.

366. Simon, *Boardwalk of Dreams*, pp. 81–2.

367. U. Obst, 'The Slum Hispanics Call Home', *Press of Atlantic City*, 8 and 9 June 1981.

368. Interview with J. David Alcantara, ACPOHI.

369. P. Ackerman, 'Census '90, Area Sees Increase in Asians, Casinos Offer them Jobs, Opportunity', *Press of Atlantic City*, 13 February 13, 1991, p. A6.

370. S. L. Johnson, 'Kin and Casinos: Changing Family Networks in Atlantic City', *Current Anthropology*, 26:3 (June 1985), pp. 397–9.

371. J. LaPolla, 'The Changing Face of Atlantic City: The New Immigrants', *Atlantic City Press*, 18 April 1993, p. A1.

372. Interview with Joseph Pham, 19 May 2003, ACPOHI.

373. Ibid.

374. Interview with Hasumati Patel, 4 November 2002, ACPOHI.

375. Interview with Chittubhai M. Patel, 4 November 2002, ACPOHI.

376. Interview with Joseph Pham, ACPOHI.

377. Interview with Martha Lopez, 16 May 2003, ACPOHI.

378. Interview with Jean Baptiste Noel, 4 November 2002, ACPOHI.

379. Interview with Asuncion Centeno, 17 June 2003, ACPOHI.

380. Interview with Carol N., June 2003, ACPOHI.

381. Interview with Jean Baptiste Noel, ACPOHI.

382. Interview with Mashiuz Alan, 4 November 2002, ACPOHI.

383. J. Olshan, 'Asian, Hispanic populations up in county', *Atlantic City Press*, 10 March 2001; all census information derived from reports posted at the United States Census Bureau, www.census.gov (accessed 11 October 2007).

384. www.census.gov; ACDPED, *Atlantic County Master Plan*, p. 25.

385. Bureau of Economic Research, Rutgers, the State University of New Jersey, *Limitations in the Workplace: A Survey & Study of Atlantic City Casinos* (New Brunswick, NJ: Rutgers University, 1998), p. 20; interview with Tom Gitto, ACPOHI.

386. Interview with Isias Gomes, 10 August 2005, ACPOHI.

387. *Michael Pollock's Gaming Industry Observer*, 9 September 1996; interview with Tom Gitto, ACPOHI.

388. Interview with David Alcantara, ACPOHI.

389. Interview with Russelle Patterson, ACPOHI.

390. T. Peele, 'Richness of Diversity Defines Lower Chelsea', *Press of Atlantic City*, 31 December 1998.

391. Interview with Steven Perskie, ACPOHI; B. Hickey, 'Across the Bridge to Chelsea Heights', *Atlantic City Press*, 29 December 1998.

392. [Anon.], 'Diversity', *The Herald* (Atlantic City High School Yearbook, 1999), p. 8.

393. R. Shopes, 'Atlantic City's Chelsea Flourishes with Ethnic Change', *Atlantic City Press*, 4 August 1997, p. A1; J. Olshan, 'Asian Population Grows Bigger, But Not Together: Culture, Language Are Community Barriers', *Atlantic City Press*, 25 March 2001, p. A1, A7.

394. Interview with Marta Lopez, ACPOHI.

395. Interview with Chhitubhai Patel, ACPOHI.

396. Interview with Hasmati Patel, 4 November 2002, ACPOHI.

397. Shopes, 'Atlantic City's Chelsea Flourishes with Ethnic Change'; interview with Carol Nhan, ACPOHI; interview with Chittubhai Patel, ACPOHI.

398. Interview with H. Mayra Momperousse, 21 June 2005, ACPOHI.

399. Interview with Mashiuz Alan, 4 November 2002, ACPOHI.

400. Interview with Rashmika and Mahesh Gandhi, 4 November 2002, ACPOHI.

401. Interview with Chhitubhai Patel and Marta Lopez, ACPOHI.

402. Interview with Noel Baptiste, ACPOHI.

403. Interview with Chittubhai Patel, 4 November 2002, ACPOHI.

404. Interview with Barbara Devlin, ACPOHI; interview with Carlos Flores, 4 November 2002, ACPOHI.

405. Interview with Aura Sprague Osorno, ACPOHI; interview with Martha Lopez, ACPOHI.

406. NJCCC, *Casino Gambling in New Jersey*, p. 26.

407. NGIS, *The National Gambling Impact Study Commission: Final Report* (Washington, DC: NGIS, 1999), chs 7, 8, available online at http://govinfo.library.unt.edu/ngisc/ (accessed 11 October 2007).

408. LaPolla, 'The Changing Face of Atlantic City'.

409. Interview with Carol N., ACPOHI; interview with Chhitubai Patel, ACPOHI.

410. Interview with Carol N., ACPOHI; interview with Richard Lopez, ACPOHI; interview with Martha Lopez, ACPOHI.
411. Interview with Richard Lopez, ACPOHI; R. S. Anson, 'Are Casinos a Bad Bet?' *Saturday Review* (June 1980), pp. 28–33; Anastasia, 'Monopoly'.
412. J. Glick, 'Some Area Immigrants Feeling More at Home/American Dream of Owning a House is Reality for Some Families', *Press of Atlantic City*, 8 November 2004.
413. Johnson, 'Kin and Casinos'.
414. Interview with Joseph Pham, ACPOHI.
415. Interview with Cathanina Tran, 7 June 2005, ACPOHI.
416. L. T. Saito, *Ethnic Identity and Motivation: Socio-Cultural Factors in the Educational Achievement of Vietnamese American Students* (New York: LFB Scholarly Publishing LLC, 2002), pp. 26–7.
417. Interview with Carol N., ACPOHI.
418. Interview with Cathanina Tran, ACPOHI.
419. Ibid.
420. Interview with Peter Pham and Thu Ngo, ACPOHI.
421. *Atlantic City Report*, Spring 2003; [Anon.], 'ACPD Diversity: High-Level Concern', *Press of Atlantic City*, 8 February 2002, p. A8.
422. Interview with Chhitubhai Patel, ACPOHI.
423. Interview with Aura Sprague Osorno, 1 July 2003, ACPOHI.
424. Interview with Luz Prado, 18 May 2005, ACPOHI.
425. Interview with Martha Lopez, ACPOHI.
426. Interview with Richard Lopez, ACPOHI.
427. This affirms recent ethnography that suggests there was no real adoption of gender equality within immigrant social structures upon moving to the US. See P. Pessar, 'Engendering Migration Studies: The Case of New Immigrants in the United States', in P. Hondagenu-Sotelo (ed.), *Gender and U.S. Immigration: Contemporary Trends* (Berkeley, CA: University of California Press, 2003), pp. 20–42; Y. Le Espiritu, 'Gender and Labor in Asian Immigrant Families', in Hondagenu-Sotelo (ed.), *Gender and U.S. Immigration*, pp. 81–100; P. Kurien, 'Gendered Ethnicity: Creating a Hindu Indian Identity in the United States', in Hondagenu-Sotelo (ed.), *Gender and U.S. Immigration*, pp. 151–73.
428. M. Zhou, 'Assimilation, The Asian Way', in T. Jacoby (ed.), *Reinventing the Melting Pot: The New Immigrants and What it Means to Be American* (New York: Basic Books/Perseus Book Group, 2004), pp. 148–52; K. Lydersen, *Out of the Sea and into The Fire: Immigration from Latin America to the U.S. in the Global Age* (Monroe, ME: Common Courage Press, 2005), p. 172.
429. N. S. Chinchilla and N. Hamilton, 'Central American Immigrants: Diverse Populations, Changing Communities' in D. G. Guttierez (ed.), *The Columbia History of Latinos in the United States Since 1960* (New York: Columbia University Press, 2004), pp. 187–228.
430. Interview with Joseph Pham, ACPOHI.
431. Interview with Jagdish Patel and Chittubai Patel, ACPOHI.
432. Stockton Institute for Gaming Management at The Richard Stockton College of New Jersey (SIGMA), *Front-Line Employees in Atlantic City's Gaming Industry: Issues and Concerns* (Pomona, NJ: SIGMA, 2006), slides 38–9, available online at

http://intraweb.stockton.edu/eyos/page.cfm?siteID=114&pageID=2 (accessed 11 October 2007); interview with Joseph Pham, ACPOHI.

433. For a positive account, see Heneghan, 'Economic Aspects of Casino Gaming in Atlantic City'.

434. D. Johnston, 'America Inc. Buys Out Murder Inc.' in J. Vogel (ed.), *Crapped Out* (Monroe, ME: Common Curtis Press, 1997), p. 22; O'Brien, *Best Bet*, pp. 62–87.

435. See F. Zephir, *The Haitian Americans* (Westport, CT: Greenwood Press, 2004): 'The Haitian immigrant has a special attitude. He is ready to make sacrifices. He sees money and his current situation in light of what he has left behind.'

436. Interview with Carmen DeBasilio, 17 June 2003, ACPOHI; interview with Aura Sprague Osrono, 17 June 2003, ACPOHI; interview with Jean Baptist Noel, 17 June 2003, ACPOHI; interview with J. Patel, 17 June 2003, ACPOHI; interview with Rosa Velasco, 17 June 2003, ACPOH; W. Clayson, 'Cubans in Las Vegas: Ethnic Identity, Success, and Urban Life the Late Twentieth Century', *Nevada Historical Society Quarterly*, 38:1 (1995), pp. 13–15.

437. SIGMA, *Front-Line Employees*, slide 41.

438. CRDA, *The Rebirth of a City*.

439. City of Atlantic City, *Atlantic City Report* (Atlantic City, NJ: City of Atlantic City, Winter 1994).

440. NJCCC, 'Operating Statistics, 1990–1999'.

441. Ibid.

442. NJCCC, *Annual Report* (1994), pp. 3–6.

443. Ibid., pp. 9–10; N. Casiello Jr., B. Aaron and K. Shanon, 'Regulatory Relaxation: New Legislation Aimed at Reducing Red Tape', *New Jersey Casino Journal* (January 1995).

444. [Anon.], 'What's News', *New Jersey Casino Journal* (January 1995), p. 21.

445. Eadington, 'The Casino Gaming Industry', pp. 23–35; Ochrym, 'Gambling in Atlantic City', pp. 591–6; M. Heller, 'The Changing Structure of American Gambling in the Twentieth Century', *Journal of Social Issues*, 35:3 (Summer 1979), pp. 87–114; Rothman, *Neon Metropolis*, pp. 23–5.

446. O'Brien, *Bad Bet*, p. 90; Simon, *Boardwalk of Dreams*, p. 205.

447. Gros, 'The Heartbeat of the Taj', pp. 12–13; Harrah's Entertainment Inc., 'This is What Makes Harrah's A Place Like Nowhere Else' [advertisement], *New Jersey Casino Journal* (February 1994), p. 31.

448. R. Gros, 'Going Global: New Castle Marketing Team Refocuses Efforts to Include the International Arena', *New Jersey Casino Journal* (February 1994), pp. 20–1.

449. W. B. Turner, and S. M. Renner, *Atlantic City: Worthy of a Second Look* (New York: Saloman Brothers/United States Equity Research-Gaming, 1995), pp. 1–10.

450. Ibid., pp. 10–13.

451. D. Wittkowski, 'Atlantic City Airport Stunted by Few, Costly Flights', *Press of Atlantic City*, 5 September 1995.

452. Turner and Renner, *Atlantic City*, pp. 18–26.

453. O'Brien, *Bad Bet*, p. 81.

454. R. Gros, 'Is Atlantic City Blowing its Very Last Chance?', *New Jersey Casino Journal* (March 1995), pp. 70–7; [Anon.], 'Atlantic City Redevelopment Update', *Press of Atlantic City*, 4 December 1995, p. C1.

455. [Anon.], 'What's News' (1995); S. Herriott, 'The Boardwalk Experience', *New Jersey Casino Journal* (January 1996), p. 20; R. Gros, 'Kiss and Make Up', *New Jersey Casino Journal* (January 1996), p. 34; Rothman, *Neon Metropolis*, 108–11.

456. Gros, 'Is Atlantic City Blowing its Very Last Chance?', pp. 70–7.

457. Turner and Renner, *Atlantic City*, pp. 25–6; oral history interview with James Whelan; Gros, 'Is Atlantic City Blowing its Very Last Chance?', pp. 70–7.

458. *New Jersey Casino Journal* (January 1996), p. 22; NJCCC, 'Annual Operating Statistics, 1990–1999'; K. Johnson, 'With Cash Rolling in, Atlantic City Raises Stakes', *New York Times*, 24 June 1996, pp. A1, B5.

459. [Anon.], 'Second Time around the Island' [interview with James Whelan] *New Jersey Casino Journal* (January 1995), pp. 10–13, 38–9, 44; oral history interview with James Whelan; [Anon.], 'Wynn, Trump Vie for 13 Atlantic City Casino', *New Jersey Casino Journal* (January 1995), pp. 30, 48.

460. NJCCC, *Annual Report* (1995), p. 5; Johnson, 'With Cash Rolling in, Atlantic City Raises Stakes'; D. C. Johnston, 'Coming Back to Atlantic City; Welcome Set for Wynn's Las Vegas-Scale Project', *New York Times*, 27 June 1995 [Wynn quote].

461. R. Gros, 'The Light at the End of the Tunnel', *New Jersey Casino Journal* (March 1996), pp. 14–22, 27.

462. [Anon.], 'Inside the Industry'; R. Gros, 'Donald Trump: King of the Realm', *New Jersey Casino Journal* (May 1996), pp. 10–19, 42.

463. NJCCC, *Annual Report* (1996), pp. 4–5; B. Pulley, 'As Atlantic City Thrives, Whitman May Call a Casino Bluff', *New York Times*, 29 June 1996.

464. Johnson, 'With Cash Rolling In', *New York Times*, 24 June 1996; Brett Pulley, 'Tense Talks Behind a Casino Road and Tunnel Project', *New York Times*, 2 March 1997; Associated Press report, *Asbury Park Press*, 3 November 1998.

465. [Anon.], 'From Wall Street to the Boardwalk: Success Gets Measured in Different Ways', *Michael Pollack's Gaming Industry Observer, Atlantic City Edition*, 2:9 (May 1997), p. 20; CRDA, *1997 Annual Report*.

466. New Jersey General Assembly, *Committee Meeting of the Senate Transportation Committee and Assembly Transportation and Communications Committee* [on] *Senate Bill No. 1948 and Assembly Bill No. 2798 (Testimony on the Proposal to "Increases New Jersey Transportation Trust Fund Authority Spending Cap by $200 Million for Fiscal Year 1998")*, pp. 7–8, 14–16, available online at http://www.njleg.state.nj.us/legislativepub/pubhear/041097t.htm (accessed 12 October 2007),

467. Ibid., pp. 29–30.

468. Ibid., pp. 32–5.

469. [Anon.], 'What's News', *Casino Journal* (January 1997), p. 8; [Anon.], 'The Casino Association of New Jersey: R.I.P.', *Casino Journal* (January 1997), p. 37.

470. ACCVA, *The New Atlantic City Convention Center: America's New Northeast Business Address* [brochure] (1–3 May 1997).

471. R. Smothers, 'Convention Center Leads Effort To Broaden the Revival of a City', *New York Times*, 3 May 1997, p. 25.

472. Smothers, 'Convention Center Leads Effort'; [Anon.], 'The Hotel Equation', *New Jersey Casino Journal* (November 1992); Gros, 'The Light at the End of the Tunnel', pp. 14–22, 27.

473. Interview with Steve Perskie, ACPOHI; interview with James McCullough, ACPOHI.

474. ACDPED, *Atlantic County Master Plan*, p. 69.

475. Interview with Pierre Hollingsworth, ACPOHI; NGIS Commission, Testimony of Pierre Hollingsworth, 20 August 1997, available online at http://govinfo. library.unt.edu/ngisc/meetings/aug2097/aug20p10.html (accessed 11 October 2007); Simon, *Boardwalk of Dreams*, p. 210; T. Peele, 'Westside Residents Unsure of Neighborhood's Future', *Press of Atlantic City*, 19 February 1996; Philly Roads, *Atlantic City–Brigantine Connector: Historical Overview*, http://www.phillyroads. com/roads/ac-brigantine/ (accessed 12 October 2007).

476. S. Lopez, 'In the Name of Her Father', *Time*, 14 July 1997.

477. B. Kent, 'Groundbreaking Is Set for Atlantic City Tunnel', *New York Times*, 1 November 1998; D. Razler, 'Atlantic County: Tunnel Groundbreaking: A Harbinger of Casinos "Second Wave" – 1998 Year in Review', *Press of Atlantic City*, 28 December 1998; Associated Press report, *Asbury Park Press*, 3 November 1998; Office of the Governor, 'Governor Breaks Ground for Atlantic City Tunnel: Cites Economic Benefits and Traffic Improvements from Project' [news release], 4 November 1998.

478. Associated Press, 'Top Court Gives OK to Funds for Tunnel', *Press of Atlantic City*, 3 August 1999; Joe Weinert, 'Casino Notes', *Press of Atlantic City*, 8 August 1999.

479. Associated Press, 'Top Court Gives OK to Funds for Tunnel', *Press of Atlantic City*, 3 August 1999.

480. Reifer, 'Casino Reinvestment Revisited', pp. 18–19.

481. D. Wittkowski, 'Suit Against A.C. Tunnel Dismissed', *Press of Atlantic City*, 23 July 1999; D. Wittkowski, 'Wall Street Lukewarm to Bond for A.C. Tunnel Financing', *Press of Atlantic City*, 7 May 1999, p. E1; D. Wittkowski, 'A.C. Tunnel Hits New Roadblock', *Press of Atlantic City*, 20 December 2000; Philly Roads, *Atlantic City– Brigantine Connector: Historical Overview*.

482. Atlantic City–Brigantine Connector Project, *Community Connection Bulletin* (July 1999), Transportation-Tunnel Subject File, Heston Room, Atantic City Free Public Library.

483. SJTA, 'Atlantic City–Brigantine Connector Grand Opening July 27, 2001' [press release], 27 July 2001; D. Wittkowski, 'Atlantic City Expressway Tunnel Connector Opening/Tunnel Opens Finally/Ho Hum Celebration for Atlantic City Road Beset by Delays', *Press of Atlantic City*, 1 August 2001; D. Wittkowski, 'Year Later, Tunnel on Road to Success', *Press of Atlantic City*, 31 July 2002.

484. NJCCC, *Annual Report* (1997), pp. 8–9; *Michael Pollack's Gaming Industry Observer*, 12 February 1998; J. Weinert, ''98 Meant Business: Casinos Focused on Projects and Profits', *Press of Atlantic City*, 27 December 1998, p. F1; L. Mansnerus, 'Great Expectations; Money Has Poured into Atlantic City. But a Second Wave, Ever Poised, Still Hasn't Broken', *New York Times*, 2 April 2000.

485. [Anon.], 'Playing Monopoly Big Time', *Casino Journal* (May 1996).

486. NJCCC, *Annual Report* (1998), p. 14; Weinert, ''98 Meant Business'; [Anon.], 'What's News' (1997), p. 37.

487. F. Legato, 'Harrah's and Showboat: A Marriage of Marketing', *New Jersey Casino Journal* (May 1998), pp. 68–71.

488. Shook, *Jackpot!*, pp. 147–53; Legato, 'Harrah's and Showboat'; Schwartz, *Suburban Xanadu*, pp. 215–16.

489. [Anon.], 'Best Gaming Employers: Harrah's Receives Recognition for Demonstrating Link between Morale, Bottom Line', *Michael Pollack's Gaming Industry Observer*, 29 January 1998; [Anon.], 'Harrah's Structure Gets 'A' from Academicians, Analysts', *Michael Pollack's Gaming Industry Observer*, 26 November 1999; M. Brown, 'The Human Factor', *Casino Journal* (May 1998), pp. 79–82; M. Brown, 'Labor Pains', *Casino Journal* (May 1998), pp. 84–5; conversation with Barbara Devlin, 17 July 2007.

490. Shook, *Jackpot!*, p. 135.

491. NJCCC, 'Annual Operating Statistics, 2000–2006', available online at http://www.state.nj.us/casinos/financia/histori/ (accessed 10 October 2007).

492. Harrah's Entertainment Inc., *Setting the Standard: 2002 Annual Report* (2002), pp. 2–5.

493. *Michael Pollack's Gaming Industry Observer*, 12 February 1998; R. Gros, 'Just a Day at the Beach ... Sort of', *Casino Journal* (March 1998), pp. 76–7.

494. HERE Local 54, 'Testimony of Hotel Employees and Restaurant Employees International Union (HERE) and HERE Local 54', [videotape] for NGIS hearings, 21–22 January 1998.

495. Ibid.

496. Ibid.

497. NJCCC, *Casino Gambling in New Jersey*, pp. 17–18, 22–24, A3.

498. O'Brien, *Bad Bet*, p. 91.

499. Bureau of Economic Research, Rutgers University, *Limitations in the Workplace*, pp. 23–7; NGIS, *Final Report*, pp. 7–8.

500. New Jersey Department of Labor, *Employment and the Economy: Atlantic Coastal Region 128* (Trenton, NJ: New Jersey Department of Labor, March 1998); Nelson, 'Casino Gambling In Atlantic City: A Sure Bet for Whom?'.

501. A. Rosenberg, 'A.C. Casinos' 25 Years: An Era of Mixed Payoffs', *Philadelphia Inquirer*, 20 June 2007, p. A01.

502. Simon, *Boardwalk of Dreams*, p. 220.

503. Nelson, 'Casino Gambling In Atlantic City'; O'Brien, *Bad Bet*, p. 81; Goodman, *The Luck Business*.

504. B. Hickey, 'Westside's Story is Full of Good Memories', *Press of Atlantic City*, 15 December 1998.

505. Pollock, *Hostage to Fortune*; Sternlieb and Hughes, *The Atlantic City Gamble*.

506. NJCCC, *Casino Gambling in New Jersey*, pp. 55–6; United States and New Jersey crime statistics compiled by FBI Uniform Crime Reports, http://www.disaster-center.com/crime/; City of Atlantic City, 'What a Difference a Decade Makes: A.C.'s 10-Year Tally of Accomplishments', *Atlantic City Report* (Fall 1993).

507. NJCCC, *Casino Gambling in New Jersey*, pp. 24–5; NJCCC, *Annual Report* (1991), p. 9; Bureau of Economic Research, Rutgers University, *Limitations in the Workplace*, p. 21.

508. T. Barlas, 'Gaming's Reach: Real People, Real lives ... Five Local Portraits', *Press of Atlantic City*, 26 May 1998, pp. A6–A7.

509. Rosenberg, 'A.C. Casinos' 25 Years', p. A01.

510. NJCCC, *Annual Report* (1992), p. 8; D. Heneghan, 'Minorities, Women Push Action to Achieve Casino Set-Aside Goals', *Press of Atlantic City*, 15 December 1992, p. C1.

511. NJCCC, *Annual Report* (1988), p. 6; NJCCC, *Annual Report* (1993), p. 15; R. Gros, 'Casino Association Forms Purchasing Cooperative', *New Jersey Casino Journal* (June 1992), p. 8.

512. Heneghan, 'Minorities, Women Push Action'.

513. S. Herriott and R. Gros, 'Acting Affirmatively: The Status of Minority and Women Employment Is Improving … but Is It at Anyone's Expense?', *New Jersey Casino Journal* (November 1995), pp. 16–20; oral history interview with Harry Hasson, 22 March 2007.

514. Simon, *Boardwalk of Dreams*, pp. 210–22.

515. ACOPPED, *Growth Trends: Atlantic County, NJ 1993–1994*; T. Russell, 'Region Enjoys Diversified Growth', *Press of Atlantic City*, 21 June 1998; D. P. Lee, 'The Casino Gamble: 25 Years Later, Atlantic City Casinos Brought Progress, but at a Price', *Press of Atlantic City*, 25 May 2003.

516. ACDPED, *Atlantic County Master Plan*, pp. 6–9; interview with James 'Sonny' McCullough, ACPOHI.

517. [Anon.], 'Food Operations', *Michael Pollock's Gaming Industry Observer*, 2:5 (17 March 1997); ACDPED, *Atlantic County Master Plan*, pp. 12, 38.

518. Barlas, 'Gaming's reach'; M. Epifianio (ed.), *20th Anniversary of Casino Gaming in Atlantic City: 1978–1998: 20 Years and Lady Luck Is Still Smiling on Atlantic City* (1998); NJCCC, *Casino Gambling in New Jersey*, p. 22; J. Micale, *Economic Impact Generated by a Typical New Large Scale Casino/Hotel* (Atlantic City, NJ: Atlantic City Department of Planning and Development, 1999).

519. Mansnerus, 'Great Expectations'.

520. Interview with Daniel Heneghan, ACPOHI; Barlas, 'Gaming's Reach'; NJCCC, *Casino Gambling in New Jersey*, p. 22; Micale, *Economic Impact*.

521. Oral history interview with Harry Hasson.

522. NJCCC, *Annual Report* (1989), p. 9; NJCCC, *Annual Report* (1999), pp. 15–16; NJCCC, *Annual Report* (2003), p. 27.

523. J. Ryan, *A Chartbook of County Social & Health Indicators* (Trenton, NJ: New Jersey Department of Health and Senior Services, 1996), pp. 34–5; Y. Hailu, A. Mammo and A. Kline, *A Chartbook of Social and Health Indicators in New Jersey* (Trenton, NJ: New Jersey Department of Health and Senior Services, 2003), pp. 19–20; NGIS, *Final Report*, pp. 7-11, 7-12.

524. Ryan, *Chartbook of County Social & Health Indicators*; Hailu, Mammo and Kline, *Chartbook of Social and Health Indicators*.

525. Interview with Nanette Stuart, ACPOHI.

526. Hailu, Mammo and Kline, *Chartbook of Social and Health Indicators*, p. 65.

527. NGIS, *Final Report*, pp. 7-18 to 7-25; H. Lesieur, R. Klein and M. Rimm, 'Pathological and Problem Gambling among New Jersey High School Students', [study conducted for the Council on Compulsive Gambling of New Jersey, Inc., Trenton, NJ]; Council of Compulsive Gambling of New Jersey, Inc., 'Correlation between Gambling and Bankruptcy Holding Strong' [press release, 23 August 2001].

528. Annual statistics provided by the Council on Compulsive Gambling of New Jersey, Inc.; Subcommittee on Technology, Terrorism & Government Information, Senate Judiciary Committee 'Testimony of James R. Hurley, Chairman, New Jersey Casino Control Commission', 23 March 1999, available online at http://judiciary.senate. gov/oldsite/32399jrh.htm (accessed 13 October 2007); NJCCC, *Annual Report* (2002), p. 5.

529. Interview with Steve Perskie, ACPOHI.

530. NJCCC, 'Annual Operating Statistics, 1990–1999'; City of Atlantic City, *Developer's Package 1999* (Atlantic City, NJ: City of Atlantic City Planning and Development Division, 1999), pp. 8, 13; *Gaming Industry Observer*, 23 April 1999.

531. [Anon.], 'Win per Employee Rises; So Does Emphasis on Full-Time Employment', *Michael Pollack's Gaming Industry Observer*, 5 February 1999; *Michael Pollack's Gaming Industry Observer* 19 February 1999.

532. [Anon], '1995: Time to Consolidate' [editorial], *New Jersey Casino Journal* (January 1995), p. 6.

533. NJCCC, *Annual Report* (1999), pp. 4, 10–17.

534. *Michael Pollack's Gaming Industry Observer*, 9 May 1999; NJCCC, 'Annual Operating Statistics, 1990–1999'; J. Weinert, 'Casino Notes', *Press of Atlantic City*, 8 August 1999, p. F1.

535. A. Pollack, 'Arthur Goldberg, Builder of Casino Empire, Dies at 58', *New York Times*, 20 October 2000; NJCCC, *Annual Report* (2001), p. 12.

536. City of Atlantic City, *Developer's Package 1999*, p. 11; interview with Dennis Ricci, ACPOHI.

537. T. Peele, 'Atlantic City Votes on Deal With MGM', *Press of Atlantic City*, 6 January 2000.

538. T. Faherty, 'MGM Buys Mirage: Mirage and MGM Merge in Atlantic City', *Press of Atlantic City*, 7 March 2000, p. A3; T. Barlas, 'MGM Buys Mirage: Bombastic Return Ends like a Mirage: Wynn's Proposals Brought Hope, But No Construction', *Press of Atlantic City* 7 March 2000, p. A3.

539. Faherty, 'MGM Buys Mirage'.

540. *Michael Pollack's Gaming Industry Observer*, 13 March 2000, 3 April 2000; Mansnerus, 'Great Expectations'.

541. T. Peele, 'Victors View the Atlantic City Election Results as a Mandate', *Press of Atlantic City*, 14 May 1998, p. C1; J. Weinert, 'Casinos Hope for Mayoral Support', *Press of Atlantic City*, 18 November 2001, p. A1.

542. I. Petersen, 'Homeless, Not Scandal, Shakes Up Atlantic City', *New York Times* 11 November 2001; I. Peterson, 'Metro Briefing New Jersey: Atlantic City; Whelan Concedes Election', *New York Times*, 14 November 2001, p. D-8.

543. Weinert, 'Casinos Hope for Mayoral Support'.

544. M. Busler, 'Langford Has the Opportunity to Unite Atlantic City', [editorial] *Press of Atlantic City*, 19 November 2001, p. A11.

545. J. Weinert, 'Small City Home to Mighty Industry', *Press of Atlantic City*, 28 May 2002.

546. *Michael Pollack's Gaming Industry Observer*, 14 May 2001.

547. J. Weinert, 'Casinos Expect Financial Hit in Wake of Attacks', *Press of Atlantic City*, 13 September 2001; J. Weinert, 'Week Later, Casinos Still Feel Pinch', *Press of Atlantic City*, 19 September 2001.

548. K. D. Grimsley, 'Tourists Gamble Closer to Home: Business Is Brisk at Casinos Not Dependent on Air Travel', *Washington Post*, 30 September 2001, p. A08; Weinert, 'Week Later'.

549. NJCCC, *Annual Report* (2001), pp. 4–5, 18; J. Weinert, 'A.C. Not Envying Las Vegas These Days', *Press of Atlantic City*, 7 October 2001; SJTA, *2001 Annual Report*, p. 9.

550. J. Martin, 'At Freedom's Edge: Liberty, Security and The Patriot Act', *Newark Star Ledger*, 28 August 2005.

551. Casino Watch, Inc., 'Crime: Money Laundering in the Casinos', http://www.casinowatch.org/crime/money_laundering.html, January 2005 (accessed 13 October 2007).

552. J. N. Rose, 'Casinos Stuck under New Anti-Terrorism Laws', http://www.gamblingandthelaw.com/columns.html, 2005 (accessed 13 October 2007).

553. NJCCC, *Annual Report* (2002), p. 9; [Anon.], 'From Trenton to the Boardwalk ... ', *Michael Pollack's Gaming Industry Observer*, 4 February 2002.

554. P. Saharko, 'Gormley Proposes Tax Breaks for Casinos', *Press of Atlantic City*, 17 February 2001; J. Urgo, 'Law Lets Casinos Openly Offer Free Booze', *Philadelphia Inquirer*, 15 August 2002.

555. J. Weinert, 'Budget Plan Pounds Casinos: Industry Vows to Fight $135 Million in New Taxes on Revenues, Comps', *Press of Atlantic City*, 4 February 2003, p. A1; D. Kinney and J. Donohue, 'Both Sides Agree on $24 Billion Budget: Threat of Government Shutdown Keeps Lawmakers in Negotiations through the Day', *The Star-Ledger*, 1 July 2003, p. 1.

556. C. Hedges, 'Casino Boss Who Started With a Bucket of Coins', *Borgata Style*, 'The Borgata' subject file, Heston Room, Atlantic City Free Public Library; J. Weinert, 'New Gaming Hall Will Make Debut in the Wee Hours', *Press of Atlantic City*, 2 July 2003, p. A1. *New York Times*, 26 August 2003; *Michael Pollack's Gaming Industry Observer*, 28 July 2003.

557. [Anon.], 'Colony Paid Fair Price for Aging Resorts Property', *Michael Pollack's Gaming Industry Observer*, 4 December 2000; *Michael Pollack's Gaming Industry Observer* 3 April 2000, 16 July 2001; [Anon.], 'Who Will Feel Borgata's Bite?', *Michael Pollack's Gaming Industry Observer*, 6 August 2001; S. Sataline, 'Atlantic City Reinvents Itself as Vegas East ; Faced with Competition, Resort Town Embarks on Biggest Building Boom in 24 Years. But Will it Work?', *Christian Science Monitor*, 22 August, 2002, p. 3.

558. [Anon.], 'Borgata Analysis: Old Definitions Useless in New Era', *Michael Pollack's Gaming Industry Observer*, 2 December 2002; R. Strauss, 'Atlantic City Places Money on New Image; Casinos Refurbishing, Seeking Big Spenders', *Washington Post*, 21 July 2003, p. A.03.

559. A. Bary, 'Rolling the Dice: Will Borgata Rejuvenate Atlantic City?', *Barron's*, 21 July 2003, pp. 20–4.

560. NJCCC, 'Annual Operating Statistics, 2000–2006'; K. Ball, 'Q & A with Mark Juliano', *Trump Magazine* (Spring 2006), p. 56; NJCCC, *Annual Report* (2006), p. 3.

561. Strauss, 'Atlantic City Places Money'; C. Binkley, 'Atlantic City Gets a Vegas Makeover – First New Casino in 13 Years Spurs Push for Hipper Gamblers; Next, an Imax at the Tropicana', *Wall Street Journal*, 26 June 2003, p. D1; A. Rosenberg, 'Where Naughty is Looking Nice', *Philadelphia Inquirer*, 8 June 2003, p. B01.

562. Interview with Paul Tjoumakaris, ACPOHI; J. Weinert, 'Borgata Building Team to Manage A.C. Resort', *Press of Atlantic City*, 7 December 2001.

563. Interview with Paul Tjoumakaris, ACPOHI.

564. *Michael Pollack's Gaming Industry Observer*, 28 July 2003.

565. J. Weinert, 'Borgata No Help to Casino Revenue', *Press of Atlantic City*, 13 August 2003, p. A1.

566. *Michael Pollack's Gaming Industry Observer*, 28 February 2004, 14 April 2004, 20 May 2004.

567. SJTA, 'Atlantic City Visit-Trips, 2006 Annual', available online at www.sjta.org (accessed 14 October 2007).

568. J. Harrison, 'Laying it on the Table: What Does the Comeback of Table Games Mean to Atlantic City?', *Casino Connection*, 2:3 (March 2005), pp. 24–7, available online at http://www.casinoconnectionac.com/articles/Laying_It_On_The_Table (accessed 14 October 2007).

569. In January 2004, Park Place Entertainment officially changed its name to Caesar's Inc. following a stockholder vote to capitalize on Caesar's brand name recognition; G. Rivlin, 'Atlantic City Aiming Higher As Casinos Slip', *New York Times*, 19 March 2007, Metropolitan Section 1; S. Citron, 'Atlantic City's Hot Makeover', *Baltimore* (July 2005), pp. 72–6; NJCCC, 'Annual Operating Statistics, 2000–2006'; 'Historical US Inflation Rate 1914–Present', www.InflationData.com (accessed 14 October 2007); D. DeLuca, 'The New Sounds of Atlantic City – Promoters are Bringing in Rock and Hip-Hop Acts such as Eminem to revive the Resort's Dowdy Image', *Philadelphia Inquirer*, 10 July 2005.

570. NJCCC, 'Annual Operating Statistics, 2000–2006'.

571. NJCCC, *Annual Report* (2004), p. 18.

572. Interview with Selina Jahan, 28 June 2005, ACPOHI.

573. Interview with Tom Gitto, ACPOHI.

574. J. Urgo, 'A.C. casinos and union locked in for long battle', 16 October 2004, *Philadelphia Inquirer*, p. A01; J. S. Haught, 'Atlantic City's Casino Strike Is Over / Agreement Reached Late Monday', *Press of Atlantic City*, 2 November 2004, p. A1; M. DeAngelis, 'Casino Labor Strike: Local 54 Deal Brings Welcome Quiet to Boardwalk', *Press of Atlantic City*, 3 November 2004, p. C1.

575. D. Wittkowski, 'Strike Splits Casinos' Win: Five of Seven Struck Casinos Show Decline – Five Non-Walkout Houses Show Increases', *Press of Atlantic City*, 11 November 2004, p. A1; J. Brand, 'Casino Labor Strike / Jackson Motivated Wet, Weary Pickets In Atlantic City', *Press of Atlantic City*, 23 October 2004, p. B1.

576. NJCCC, *Annual Report* (2001), p. 28; NJCCC, *Annual Report* (2004), pp. 26–7.

577. NJCCC, 'Annual Operating Statistics, 2000–2006'; NJCCC, *Annual Report* (2004), p. 4.

578. Interview with Edna Hall, ACPOHI; interview with James 'Sonny' McCullough, ACPOHI.

579. K. Adams, 'Quick-Takes: The Month's Trends in a Glance – September 2004', *Casino City Times*, 30 September 2004, available online at http://adams.casinocitytimes. com/articles/15740.html (accessed 14 October 2007); D. Wittkowski, 'Harrah's–Caesar's Merger Gets OK From Casino Board', *Press of Atlantic City*, 25 May 2005, p. A1.

580. Wittkowski, 'Harrah's–Caesar's Merger' p. A1; NJCCC, 'Annual Operating Statistics, 2000–2006'.

581. D. Berns, 'Casino Consolidation: Raising the Stakes', *Las Vegas Review-Journal*, 9 January 2005, p. 29A; Wittkowski, 'Harrah's–Caesar's Merger'.

582. H. Stutz, 'Mergers and Acquisitions: Harrah's Priority: Reduce Debt', *Las Vegas Review-Journal*, 21 December 2006; P. Sanders and D. K. Berman, 'Harrah's Accepts Buyout Offer, Proceeds With Internal Revamp', *Wall Street Journal*, 20 December 2006, p. C6; N. Alster, 'Your Debt May Become My Advantage', *New York Times*, 1 July 2007, pp. 3–6.

583. J. Whelan and J. Martin, 'Special Budget Talks Fail to Curtail State Shutdown', *Star Ledger* (Newark, NJ), 5 July 2006, News 1; R. Siegel (host), 'Jersey Shutdown Hits Resort Casinos', *All Things Considered*, National Public Radio, 5 July 2006; 'From the Desk of C. Robert McDevitt' [letter to Local 54 employees], www.hereLocal54.org (accessed 14 October 2007).

584. [Anon.], 'New Jersey Update ... Casino Closings Offered Good News for Atlantic City at Important Moment', *Michael Pollack's Gaming Industry Observer*, 17 July 2006.

585. D. Wittkowski, 'Philadelphia Slot Parlors Put Dent in Atlantic City Revenue', *Press of Atlantic City*, 10 February 2007, p. A1; Rivlin, 'Atlantic City Aiming Higher'; J. DeHaven, 'Gamblers Betting Less on Atlantic City', *Star-Ledger*, 12 June 2007, p. 60.

586. Schwartz, *Roll the Bones*, pp. 433–6.

587. C. Reidy, 'Rolling the Dice: Pequot Casino Opens with Hopes of Giving Connecticut Luck', *Boston Globe*, 16 February 1992, p. 12.

588. 'Mashantucket Pequot Gaming Enterprise Inc.', https://www.fundinguniverse. com/company-histories/Mashantucket-Pequot-Gaming-Enterprise-Inc-Company-History.html (accessed 15 October 2007); Reidy, 'Rolling the Dice', p. 12.

589. J. Benedict, *Without Reservation: How a Controversial Indian Tribe Rose to Power and Built the World's Largest Casino* (New York: HarperCollins, 2001), pp. 198–221.

590. K. Eisler, *Revenge of the Pequots: How a Small Native American Tribe Created the World's Most Profitable Casino* (New York: Simon & Schuster, 2001), pp. 156–91.

591. L. Horan, 'Connecticut Indian Tribe Set to Open Gambling Casino', *Reuters*, 13 February 1992; Eisler, *Revenge of the Pequots*, pp. 174–5.

592. H. Waldman, 'Slot Money Would Boost Poor Cities', *Hartford Courant*, 4 February 1993, p. A1.

593. C. Boger, Jr., D. Spears, K. Wolfe and L. Lee, 'Economic Impacts of Native American Casino Gaming', in C. Hsu (ed.), *Legalized Casino Gaming in the United States*, pp. 140–2.

594. Eisler, *Revenge of the Pequots*, pp. 212–13.

595. Ibid., pp. 171–81; H. Waldman and M. Jackman, 'Attorney General Rules Slot Machine Pact is Legal: Ruling Backs Weicker's Slot-Machine Pact With Tribe', *Hartford Courant*, 12 February 1993.

596. D. Collins, 'Casinos Dominate Regional Employment Scene', *The Day* (New London, CT), 23 February 1997.

597. P. Zielbauer, 'Study Finds Pequot Business Lifts Economy', *New York Times*, 29 November 2000, p. B5; R. Nykiel, 'A Special Look at Indian Gaming', *UNLV Gaming Research and Review Journal*, 8:2 (2004), pp. 51–6; J. Mead, 'The Big Gamble', *New York Times*, 23 March 2003, p. 14; J. Marsden, 'Tribes Ripple Effect Muted: Report: Two Casinos Bring State One Job for Every Three of Theirs', *Hartford Courant*, 14 June 2007, available online at http://www.hotel-online.com/News/2007_Jun_14/ k.HCG.1181839709.html (accessed 15 October 2007).

598. R. Hamilton, 'Tribe Invests Downtown in an Old Industrial City', *New York Times*, 15 January 2003, p. C5.

599. Benedict, *Without Reservation*, pp. 201–11.

600. K. Florin, 'Indian Gambling Has Become Major Force in Industry', *The Day*, 20 September 2002; K. Florin, 'Every Square Foot Adds Up to Profit at Mohegan Sun, Foxwoods', *The Day*, 1 January 2004, p. 1A.

601. *Michael Pollack's Gaming Industry Observer*, 26 November 1999; Shook, *Jackpot!*, pp. 203–11.

602. J. Gordon, 'Gambling on Family Fun', *New York Times*, 5 October 2003; p. 14CN.

603. S. S. Hsu, 'Mississippi's Reversal of Fortune; In Casino Towns, Aid and Speculation Fuel a Post-Katrina Boom', *Washington Post*, 10 March 2006, p. A01.

604. D. S. Nuwer and G. O'Brien, 'Mississippi's Oldest Pasture' in D. von Herrman (ed.), *Resorting to Casinos: The Mississippi Gambling Industry* (Jackson, MS: University Press of Mississippi, 2006), pp. 11–25; M. Nelson and J. L. Mason, 'Mississippi: The Politics of Casino Gambling', in von Herrman (ed.), *Resorting to Casinos*, pp. 26–47.

605. AGA, *Casino Gaming in America: Key Findings of the National Gambling Impact Study Commission (1997–99)*, available online at http://www.americangaming.org/ assets/files/studies/aga_casino_gaming_2005.pdf (accessed 15 October 2007), p. 6.

606. Nelson and Mason, 'Mississippi: The Politics of Casino Gambling', pp. 26–40.

607. Ibid., pp. 31–2; K. Russell, 'Paul Harvey: The Good Shepard of Mississippi's Gaming Billions', *Mississippi Business Journal*, 5 May 1997.

608. AGA, *Casino Gaming in America*, p. 6; S. Powers, 'Casino Revenue Pumps Up Government Coffers', *Coast Business Journal* (Gulfport, MS), 12 August 1996.

609. K. Russell, 'Survival of Fittest Emerges as Theme of State Casino Market', *Mississippi Business Journal* (Jackson, MS), 5 May 1997.

610. J. Plume, 'Mississippi Casinos Approach a Defining Moment as "Las Vegas" of the South' & 'Mississippi Casinos Evolve Quickly', *Casino Journal* (May 1998), pp. 44–56.

611. K. J. Meyer-Arendt, 'From the River to the Sea: Casino Gaming in Mississippi', in K. Meyer-Arendt (ed.), *Casino Gaming in America: Origins, Trends, and Impacts* (New York: Cognizant Communication, 1998), pp. 166–7.

612. D. von Herrman, R. Ingram, W. C. Smith, 'Gaming in the Mississippi Economy: A Marketing, Tourism, and Economic Perspective' (University of Southern Mississippi,

2000), available online at http://www.usm.edu/dewd/pdf/Gamingstudy.pdf (accessed 15 October 2007), pp. 2–27.

613. Nelson and Mason, 'Mississippi: The Politics of Casino Gambling', pp. 27–8; von Herrman, Ingram and Smith, 'Gaming in the Mississippi Economy', pp. 25–6; AGA, *Casino Gaming in America*, pp. 6–7.

614. Meyer-Arendt, 'From the River to the Sea', pp. 59–162; von Herrman, Ingram and Smith, 'Gaming in the Mississippi Economy', pp. 12–13; Shook, *Jackpot!*, p. 214.

615. S. W. Austin and R. T. Middleton IV, 'Racial Politics of Casino Gaming in the Delta', in von Herrman (ed.) *Resorting to Casinos*, pp. 47–66; P. Kilborn, 'Casinos Revive a Town, but Poverty Persists', *New York Times*, 20 October 2002, p. 1.1.

616. L. Parker, 'Abandoned Education: Tunica's Schools Struggle with Leftovers and Neglect', *APF Reporter* [Alicia Patterson Foundation], 18:2 (1997), available online at http://www.aliciapatterson.org/APF1802/Parker/Parker.html (accessed 15 October 2007).

617. Kilborn, 'Casinos Revive a Town'.

618. D. von Herrmann, 'Afterword', in von Herrman (ed.), *Resorting to Casinos*, pp. 167–9.

619. K. Chu, 'Gulf Coast Casinos Hit Revenue Jackpot', *USA Today*, 1 August 2007; G. Rivlin, 'Casinos Booming in Katrina's Wake as Cash Pours in', *New York Times*, 16 July 2007, Business p. 1; Mississippi State Tax Commission, *Miscellaneous Tax Bureau Casino Gross Gaming Revenues*, available online at http://www.mstc.state. ms.us/taxareas/misc/gaming/stats/GamingGrossReveues.pdf (accessed 16 October 2007).

620. On this point for Atlantic City, see Schwartz, *Suburban Xanadu*, p. 181.

621. Austin and Middleton, 'Racial Politics of Casino Gaming in the Delta', pp. 47–66.

622. J. Sullivan and T. Moore, 'Slots Bill Aim: Pa. Gamblers Spend it Here', *Philadelphia Inquirer*, 27 June 2004.

623. Pennsylvania General Assembly, *The General Assembly of Pennsylvania House Bill No. 2330 Session of 2004, Amending Title 4 (Amusements) of the Pennsylvania Consolidated Statutes, Authorizing Certain Racetrack and Other Gaming; Providing for the Powers and Duties of the Pennsylvania Gaming Control Board; Conferring Powers and Imposing Duties on the Department of Revenue, the Department of Health, the Office of Attorney General, the Pennsylvania State Police and the Pennsylvania Liquor Control Board; Establishing the State Gaming Fund, the Pennsylvannia Race Horse Development, Fund, the Pennsylvania Gaming Economic Development and Tourism Fund, the Compulsive Problem Gambling Treatment Fund and the Property Tax Relief Fund, Providing for Enforcement; Imposing Penalties; Making Appropriations; and Making Related Appeals* (2004), available online at http://www.pgcb.state.pa.us/legislation/HB2330P4272.pdf (accessed 16 October 2007); T. Barnes, 'Board Ready to Roll the State of Gambling', *Pittsburgh Post-Gazette*, 26 July 2004, p. A-1; Tom Barnes, Forces Vow Last Stand in House: Gambling Bill Clears Senate', *Pittsburgh Post-Gazette*, 3 July 2004, p. A-1.

624. *Michael Pollack's Gaming Industry Observer*, 30 May 2005; Barnes, 'Board Ready to Roll the State of Gambling'.

625. Demaris, *Boardwalk Jungle*, pp. 261–8.

626. J. Shields and S. Parmley, 'Why Trump Lost Gamble on Slot Site', *Philadelphia Inquirer*, 2 February 2007, p. A01; J. Shields, Simple tax-revenue numbers can be dazzling, but opponents say that the economic and social costs are equally spectacular' (*Philadelphia Inquirer*, 13 May 2007, p. B01).

627. DeHaven, 'Gamblers Betting Less on Atlantic City', p. 60.

628. NJCCC, 'CCC Announces June 2007 Casino Revenue' [press release], 10 July 2007, available online at http://www.state.nj.us/casinos/home/news/200706_revenue. pdf (accessed 16 October 2007); Pennsylvania Gaming Control Board, 'Gaming Revenues' [week of 25 June–1 July], available online on http://www.pgcb.state. pa.us/gaming_revenue/2007_06–25_gaming_rev.pdf (accessed 16 October 2007).

629. A. Baker, 'Tourism Commission Renews Opposition to Slots In Md.', *The Dispatch* (Ocean City, MD), 10 August 2007, available online at http://www.mdcoastdispatch.com/article.php?cid=30&id=1120 (accessed 16 October 2007).

630. 'Ocean City says slots are threat to town', *Baltimore Sun* forum, 18 August 2007, http://www.topix.com/forum/source/baltimore-sun/TP6F0IHLNITI7U7BC (accessed 16 October 2007).

631. Associated Press, 'Sands Casino to Close After 26 Years', 10 November 2006.

632. [Anon.], 'Corporate Trends...The New Breed of Acquirers: Is a Good Deal for Investors A Good Deal for Industry?', *Michael Pollack's Gaming Industry Observer*, 16 October 2006; Reuters, 'Harrah's to Open Biloxi Margaritaville Casino' 15 May 2007, available online at http://www.topix.net/forum/com/het/TD4532QRK7B1U17OO (accessed 16 October 2007); P. Kravitz, 'Pinky's Corner: Boardwalk vs. Marina District', *Atlantic City Weekly*, 22 March 2007, available online at http://www. acweekly.com/view.php?id=6187&issue_id=172 (accessed 16 October 2007).

633. [Anon.], 'Layoffs at Tropicana Raise Serious Questions for Atlantic City' [editorial], *Press of Atlantic City*, 20 June 2007.

634. W. Yung III, 'Layoffs Ensure Trop's Continued Success' [letter to the editor], *Press of Atlantic City*, 27 June 2007; S. Parmley, 'Some Question Columbia-Sussex' Management of the Tropicana Casino & Resort, Atlantic City', *Philadelphia Inquirer*, 10 August 2007, available online at http://www.hotel-online.com/News/PR2007_ 3rd/Aug07_TropAC.html (accessed 16 October 2007); [Anon.], 'Tropicana Makeover on Hold for Now', *TMC Net*, 17 August 2007, http://www.tmcnet.com/ usubmit/2007/08/17/2871015.htm (accessed 16 October 2007).

635. A. Meister, *Casino City's Indian Gaming Industry Report* (Newton, MA: Casino City Press, 2006), p. 33.

636. United Auto Workers, 'Casino Workers Rally Aug. 9 to Support UAW Bargainers at Caesars' [news release], 8 August 2007, available online at http://www.uaw.com/ news/newsarticle.cfm?ArtId=485 (accessed 16 October 2007); M. Rao, 'Tropicana Dealers Vote for UAW's Representation', *Press of Atlantic City*, 27 August 2007, available online at http://www.pressofatlanticcity.com/news/local/atlantic_city/ story/7498349p-7394926c.html (accesed 16 October 2007); D. Wittkowski, 'Electronic Table Games Coming to Atlantic City', *Press of Atlantic City*, 19 July 2007, available online at http://www.pressofatlanticcity.com/top_three/story/7491875p-7387519c.html (accessed 16 October 2007).

637. F. Norris, 'Bad Gamble: Trump Stock Falls Again', *New York Times*, 6 July 2007, p. C1; W. Parry, 'No Deal for Trump's Casino Company', *USA Today*, 2 July 2007;

NJCCC, 'Annual Operating Statistics 1990–1999'; NJCCC, 'Annual Operating Statistics 2000–2006'; NJCCC, 'CCC Announces June 2007 Casino Revenue'.

638. Blair, *Donald Trump*, pp. 218–19.

639. Associated Press, 'MGM Mirage Growth Mania Grips Atlantic City Casinos', 20 July 2007, available online at http://www.advfn.com/news_Growth-mania-grips-Atlantic-City-casinos_21531491.html (accessed 16 October 2007).

640. Development Update (2007), Casinos – General Subject File, Heston Room, Atlantic City Free Public Library.

641. Interview with Steve Perskie, ACPOHI.

642. D. Wittkowski, 'Wynn Eyes Atlantic City for New Casino', *Press of Atlantic City*, 10 August 2007.

643. F. Szasz, 'Quotes about History', *History News Network*, http://hnn.us/articles/1328.html (accessed 16 October 2007).

644. Wittkowski, 'Wynn Eyes Atlantic City'.

645. United States Attorney's Office, District of New Jersey, 'Atlantic City Council President, Camden Councilman Plead Guilty to Extortion; Contractor Admits Drug Charges' [news release], 30 August 2006, available online at http://www.usdoj.gov/usao/nj/press/files/call0830_r.htm (accessed 16 October 2007).

646. NJCCC, 'Casino Control Commission – License Division Employment by Atlantic City Casino Licensees by Zip Code and License Category', http://www.state.nj.us/casinos/licens/licenrep/emp_casino_zip.html (accessed 16 October 2007); NJCCC, *Annual Report* (2006), p. 20.

647. Interview with Nannette Stuart, ACPOHI.

648. Hailu, Mammo and Kline, *A Chartbook of Social and Health Indicators in New Jersey*, pp. 64–7.

BIBLIOGRAPHY

Periodicals

APF Reporter [Alicia Patterson Foundation]

Asbury Park Press.

Atlantic City Action.

Atlantic City Magazine.

Atlantic City Weekly.

Baltimore.

Baltimore Sun.

Black Atlantic City Magazine.

Black New Jersey Magazine.

Black News and Events.

Boston Globe.

Casino Connection.

Casino Chronicle.

Casino City Times.

New Jersey Casino Journal.

Christian Century.

Christian Science Monitor.

Coast Business Journal.

Hartford Courant.

Las Vegas Review-Journal.

Michael Pollock's Gaming Industry Observer.

Mississippi Business Journal.

New York Times.

New York Magazine.

New Jersey Casino Journal.

New Jersey Monthly.

Nation's Business.

New Jersey Reporter.

Philadelphia Inquirer.

Pittsburgh Post-Gazette.

Press of Atlantic City.

The Bulletin (Philadelphia, PA).

The Day (New London, CT).

The Dispatch (Ocean City, MD).

The Star Ledger (Newark, NJ).

USA Today.

Wall Street Journal.

Washington Post.

Time Magazine.

Trump Magazine.

Primary Sources

Ackerman, P. 'Census '90, Area Sees Increase in Asians, Casinos Offer them Jobs, Opportunity', *Press of Atlantic City*, 13 February 13, 1991, p. A6.

Adams, K., 'Quick-Takes: The Month's Trends in a Glance –September 2004', *Casino City Times*, 30 September 2004, available online at http://adams.casinocitytimes.com/articles/15740.html (accessed 14 October 2007).

Alster, N., 'Your Debt May Become My Advantage', *New York Times*, 1 July 2007, pp. 3–6.

American Gaming Association (AGA), *Casino Gaming in America: Key Findings of the National Gambling Impact Study Commission (1997–99)*, available online at http://www.americangaming.org/assets/files/studies/aga_casino_gaming_2005.pdf (accessed 15 October 2007).

Anastasia, G., 'Monopoly: The Resorts Game in Atlantic City', *Philadelphia Inquirer*, 16 June 1985.

Anderson, D., 'Who Will Rebuild Atlantic City?', *Atlantic City Magazine* (May 1982), pp. 88–93, 104–6.

[Anon.], 'Millions Made by Racketeers', *Press of Atlantic City*, 19 January 1930.

—, 'Gambling Comes to Atlantic City', *Christian Century*, 24 January 1979.

—, 'Up With the Downs', *Atlantic City Action*, 10:2 (October 1979).

—, Interview with J.H. Lyles-Belton, *Black Atlantic City* (March/April 1982).

—, 'City vs. Casino is really a Failure to Communicate', *Black News and Events*, 5–18 June 1987.

—, '1987 Year in Review', *New Jersey Casino Journal* (January 1988).

—, 'DGE Takes on Donald Trump', *New Jersey Casino Journal* (January 1988), p. 54.

—, 'Interview with Jack Pratt, Chairman Pratt Hotel Corporation', *New Jersey Casino Journal* (July 1988), pp. 38–41.

—, 'Why Does It Always Have to Be "We" vs. "Them" in Atlantic City?' [editorial], *Press of Atlantic City*, 16 October 1988, p. D3.

—, 'Interview with Steve Wynn', *New Jersey Casino Journal* (November 1988), pp. 19–20, 48–9, 53–9.

—, 'Interview with Tom Carver', *New Jersey Casino Journal* (November 1988), pp. 23–35.

—, 'Humpty-Dumpty Rules in Trenton and Ruins Atlantic City' [editorial], *New Jersey Casino Journal* (December 1988), pp. 6–7.

—, 'Probe Will Kill', *Black News and Events*, December 1988.

—, 'Visions of a New School', *The Herald* (Atlantic City High School Yearbook, 1988).

—, 'Success After High School, *The Herald* (Atlantic City High School Yearbook, 1988).

—, 'Interview with Phil Satre, President/CEO of Harrah's Gaming Group & Ron Lenczycki, Pres GM of Harrah's Marina', *New Jersey Casino Journal* (January 1989), pp. 19–20, 22–3, 55.

—, 'Trump Traits' [editorial], *New Jersey Casino Journal* (February 1989), p. 8.

—, 'If We Only Knew Then What We Know Now!' [interview with Brendan Byrne], *New Jersey Casino Journal* (June 1989), pp. 40–6.

—, 'Executive Forum: Merv Griffin's Resorts' Hotel and Casino: VP Operations Al Luciani', *New Jersey Casino Journal* (January 1990), pp. 10–11.

—, 'A Matter of Semantics?' [editorial], *New Jersey Casino Journal* (February 1990), pp. 23–6.

—, 'Las Vegas, N.J.? Keep it Out There', *Asbury Park Press*, 3 March 1990, p. A8 (via the *Press of Atlantic City*).

—, 'Jim Whelan for Mayor: The Fudge Factor', *New Jersey Casino Journal* (May 1990), p. 6.

—, 'Harrah's Marina: The People Place', *New Jersey Casino Journal* (June 1990), pp. 26–36.

—, 'Ed Tracy, Trump's Top Atlantic City Executive: "We Will Survive", *Press of Atlantic City*, 30 September 1990, p. F1.

—, 'Dear Steve … We've Got a Problem', *New Jersey Casino Journal* (October 1990).

—, 'Interview with Jim Whelan', *New Jersey Casino Journal* (October 1990), pp. 18–22, 60.

—, Interview with Steve Wynn, *New Jersey Casino Journal* (June 1991), pp. 26–9.

—, 'Interview with Phil Satre [CEO Promus]', *New Jersey Casino Journal* (June 1991), pp. 14–17, 19.

—, 'Exclusive Interview: Henry Gluck' [Chair, Caesars World], *New Jersey Casino Journal* (July 1991).

—, 'The Stabilizer' [interview with Nicholas Ribis, CEO of Trump Hotel and Casino Reports], *New Jersey Casino Journal* (December 1991).

—, 'From Trenton to the Boardwalk...', *Michael Pollack's Gaming Industry Observer*, 4 February 2002.

—, 'Up Up and Away in Atlantic City: Interview with Gov. James Florio', *New Jersey Casino Journal* (March 1992).

—, 'Gormley's Guns', *New Jersey Casino Journal* (May 1992).

—, 'Bally's Bounces Back: Interview with Richard Gillman', *New Jersey Casino Journal* (August 1992), pp. 11–13.

—, 'Inside the Industry', *New Jersey Casino Journal* (August 1992), p. 22.

—, 'The Hotel Equation', *New Jersey Casino Journal* (November 1992).

—, 'The Year that Was: 1992', *New Jersey Casino Journal* (January 1993), pp. 24–9.

—, 'Leaps and Bounds: How Harrah's Atlantic City Spurred Promus Expansion' [interview with Ron Lenczycki], *New Jersey Casino Journal* (April 1993), pp. 12, 13, 22.

—, 'The Foxwoods Phenomenon: Does it Threaten Atlantic City?' [interview with Michael 'Mickey' Brown, Foxwoods President and CEO], *New Jersey Casino Journal* (July 1993), pp.11–12.

—, 'Interview with James Whelan, '*New Jersey Casino Journal* (January 1995), pp. 10–13.

—, 'Second Time around the Island' [interview with James Whelan] *New Jersey Casino Journal* (January 1995), pp. 10–13, 38–9, 44.

—, '1995: Time to Consolidate' [editorial], *New Jersey Casino Journal* (January 1995), p. 6.

—, 'What's News', *New Jersey Casino Journal* (January 1995), p. 21.

—, 'Wynn, Trump Vie for 13 Atlantic City Casino', *New Jersey Casino Journal* (January 1995), pp. 30, 48.

—, 'Let's Kill Two Canards', *New Jersey Casino Journal* (March 1995), p. 6.

—, 'Atlantic City Redevelopment Update', *Press of Atlantic City*, 4 December 1995, p. C1.

—, 'Playing Monopoly Big Time', *New Jersey Casino Journal* (May 1996).

—, 'The Casino Association of New Jersey: R.I.P.', *Casino Journal* (January 1997), p. 37.

—, 'What's News', *Casino Journal* (January 1997), p. 8.

—, 'Food Operations', *Michael Pollock's Gaming Industry Observer*, 2:5 (17 March 1997).

—, 'From Wall Street to the Boardwalk: Success Gets Measured in Different Ways', *Michael Pollack's Gaming Industry Observer, Atlantic City Edition*, 2:9 (May 1997), p. 20.

—, 'Best Gaming Employers: Harrah's Receives Recognition for Demonstrating Link between Morale, Bottom Line', *Michael Pollack's Gaming Industry Observer*, 29 January 1998.

—, 'Win per Employee Rises; So Does Emphasis on Full-Time Employment', *Michael Pollack's Gaming Industry Observer*, 5 February 1999.

—, 'Harrah's Structure Gets 'A' from Academicians, Analysts', *Michael Pollack's Gaming Industry Observer*, 26 November 1999.

—, 'Diversity', *The Herald* (Atlantic City High School Yearbook, 1999), p. 8.

—, 'Colony Paid Fair Price for Aging Resorts Property', *Michael Pollack's Gaming Industry Observer*, 4 December 2000.

—, 'Who Will Feel Borgata's Bite?', *Michael Pollack's Gaming Industry Observer*, 6 August 2001.

—, 'ACPD Diversity: High-Level Concern', *Press of Atlantic City*, 8 February 2002, p. A8.

—, 'Borgata Analysis: Old Definitions Useless in New Era', *Michael Pollack's Gaming Industry Observer*, 2 December 2002.

—, 'New Jersey Update ... Casino Closings Offered Good News for Atlantic City at Important Moment', *Michael Pollack's Gaming Industry Observer*, 17 July 2006.

—, 'Corporate Trends ...The New Breed of Acquirers: Is a Good Deal for Investors A Good Deal for Industry?', *Michael Pollack's Gaming Industry Observer*, 16 October 2006.

—, 'Layoffs at Tropicana Raise Serious Questions for Atlantic City' [editorial], *Press of Atlantic City*, 20 June 2007.

—, 'Tropicana Makeover on Hold for Now', *TMC Net*, 17 August 2007, http://www.tmcnet.com/usubmit/2007/08/17/2871015.htm (accessed 16 October 2007).

Anson, R. S., 'Are Casinos a Bad Bet?' *Saturday Review* (June 1980), pp. 28–33.

Associated Press, 'Top Court Gives OK to Funds for Tunnel', *Press of Atlantic City*, 3 August 1999.

—, 'Wynn's 30-Story Mirage Shadows Casinos in Las Vegas', *Press of Atlantic City*, 19 November 1989, p. 19, Marketplace p. F1.

—, 'Trump Recruits in Gary, A Potential Casino City', *Press of Atlantic City*, 10 December 1989, p. A10.

—, 'Resorts Files its Reorganization Plan', *Press of Atlantic City*, 23 December 1989, p. B4.

—, 'Sands Casino to Close After 26 Years', 10 November 2006.

—, 'MGM Mirage Growth Mania Grips Atlantic City Casinos', 20 July 2007, available online at http://www.advfn.com/news_Growth-mania-grips-Atlantic-City-casinos_21531491.html (accessed 16 October 2007).

Atlantic City–Brigantine Connector Project, *Community Connection Bulletin* (July 1999), Transportation-Tunnel Subject File, Heston Room, Atantic City Free Public Library.

Atlantic City Casino Association (ACCA), *Annual Report*(s) (Atlantic City, NJ: Atlantic City Casino Association, 1985–9).

—, *News and Views*, 1:6 (November 1986).

Atlantic City Casino Hotel Association (ACCHA), *Annual Report*(s) (Atlantic City, NJ: Atlantic City Casino Hotel Association, 1982–4).

Atlantic City Charter Study Commission, *Atlantic City on the Brink of Survival* (Atlantic City, NJ: Atlantic City Charter Study Commission, 1976).

Atlantic City Convention and Visitor's Association (ACCVA), *The New Atlantic City Convention Center: America's New Northeast Business Address* [brochure] (1–3 May 1997).

Atlantic City Corridor Project, 'The Gateway to Economic Prosperity' [poster], The Corridor Subject File, Heston Room, Atlantic City Free Public Library.

Atlantic City Free Public Library guide: 'Proposed A.C. Casino-Hotels' (as of 5/1/1979), Casinos Subject File, Heston Room, Atlantic City Free Public Library.

Atlantic City High School, *The Herald* [Atlantic City High School Yearbook] (Atlantic City, NJ: Atlantic City High School 1979–2000).

Atlantic City Memory Webpage, http://iloveac.com/memory.php (accessed 7 January 2007).

Atlantic City Project Oral History Interviews (ACPOHI), MS J. R. Karmel, Heston Room, Atlantic City Free Public Library.

Atlantic County Chamber of Commerce, *Membership Bulletin*, May 1977, Chamber of Commerce Subject File, Heston Room, Atlantic City Free Public Library.

—, *Gambling's Impact 1976–1990* [brochure] (November 1991).

Atlantic County Department of Planning, *Growth Trends Report: Atlantic County, NJ* (Atlantic County, NJ: Atlantic County Department of Planning, 4th quarter, 1981).

—, *1988 Growth Trends* (Atlantic County, NJ: Atlantic County Department of Planning, 1988).

Atlantic County Department of Planning and Economic Development (ACDPED), *Atlantic County Master Plan* (Atlantic County, NJ: Department of Planning and Economic Development, 2000).

Atlantic County Office of Policy, Planning and Economic Development (ACOPPED), *Growth Trends: Atlantic County, NJ 1993–1994 Annual Issue* (Atlantic City, NJ: ACCOPED,, 1994).

Baker, A., 'Tourism Commission Renews Opposition to Slots In Md.', *The Dispatch* (Ocean City, MD), 10 August 2007, available online at http://www.mdcoastdispatch. com/article.php?cid=30&id=1120 (accessed 16 October 2007).

Ball, K., 'Q & A with Mark Juliano', *Trump Magazine* (Spring 2006), p. 56.

Barlas, T., 'Gaming's Reach: Real People, Real lives ... Five Local Portraits', *Press of Atlantic City*, 26 May 1998, pp. A6–A7.

—, 'MGM Buys Mirage: Bombastic Return Ends like a Mirage: Wynn's Proposals Brought Hope, But No Construction', *Press of Atlantic City* 7 March 2000, p. A3.

Barnes, T., 'Board Ready to Roll the State of Gambling', *Pittsburgh Post-Gazette*, 26 July 2004, p. A-1.

Bary, A., 'Rolling the Dice: Will Borgata Rejuvenate Atlantic City?', *Barron's*, 21 July 2003, pp. 20–4.

Berns, D., 'Casino Consolidation: Raising the Stakes', *Las Vegas Review-Journal*, 9 January 2005, p. 29A.

Binkley, C. 'Atlantic City Gets a Vegas Makeover – First New Casino in 13 Years Spurs Push for Hipper Gamblers; Next, an Imax at the Tropicana', *Wall Street Journal*, 26 June 2003, p. D1.

Bontempo, D., 'The Merchant of Venice', *Casino Connection* 2:4 (April 2005), p. 28, available online at http://www.casinoconnectionac.com/articles/The_Merchant_of_Venice (accessed 11 October 2007).

—, 'It's No Bluff! Poker Comes to the Atlantic City Boardwalk', *New Jersey Casino Journal* (June 1993), pp. 10–12.

Brand, J., 'Casino Labor Strike / Jackson Motivated Wet, Weary Pickets In Atlantic City', *Press of Atlantic City*, 23 October 2004, p. B1.

Brown, M., 'The Human Factor', *Casino Journal* (May 1998), pp. 79–82.

—, 'Labor Pains', *Casino Journal* (May 1998), pp. 84–5.

Bureau of Economic Research, Rutgers, the State University of New Jersey, *Limitations in the Workplace: A Survey & Study of Atlantic City Casinos* (New Brunswick, NJ: Rutgers University, 1998).

Busler, M., 'Langford Has the Opportunity to Unite Atlantic City' [editorial], *Press of Atlantic City*, 19 November 2001, p. A11.

Caesar's Boardwalk Regency, 'Press Release', 28 April 1989, Caesar's, Subject File, Heston Room, Atlantic City Free Public Library.

Caesar's Casino Hotel, 'Fact Sheet' [on its new garage], 1990, Caesar's Subject File, Heston Room, Atlantic City Free Public Library.

Casiello, N., Jr., B. Aaron and K. Shanon, 'Regulatory Relaxation: New Legislation Aimed at Reducing Red Tape', *New Jersey Casino Journal* (January 1995).

Casino Association of New Jersey (CANJ), *The 1990s – Promise of a New Decade: 1989 Annual Report* (Atlantic City, NJ: CANJ, 1989).

Casino Reinvestment Development Authority (CRDA), *Annual Report* (Atlantic City, NJ: CRDA, 1986).

—, 'Corridor Approved as New Gateway for Atlantic City: Governor Hails Resort's 'New Front Door' [press release], 1993, Convention Center Subject File, Heston Room, Atlantic City Free Public Library.

—, *The Rebirth of a City: 1996 Annual Report – Casino Reinvestment Development Authority*, (Atlantic City, NJ: CRDA, 1997).

—, *1997 Annual Report* (Atlantic City, NJ: CRDA, 1998).

Chu, K., 'Gulf Coast Casinos Hit Revenue Jackpot', *USA Today*, 1 August 2007.

Citron, S., 'Atlantic City's Hot Makeover', Baltimore (July 2005), pp. 72–6.

City of Atlantic City, *Atlantic City: Building for Tomorrow* (Atlantic City, NJ: Atlantic City Department of Planning and Development, 1991).

—, *Atlantic City Report* (s), (Atlantic City, NJ: City of Atlantic City 1994–2003).

—, *Developer's Package 1999* (Atlantic City, NJ: City of Atlantic City Planning and Development Division, 1999), pp. 8, 13.

Collins, D. 'Casinos Dominate Regional Employment Scene', *The Day* (New London, CT), 23 February 1997.

Committee to Re-build Atlantic City (CRAC), *Help Yourself. Help Atlantic City. Help New Jersey* [brochure] (Atlantic City, NJ, 1976).

Council of Compulsive Gambling of New Jersey, Inc., 'Correlation between Gambling and Bankruptcy Holding Strong' [press release, 23 August 2001].

DeAngelis, M., 'Casino Labor Strike: Local 54 Deal Brings Welcome Quiet to Boardwalk', *Press of Atlantic City*, 3 November 2004, p. C1.

DeHaven, J., 'Gamblers Betting Less on Atlantic City', *Star-Ledger*, 12 June 2007, p. 60.

DeLuca, D., 'The New Sounds of Atlantic City – Promoters are Bringing in Rock and Hip-Hop Acts such as Eminem to revive the Resort's Dowdy Image', *Philadelphia Inquirer*, 10 July 2005.

Demetriou, A., et. al.,*The Atlantic City Master Plan* (Office of Angelos C. Demetriou, A.I.A., 1978).

DiStephan, D., 'Culture Shock Stuns Foreign Workers Recruited by Trump', *Press of Atlantic City*, 20 March 1990, p. C1.

—, 'Whelan Sees "Demoralized" A.C.', *Press of Atlantic City*, 16 April 1990, p. C1.

Donohue, J., D. Heneghan and J. Froonjian, 'Casinos, Politicians Hail Perskie Nomination', *Press of Atlantic City*, 23 August 1990.

Economic Research Associates, *Impact of Casino Gambling on the Redevelopment Potential of the Uptown Urban Renewal Site and on the Economy of Atlantic City* (Atlantic City, NJ: Economic Research Associates, 1976).

Faherty, T., 'MGM Buys Mirage: Mirage and MGM Merge in Atlantic City', *Press of Atlantic City*, 7 March 2000, p. A3.

Florin, K., 'Indian Gambling Has Become Major Force in Industry', *The Day*, 20 September 2002.

—, 'Every Square Foot Adds Up to Profit at Mohegan Sun, Foxwoods', *The Day*, 1 January 2004, p. 1A.

Fowler, A., 'Mayor James Usry Standing Tall in Atlantic City', *Black New Jersey* (June 1987), pp. 1, 3.

Frelinghysen, R. P., 'What Has Gone Wrong in the Plan?', *New York Times*, 19 October 1986, [New Jersey] p. 26.

Froonijian, J., 'Taj Saps Casino Workers/Hearings Check Labor Shortage', *Press of Atlantic City*, 21 March 1990, p .A1.

Gambling Study Commission, *Report to the Governor and Legislature*, 5 February 1973 (Trenton, NJ: New Jersey General Assembly, 1973), Heston Room, Atlantic City Free Public Library.

—, *Public Hearing Before Senate Judiciary and Assembly State Government Committee on Senate Concurrent Resolutions 2011, 2012, & 2013 and Assembly Concurrent Resolutions 2015, 2016, 2017, 11 April 1973* (Trenton, NJ: New Jersey General Assembly, 1973), Heston Room, Atlantic City Free Public Library.

—, *Public Hearing before Assembly Judiciary, Law, Public Safety & Defense Committee on Assembly Concurrent Resolution No. 128* [on referendum to amend constitution for gambling] (Trenton, NJ: New Jersey General Assembly 1974), Heston Room, Atlantic City Free Public Library.

Gordon A., 'Crime War Waged in Atlantic City', *New York Times*, 16 January 1949.

Gordon, J., 'Gambling on Family Fun', *New York Times*, 5 October 2003; p. 14CN.

Greater Atlantic City Convention and Visitor's Bureau, 'Atlantic City's $1 Billion Renaissance' [press release], 14 December 1993, Convention Center Subject File, Heston Room, Atlantic City Free Public Library.

Grimsley, K. D., 'Tourists Gamble Closer to Home: Business Is Brisk at Casinos Not Dependent on Air Travel', *Washington Post*, 30 September 2001, p. A08.

Gros, R., 'Junkets: Bang for Your Bucks', *New Jersey Casino Journal* (June 1989), pp. 10–13, 68.

—, 'The Grass is Greener: Human Resource Departments Face the Taj Mahal Challenge', *New Jersey Casino Journal* (January 1990), pp. 20–2.

—, 'Where Have All the Players Gone?', *New Jersey Casino Journal* (July 1990), pp. 32–9.

—, 'Casinos in Crisis', *New Jersey Casino Journal* (September 1990), pp. 15–30.

—, 'Casino Association Forms Purchasing Cooperative', *New Jersey Casino Journal*, (June 1992), p. 8.

—, 'CRDA's Nick Amato Describes Agency's New Purpose' *New Jersey Casino Journal* (July 1992), pp. 10–11, 22.

—, 'Gaming's Greatest Comeback: Donald Trump's Amazing Turnaround' [interview with Donald Trump], *New Jersey Casino Journal* (September 1992), pp. 14–21, 42–3.

—, 'What's Going on in Gaming?' *New Jersey Casino Journal* (November 1992), pp. 10–25.

—, 'Going Global: New Castle Marketing Team Refocuses Efforts to Include the International Arena', *New Jersey Casino Journal* (February 1994), pp. 20–1.

—, 'The Heartbeat of the Taj', *New Jersey Casino Journal* (May 1994), pp. 12–13.

—, 'Is Atlantic City Blowing its Very Last Chance?', *New Jersey Casino Journal* (March 1995), pp. 70–7.

—, 'Kiss and Make Up', *New Jersey Casino Journal* (January 1996), p. 34.

—, 'The Light at the End of the Tunnel', *New Jersey Casino Journal* (March 1996), pp. 14–22, 27.

—, 'Donald Trump: King of the Realm', *New Jersey Casino Journal* (May 1996), pp. 10–19, 42.

—, 'Just a Day at the Beach … Sort of', *Casino Journal* (March 1998), pp. 76–7.

Gros, R., M. Epifano and G. Schnorius, 'Setting the Tables', *New Jersey Casino Journal* (November 1993), pp. 14–17.

Gros R., and G. Fine, 'Continuous Improvement: Showboat's Steady Progress Yields Dynamic Results', *New Jersey Casino Journal* (February 1993).

Hailu, Y., and A. Mammo and A. Kline, *A Chartbook of Social and Health Indicators in New Jersey* (Trenton, NJ: New Jersey Department of Health and Senior Services, 2003).

Hamilton, R., 'Tribe Invests Downtown in an Old Industrial City', *New York Times*, 15 January 2003, p. C5.

Harrah's Entertainment Inc., 'Profile of Competition' [business memo], 'Casinos – General' Subject File, Heston Room, Atlantic City Free Public Library.

—, *Setting the Standard: 2002 Annual Report* (2002).

—, 'This is What Makes Harrah's A Place Like Nowhere Else' [advertisement], *New Jersey Casino Journal* (February 1994), p. 31.

Harrison, J., 'Laying it on the Table: What Does the Comeback of Table Games Mean to Atlantic City?', *Casino Connection*, 2:3 (March 2005), pp. 24–7, available online at http://www.casinoconnectionac.com/articles/Laying_It_On_The_Table (accessed 14 October 2007).

Hasson, H., Oral history interview, 22 March 2007.

Haught, J. S., 'Atlantic City's Casino Strike Is Over / Agreement Reached Late Monday', *Press of Atlantic City*, 2 November 2004, p. A1.

Hedges, C., 'Casino Boss Who Started With a Bucket of Coins', *Borgata Style*, 'The Borgata' subject file, Heston Room, Atlantic City Free Public Library.

Heneghan, D. 'Griffin-Trump Deal Turns Executive Revolving Door', *Press of Atlantic City*, 30 November 1988, p. E1.

—, 'Griffin Buys Resorts', *Press of Atlantic City*, 16 November 1988, p. A1.

—, 'Union Has No Place In Atlantis Hearings', *Press of Atlantic City*, 26 March 1989, p. C2.

—, 'Atlantis Sold, Trump Will Close Elsinore's Casino', *Press of Atlantic City*, 16 April 1989.

—, 'Trump Hits Griffin's Plan for Restructuring Resorts', *Press of Atlantic City*, 14 November 1989.

—, 'Taj Will "Trump" All: Huge Casino Drawing Close to Completion', *Press of Atlantic City*, 3 December 1989.

—, 'And Casinos Floated in a Sea of 'Junk', *Press of Atlantic City*, 31 December 1989, p. F1.

—, 'Casinos Warn Moonlighting Workers: Claridge, Bally's Park Place: Defectors to Taj Will be Fired', *Press of Atlantic City*, 24 January 1990.

—, 'Taj Will Reshape Market: A.C. Casinos Also Fearful of "Gary Gaming"', *Press of Atlantic City*, 30 January 1990, p. C6.

—, 'Casino Commission Cuts Staff, Will Save $1.35 million', *Press of Atlantic City*, 17 February 1990.

—, 'Resort's License Renewed Vote Unanimous Despite Troubles', *Press of Atlantic City*, 22 February 1990, p. A1.

—, 'Trump Opens Taj with a Flourish / After Tour, Florio Vows to Help City', *Press of Atlantic City*, 6 April 1990, p. A1.

—, 'Taj Slots Shut Down Indefinitely/Major Modifications Planned for Casino', *Press of Atlantic City*, 7 April 1990, p. A1.

—, 'Taj Wins $4.9 Million in 6 days/Overall Casino Win up 3.6% for Week', *Press of Atlantic City*, 10 April 1990, p. A1.

—, 'A.C. Casino Industry Struggling, Exec. Says', *Press of Atlantic City*, 2 August 1990, p. A1.

—, 'Taj Squeezing Trump, Other Casinos/AC Competition, Bleak Economy Contribute to Weak Win Figures', *Press of Atlantic City*, 5 September 1990.

—, 'Hundreds Face Layoffs as Casinos Feel the Squeeze', *Press of Atlantic City*, 18 September 1990.

—, 'The Opening of Two Casinos Hikes Revenues in Las Vegas, but New Facility Had No Similar Impact in A.C.', *Press of Atlantic City*, 24 October 1990, p. A1.

—, 'Taj Officials Promise Stability/But CCC Wants to See Proof That Restructuring Will Work', *Press of Atlantic City*, 4 December 1990.

—, 'Casinos End Difficult Year With a Little Hope For Better 1991: Opening of Taj Stressed Industry', *Press of Atlantic City*, 27 December 1990, p. C1.

—, 'Minorities, Women Push Action to Achieve Casino Set-Aside Goals', *Press of Atlantic City*, 15 December 1992, p. C1.

Heneghan D., and D. Spatz, 'Trump Opens Taj With a Flourish/After Tour Florio Vows to Help City', *Press of Atlantic City* , 6 April 1990.

HERE Local 54, 'Testimony of Hotel Employees and Restaurant Employees International Union (HERE) and HERE Local 54', [videotape] for NGIS hearings, 21–22 January 1998.

Herriott, S., 'The Boardwalk Experience', *New Jersey Casino Journal* (January 1996), p. 20.

Herriott, S., and R. Gros, 'Acting Affirmatively: the Status of Minority and Women Employment is Improving ... But Is it at Anyone's Expense?', *New Jersey Casino Journal* (November 1995), pp. 16–20.

Hickey, B., 'Across the Bridge to Chelsea Heights', *Atlantic City Press*, 29 December 1998.

—, 'Westside's Story is Full of Good Memories', *Press of Atlantic City*, 15 December 1998.

Horan, L., 'Connecticut Indian Tribe Set to Open Gambling Casino', *Reuters*, 13 February 1992.

Hospitals Subject File, Heston Room, Atlantic City Free Public Library.

Hsu, S. S., 'Mississippi's Reversal of Fortune; In Casino Towns, Aid and Speculation Fuel a Post-Katrina Boom', *Washington Post*, 10 March 2006, p. A01.

Johnson. K., 'With Cash Rolling in, Atlantic City Raises Stakes', *New York Times*, 24 June 1996, pp. A1, B5.

Johnston, D. C., 'Coming Back to Atlantic City; Welcome Set for Wynn's Las Vegas-Scale Project', *New York Times*, 27 June 1995.

Kent, B., 'Groundbreaking Is Set for Atlantic City Tunnel', *New York Times*, 1 November 1998.

Kershenblatt, B., 'The Casinos of the Thirties: You Had to Know Uncle Dan', *The Bulletin* (Philadelphia), 23 October 1980.

Key, P., 'Boardwalk Borrowing: Are Casinos Floating Debt Now Only to Founder Later?', *Press of Atlantic City*, 21 May 1989, Marketplace p. 1.

—, 'Taj Mahal Works Hard for Workforce', *Press of Atlantic* City, 29 November 1989, p. A13.

—, '"Destination Marketing" May Have its Day', *Press of Atlantic City*, 28 January 1990, p. BF19.

Kilborn, P., 'Casinos Revive a Town, but Poverty Persists', *New York Times*, 20 October 2002, p. 1.1.

Kinney, D., and J. Donohue, 'Both Sides Agree on $24 Billion Budget: Threat of Government Shutdown Keeps Lawmakers in Negotiations through the Day', *The Star-Ledger*, 1 July 2003, p. 1.

Kravitz, P., 'Pinky's Corner: Boardwalk vs. Marina District', *Atlantic City Weekly*, 22 March 2007, available online at http://www.acweekly.com/view.php?id=6187&issue_id=172 (accessed 16 October 2007).

Lalli, S., 'Fantasy becomes reality at Mirage', *New Jersey Casino Journal* (December 1989), pp. 48–52.

LaPolla, J., 'The Changing Face of Atlantic City: The New Immigrants', *Atlantic City Press*, 18 April 1993, p. A1.

Laymon, R., 'Theme Song: Taj Mahal Borrow's Disney's Theme-Park Techniques', *Press of Atlantic City*, 5 April 1990, p. A15.

Lee, D. P., 'The Casino Gamble: 25 Years Later, Atlantic City Casinos Brought Progress, But at a Price', *Press of Atlantic City*, 25 May 2003.

Legato, F., 'Harrah's and Showboat: A Marriage of Marketing', *Casino Journal* (May 1998), pp. 68–71.

Lesieur, Henry and Klein, Robert and Rimm, Marty, 'Pathological and Problem Gambling among New Jersey High School Students', [study conducted for the Council on Compulsive Gambling of New Jersey, Inc., Trenton, NJ].

Linsalata, P., 'Trump Claims Win over Sands', *Press of Atlantic City*, 21 March 1989, p. A1.

Linz, C., 'Unions Take Conventions Elsewhere / Cite Dirt, Crime Rate, Lack of Air Connections', *Press of Atlantic City*, 5 October 1988, p. B1.

—, 'Six Million Cost Reached on Final Tract for Convention Center', *Press of Atlantic City*, 6 October 1988, p. C2.

—, 'Inlet Project Passes Another Obstacle', *Press of Atlantic City*, 8 October 1988, p. A1.

—, 'Trump Shifts Etess to Taj Mahal as Site Work Resumes', *Press of Atlantic City*, 22 December 1988, p. C8.

Linz, C.and K. Shelly, 'Chelsea Group Wants to Block Inlet Bonding', *Press of Atlantic City*, 30 September 1988, p. B1.

Lopez, S., 'In the Name of Her Father', *Time*, 14 July 1997.

Mansnerus, L., 'Great Expectations; Money Has Poured into Atlantic City. But a Second Wave, Ever Poised, Still Hasn't Broken', *New York Times*, 2 April 2000.

Marsden, J., 'Tribes Ripple Effect Muted: Report: Two Casinos Bring State One Job for Every Three of Theirs', *Hartford Courant*, 14 June 2007, available online at http://www.hotel-online.com/News/2007_Jun_14/k.HCG.1181839709.html (accessed 15 October 2007).

Martin, J., 'At Freedom's Edge: Liberty, Security and The Patriot Act', *Newark Star Ledger*, 28 August 2005.

'Mashantucket Pequot Gaming Enterprise Inc.', https://www.fundinguniverse.com/company-histories/Mashantucket-Pequot-Gaming-Enterprise-Inc-Company-History.html (accessed 15 October 2007).

McCoy, P., 'Senator to Seek a Ban on New Casinos in Atlantic City', *Press of Atlantic City*, 3 October 1989, p. A1.

McDevitt, C. R., 'From the Desk of C. Robert McDevitt' [letter to Local 54 employees], www.hereLocal54.org (accessed 14 October 2007).

McLaughlin, J., 'The Great Casino Experiment', *New Jersey Monthly* (June 1981), pp. 48–50, 96–100.

Mead, J., 'The Big Gamble', *New York Times*, 23 March 2003, p. 14.

Meister, A., *Casino City's Indian Gaming Industry Report* (Newton, MA: Casino City Press, 2006).

Micale, J., *Economic Impact Generated by a Typical New Large Scale Casino/Hotel* (Atlantic City, NJ: Atlantic City Department of Planning and Development, 1999).

Mississippi State Tax Commission, *Miscellaneous Tax Bureau Casino Gross Gaming Revenues*, available online at http://www.mstc.state.ms.us/taxareas/misc/gaming/stats/GamingGrossReveues.pdf (accessed 16 October 2007).

National Gambling Impact Study (NGIS) Commission, Testimony of Pierre Hollingsworth, 20 August 1997, available online at http://govinfo.library.unt.edu/ngisc/meetings/aug2097/aug20p10.html (accessed 11 October 2007).

—, *The National Gambling Impact Study Commission: Final Report* (Washington DC: NGIS, 1999), available online at http://govinfo.library.unt.edu/ngisc/ (accessed 11 October 2007).

New Jersey Casino Control Commission (NJCCC), *Annual Report*(s) (1978–2006).

—, *Housing Obligation of Atlantic City Casinos* [hearing proceedings], 22 July 1981 (Trenton, NJ: NJCCC, 1981).

—, *Personal and Confidential* [1986 brochure on applying for casino employee licenses], 'Casinos-General' Subject File, Heston Room, Atlantic City Free Public Library.

—, 'Annual Operating Statistics, 1978–1989', available online at http://www.state.nj.us/casinos/financia/histori/ (accessed 10 October 2007).

—, *Years of Change 1990–1994: A Report by the New Jersey Casino Control Commission* (Atlantic City, NJ: NJCCC, 1995).

—, *Casino Gambling in New Jersey: A Report to the National Gambling Impact Study Commission* (Atlantic City, NJ: NJCCC, January 1998).

—, 'Annual Operating Statistics, 1990–1999', available online at http://www.state.nj.us/casinos/financia/histori/ (accessed 10 October 2007).

—, 'Annual Operating Statistics, 2000–2006', available online at http://www.state.nj.us/casinos/financia/histori/ (accessed 10 October 2007).

—, 'CCC Announces June 2007 Casino Revenue' [press release], 10 July 2007, available online at http://www.state.nj.us/casinos/home/news/200706_revenue.pdf (accessed 16 October 2007).

—, 'Casino Control Commission – License Division Employment by Atlantic City Casino Licensees by Zip Code and License Category', http://www.state.nj.us/casinos/licens/licenrep/emp_casino_zip.html (accessed 16 October 2007).

New Jersey Department of Commerce and Economic Development, *An Economic Profile of Atlantic County* (Trenton, NJ: New Jersey Department of Commerce, 1982).

New Jersey Department of Labor, *Labor Market Information Review*, October 1978 (Atlantic City Labor Area).

—, *Growth Trends Report: Atlantic County, NJ* (Trenton, NJ: New Jersey Labor Department, 4th quarter, 1979).

—, *Atlantic County Wage Survey of Selected Occupations: Casino Versus Non-Casino Wages* (Trenton, NJ: New Jersey Department of Labor and Industry, Division of Planning and Research, 1980).

—, *Growth Trends Report: Atlantic County, NJ* (Trenton, NJ: New Jersey Department of Labor, 4th quarter, 1981).

—, *Growth Trends Report: Atlantic County, NJ* (Trenton, NJ: New Jersey Department of Labor, 4th quarter, 1982).

—, *Regional Labor Market Review, Atlantic Coastal Region: Atlantic, Cape May, Monmouth and Ocean Counties* (Trenton, New Jersey: New Jersey Department of Labor, 1984).

—, *Growth Trends Report: Atlantic County, NJ* (Trenton, NJ: New Jersey Department of Labor, 2nd quarter, 1989).

—, *Employment and the Economy: Atlantic Coastal Region 128* (Trenton, NJ: New Jersey Department of Labor, March 1998).

New Jersey General Assembly, *Public Hearing before the Senate and Assembly Judiciary Committees on Senate Concurrent Resolution No. 39 – Proposing a Constitutional Amendment to Permit the Legislature to Authorize the Operation of Gambling Games in Atlantic City and to License and Tax Such Operations*, 19 March 1970 (Trenton, NJ: New Jersey General Assembly, 1970), Heston Room, Atlantic City Free Public Library.

—, *Public Hearing before the Senate Judiciary Committee on Senate Concurrent Resolution No. 74 – Proposing to Amend the Constitution of the State of New Jersey to Permit the Legislature to Authorize by Law the Operation of Gambling games in Atlantic City*, 7 April 1971 (Trenton, NJ: New Jersey General Assembly, 1971), Heston Room, Atlantic City Free Public Library.

—, *Public Hearing before Assembly State Government and Federal and Interstate Relations Committee on ACR-126 (which Proposes an Amendment to the Constitution to Permit Gambling Casinos in Atlantic City)* (Trenton, NJ: New Jersey General Assembly, 1976).

—, *Casino Control Act* (Trenton, NJ: New Jersey General Assembly, 1977), available online at http://www.state.nj.us/casinos/actreg/act/ (accessed 10 October 2007).

—, *Public Hearing before Assembly Legislative Oversight Committee on the Licensing of Casino Employees*, 29 October 1979 (Trenton, NJ: New Jersey General Assembly, 1979).

—, *Public Hearing before Assembly Independent Authorities Committee: Current and Future Manpower Needs of the Casino Industry, the Availability of Qualified Casino Employees to Meet those Needs and the Impact on the Casino Employees Labor Pool* [hearing transcript] (Trenton, NJ: New Jersey General Assembly, 1990).

—, *Committee Meeting of the Senate Transportation Committee and Assembly Transportation and Communications Committee* [on] *Senate Bill No. 1948 and Assembly Bill No. 2798 (Testimony on the Proposal to "Increases New Jersey Transportation Trust Fund Authority*

Spending Cap by $200 Million for Fiscal Year 1998"), available online at http://www.njleg.state.nj.us/legislativepub/pubhear/041097t.htm (accessed 12 October 2007).

—, 'Testimony of James R. Hurley, Chairman, New Jersey Casino Control Commission, before the Subcommittee on Technology, Terrorism & Government Information, Senate Judiciary Committee', 23 March 1999, available online at http://judiciary.senate.gov/oldsite/32399jrh.htm (accessed 13 October 2007).

Norris, F. 'Bad Gamble: Trump Stock Falls Again', *New York Times*, 6 July 2007, p. C1.

Obst, U., 'The Slum Hispanics Call Home', *Press of Atlantic City*, 8 and 9 June 1981.

O'Donnell, J., *Trumped! The Inside Story of the Real Donald Trump* (New York: Simon & Schuster, 1991), pp. 15, 17, 22, 34, 123, 140–1.

Office of the Governor, 'Governor Breaks Ground for Atlantic City Tunnel: Cites Economic Benefits and Traffic Improvements from Project' [news release], 4 November 1998.

Oldroyd, J. W., *Master Plan, City of Absecon* (Pleasantville, NJ: Oldroyd Planning Group, 1993).

Olshan, J., 'Asian, Hispanic Populations up in County', *Atlantic City Press*, 10 March 2001.

—, 'Asian Population Grows Bigger, But Not Together: Culture, Language Are Community Barriers', *Atlantic City Press*, 25 March 2001, p. A1, A7.

Painton, P., 'Boardwalk of Broken Dreams', *Time*, 25 September 1989, pp. 64–9.

Parker, L., 'Abandoned Education: Tunica's Schools Struggle with Leftovers and Neglect', *APF Reporter* [Alicia Patterson Foundation], 18:2 (1997), available online at http://www.aliciapatterson.org/APF1802/Parker/Parker.html (accessed 15 October 2007).

Parmley, S., 'Some Question Columbia-Sussex' Management of the Tropicana Casino & Resort, Atlantic City', *Philadelphia Inquirer*, 10 August 2007, available online at http://www.hotel-online.com/News/PR2007_3rd/Aug07_TropAC.html.

Parry, W. 'No Deal for Trump's Casino Company', *USA Today*, 2 July 2007.

Peele, T, 'Westside Residents Unsure of Neighborhood's Future', *Press of Atlantic City*, 19 February 1996.

—, 'Victors View the Atlantic City Election Results as a Mandate', *Press of Atlantic City*, 14 May 1998, p. C1.

—, 'Richness of Diversity Defines Lower Chelsea', *Press of Atlantic City*, 31 December 1998.

—, 'Atlantic City Votes on Deal With MGM', *Press of Atlantic City*, 6 January 2000.

Pennsylvania Gaming Control Board, 'Gaming Revenues' [week of 25 June–1 July], available online on http://www.pgcb.state.pa.us/gaming_revenue/2007_06–25_gaming_rev.pdf (accessed 16 October 2007).

Pennsylvania General Assembly, *The General Assembly of Pennsylvania House Bill No. 2330 Session of 2004, Amending Title 4 (Amusements) of the Pennsylvania Consolidated Statutes, Authorizing Certain Racetrack and Other Gaming; Providing for the Powers and Duties of the Pennsylvania Gaming Control Board; Conferring Powers and Imposing Duties on the Department of Revenue, the Department of Health, the Office of Attorney General, the Pennsylvania State Police and the Pennsylvania Liquor Control Board; Establishing the State Gaming Fund, the Pennsylvania Race Horse Development, Fund, the Pennsylvania Gaming Economic Development and Tourism Fund, the Compulsive Problem Gambling Treatment Fund and the Property Tax Relief Fund, Providing for Enforcement; Imposing Penalties; Making Appropriations; and Making Related Appeals* (2004), available online at http://www.pgcb.state.pa.us/legislation/HB2330P4272.pdf (accessed 16 October 2007).

Petersen, I., 'Homeless, Not Scandal, Shakes Up Atlantic City', *New York Times*, 11 November 2001.

—, 'Metro Briefing New Jersey: Atlantic City; Whelan Concedes Election', *New York Times*, 14 November 2001, p. D-8.

Philly Roads, *Atlantic City–Brigantine Connector: Historical Overview*, http://www.phillyroads.com/roads/ac-brigantine/ (accessed 12 October 2007).

Plume, J., 'Mississippi Casinos Approach a Defining Moment as "Las Vegas" of the South' and 'Mississippi Casinos Evolve Quickly', *Casino Journal* (May 1998), pp. 44–56.

Pollack, A., 'Arthur Goldberg, Builder of Casino Empire, Dies at 58', *New York Times*, 20 October 2000.

Powers, S., 'Casino Revenue Pumps Up Government Coffers', *Coast Business Journal* (Gulfport, MS), 12 August 1996.

Pulley, B., 'As Atlantic City Thrives, Whitman May Call a Casino Bluff', *New York Times*, 29 June 1996.

Rao, M., 'Tropicana Dealers Vote for UAW's Representation', *Press of Atlantic City*, 27 August 2007, available online at http://www.pressofatlanticcity.com/news/local/atlantic_city/story/7498349p-7394926c.html (accesed 16 October 2007).

Razler, D., 'Atlantic County: Tunnel Groundbreaking: A Harbinger of Casinos "Second Wave" – 1998 Year in Review', *Press of Atlantic City*, 28 December 1998.

Rehrmann, L., 'New A.C. High School Planning Continues', *Press of Atlantic City*, 18 October 1988, p. B4.

Reidy, C., 'Rolling the Dice: Pequot Casino Opens with Hopes of Giving Connecticut Luck', *Boston Globe*, 16 February 1992, p. 12.

Reifer, M., 'It's Crunch Time in Fun City', *New Jersey Casino Journal* (May 1986), p. 17.

—, 'Justice and the Regulators', *New Jersey Casino Journal* (February 1988), pp. 34–5.

—, 'Casino Reinvestment Revisited: A Sacrifice of Principle', *New Jersey Casino Journal* (June 1988), p. 19.

—, 'A How-Not-To Guide to State & Local Management of Casino Gaming or How "Moral Opprobrium" can Falsify Facts and Preclude Rational Thought', *New Jersey Casino Journal* (July 1988), pp. 17–19, 82–6.

—, 'Casino Industry Profitability: The Myth and Reality', *New Jersey Casino Journal* (October 1988), pp. 16–18.

—, 'Who Really Killed the Atlantis?', *New Jersey Casino Journal* (May 1989), pp. 14–18.

—, 'A Bad Idea for a Worse Objective', *New Jersey Casino Journal* (October 1989), pp. 24–5.

—, 'CRDA: The Casino Reinvestment Obligation Revisited', *New Jersey Casino Journal* (December 1989), pp. 10–11, 24.

—, 'The Wave of the Future?', *New Jersey Casino Journal* (August 1992), p. 6.

—, 'Time for a New Deal', *New Jersey Casino Journal* (August 1993).

—, 'Atlantic City Under Whitman: Reason to Believe', *New Jersey Casino Journal* (February 1994).

Reifer M., and A. Fine, '1993: Year In Review', *New Jersey Casino Journal* (February 1994).

Reuters, 'Harrah's to open Biloxi Margaritaville casino' 15 May 2007, available online at http://www.topix.net/forum/com/het/TD4532QRK7B1U17OO (accessed 16 October 2007).

Rivlin, G., 'Atlantic City Aiming Higher As Casinos Slip', *New York Times*, 19 March 2007, Metropolitan Section 1.

— 'Casinos Booming in Katrina's Wake as Cash Pours in', *New York Times*, 16 July 2007, Business p. 1.

Roffman, M. B., 'Casino Gaming in the United States: Las Vegas on a Roll, Atlantic City Trouble Ahead with a Capital 'T', *New Jersey Casino Journal* (June 1988), pp. 30–1.

Rose, J. N., 'Casinos Stuck under New Anti-Terrorism Laws', http://www.gamblingandthelaw.com/columns.html, 2005 (accessed 13 October 2007).

Rosenberg, A., 'Where Naughty is Looking Nice', *Philadelphia Inquirer*, 8 June 2003, p. B01.

Ross P., and S. P Haven, 'The Little City That Could', *New York Magazine*, 20 June 1977, pp. 34–40.

Rubeli, P., 'A Bill of Rights for the Atlantic City Casino Industry', *New Jersey Casino Journal* (December 1988), pp. 20–1.

Russell, D., and L. DiMeo, 'Atlantic City's Bet on Gambling: Who Won What?', *Atlantic City* (January 1987).

Russell, K., 'Paul Harvey: The Good Shepard of Mississippi's Gaming Billions', *Mississippi Business Journal*, 5 May 1997.

—, 'Survival of Fittest Emerges as Theme of State Casino Market', *Mississippi Business Journal*, 5 May 1997.

Russell, T., 'Region Enjoys Diversified Growth', *Press of Atlantic City*, 21 June 1998.

Ryan, J., *A Chartbook of County Social & Health Indicators* (Trenton, NJ: New Jersey Department of Health and Senior Services, 1996).

Saharko, P., 'Gormley Proposes Tax Breaks for Casinos', *Press of Atlantic City*, 17 February 2001.

Sanders, P., and D. K. Berman, 'Harrah's Accepts Buyout Offer, Proceeds With Internal Revamp', *Wall Street Journal*, 20 December 2006, p. C6.

Sataline, S., 'Atlantic City Reinvents Itself as Vegas East ; Faced with Competition, Resort Town Embarks on Biggest Building Boom in 24 Years. But Will it Work?', *Christian Science Monitor*, 22 August, 2002, p. 3.

Schwarz S., 'Atlantic City Had a Casino – 81 Years Ago!' *Press of Atlantic City*, 19 August 1979.

—, 'A Bad Risk: Casinos Don't Pay Off In Atlantic City, N.J., "Experiment"', *Wall Street Journal*, 28 March 1986.

—, 'Wynn Dumps $110 million Claridge Deal', *Press of Atlantic City*, 26 October 1988, p. A1.

Shabazz, K., 'Jackson Came, He Saw and He Conquered', *Black News and Events*, 3–16 June, 1988.

Shelly, K., '$3.9 Million Taj Tax Check Delivered to Whelan', *Press of Atlantic City*, 6 November 1990, p. B1.

Shields, J., and S. Parmley, 'Why Trump Lost Gamble on Slot Site', *Philadelphia Inquirer*, 2 February 2007, p. A01.

Shopes, R., 'Atlantic City's Chelsea Flourishes with Ethnic Change', *Atlantic City Press*, 4 August 1997, p. A1.

Siegel R. (host), 'Jersey Shutdown Hits Resort Casinos', *All Things Considered*, National Public Radio, 5 July 2006.

Sledek, S. and M., Collection of Sands Casino Memorabilia, Heston Room, Atlantic City Free Public Library.

Sless, B., 'How Serious is the Casinos' Long-Term Debt Problem?', *New Jersey Casino Journal* (May 1989).

—, 'Comps Largest Expense After Salaries', *New Jersey Casino Journal* (September 1988), pp.16–17.

—, 'How Serious is the Casinos' Long-Term Debt Problem?', *New Jersey Casino Journal* (May 1989), pp. 26, 39.

Sloan, G., 'Atlantic City Stakes its Future on Rebuilding Plan', *USA Today*, 19 April 1993.

Slusher, G. M., *The Casino Gaming Industry and its Impact on Southern New Jersey* (Atlantic County, NJ: Atlantic County Division of Economic Development, 1991).

Smothers, R., 'Convention Center Leads Effort To Broaden the Revival of a City', *New York Times*, 3 May 1997, p. 25.

South Jersey Transit Authority (SJTA), 'Atlantic City–Brigantine Connector Grand Opening July 27, 2001' [press release], 27 July 2001.

—, *2001 Annual Report* (Atlantic City, NJ: SJTA, 2002).

—, 'Atlantic City Visit-Trips, 2006 Annual', available online at www.sjta.org (accessed 14 October 2007.

Spatz, D., 'In Hyde and Etess, Casino World Has Lost Two Class Acts', *Press of Atlantic City*, 12 October 1989, p. C6.

—, 'Bally's Out to Soften Taj's Effect/Plans Lineup to Pull Customers Its Way', *Press of Atlantic City*, 3 March 1990.

Stockton Institute for Gaming Management at The Richard Stockton College of New Jersey (SIGMA), *Front-Line Employees in Atlantic City's Gaming Industry: Issues and Concerns* (Pomona, NJ: SIGMA, 2006), available online at http://intraweb.stockton.edu/eyos/page.cfm?siteID=114&pageID=2 (accessed 11 October 2007).

Strauss, R., 'Atlantic City Places Money on New Image; Casinos Refurbishing, Seeking Big Spenders', *Washington Post*, 21 July 2003, p. A.03.

Stutz, H., 'Mergers and Acquisitions: Harrah's Priority: Reduce Debt', *Las Vegas Review-Journal*, 21 December 2006.

Sullivan, J., and T. Moore, 'Slots Bill Aim: Pa. Gamblers Spend it Here', *Philadelphia Inquirer*, 27 June 2004.

Szasz, F., 'Quotes about History', *History News Network*, http://hnn.us/articles/1328.html (accessed 16 October 2007).

Tanfani, J, and R. Ellis, 'Some Folks Resist Inlet Home Razing', *Press of Atlantic City*, 26 November 1988, p. A1.

Trump, D., 'Trump Sounds Off', *Press of Atlantic City*, 28 May 1989, p. E1.

Tucker, A., 'Hurricane has Gone, as has Familiar Landscape of Biloxi', *Baltimore Sun*, 2 September 2005.

Turner, W. B, and S. M. Renner, *Atlantic City: Worthy of a Second Look* (New York: Saloman Brothers/United States Equity Research-Gaming, 1995).

Tuthill, M., 'Is Gambling Good for Business? You bet!', *Nation's Business*, August 1980.

United Auto Workers, 'Casino Workers Rally Aug. 9 to Support UAW Bargainers at Caesars' [news release], 8 August 2007, available online at http://www.uaw.com/news/newsarticle.cfm?ArtId=485 (accessed 16 October 2007).

United States Attorney's Office, District of New Jersey, 'Atlantic City Council President, Camden Councilman Plead Guilty to Extortion; Contractor Admits Drug Charges' [news release], 30 August 2006, available online at http://www.usdoj.gov/usao/nj/press/files/call0830_r.htm (accessed 16 October 2007).

United States: Uniform Crime Report – State Statistics from 1960–2006, available online at http://www.disastercenter.com/crime (accessed 11 October 2007).

United States Census Bureau, www.census.gov (accessed 11 October 2007).

Urgo, J., 'Law Lets Casinos Openly Offer Free Booze', *Philadelphia Inquirer*, 15 August 2002.

—, 'A.C. Casinos and Union Locked in for Long Battle', 16 October 2004, *Philadelphia Inquirer*, p. A01.

Vis, D., 'Comps Hurt A.C. Quest for New Hall', *Press of Atlantic City*, 22 August 1989, p. A1.

—, 'Atlantic City's New Convention Hall: An Investment in Debt Casino Owners, State Officials Agree Won't Pay for Itself', *Press of Atlantic City*, 27 August 1989, p. B1.

—, 'Publication Predicts Trouble for Trump', *Press of Atlantic City*, 7 February 1990, p. B1.

von Herrman, D., R. Ingram and W. C. Smith, 'Gaming in the Mississippi Economy: A Marketing, Tourism, and Economic Perspective' (University of Southern Mississippi, 2000), available online at http://www.usm.edu/dewd/pdf/Gamingstudy.pdf (accessed 15 October 2007).

Waldman, H., 'Slot Money Would Boost Poor Cities', *Hartford Courant*, 4 February 1993, p. A1.

Waldman, H., and M. Jackman, 'Attorney General Rules Slot Machine Pact is Legal: Ruling Backs Weicker's Slot-Machine Pact With Tribe', *Hartford Courant*, 12 February 1993.

Weinert, J., "98 Meant Business: Casinos Focused on Projects and Profits', *Press of Atlantic City*, 27 December 1998, p. F1.

—, 'Casino Notes', *Press of Atlantic City*, 8 August 1999, p. F1.

—, 'Casinos Expect Financial Hit in Wake of Attacks', *Press of Atlantic City*, 13 September 2001.

—, 'Week Later, Casinos Still Feel Pinch', *Press of Atlantic* City, 19 September 2001.

—, 'A.C. Not Envying Las Vegas These Days', *Press of Atlantic City*, 7 October 2001.

—, 'Casinos Hope for Mayoral Support', *Press of Atlantic City*, 18 November 2001, p. A1.

—, 'Borgata Building Team to Manage A.C. Resort', *Press of Atlantic City*, 7 December 2001.

—, 'Small City Home to Mighty Industry', *Press of Atlantic City*, 28 May 2002.

—, 'Budget Plan Pounds Casinos: Industry Vows to Fight $135 Million in New Taxes on Revenues, Comps', *Press of Atlantic City*, 4 February 2003, p. A1.

—, 'New Gaming Hall Will Make Debut in the Wee Hours', *Press of Atlantic City*, 2 July 2003, p. A1.

—, 'Borgata No Help to Casino Revenue', *Press of Atlantic City*, 13 August 2003, p. A1.

Weinberg, D., 'The $200 Million Season', *New Jersey Monthly*, March 1979.

Wittkowski, D., 'Atlantic City Airport Stunted by Few, Costly Flights', *Press of Atlantic City*, 5 September 1995.

—, 'Suit Against A.C. Tunnel Dismissed', *Press of Atlantic City*, 23 July 1999.

—, 'Wall Street Lukewarm to Bond for A.C. Tunnel Financing', *Press of Atlantic City*, 7 May 1999, p. E1.

—, 'A.C. Tunnel Hits New Roadblock', *Press of Atlantic City*, 20 December 2000.

—, 'Atlantic City Expressway Tunnel Connector Opening/Tunnel Opens Finally/Ho Hum Celebration for Atlantic City Road Beset by Delays', *Press of Atlantic City*, 1 August 2001.

—, 'Year Later, Tunnel on Road to Success', *Press of Atlantic City*, 31 July 2002.

—, 'Strike Splits Casinos' Win: Five of Seven Struck Casinos Show Decline – Five Non-Walkout Houses Show Increases', *Press of Atlantic City*, 11 November 2004, p. A1.

—, 'Harrah's–Caesar's Merger Gets OK From Casino Board', *Press of Atlantic* City, 25 May 2005, p. A1.

—, 'Philadelphia Slot Parlors Put Dent in Atlantic City Revenue', *Press of Atlantic City*, 10 February 2007, p. A1.

—, 'Electronic Table Games Coming to Atlantic City', *Press of Atlantic City*, 19 July 2007, available online at http://www.pressofatlanticcity.com/top_three/story/7491875p-7387519c.html (accessed 16 October 2007).

—, 'Wynn Eyes Atlantic City for New Casino', *Press of Atlantic City*, 10 August 2007.

Yung III, W., 'Layoffs Ensure Trop's Continued Success' [letter to the editor], *Press of Atlantic City*, 27 June 2007.

Zielbauer, P., 'Study Finds Pequot Business Lifts Economy', *New York Times*, 29 November 2000, p. B5.

Secondary Sources

Alcamo, J., *Atlantic City: Behind the Tables* (Grand Rapids, MI: Gollehon, 1991).

Austin, S. W., and R. T. Middleton IV, 'Racial Politics of Casino Gaming in the Delta', in D. von Herrman (ed.), *Resorting to Casinos: The Mississippi Gambling Industry* (Jackson, MS: University Press of Mississippi, 2006), pp. 47–66.

Benedict, J., *Without Reservation: How a Controversial Indian Tribe Rose to Power and Built the World's Largest Casino* (New York: HarperCollins, 2001).

Blair, G., *The Trumps: Three Generations That Built an Empire* (New York: Simon & Schuster, 2000).

—, *Donald Trump: Master Apprentice* (New York: Simon & Schuster, 2005).

Boger, Jr. C, D. Spears, K. Wolfe and L. Lee, 'Economic Impacts of Native American Casino Gaming', in C. Hsu (ed.), *Legalized Casino Gaming in the United States* (Binghamton, NY: Haworth Hospitality Press, 1999), pp. 140–2.

Casino Watch Inc., 'Crime: Money Laundering in the Casinos', January 2005, http://www.casinowatch.org/crime/money_laundering.html (accessed 13 October 2007).

Chinchilla, N. S., and N. Hamilton, 'Central American Immigrants: Diverse Populations, Changing Communities', in D. G. Guttierez (ed.), *The Columbia History of Latinos in the United States Since 1960* (New York: Columbia University Press, 2004), pp. 187–228.

Clayson, W., 'Cubans in Las Vegas: Ethnic Identity, Success, and Urban Life the Late Twentieth Century', *Nevada Historical Society Quarterly* 38:1 (1995).

D'Amato, G. A., and V. G. Levi, *Chance of a Lifetime: Nucky Johnson, Skinny D'Amato, and How Atlantic City Became the Naughty Queen of Resorts* (West Creek, NJ: Down the Shore, 2001).

Davis, E., *Atlantic City Diary: A Century of Memories, 1880-1985* (Atlantic City, NJ: Atlantic City News Agency, 1989).

Demaris, O., *The Boardwalk Jungle* (New York: Bantam, 1986).

Eadington, W., 'The Casino Gaming Industry: A Study of Political Economy', *Annals of the American Academy* 474 (July 1984), pp. 23–35.

Eisler, K., *Revenge of the Pequots: How a Small Native American Tribe Created the World's Most Profitable Casino* (New York: Simon & Schuster, 2001).

Epifianio, M. (ed.), *20th Anniversary of Casino Gaming in Atlantic City: 1978–1998: 20 Years and Lady Luck Is Still smiling on Atlantic City* (1998).

Frisch, M., *A Shared Authority: Essays on the Craft and Meaning of Oral and Public History* (Albany, NY: State University of New York Press, 1991).

George, N., 'Will the Gamble Pay Off?', *Black Enterprise* (March 1983), pp. 59–62.

Godfrey, B. S., and J. Richardson, 'Loss, Collective Memory and Transcripted Oral Histories', *International Journal of Social Research Methodology*, 7:4 (2004), pp. 143–55.

Goodman, R., *The Luck Business: The Devastating Consequences and Broken Promises of America's Gambling Explosion* (New York: Simon & Schuster, 1995).

Gutiérrez, D. G. (ed.), *The Columbia History of Latinos in the United States Since 1960* (New York: Columbia University Press, 2004).

Heller, M., 'The Changing Structure of American Gambling in the Twentieth Century', *Journal of Social Issues* 35:3 (Summer 1979), pp. 87–114.

Heneghan, D., 'Economic Impacts of Casino Gambling in Atlantic City', in C. Hsu (ed.) *Legalized Casino Gaming in the United States* (Binghamton, NY: Haworth Hospitality Press, 1999), pp. 113–34.

Hondagenu-Sotelo, P. (ed.), *Gender and U.S. Immigration: Contemporary Trends* (Berkeley, CA: University of California Press, 2003).

Hsu, C. (ed.), *Legalized Casino Gaming in the United States* (Binghamton, NY: Haworth Hospitality Press, 1999).

Johnson, N., *Boardwalk Empire: The Birth, High Times, and Corruption of Atlantic City* (Medford, NJ: Plexus Publishing, 2002).

Johnson, S. L., 'Kin and Casinos: Changing Family Networks in Atlantic City', *Current Anthropology*, 26:3 (June 1985).

Johnston, D., 'America Inc. Buys Out Murder Inc.' in J. Vogel (ed.), *Crapped Out* (Monroe, ME: Common Curtis Press, 1997).

Kurien, P., 'Gendered Ethnicity: Creating a Hindu Indian Identity in the United States', in P. Hondagenu-Sotelo, Gender and U.S. Immigration: Contemporary Trends (Berkeley, CA: University of California Press, 2003), pp. 151–73.

Le Espiritu, Y., 'Gender and Labor in Asian Immigrant Families', in P. Hondagenu-Sotelo, *Gender and U.S. Immigration: Contemporary Trends* (Berkeley, CA: University of California Press, 2003), pp. 81–100.

Lee, B., and J. Chelius, 'Government Regulation of Labor–Management Corruption: The Casino Industry Experience in Atlantic City', *Industrial and Labor Relations Review*, 42:4 (July 1989), pp. 536–48.

Levi, V. G., *Atlantic City: 125 Years of Ocean Madness* (Berkeley, CA: Ten Speed Press, 1979).

Lydersen, K., *Out of the Sea and into The Fire: Immigration from Latin America to the U.S. in the Global Age* (Monroe, ME: Common Courage Press, 2005), p. 172.

Mahan, G., *The Company that Bought the Boardwalk: A Reporter's Story of Resorts International* (New York: Random House, 1980).

Meyer-Arendt, K. J., 'From the River to the Sea: Casino Gaming in Mississippi', in K. Meyer-Arendt (ed.), *Casino Gaming in America: Origins, Trends, and Impacts* (New York: Cognizant Communication, 1998).

Morrison, R., *High Stakes to High Risk: The Strange Story of Resorts International and the Taj Mahal* (Ashtabula, OH: Lake Erie Press, 1994).

Nelson, M. K., 'Casino Gambling in Atlantic City: A Sure Bet For Whom', American Planning Association (APA) 1999 Proceedings, http://design.asu.edu/apa/proceedings99/Nelson/Nelson.htm (accessed 8 October 2007).

Nelson, M., and J. L. Mason, 'Mississippi: The Politics of Casino Gambling', in D. von Herrman (ed.), *Resorting to Casinos: The Mississippi Gambling Industry* (Jackson, MS: University Press of Mississippi, 2006), pp. 26–47.

Nuwer, D. S., and G. O'Brien, 'Mississippi's Oldest Pasture', in D. von Herrman (ed.), *Resorting to Casinos: The Mississippi Gambling Industry* (Jackson, MS: University Press of Mississippi, 2006), pp. 11–25.

Nykiel, R. 'A Special Look at Indian Gaming', *UNLV Gaming Research and Review Journal*, 8:2 (2004), pp. 51–6.

O'Brien, T., *Bad Bet: The Inside Story of the Glamour, Glitz, and Danger of America's Gambling Industry* (New York: Times Business, 1996).

Ochrym, R., 'Gambling in Atlantic City: The "Grand Vision" Blurs', *National Civic Review*, 72:11 (December 1983), pp. 591–6.

Pessar, P., 'Engendering Migration Studies: The Case of New Immigrants in the United States', in P. Hondagenu-Sotelo, *Gender and U.S. Immigration: Contemporary Trends* (Berkeley, CA: University of California Press, 2003), pp. 20–42.

Philly Roads, *Atlantic City–Brigantine Connector: Historical Overview*, http://www.phillyroads.com/roads/ac-brigantine/ (accessed 12 October 2007).

Pollack, M., *Hostage to Fortune: Atlantic City and Casino Gambling* (Princeton, NJ: Center for Analysis of Public Issues, 1987).

Portelli, A., *The Death of Luigi Trastulli and Other Stories: Form and Meaning in Oral History* (Albany, NY: State University of New York Press, 1991).

Ritchie, D. A., *Doing Oral History: A Practical Guide*, 2nd edn (New York: Oxford University Press, 2003).

Rose, J. N., 'Casinos Stuck under New Anti-Terrorism Laws', http://www.gamblingand thelaw.com/columns.html, 2005 (accessed 13 October 2007).

Rosenberg, A., 'A.C. Casinos' 25 Years: An Era of Mixed Payoffs', *Philadelphia Inquirer*, 20 June 2007, p. A01.

Rothman, H., *Neon Metropolis: How Las Vegas Started the Twenty-First Century* (New York: Routledge, 2003).

Rubinstein, J., 'Casino Gambling in Atlantic City: Issues of Development and Redevelopment', *Annals of the American Academy of Political and Social Science*, 474 (July 1984), pp. 61–71.

Rudd, D. P., 'Social Impacts of Atlantic City Casino Gaming', in C. Hsu (ed.) *Legalized Casino Gaming in the United States* (Binghamton, NY: Haworth Hospitality Press, 1999), pp. 201–20.

Saito, L. T., *Ethnic Identity and Motivation: Socio-Cultural Factors in the Educational Achievement of Vietnamese American Students* (New York: LFB Scholarly Publishing LLC, 2002).

Schwartz, D. G., *Jurisdiction Summary: Atlantic City* (Center for Gaming Research, University of Nevada, Las Vegas, 2001–6), available online at http://gaming.unlv.edu/ subject/atlanticcity.html (accessed 10 October 2007).

—, Suburban Xanadu: The Casino Resort on the Las Vegas Strip and Beyond (New York: Routledge, 2003).

—, *Roll the Bones: The History of Gambling* (New York: Gotham, 2006).

—, 'The Road Not Taken', *Casino Connection*, 3:1 (January 2006), p. 70, available online at http://www.casinoconnectionac.com/articles/The_Road_Not_Taken (accessed 11 October 2007).

—, 'Bunny on the Boardwalk', *Casino Connection*, 3:12 (December 2006), p. 64, available online at http://www.casinoconnectionac.com/articles/Bunny_on_the_Boardwalk (accessed 11 October 2007).

Simon, B., *Boardwalk of Dreams: Atlantic City and the Fate of Urban America* (New York: Oxford University Press, 2004).

Snook, R., *Jackpot! Harrah's Winning Secrets for Customer Loyalty* (Hoboken, NJ: John Wiley & Sons, 2003).

Sternlieb, G. and J. Hughes, *The Atlantic City Gamble* (Cambridge, MA: Harvard University Press, 1983).

Stitt, G., M. Nichols and D. Giacopassi, 'Does the Presence of Casinos Increase Crime? An Examination of Casino and Control Communities', *Crime & Delinquency*, 49:2 (April 2003), pp. 253–84.

Teske, P., and B. Sur, 'Winners and Losers: Politics, Casino Gambling, and Development in Atlantic City', *Policy Studies Review*, 10:2 (Spring/Summer 1991), pp. 130–7.

Teskea, M., et al, *A City Revitalized: The Elderly Lose at Monopoly* (Lanham, MD: University Press of America, 1983).

Tonkin, E., *Narrating Our Pasts: The Social Construction of Oral History* (Cambridge: Cambridge University Press, 1992).

Van Meter, J., *The Last Good Time: Skinny D'Amato, the Notorious 500 Club, and the Rise and Fall of Atlantic City* (New York: Crown, 2003).

Vogel, J. (ed.), *Crapped Out* (Monroe, ME: Common Curtis Press, 1997).

von Herrmann, D., 'Afterword', in D. von Herrman (ed.), *Resorting to Casinos: The Mississippi Gambling Industry* (Jackson, MS: University Press of Mississippi, 2006), pp. 167–9.

— (ed.), *Resorting to Casinos: The Mississippi Gambling Industry* (Jackson, MS: University Press of Mississippi, 2006).

Wortman, J., 'Personal Recollections of the New Jersey Gambling "Experiment" in Atlantic City', in C. Hsu (ed.), *Legalized Casino Gaming in the United States* (Binghamton, NY: Haworth Hospitality Press, 1999), pp. 25–39.

Yerkes, P., 'Wheel of Misfortune: Atlantic City, Ten Years Later', *New Jersey Reporter* (October 1986), pp. 15–19, 30.

Zephir, F., *The Haitian Americans* (Westport, CT: Greenwood Press, 2004).

Zhou, M., 'Assimilation, The Asian Way', in T. Jacoby (ed.), *Reinventing the Melting Pot: The New Immigrants and What it Means to Be American* (New York: Basic Books/ Perseus Book Group, 2004), pp. 148–52.

INDEX

For Product Safety Concerns and Information please contact our EU
representative GPSR@taylorandfrancis.com
Taylor & Francis Verlag GmbH, Kaufingerstraße 24, 80331 München, Germany

www.ingramcontent.com/pod-product-compliance
Ingram Content Group UK Ltd.
Pitfield, Milton Keynes, MK11 3LW, UK
UKHW021633240425
457818UK00018BA/385